A Lion Amongst the Cattle

HEINEMANN SOCIAL HISTORY OF AFRICA SERIES
Series Editors: Allen Isaacman and Jean Hay

African Workers and Colonial Racism: *Mozambican Strategies and Struggles in Lourenço Marques, 1877-1962*   JEANNE PENVENNE

Agriculture and Apartheid: *Agrarian Struggle and Transformation in Rural South Africa*   JONATHAN CRUSH AND ALAN JEEVES (EDITORS)

Are We Not Also Men? *The Samkange Family and African Politics in Zimbabwe*   TERENCE RANGER

Burying SM: *The Politics of Knowledge and the Sociology of Power in Africa*   DAVID COHEN AND E. S. ATIENO ODHIAMBO

Colonial Conscripts: *The* Tirailleurs Sénégalais *in French West Africa, 1875-1960*   MYRON ECHENBERG

Cotton is the Mother of Poverty: *Peasants, Work, and Rural Struggle in Mozambique*   ALLEN ISAACMAN

Cotton, Colonialism and Social History in Sub-Saharan Africa   ALLEN ISAACMAN AND RICHARD ROBERTS (EDITORS)

Cutting Down Trees: *Gender, Nutrition, and Agricultural Change in the Northern Province of Zambia, 1890-1990*   HENRIETTA MOORE AND MEGAN VAUGHAN

Drink, Power and Cultural Change: *A Social History of Alcohol in Ghana*   EMMANUEL AKYEAMPONG

Feasts and Riot: *Revelry, Rebellion, and Popular Consciousness on the Swahili Coast, 1856-1888*   JONATHON GLASSMAN

Gender, Ethnicity and Social Change on the Upper Slave Coast: *A History of the Anlo Ewe*   SANDRA GREENE

In Pursuit of History: *Fieldwork in Africa*   CAROLYN KEYES ADENAIKE AND JAN VANSINA (EDITORS)

Insiders and Outsiders: *The Indian Working Class of Durban, 1910-1990*   BILL FREUND

Law in Colonial Africa   KRISTIN MANN AND RICHARD ROBERTS (EDITORS)

A Lion Amongst the Cattle: *Reconstruction and Resistance in the Northern Transvaal*   PETER DELIUS

Money Matters: *Instability, Values, and Social Payments in the Modern History of West African Communities*   JANE GUYER (EDITOR)

The Moon is Dead! Give Us Our Money! *The Cultural Origins of an African Work Ethic, Natal, South Africa, 1843-1900*   KELETSO E. ATKINS

Peasants, Traders, and Wives: *Shona Women in the History of Zimbabwe, 1870-1939*   ELIZABETH SCHMIDT

The Realm of the Word: *Language, Gender, and Christianity in a Southern African Kingdom*   PAUL LANDAU

"We Spend Our Years as a Tale That is Told": *Oral Historical Narrative in a South African Chiefdom*   ISABEL HOFMEYR

Women of Phokeng: *Consciousness, Life Strategy, and Migrancy in South Africa, 1900-1983*   BELINDA BOZZOLI (with the assistance of MMANTHO NKOTSOE)

Work, Culture and Identity: *Migrant Laborers in Mozambique and South Africa, 1860-1910*   PATRICK HARRIES

A Lion Amongst the Cattle

Reconstruction and Resistance in the Northern Transvaal

Peter Delius

HEINEMANN
Portsmouth, NH

RAVAN PRESS
Johannesburg

JAMES CURREY
Oxford

Ravan Press (Pty) Ltd
PO Box 145
Randburg 2125
South Africa

Heinemann
361 Hanover Street
Portsmouth
NH 03801-3912
United States of America

James Currey
73 Botley Road
Oxford
OX2 OBS
United Kingdom

Published in South Africa by Ravan Press 1996
Published in the United States by Heinemann 1996
Published in the United Kingdom by James Currey Publishers 1996

© Peter Delius 1996

Ravan Press: ISBN 0 86975 489 0

Heinemann: ISBN (cloth) 0 435 074164
                    ISBN (paper) 0 435 074156

James Currey   ISBN (cloth) 0 85255 675 6
                    ISBN (paper) 0 85255 625 X

Library of Congress Cataloging-in-Publication Data on file at the Library of
Congress.

British Library Cataloguing in Publication Data on file at the British Library.

Cover and text design, DTP by Ingrid Obery, Media and Publishing Services
Repro by Positive Proof
Printed and bound by Galvin & Sales, Cape Town

Contents

*Representing the Reserves?; Questions and
Answers.*

Chapter 1

*Introduction; Divide and Rule; The Boer
War and Reconstruction; Native
Commissioners; Chiefly Rule; Migrants;
Chiefs, Commoners and Conflicts;
Childhood and Education; Marriage and
Migrancy; Migrant Associations; Malaita;
Elite Ethnic Associations; Conclusion.*

Chapter 2

*Introduction; 'The Problem Lies in the
Reserves'; Trust and Tribulation; The
Sebataladi Motor Cottage Association; The
Sekhukhuneland Student Association; 'A
New Era of Reclamation'; Conclusion.*

Chapter 3

*Introduction; Boipušo – Self Rule; The ANC
and Resistance in the Reserves; Migrant
Organisation; Migrants, Unions and*

List of illustrations

Maps

Plates

*In memory of my father
Anthony Delius*

Preface

This book takes up where my history of the Pedi Kingdom in the nineteenth century – *The Land Belongs to Us* – left off.[1] And its form has been shaped not only by the content but also by the audience reached by the earlier study. *The Land Belongs to Us* started life as a PhD thesis and at another time might have remained restricted to a university-based readership. But in South Africa in the early 1980s there was broader demand for writing which contested the prevailing views of the past. Ravan Press was sensitive to this need and started to publish the work of a burgeoning new generation of graduate students. My thesis, very little changed in content from the austere blue-bound volume which was housed in the vaults of the University of London, was given a livelier title, wrapped in a colourful cover and sent out in search of readers.

It found an initial modest market amongst academics and history enthusiasts. But over time, despite the almost complete absence of local distribution, the book started to circulate in the Northern Transvaal. It was bought by individuals with a strong interest in the history of the region – often school teachers – and by people active in a range of non-governmental organisations working in Sekhukhuneland. Eventually a retired teacher made a modest return from selling copies of the book at schools in nearby villages until the print run was exhausted.

This constituency was of course far from a mass readership but it was nonetheless considerably wider than the book had in all truth been designed to serve. During my travels to Sekhukhuneland in subsequent years I had numerous opportunities to talk to people who had read the book and to get their – usually constructive – comments and criticisms. Responses from students, reviewers and general readers provided further guidance as to which sections of the text had captured people's interest. I also became heavily involved in a range of attempts by the Wits History Workshop to popularise historical material.

When I decided to write this book I was influenced by these experiences and thus had a rather disparate audience in mind. I tried to write a history which could reach general readers curious about this range of historical processes as well as people living and working in the region and individuals grappling with understanding the contours of conflict and change in the countryside in South Africa and beyond. Catering to this imagined audience has inevitably involved compromises in the presentation of the material. Some academics, for example, may wish for a fuller treatment of the specialised debates which a wider readership assured me they found the most alienating aspect of my earlier study.[2] Other readers may still find the prose too ponderous and the material too dense in places. Individuals particularly concerned with local history may lament the lack of detail on their own relatives, villages and experiences. Nevertheless my hope is that a diverse readership will find sufficient of interest to persevere with the book.

Acknowledgements and thanks are due to the large number of people who have helped this book on its way. Godfrey Mogaramedi Sekhukhune encouraged me to start the research but sadly did not live to read the result. Isaac Segopotše Sekhukhune gave unstintingly of his time, insights and networks. Stephen Sekgothe Mothubatse shepherded me around Mohlaletse and did his best to educate me about the past and the present. Cedric Monare Rachidi, Philip Mbiba and the late Philip Mnisi played a major role in the oral research for this study and shared with me their rich understanding of Sekhukhuneland.

In the almost ten years of this book's gestation I have been fortunate to work with a number of graduate students who tackled related topics and whose work is reflected in both notes and text. But I owe a particular debt of gratitude to Edwin Ritchken and Stefan Schirmer whose work overlapped with my own and who generated a stream of questions and answers which had a powerful effect on my thinking. Ron Anderson generously gave me access to material he painstakingly collected on the trials relating to the 1986 witch-hunts in Sekhukhuneland and Sekibakiba Peter Lekgoathi assisted with the translation of key documents and contributed important perspectives on struggles around education in the Northern Transvaal.

Thanks are also due to those who bravely joined in the battle to disentangle my prose and to sharpen my arguments. Harriet Perlman read draft after draft without (visibly) blanching and provided invaluable suggestions for improvements. Belinda Bozzoli made copious and telling comments on the penultimate draft of the manuscript. Deborah James read many of the chapters and clarified key issues. Edward Breslin's comments, and our collaboration on other projects, deepened my understanding of the contemporary resonances of this history. William Beinart was generous with his insights – especially in relation to conservation.

Over years of research and writing I accumulated many other debts of gratitude to people who, variously and sometimes severally, commented on papers, drafts or arguments, gave me access to their own work, assisted with finding informants, helped with translation, did interviews and made suggestions about relevant documents and photographs. An incomplete list of the people I am beholden to includes: Dave Anderson, Adam Ashforth, Rupert Baber, Howard Barrell, Phil Bonner, Helen Bradford, Luli Callinicos, Matthew Chaskalson, Marc Epprecht, Steven Feierman, Gail Gerhart, Tony Harding, Barbara Harmel, Jean Hay, Baruch Hirson, Jonathan Hyslop, Allen Isaacman, Alan Jeeves, Tom Karis, Paul la Hausse, Hugh Macmillan, Sarah Madrid, Tiny Mankge, Anna Maponya, Shula Marks, Rob McCutcheon, Kgaugelo Mokgoatšana, Rachidi Molapo, the late Moss Molepo, Mothodi Nchabeleng, Thiatu Nemutanzhela, Isak Niehaus, John Perlman, John Phala, Deborah Posel, Christonie Roote, Selelepoo Sebaka, Karin Shapiro, Mamatši Sekhukhune, John Sender, Jill Straker, Stanley Trapido, Charles van Onselen and Gavin Williams.

A partial list of people who gave me succour and support during my innumerable trips to Sekhukhuneland includes: Elizabeth and Peter Anderson, Belinda Blaine, Tony Harding, *Tona* B.K. Hlakudi, Tanya Honig, Mma Marishane, Ina Perlman, Johann Rissik, Colleen Saunders, *Kgošikgolo* K.K. Sekhukhune, the late Joseph Ramphelane Sekhukhune, the late Christina Nomalizo Sekhukhune, Richard Magerule Sekonya and Franz Temba.

My research would have ground rapidly to a halt without material assistance from a number of benefactors. The Chairman's Fund provided vital support as did the Institute of Research Development and the Centre for Science Development. The Institute of Advanced Social Research, Wits University, supplied and housed tapes. The Rhodes Chair, Oxford University, and the Canadian Research Consortium on Southern Africa in conjunction with Queens University helped make possible periods of reflection and research in the United Kingdom and Canada respectively. Of course, the opinions and conclusions contained in this study do not necessarily represent the views of either the individuals or the institutions listed above.

Without the emotional and practical support of my wife Harriet I doubt this book would have seen the light of day. And while the arrival of our daughters Sarah and Emma sometimes threatened to scupper this study, their rumbustious presence immeasurably enriched the life of its author.

Notes

1. P. Delius, *The Land Belongs To Us* (Ravan Press, 1983, and Heinemann and University of California Press, 1984).
2. They may find partial relief in some of the endnotes which enlarge on issues and debates touched on in the text.

Glossary of key words

Contemporary Northern Sotho orthography is used in the text in most instances. The exceptions are individual names where I have reproduced people's own usage and quotations from documents.

Baditšaba – people of the community, 'traditionalists'
Baheitene – heathens
Bakgomana – royals, members of the chiefly lineage
Bašemane (sing. *mošemane*) – boys
Basetsana (sing. *mosetsana*) – girls
Batala – commoners
Batseta (sing. *motseta*) – intermediaries
Bodika – the first session of male initiation
Bogadi (pl. *magadi*) – bridewealth
Bogoši – the chieftainship, kingdom
Bogwera – the second session of male initiation
Boipušo – self-rule, Bantu Authorities
Bopedi –- Sekhukhuneland
Byale – female initiation
Koma – initiation
Kgoro (pl. *dikgoro*) – ward, subsection of a village/chiefdom
Kgoši (pl. *dikgoši, magoši*) – chief
Kgošana (pl. *dikgošana, magošana*) – subordinate chief, headman
Kgošikgolo – King, Paramount Chief
Khuduthamaga – executive/central committee
Lapa – household, courtyard
Lešokeng – urban area, in the wilderness
Majakane – Christians
Makgoweng – urban areas, the place of the whites
Mašoboro (sing. *lešoboro*) – uninitiated boys
Mathumaša (sing. *lethumaša*) – uninitiated girls
Mohumagadi – chief wife, queen
Megodišano – rotating saving associations
Mošate – chief's headquarters
Ngaka (pl. *dingaka*) – diviner, herbalist
Rondavel – round hut

Skeleton genealogy of Pedi Royals

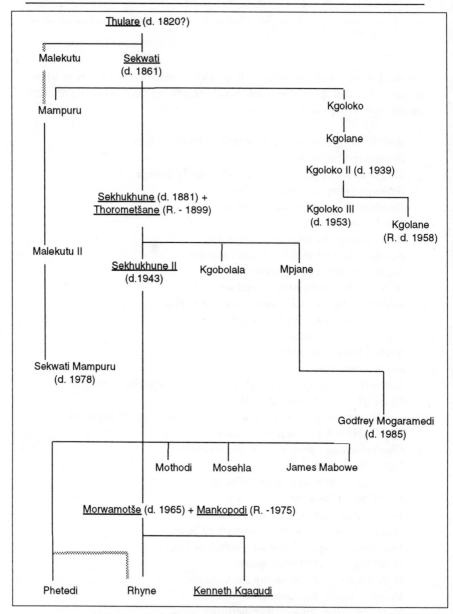

Underlined = *Kgošikgolo*; R. = Regent; d. = died; + = married
〰〰〰 = claimed sociological parentage

MAP 1
The Transvaal

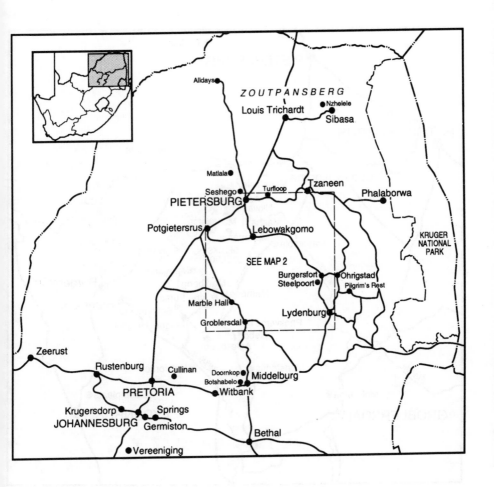

MAP 2
Sekhukhuneland

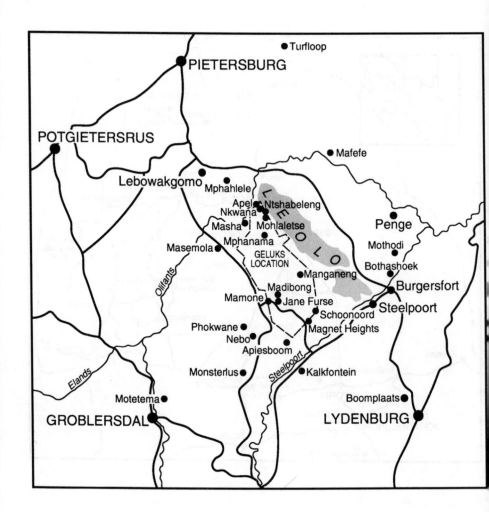

Introduction

The first day of South Africa's first democratic election dawned in Sekhukhuneland in the Northern Transvaal.[1] It was supposed to be an opportunity for the old and the frail to go to the polls early and thus avoid the crush expected later. Instead, administrative chaos produced a protracted ordeal:

> All day Tuesday, the aged and infirm sat around patiently waiting to vote. By nightfall they had to be dispersed. They were back again before dawn on Wednesday morning. Most of them, hobbling and illiterate but determined, finally got to vote ten hours later. Two whole days sitting in the sun, just to make a cross on a … ballot paper.[2]

In other parts of the district the polls only opened on the Friday evening, a day after the election was scheduled to have ended.

The perseverance of people in these trying circumstances testified to their determination to have a say at last. But their wait while the rest of the country voted was also symbolic of the fact that the people of Sekhukhuneland, like those in other rural communities, had long been last in line for a share of national resources. This position has ensured them a leading place in the statistics of relative poverty and deprivation.[3]

Journalists who made their way to Sekhukhuneland in April 1994 were intent on observing the election in a backwater, a place off the map and off the beaten track. But some of the old men and women who endured heat, hunger and fatigue in the voting queues had a rather different image of the land upon which they stood. They were in the heartland of the once powerful Pedi Kingdom which, under the leadership of Sekwati and Sekhukhune, had played a pivotal role in the nineteenth-century history of the Transvaal. It had held the Zulu, the Swazi, the Boers and the British at bay and had provided a haven in a dangerous and turbulent world. In historic maps of the Transvaal it was marked in bold letters – a place at the forefront of the hopes and fears of statesmen, missionaries and, ultimately, major-generals.[4]

1

Conquest by an Imperial army in 1879 ruptured this refuge but did not produce an easy acceptance of a colonial order. In the twentieth century Sekhukhuneland was the site of bitter and protracted struggles between outsiders attempting to restructure the society, and various forms of popular resistance and innovation.[5] This contest erupted into open revolt in 1958, when migrant workers and villagers battled to defend the few freedoms that remained to them, and again in 1986, when youthful 'comrades' set out to purge their communities of the influences of apartheid. These events briefly catapulted Sekhukhuneland on to the front pages of national newspapers, sent shivers of alarm through white society and prompted some activists to reflect on the problems and possibilities of the countryside.

A portrait of these revolts forms the heart of this book. They involve decisive moments in the history of the region which cast old and new conflicts into sharp relief and which expose neglected dimensions of South Africa's peculiar path of racially structured industrialisation.

The divisions, interpretations and aspirations which shaped these events are part of the heritage of the government brought to life by the slow-moving queues of the 1994 election. It remains an open question whether a new order will be underpinned by a democratic popular culture and make a material difference to the lives of people in places like Sekhukhuneland. But this conundrum will be resolved in conditions partly created by this long history of contestation.

Representing the Reserves?

The central focus of this book is on the twentieth-century experiences of communities living on land which had once formed the core of the Pedi Kingdom. After the kingdom's defeat, fragments of its former domain were set aside for African occupation. The 1913 and 1936 Land Acts added to this 'reserve' although the area remained puny in comparison to the land ruled at the height of the kingdom's power. Sekhukhuneland thus became part of the patchwork of reserve areas etched into South African geography through a history of resistance, defeat and the elaboration of a segregationist social order. These regions have over the years been the object of diverse and even contradictory depictions. As fears subsided that the reserves might allow Africans to relaunch military resistance, they were increasingly portrayed within white society as rural idylls. It was suggested that they were home to contented tribesmen and bare-breasted maidens who lived in picturesque rondavels under the rule of imposing chiefs and in the thrall of exotic witchdoctors. Here, according to this portrayal, they pursued a languid interest in farming and a passion for cattle, although this relaxed lifestyle was from time

to time interspersed with trips to town to earn money to buy particularly al-
luring goods.

But this picture postcard perspective jostled with other, bleaker images.
From the 1930s, radical commentators argued that these societies constituted
the shock absorbers of South African industrialisation. They bore the burden
of nurturing new generations of migrant workers, sustained their families
during their long absences from home and cared for those discarded by the
mines and the factories – the old, the disabled and the dying. Warnings were
sounded from diverse quarters that this was taking a terrible toll on these
communities and that economic, social and ecological disaster loomed. There
was much that was persuasive in this representation, but it was a mono-
chrome portrait presenting reserve communities as helpless victims caught up
in uncontrollable currents. Anthropologists conveyed a much richer sense of
the composition and culture of local-level society but, until the 1960s, the
burdens of structural functionalism and of the ethnographic present limited
the impact of their work on intellectuals and activists trying to define or engage with wide-ranging processes of change.[6] The latter were left with
catch-all and external categories like 'tribesman', 'peasant' or 'proletarian'.
These formulations were not without some explanatory power, but could not
capture the identities within, or the content of, struggles and transformations
in the countryside.

As a result the communities in the reserves were, at best, cast in a supporting, suffering role in South African history. They did not feature in the
dominant narratives of conflict and change in the twentieth century. And
when their 'unruly' behaviour – as in the widespread revolts of the 1950s –
forced scholars to pay them some attention, they were gently chided for being
'isolated ... parochial peasants' grieving for a world which had 'long been
subverted'.[7]

In recent decades the foundations have been laid for a rather different historical reconstruction. There is a growing body of argument and evidence
which shows that while societies in the reserves have been fundamentally refashioned by the intersecting forces of racism and capitalism, their struggles
have in turn helped to shape the particular nature of both rural and urban society. A continuing, though sometimes strained, dialogue between historians,
anthropologists and sociologists has played a part in fostering a concern with
the interplay between the dynamics of local-level society and wider processes
of change. It has – as expressed by the Comaroffs in their own special dialect
– contributed to a widening

> refusal to separate culture from political economy, insisting instead on
> the simultaneity of the meaningful and the material in all things [and
> while recognising] the brute realities of colonialism and its aftermath,

[not] assuming that they have robbed African peoples of their capacity to act on the world.[8]

This perspective has also been influenced by a broader recognition that:

> In Africa the encounters of the past are very much part of the present ... Africa's crisis derives from a complex history that demands a complex analysis; a simultaneous awareness of how colonial powers exercised power and the limits of that power, an appreciation of the intensity with which that power was confronted and the diversity of the futures that people sought for themselves.[9]

Questions and Answers

The story told in this book starts with a sketch of Sekhukhuneland in the 1930s which underscores the profound consequences of conquest and colonial control. In this picture the fundamental restructuring of both economy and society around migrant labour stands out in starkest relief. But economic dependence did not readily translate into colonial hegemony. Pedi men and women battled to retain elements of cultural, political and economic autonomy. This protracted tussle cannot, however, be reduced to a simple contest between resistor and oppressor. Cleavages of religion, gender, generation and between chiefs and commoners shaped the contours of conflict and provide recurring refrains in the ensuing history. And a rich and changing repertoire of remembered pasts and imagined futures was elaborated by both rulers and ruled and provided the language and substance of dispute.[10]

From the late 1930s the shifting policies and practices of conservation, segregation and apartheid sent shock waves through the region and set in motion forms of popular resistance which climaxed in the Sekhukhuneland Revolt of 1958 – a last-ditch defence of a residual autonomy pioneered by migrant workers. Under siege in both town and countryside, and drawing on a long lineage of migrant organisation, these workers formed an organisation called Sebatakgomo which played a prominent part in the mounting resistance.

The revolt was a testament to both the intensity of a popular rejection of expanded state intervention and to the depth of the fissures within local-level society. The dramatic confrontations that resulted may appear as atypical distractions to historians concerned to assert the significance of 'hidden struggles' or the covert 'weapons of the weak'. But the great advantage of these events is that, at a decisive moment in the history of the region, they allow us to hear the voices and listen to the ideas of people who might otherwise have remained muffled by official disinterest.[11]

In 1958 the state was forced to beat an undignified retreat. But popular victory celebrations were shortlived, as multiple processes of change overwhelmed local defences and eroded the forms of autonomy which the rebels had fought so hard to defend. In 1986 in profoundly changed circumstances the youth emerged as the cutting edge of struggle and violent resistance resumed. The 'comrades' were armed with a political agenda which diverged markedly from that of the earlier rebels. But it was also crafted from a combination of the dominant debates within the villages and broader diagnoses of social and political malaise.

A Lion Amongst the Cattle charts the changing relationship of the Communist Party and the African National Congress to the countryside and explores the importance of migrant workers in the processes of political cross-fertilisation which contributed both to the revolt in 1958 and to the decision to launch Umkhonto we Sizwe in 1961. It traces the growing interaction of township and rural youth from the 1970s and the part this played in linking insurrection in the cities and in Sekhukhuneland during the 1980s. But interconnection did not result in uniformity of understanding and action. This is borne out by an examination of the content and form of each of the revolts and by exploring why the 1986 rebels, who began by targeting obvious symbols of the apartheid order, turned to killing witches in some villages.

The book also shows that while Sekhukhuneland – and areas like it – were sidelined by the focus of resources and attention on urban areas, they were far from being passive objects of policy or strangers to the discourses of development. The following chapters explore the contending ideas about continuity and change that were generated within the region. Pedi migrants and villagers have, for example, long debated the role and practice of chieftainship, democracy and the market. They have also been subjected to (and sometimes able to subvert) a succession of attempts to restructure the society. Part of what is striking about contemporary controversies over rural development is the strong, though often unintended, echoes of earlier formulations.

The story told in *A Lion Amongst the Cattle* was pieced together over several years in a fashion described in some detail at the end of the book. (For a discussion of methodology and sources, see Appendix 1.) The nature and context of the research had important consequences for both the form and content of the narrative, and some readers may wish to be alerted to these filters before stepping into this history. Others will be content to wait until later or to forgo this perspective altogether. Nonetheless it should be noted at the outset that the book is largely based on 180 interviews conducted mainly between 1987 and 1992 in Sekhukhuneland. Many of these encounters were three-way conversations, and Isaac Sekhukhune, Stephen Mothubatse, Cedric Rachidi, Philip Mbiba and Philip Mnisi contributed their own questions and perspectives to the project. Oral material is the foundation of the book but has been combined with a wide range of documentary sources and enhanced by histories of key episodes written in Sepedi by Mothodi Nchabeleng and John Phala. And my own observations and conversations during stays in the area over almost twenty years have left their mark.

. Where possible I have allowed people to speak for themselves, and sections of the book are a compendium of quotations. But this, of course, does not mean that the men and women whose voices sound through the text would have told the story in the way that I have or agree with all or even most of my conclusions. I do hope, however, that they recognise in this book an attempt at reciprocity. Enriched by their memories I have tried to tell a story that reflects some, at least, of the vividness of their lives.[12]

Notes

1. Sekhukhuneland refers to the area lying between the Olifants River in the north and the Steelpoort River in the south-east which formed the core area of the Pedi Kingdom from 1830 to 1879. It should not be confused with the very much smaller magisterial district of Sekhukhuneland which was demarcated after the conquest of the kingdom.
2. *Weekly Mail*, 29/4/1994.
3. The Northern Transvaal, for example, scores lowest of all the regions in South Africa (0,59) on a Human Development Index consisting of life expectancy, literacy and GDP per capita. Amongst the many sombre statistics on the region are figures which show that it has the highest percentage of children living in poverty (74,15%). For these and other figures see Development Bank of South Africa, *Statistics on Living Standards and Development; Regional Poverty Profile; Eastern and Northern Transvaal* (Midrand, 1993); The Project on Living Standards and Development, *South Africans Rich and Poor* (Cape Town, 1994); Operation Hunger, *Annual Report,* 1995, pp. 20-3.
4. P. Delius, *The Land Belongs To Us* (Johannesburg, 1983).
5. This is not to suggest that these were autonomous processes and ideologies. The forms of resistance and models of appropriate transformations were, as will be explored later, profoundly affected by experience of the practices and discourses of Christianity, colonialism and capitalism. And despite the asymmetry of power relations this was far from a one-way process as the arguments, diagnoses and narratives of diverse members of African communities also had an effect on the policy and practice of industry, church and state. For a valuable discussion of the strengths and weaknesses of the focus on resistance in recent historical writing about Africa see F. Cooper, 'Conflict and Connection,' *American Historical Review*, 99, 5, 1994.
6. An influential article which drew on a lineage of leftwing analysis of migrant labour and the reserves is H. Wolpe, 'Capitalism and Cheap Labour Power', *Economy and Society* 1, 4, 1972. Particularly rich anthropological perspectives in works published before 1960 are to be found in M. Hunter, *Reaction to Conquest* (London, 1936) and the voluminous publications of I. Schapera including *Migrant Labour and Tribal Life* (London, 1947). For a pioneering and influential account from a 'liberal' historian see W.M. Macmillan, *Complex South Africa* (London, 1930). For a valuable overview of the now substantial literature on migrant labour see P. Harries, *Work, Culture and*

Identity (Johannesburg, 1994), pp. xi-xxiii; and for a perceptive overview of transformations in the reserves see W. Beinart, *Twentieth Century South Africa* (Oxford, 1994).

7.   T. Lodge, *Black Politics in South Africa since 1945* (Johannesburg, 1983), p. 290.

8.   J. and J. Comaroff (eds.) *Modernity and its Malcontents* (Chicago, 1993), p. xiv. As this scholarship has gathered momentum the simple oppositions which underpinned dyads like resistor and oppressor, resistance and collaboration and the dichotomy between peasant and proletarian have appeared decreasingly helpful. The concern with the 'dialectic of articulation between a local system and its encompassing context' which was central to some earlier work has been enriched by a growing concern with culture and consciousness. And struggles within African societies informed by gender, generation, ethnicity and religion have come into still sharper focus. This work has revealed a multitude of historical travellers with a diversity of imagined destinations employing a wide variety of strategies who have defied crude classification. But, while it is possible to lump together literature which has contributed to this broad understanding, it would also be possible to split it along a variety of fault lines of methodology, analysis and conclusion. There is now a considerable body of writing falling into this category, but which cannot be cited here in full. However, relevant recent books which explore and elaborate many of these issues in a South African context include W. Beinart, *Twentieth Century*; W. Beinart and C. Bundy, *Hidden Struggles in Rural South Africa* (London, 1987); H. Bradford, *A Taste of Freedom* (London, 1987); P. Bonner, P. Delius and D. Posel (eds.), *Apartheid's Genesis 1935-1962* (Johannesburg, 1993); B. Bozzoli, *Women of Phokeng* (Johannesburg, 1991); J. Brown *et al.*, *History From South Africa* (Philadelphia, 1991); J. and J. Comaroff, *Of Revelation and Revolution* (Chicago, 1991); P. Harries, *Work, Culture and Identity*; C. Murray, *Black Mountain* (Johannesburg, 1992); D. Moodie, *Going For Gold* (Berkeley, 1994); J. Peires, *The Dead Will Arise* (Johannesburg, 1989). Earlier works which began to move in these directions include W. Beinart, *The Political Economy of Pondoland* (Cambridge, 1982); P. Delius, *The Land Belongs to Us* (Johannesburg, 1983); P. Mayer, *Black Villagers in an Industrial Society* (Cape Town, 1980). The source of the above quotation is J. Comaroff, 'Dialectical Systems, History and Anthropology', *Journal of Southern African Studies*, 8, 1982, p. 146.

9.   Cooper, 'Conflict and Connection', p. 1545.

10. The centrality of migrant labour to culture, economy and society in Sekhukhuneland seems to me to place insuperable obstacles in the way of describing its inhabitants as a peasantry (which is not to deny that some peasants lived in the area). But, as the emphasis on autonomy in this paragraph suggests, the body of writing about peasantries (and more loosely rural transformations) in Africa and elsewhere has provided a rich comparative resource for this study. There is a massive literature, but particularly helpful recent works in a broader African context include A. Isaacman, 'Peasants and Rural Social Protest in Africa', *African Studies Review*, 33, 1990; S. Feierman, *Peasant Intellectuals* (Wisconsin, 1990); N. Kriger, *Zimbabwe's Guerrilla War* (Cambridge, 1992); B. Berman and J. Lonsdale, *Unhappy Valley 2* (London, 1992); E. Schmidt, *Peasants, Traders and Wives* (Portsmouth, 1992); H. Moore and M. Vaughan, *Cutting Down Trees* (Portsmouth, 1992). A comparative literature on migrant labour in Africa has also been of value. For an overview see S. Stichter, *Migrant Labourers* (Cambridge, 1985).

11   See, for example, J. Scott, *The Weapons of the Weak* (New Haven, 1985). For critical discussions of this perspective see Isaacman, 'Peasants', pp. 30-3, and Cooper, 'Conflict and Connection', pp. 1532-4.

12. Despite the diversity of interpretations and accounts encountered during my research, this book is built around a conventional historical narrative which represents the best

understanding I can achieve of both the causes and course of events. My experiences of attempting to communicate with audiences both inside and outside of the academy have led me to believe that the narrative form has considerable potential both to convey process and change over time and to communicate with diverse audiences. As has been pointed out:

> While philosophers and literary critics in recent years have exposed the artificial status of narrative, they have also given narrative form an attention which has enhanced appreciation for it. The flow of time does not have a beginning, middle and end; only stories about it do. Yet lives share the structures of narratives, and perhaps a familiarity with their beginnings, middles and ends predisposes people to cast their histories into narrative form. Historians should attend to the pervasive appeal of stories. (J. Appleby, L. Hunt and M. Jacob, *Telling the Truth about History* (New York, 1994), p. 263)

Equally, while this account seeks to be sensitive to a variety of perspectives it also seems to me to be impossible to represent the multitude of voices and visions bearing on this history in ways which are not profoundly influenced by my understanding of issues and events and my repertoire of explanations. Thus, while it might be possible to assemble a larger cast of narrators, such a device does not seem to me to solve the problem of 'narrative closure' and might even obscure the simple but crucial point that the text they inhabit has a single author. Unwary readers should, of course, be warned that the story that this book tells is both partial and personal and will no doubt be improved and/or overturned by subsequent writers. For examples of perceptive discussions of these issues which arrive at rather different solutions see Moore and Vaughan, *Cutting Down Trees* pp. xxiv-xxv; and E. Ayres, 'Narrating the New South', *Journal of Southern History*, 1985. For a fuller description of the research on which this book is based see Appendix 1 ('Research Revisited') which includes a full list of interviews.

1

Sekhukhuneland in the 1930s

On 28 November 1879, as the first light of dawn etched the outlines of
Tšate, the capital of the Pedi Kingdom, British artillery exploded into
life. Under the cover of shells thudding down amongst the thousands of huts
which nestled against the steep foothills of the Leolo Mountains, British
troops advanced on the lines of rifle pits and stone walling which formed a
protective perimeter to the town. But the redcoats were soon pinned down
under heavy fire from the Pedi defenders and, with the attack thus halted, Sir
Garnet Wolseley anxiously scanned the horizon. Then deafening cheers from
the British soldiers and sighs of relief from Wolseley and his staff signalled
the arrival of their keenly awaited allies – the Swazi army. They stood on the
heights towering behind Tšate, 'silhouetted against the skyline, with their
assegais and shields, an awesome spectacle'.[1]

The Pedi regiments were unprepared for attack from the rear and, with the
advantage of surprise, the Swazi swept down the mountainside. Pedi defenders were thus trapped between the descending Swazi and the advancing
British troops, and a terrible carnage ensued. Finally, as night fell and heavy
rain drenched the valley, the surviving Pedi defenders slipped out of the
caves in which they had found shelter and fled. The Pedi Kingdom which for
decades had proved invincible to attack had been shattered. Its subjects could
no longer shrug off demands for tax and tribute and pour scorn on settler
claims to the land. They faced a future where, in Wolseley's prediction, they
would be weaned from 'the ways of savage life into complete submission to a
civilised sovereignity'.[2] But those Pedi villagers who had survived this brutal
display of imperial power started to rebuild their homes, far from reconciled
to the modern major-general's prescriptions or convinced by his vision of
progress.[3]

9

The hundred years that followed witnessed a more protracted struggle. Missionaries, officials, politicians and a diverse band of experts set out to bend these communities to their will while Pedi men and women fought to maintain values and practices which they cherished, at the same time constructing their own agendas for change.

The setting for this contest was a beautiful but harsh landscape. Until the 1820s the Pedi capital had been located in the fertile valley of the Tubatse (Steelpoort) River and the state had exercised a loose authority over a considerable portion of the Northern and Eastern Transvaal. The heartland of the kingdom spanned a region of ecological contrast and transition. The treeless plains of the highveld were broken by the plunging valleys and steep slopes of the escarpment which in turn surrendered to the dense scrub and rock-strewn *kopjes* of the bushveld and the sub-tropical vegetation of the lowveld.

After 1820, the Tubatse Valley proved to be dangerously exposed as Ndwandwe, Swazi, Zulu and Boer armies penetrated deep into the region. The Pedi Kingdom narrowly avoided complete extinction and was rebuilt from the late 1820s under the skilful leadership of Sekwati in the area to the north between the Tubatse and Lepelle (Olifants) Rivers. This was rugged country cradled by the Sekhukhune and Strydpoort Mountains and dissected by the Leolo range, which formed numerous deep valleys and gorges. To the east of the Leolo lay lowveld, to the west mountainous bushveld which in the nineteenth century was well covered with trees and shrubs. It abounded in natural strongholds which could easily be fortified and defended. But it had limited amounts of arable land, and the mountains which provided such vital shelter also cast a rain shadow over much of the western portion. The result was that rainfall, which was concentrated in the summer months, was low and erratic. And when the rain finally came, it was often in violent electrical storms which produced flash floods and bolts of forked lightning, and left a trail of death and destruction. The British troops, marching on the Pedi heartland in 1879, were inclined to give credence to rumours of their opponents' magical powers after being subjected to a number of these awesome and lethal spectacles.[4]

Defeat in 1879 brought still further loss of land. As many Pedi had long suspected, much of the land on which they lived had been demarcated as farms by Boers and some of it had even been sold to speculators long before any effective external authority had been imposed upon them. Once their independence was breached they found not only new rulers demanding taxes but landlords claiming rents. The Pedi heartland was converted, virtually overnight, into crown land, land company farms, mission lands and, increasingly, privately owned farms.

The rent demanded by the various landlords differed. But the most important contrast was between demands for labour rent, which were common on land owned by working farmers, and the cash rents which were collected by companies and the state. The area was divided into the Nebo and Sekhukhuneland districts and three small locations set aside for African occupation. The most substantial of these was a narrow band of land hugging the foothills of the Leolo Mountains which was demarcated in 1885 and known as the 'Geluks location'. This title was not based on any spontaneous expression of joy by its inhabitants at being accorded rights to a fragment of their former domain but was derived from a mangled rendition of 'Kgoloko', the name of the then Pedi regent.[5]

While the Pedi had little choice but to accept the fact of conquest and the loss of much of their land, very few believed the new order had a sound moral basis. Most still shared the view so forcefully expressed in 1876 by Johannes Dinkwanyane, a Christian convert and Sekhukhune's brother:

> [Y]ou Boers ... do you think there is a God who will punish lying theft and deceit? ... I say *the land belongs to us* ...Your cleverness has turned to theft I say it in relation to the land because you came to this country ... ate everything up ... and said nothing to anybody ... [but] your theft has come into the open.[6]

The belief that the land had been stolen by the Boers and that this fraud had been entrenched by imperial power endured in popular consciousness. A communal system of rights in land with its legitimacy rooted in the history of the Pedi Kingdom remained a widely cherished model of an alternative order. And the scale of this model bore little relationship to the puny pockets of land in which the Pedi were corralled from the 1880s. To this day old men become animated when they discuss the *real* boundaries of *Bopedi*. Most relate their claims to the high point of Pedi power in the early nineteenth century when, under King Thulare, the state held sway over a large stretch of the Transvaal.[7] Heated debates take place, for example, over whether or not Pretoria and/or Rustenburg fall within the Pedi domain.

Defeat also resulted in profound changes in the political order. King Sekhukhune evaded capture on the day of the battle but was tracked down to the cave where he had taken refuge. He was arrested and paraded through the streets of Pretoria, after which it was intended that he would be imprisoned on Robben Island. In the event, however, he was spared incarceration on that bleak outcrop and after the successful Boer rising against British rule in 1881 was allowed to return home. In his absence a number of subordinate chiefdoms which had chafed under his control established their independence. Even more dangerously his brother and long-standing rival, Mampuru, who had assisted the Swazi and the British, set about usurping the throne. After

Sekhukhune's release he and Mampuru vied for supremacy. The conflict finally ended on 13 August 1882 when a band of assassins sent by Mampuru stabbed Sekhukhune to death. Mampuru was captured by Boer forces and, on the second attempt, hanged on 22 November 1883.[8]

During the battle for Tšate, Sekhukhune's son and designated heir, Morwamotše, stood with his back to a rock and fought until he was killed. After Sekhukhune's murder his half-brother, Kgoloko, was appointed as regent. Facing the difficult task of salvaging the remnants of royal power he responded, in part, by forging a close alliance with the newly appointed native commissioner for Lydenburg, Abel Erasmus.

Divide and Rule

Erasmus was already a man of considerable notoriety. After an early career based on hunting and land speculation he was elected as a veldcornet in 1876. After the British annexation of the Transvaal in 1877 his relationship with the new administration rapidly soured. By 1879 he stood accused of encouraging Sekhukhune to resist British demands and of murdering one of his tenants who had provided information about his activities to the authorities. His neck was saved, however, by the fear that his trial would provoke even greater disaffection than already existed amongst the burghers. On retrocession in 1881 he was once again appointed to office and played a central and controversial role in the history of the region for the next 20 years.[9]

Erasmus' primary responsibilities as native commissioner were to collect taxes, maintain order and ensure a supply of labour to the white farmers. Although the defeat of the Pedi Kingdom had removed one stumbling block to effective administration, these duties remained far from simple to perform. Kgoloko provided the native commissioner with vital assistance. He channelled labour to him, provided him with military levies and assisted in the collection of taxes. In return, Kgoloko received support from Erasmus against rivals and rebels and for the establishment of a location. The commissioner also turned a blind eye to the fact that, while Kgoloko's authority was formally restricted to the location, he exercised a considerably wider hegemony.

But the power and authority of the regent were not sufficient to ensure general compliance with the commissioner's demands. More naked forms of coercion also played a vital part. Central to these was what has been described as the 'tax raid'.[10] Each year in the winter months Erasmus undertook a tax-collecting tour of the vast area which fell under his sway. On these expeditions he was accompanied by an armed force which consisted of local veldcornets, farmers and specially recruited white and black 'constables'. Groups which denied, avoided or fell behind on their obligations suffered a wide range of penalties including whippings, fines, the confiscation of cattle and imprisonment with hard labour. By the mid-1880s, through this blend of coercion and collaboration, Erasmus had secured a steady flow of labour to the farms and revenue to the state.

As the decade drew to a close Erasmus worked diligently to supply the steadily expanding demand for labour for the farms, mines and railways. These pressures provoked mounting popular resistance both to his rule and to that of the aging and ill regent. When Kgoloko died in 1892, Erasmus moved swiftly and disastrously to appoint his client Nkopodi as chief, explaining that, while his supporters were 'not the largest in number, [they] consist entirely of kaffirs who I consider to be amongst the most trustworthy native subjects of the government'.[11]

This arbitrary action both inflamed popular sentiment and outraged members of the royal family who were intent on protecting and advancing the claims of the designated heir, Morwamotše's minor son, Sekhukhune. Conflict flared in and beyond the location but, undaunted, Erasmus set out to entrench Nkopodi's rule despite his manifest lack of support. His favourite technique was to seize large numbers of cattle, notionally in payment of fines, which were divided between the commissioner and his clients. In 1895 Nkopodi died and Erasmus appointed another close ally, Kgoloko's son Kgolane, as 'location chief'. In the course of 1896 Kgolane made a number of attempts to make his notional authority effective. A flashpoint was reached when he attempted to force men from the opposing camp to supply labour to Pretoria. Fighting ensued and threatened to develop into generalised conflict.

These disturbances finally provoked the superintendent of natives to intervene. With the wisdom of Solomon he decided to divide the location between the contending parties. But he left the execution of his judgment to Erasmus who promptly gave Kgolane and his tiny band of supporters control over the relatively fertile southern half while the supporters of Sekhukhune were consigned to the barren northern portion. A new capital was built at Mohlaletse against the rocky western slopes of the Leolo Mountains, but the majority of the population of the location refused to move. They remained in the south but denied Kgolane's authority and recognised Mohlaletse as the seat of legitimate government.

The year of 1896 was a particularly disastrous one for the Pedi heartland. Crops withered under cloudless skies and when the heavens finally darkened it was not through rain-clouds but swarms of locusts which consumed the remnants of the harvest. Worse still, in April, an African transport rider from Johannesburg arrived in the location with a team of oxen infected by the deadly and highly contagious cattle disease, Rinderpest. Officials, fearing that this plague would spread to the white farms, acted swiftly to contain it. Guards were posted and thousands of cattle shot. The carcasses were burnt and sometimes buried. Twelve hundred men were commandeered to build a fence along the Steelpoort River to contain the disease. By 1897 Erasmus could congratulate himself that the neighbouring farmers had largely escaped Rinderpest. But, in the location, 'barely any of the thousands of cattle which previously existed remained'.[12] This wholesale destruction of Pedi herds was widely believed to have been motivated by profound malice and burned itself deep into the historical consciousness of these communities.

The Boer War and Reconstruction

Sekhukhune II finally assumed office in 1899. He had spent part of the previous decade exiled in Pretoria, living with his mother Thorometšane in Marabastad, and attending an Anglican school. Shortly after his return to the location the Boer War broke out. Initially this led to increased Boer control and coercion of the African population. However, once the British army had penetrated the Transvaal, these pressures eased. Sekhukhune used this new-found freedom to launch attacks against Kgolane, other rivals and clients of Erasmus. More generally, it was used to settle scores with particularly disliked clerics, storekeepers and rent collectors. In neighbouring white farming areas, Pedi workers and tenants also took up arms. An observer noted that 'a bitter war is raging between master and servant in which quarter is unknown'.[13] By the time the British army arrived in Lydenburg in September 1900, Sekhukhune and his supporters were effectively in control of the location and its hinterland. Thereafter urged on by Lord Kitchener – and by promises that they could keep half the spoils – Sekhukhune and his supporters raided Boer cattle, and monitored and blocked the movement of Boer forces.

By 1901, however, it dawned on British officers that Sekhukhune did not see himself as a zealous servant of the Empire but as an ally doing battle with a common enemy – the Boers. He began openly collecting tribute from his subjects and demanded that the new Transvaal government should acknowledge the reversion of all farms between the Steelpoort and Olifants Rivers to the Pedi. A British intelligence officer noted that 'Sekhukhune simply wishes to be independent … although he will acknowledge England as suzerain power … and [pay] tribute in the form of hut tax to be collected by him and handed over in a lump sum.'[14]

These ambitions were, however, quickly disappointed. As the Boers were steadily bludgeoned into submission, British interest in Sekhukhune as an ally waned. Their primary concerns involved re-establishing taxation and encouraging the movement of migrant workers to the gold mines. The British had also resolved to mollify the Boers after their defeat, and were unwilling to countenance any challenge to the existing distribution of land. As a result,

Pedi claims for additional land were given short shrift. Instead, from 1904 onwards, the government imposed rents on the inhabitants of crown lands, while land companies and farmers intensified their demands. Equally galling was that the Pedi were forced to return, or pay compensation for, the cattle they had been encouraged to raid from the Boers and they were systematically stripped of their firearms. Pedi dreams of independence gave way to murmurings of revolt and finally to a grudging acceptance of the new order.

In 1906 the capricious fates dealt them yet another blow when East Coast Fever appeared amongst their cattle. Once again the response of local officials was powerfully influenced by the interests of white farmers. Over 10 700 Pedi cattle were shot and their losses eventually totalled almost 20 000 head – close to three-quarters of their entire herd.[15]

Native Commissioners

In the aftermath of the Boer War the Milner administration set about constructing a system of 'native' administration which was considerably more bureaucratic and pervasive than its predecessor in the South African Republic. Native commissioners continued to be crucial figures at a local level but their precepts and practices differed somewhat from the robust attitudes and actions of the likes of Erasmus. The appointments made in the reconstruction period were mainly of English speakers, many of whom had served as British army officers. They were confident of their racial superiority and convinced of the virtues of the British Empire. But they saw themselves as servants of the state rather than as the instruments of local farmers, and they operated within a more clearly defined segregationist framework which incorporated a strong element of paternalism. To some extent the Milner appointees shared the view of the governor that it was their duty to raise 'the black man – not to our level of civilisation – which it is doubtful whether he would ever attain – but to a much higher level than that which he at present occupies'.[16] This slow progress was to be achieved within a distinct territorial, political and cultural domain centred on the reserves.

Major D.R. Hunt, who served as native commissioner in Sekhukhuneland for 23 years exemplified this new category of official and became one of its longest survivors. The public school-educated, younger son of a middle-class family in Norfolk, he sought fulfilment and financial security in imperial service. In 1896 he came to South Africa to join the Cape Mounted Rifles. Raised on images of the Raj, he was initially dismayed by the somewhat grimier realities he encountered. But after his appointment as a sub-native commissioner in 1902 he discovered, in common with district-level officials elsewhere in the empire, that their remote domains allowed them considerable autonomy, authority and respite from a wider world of turmoil and transformation. In one description, 'they lived the life of little kings in an epoch when their home based brothers had exchanged kingship for bourgeois democracy'.[17]

Unlike Erasmus, Hunt actually lived in Sekhukhuneland. He was stationed at Schoonoord, which had been the site of the first mission station within the Pedi Kingdom. His thatched stone cottage and offices were built against the steep south-western slopes of the Leolo Mountains and shaded by an avenue of trees bequeathed him by his long-departed Lutheran predecessors. It was an island of relative tranquillity only intermittently disturbed by the clamorous voices of Lydenburg's white community or by visits from officious superiors. As the years passed by, Hunt developed a strong patrician sense of identity with 'my people' and learned a great deal about the societies over which he held sway, even if from a somewhat lofty perspective. The tax raids of the Erasmus era gave way to tax tours during which Hunt moved from village to village, accompanied by an elaborate retinue. In the early years, when he travelled round the district in a Cape cart, he would outspan and

> sit under a tree for a couple of hours and all the old fellows from the kraals would come along and talk to us and tell us the news, and we used to tell them the news and be in touch with them, and in the evening I would camp under a tree in a tent and all the old men from the neighbouring *stad* (village) would come and pay their respects. I used to talk to them and sleep in my little tent under the tree, and I was to some extent their host. I was in touch with them and we were friends.[18]

On his retirement in 1931, Hunt wrote a pioneering outline of Pedi history, *An Account of the Bapedi*, which was partly based on such discussions with elders.[19] But his world did not remain entirely immune to the forces of change, and he later lamented the arrival of motor cars which had quickened the pace of his life and left little scope for such conversation.

Hunt came to be convinced of the importance of preserving a system of chiefly rule, especially as a way of maintaining the 'tribal discipline' which he so cherished. But in the first decades of the twentieth century the basic assumption of the Department of Native Affairs was that the power of *magoši* (chiefs), and especially that of the *kgošikgolo* (paramount), should be kept in check. This view was reinforced by the Bambatha Rebellion which conjured up the spectre of chiefly-led insurrection and reawakened fears of a sinister conspiracy between Zulu and Pedi malcontents. As a result, time-honoured strategies of divide and rule continued to enjoy considerable appeal within the Department of Native Affairs. After the Boer War Kgolane was re-established as chief over the southern half of Geluks location – despite the strenuous objections of Sekhukhune – and made his new headquarters at Madibong. In 1904 he died of TB and was succeeded by his son, Kgoloko, then about 12 years old. His uncle, Marišane, was appointed regent while Kgoloko was sent to Lovedale to be educated. A levy was imposed on his nominal subjects to cover the costs involved but met considerable resistance in a context in which 'very few Bapedi in their hearts recognise Kgolokoe as their chief'.[20]

Marišane proved to be as incompetent as he was unpopular. By 1911 Hunt was arguing that

> Sekhukhune should be recognised simply as chief of Geluks Location. It is most difficult to carry on as present with nearly all the people in the southern end of the location ignoring the chief [regent] who is feeble and stupid – yet not allowed to go to the one whom they all recognise; I feel certain that the sullen discontent and unsatisfactory state of affairs will continue so long as this division is bolstered up. Sekhukhune, though a heathen, is sufficiently educated to fall in with plans for the general advancement and gradual civilisation of his people. He is amenable to advice and will rapidly fall in with the orders of government as occasion demands.[21]

Hunt was, however repeatedly overruled by senior officials. Kgoloko was brought home from school and installed as chief. Sekhukhune's formal domain thus remained restricted to the northern portion of the location, although in practice he was recognised as *kgošikgolo* by the vast majority of the inhabitants of the location as well as tenants on the surrounding farms.

During the 1920s, policy in the Native Affairs Department shifted towards 'retribalisation' and chiefs in Sekhukhuneland were given greater recognition and material reward. But the position of the paramountcy remained restricted and unresolved while Kgoloko continued to rule without popular legitimacy and support. In 1928 a local council was set up for Geluks location but was constructed on a somewhat farcical basis. Hunt dared not risk an election for the council

> because every one would have voted for Chief Sekhukhune and ... the council would have simply consisted of Sekhukhune and five of his immediate followers, to the complete collapse of Kgolokoe ... and my instructions were to keep the tribal parties on an equal basis.[22]

Hunt's response to this dilemma was to recommend the appointment of three members from each camp. This resolved his bureaucratic difficulties but ensured that most location residents had little regard for the council. Although the native commissioner was forced to maintain this elaborate administrative charade, he worked closely with Sekhukhune and attempted to minimise the corrosive effects of the situation.

Hunt believed that the greatest achievement of his administration was the establishment of a 'tribal fund' to buy farms in areas released for African land purchase under the 1913 Land Act. At his last public meeting prior to his retirement in October 1931, Hunt concluded that the 'fund is my child and I ask you to look after my child.'[23] From the time of his arrival in the area in 1908, Hunt had urged this course of action to the chiefs but encountered deep resistance to buying land. This was led by Sekhukhune's uncle and senior advisor, Bokgobelo, who 'continued steadfastly to assert that Sekhukhuneland as a whole was the property of the Bapedi and they should not buy what belonged to them'.[24] But the example of other groups who bought farms, together with the suffocatingly small location, ultimately led to a softening of this attitude. In 1922 it was finally agreed to establish a levy of £1 per taxpayer 'with a view to buying Sekhukhuneland back gradually, farm by farm'.[25] Over the next 30 years, 29 farms were purchased using the fund. But Hunt's 'child' was to prove a troublesome responsibility.

Chiefly Rule

Hunt believed that he enjoyed growing support from the Pedi, and that he was making excellent progress in shepherding his subjects gently towards modernity. He was confident that the 'chiefs have gradually lost their old powers and the tribe have come more and more to look to their local commissioner'.[26] But this was not a view widely shared in the villages under his sway.

In theory, native commissioners in the region enjoyed vast authority. Chiefs who proved recalcitrant ran the risk of a reduction in their stipends while those who challenged official authority were in grave danger of being deposed. Commoners who stepped out of line were also firmly dealt with – deportation being a common punishment. In practice, however, the commissioners had limited impact on the day-to-day life of most of their subjects. They presided over vast and populous regions and their energies, and those of the handful of staff at their disposal, were sapped by a grinding daily round of collecting revenue and issuing passes. In the late 1920s, tax tours were deemed too expensive by the Department of Native Affairs, and discontinued. Thereafter, the main contact that most individuals had with officials was when they left the area *en route* to town. Most practical administration of the area was undertaken by what remained of the system of government which had evolved within the Pedi Kingdom.[27]

In the eighteenth century the north-eastern Transvaal had been populated by a multitude of groups divided into a multiplicity of chiefdoms. These communities lived, not in scattered homesteads like the Xhosa or the Zulu, but in villages. The Pedi state emerged in the latter half of the eighteenth century when the Marota started to extend their control over the region, bringing the most powerful chiefdoms under their rule. The pre-existing rulers were not displaced but transformed into subordinate chiefs. This new relationship was cemented by the fact that these *dikgošana* (subordinate chiefs) were expected to find their senior wives from amongst the daughters and sisters of the *kgošikgolo* (the king), ensuring that future *dikgošana* would be tied to the Marota by blood.

The arrival of the royal bride was a major ceremonial event. All fires within the chiefdom were extinguished and then relit in order of rank by an ember taken from a fire kindled in the bride's new courtyard, thereby symbolising the renewal of legitimate political authority. The chief wife had the special titles of *setima-mello* (extinguisher of fires) or *lebone* (candle or lantern).

The Marota chiefdom became the final court of appeal for cases which could not be resolved in local courts or which resulted from disputes – for example over boundaries – between subordinate groups. This process of dispute settlement involved the *batseta* (intermediary) system which played a crucial role in the administration of the state. The Marota chiefdom, like other settlements in the area, was divided into sub-units called *dikgoro* which usually centred on a group of kin who lived in a distinct section of the village. A number of these *dikgoro* acted as *batseta* for subordinate chiefdoms. They hosted their representatives when they visited the capital and settled unresolved cases or referred them to the king's court. Over time they built up an expert knowledge of the affairs of the villages in their charge and of local history.

The *batseta* system proved to be both politically sensitive and an effective instrument of government which, like the system of *lebone*, endured long after the defeat of the kingdom. But, equally importantly, the substance of these relationships was continually renegotiated as the relative power of the different parties to them waxed and waned and the kingdom's context was transformed. A recurring theme in the history of the polity involved more powerful subordinate chiefdoms seeking to assert their independence from central control, while the Marota attempted to limit their autonomy.

By the 1930s official recognition had been extended only to the very apex of this system. Sekhukhune and Kgoloko were granted state recognition in Geluks location and a handful of chiefs appointed elsewhere in the region, including Sekwati Mampuru, who had built a powerful chiefdom in the Nebo district. But, unlike other areas where 'headmen' constituted the bottom rung of the system of colonial administration, the authority of the scores of *dik-*

gošana and heads of the *dikgoro* received no official endorsement and rested upon internal political processes and principles. The main interaction between the commissioners and their subjects took place only through recognised chiefs and vital aspects of social life were managed out of sight of this rarefied elevation.

The *kgošikgolo* and *dikgošana* exercised considerably more diverse forms of authority than white officials did. They helped to safeguard their subjects against witches, mediated between them and powerful royal ancestors and pitted their powers against the unremitting skies in rain-making rituals. With authority ultimately derived from the paramount, *dikgošana* and heads of *dikgoro* oversaw the process of land allocation in the locations, on 'tribal' farms and on those owned by absentee landlords. Chiefs sanctioned crucial phases in the life-cycle of communities. They initiated the planting season and presided over the harvest festival at its close. They gave permission for male and female initiation to commence and, when it was completed, welcomed the young men and women back home. In return they received modest amounts of tribute in grain, beer, cash and labour from their subjects. They benefited from the fines – usually in stock – that were imposed in their courts and the inflated bridewealth they received for their daughters. Most importantly they received payments – usually of £1 – from migrant workers on their return. These sources of income were of decisive significance for the vast majority of chiefs, who did not receive state salaries.

By the 1930s most Pedi had relinquished dreams of re-establishing independence from colonial control. But this did not mean that they were prepared to surrender those areas of autonomy that remained. While the authority of native commissioners to collect taxes and issue passes was grudgingly accepted, any attempt to extend the boundaries of officials' control produced intense opposition. Chiefs and commoners alike were content to indulge native commissioners' sense of authority so long as, in practice, the scope of their intervention remained restricted.

This principle was illustrated by the operation of the courts in the region. In theory, the commissioners' court dealt with cases which could not be resolved within chiefs' courts or which fell outside their limited civil jurisdiction. In practice, the commissioners' court was avoided as far as possible, and civil and criminal cases were settled in the local courts or referred to the Marota chiefdom. As Edward Mothubatse, who became 'tribal secretary' at Mohlaletse, recalled,

> We were trying cases at the tribal court. There were divorce cases, cases about land disputes, family conflicts … The government prohibited us from [trying] murder and assault cases. But we used to handle such cases. In our custom, for instance, if two young men were

fighting with *knobkerries* and one beat the other to death, he would pay a fine. His family would have to provide a girl to the bereaved family. The children born to that girl would be seen as belonging to the dead person. If a person struck another man's head we would make him pay a fine in cattle if it was a serious injury.[28]

Very few individuals had confidence in the commissioners' capacity to grasp or pronounce on complex social processes or desired to be exposed to the alien models of criminal justice and punishment which prevailed in his court. Individuals who by-passed the chiefs' court or rejected its judgment also risked heavy fines. Chiefs' courts not only played a vital role in settling disputes, but also provided a forum in which social values and practices were debated and redefined. And while they dealt with serious crimes in defiance of the official definition of their role, they were far from inundated with such cases in the 1930s. Native commissioners' reports and oral sources agree that there was very little serious crime in the area in the 1930s and 1940s. Hunt believed that if one excluded 'regulation-made crime, such as a man not having a pass [there was] extraordinarily little real crime'.[29]

Migrants

This political and social order was based on a migrant labour system which dominated the economy of the region. Limited amounts of arable land, combined with a capricious climate and remoteness from major markets, ensured that agriculture played a diminishing role in providing food or cash income for the villages. There were years in which good rains produced bumper harvests and allowed some crops to be offered for sale. But, as Hunt observed in 1930,

> I should say that every seven out of eight years we have to import mealies ... for sale for food. For the last six years, including this year, all the storekeepers have been riding mealies into the country as hard as they could.

Crops of sorghum and millet which had a greater resistance to drought fared rather better, and in reasonable years women 'bring them in [to traders] in small quantities, in baskets and exchange them for other goods'. But in 'some years we had nothing at all and we have had to import kaffir corn [sorghum] too'.[30] Even in years when women sold some grain to storekeepers they often had to buy it back at inflated prices later in the season when their own stores ran low.

The society's cattle reserves made a slow recovery from Rinderpest and East Coast Fever and were decimated once more by drought in the years 1924-9 when over 11 000 cattle died of starvation. When Hunt was called to give evidence before the Native Economic Commission at Lydenburg in 1930, his opening words were:

> I just want to place before the commission one fact ... a district such as Sekukuniland produces very little itself, and is very nearly dependent on what is sent from beyond its own borders. It produces very little indeed for its own living. If we in Sekukuniland had to depend for our revenue on Sekukuniland alone, I am quite certain it would be necessary to reduce the taxes, or else provide additional prison accommodation for the adult male population.[31]

The Pedi were amongst the earliest migrant labourers in South Africa. Long before the conquest of the kingdom and, indeed, partly to sustain its independence, young men left home for up to two years and returned with guns and cash. They travelled enormous distances across dangerous territory on foot. From the 1850s they found jobs on the farms and in the coastal towns of the Eastern Cape. From the 1870s until the mid-1890s, they dominated the labour market at the Kimberley diamond fields.

The last years of the nineteenth century and the first decade of the twentieth saw a partial reorientation of Pedi migrancy towards the Rand. But the diamond industry continued to be an important focus, especially after the opening of Premier Mines on the southern border of Sekhukhuneland in 1902. Premier Mines, in fact, became the single most important employer of Pedi workers until the early 1930s. But diamond mines had one major disadvantage – their vulnerability to recession. There were major reductions of the workforce in 1914 and the early 1920s and massive lay-offs after 1930. Premier Mine was effectively shut down in 1931 and thousands of Pedi workers had to seek work elsewhere – mainly on the gold mines.[32]

In the nineteenth century some Pedi youths sought employment on local farms but this practice declined with the development of coal mining at Witbank and Middelburg before the Anglo-Boer War, and the opening of tin and platinum mines from the second decade of the twentieth century which provided local though relatively low-paid employment. There was also a rapid expansion of asbestos mining in the area, and men often worked long hours coated from head to foot in white dust with no protection against the deadly fibres which would destroy the lungs and the lives of many of them.[33]

From the 1890s young men also found employment as domestic workers, initially in neighbouring towns but increasingly after 1902 in Pretoria and on the Rand. Individuals would often first take local jobs and thus acquire the skills and resources to make their own way to the higher-paying urban centres. By the early 1930s the bulk of the Pedi mineworkers were employed – often as surface workers – on the East Rand mines.[34] Hunt provided an overview of patterns of migrancy in 1930, reporting that

> my output of labour, mainly to the Eastern Rand Mines, to the Spring Mines, to the Van Ryn Estate, Van Ryn Deep and also to the Premier Mine and for house boys in Pretoria, I should say would be between 8 500 and 9 000 per year.[35]

While the overwhelming majority of young men were absent from the villages in these decades, very few women became migrant workers. Chiefs and elders within the community strongly opposed female migrancy, and the impact of political fragmentation, high bridewealth, economic depression and Christianity, which in various combinations spurred women from some other regions to the cities, operated on Pedi society in somewhat muted form. Hunt commented that 'comparatively few [women are away] … in numbers it is nothing like those who go from the Rustenburg district'. With a growing demand for female domestic workers, some Pedi women started to spend spells of time working in the suburbs of Pretoria. There were also women who left the area permanently. But the number of female migrant workers remained low and they were mainly drawn from Christian families.[36]

The first Pedi workers had seen migrancy as a way of protecting the independence of the kingdom. In the 1930s most men still regarded working in the city as a means of maintaining a primarily rural way of life. Migrancy was seen as a necessary evil which had to be undertaken not only in order in order to pay taxes but also to secure the resources to marry, build a homestead, accumulate cattle and ultimately allow for rural retirement.

Towns were regarded and described as *makgoweng* (the place of the whites) or *lešokeng* (a wilderness). Part of what defined them as such was the absence of core institutions like initiation and chieftainship and what many migrants saw as the corrosion of appropriate relationships of gender and generation amongst urban Africans. Some men stayed away for decades without remitting money or returning, while others abandoned their families and never came home. But these acts merely strengthened the majority view that towns were deeply immoral places. Most migrants saw the chiefs and especially the *kgošikgolo* as key symbols and guarantors of a rurally centred moral order. And the native commissioners, despite Hunt's confidence that their authority was waxing, were regarded as outsiders – as an advance guard of *makgoweng* best kept in quarantine.[37]

The commitment to a rural world was sustained by most men's expectation that they would ultimately secure some rights to land and livestock. By the 1930s there was considerable pressure on resources of arable land in the locations both because of internal population growth and because of the steady immigration of families from white farms. This led to the fragmentation of existing fields and the allocation of smaller, less fertile and more remote pieces of land.

It also resulted in debate about the security of tenure of land. In the past, rights granted to individuals over land were retained even if the fields lay fallow for ten years or more. But, from the 1930s, pressure grew for these lands to be reallocated to recent settlers and other landless families. Those who struggled to find land in the locations could opt to settle on crown or land company properties where there was less pressure on arable land. These families faced significant additional rent payments and stock charges but otherwise suffered little interference from land companies or the state. And families which could not, or would not, meet those payments had the option of entering into one of the variety of labour tenant arrangements which existed on white farms. Labour tenants sometimes were able to secure access to a better quality of arable land and grazing by settling outside the Pedi heartland. But these advantages were bought at the cost of considerable concessions to their independence from white authority.[38]

Chiefs, Commoners and Conflicts

Although it was still possible for most men to gain access to land and livestock, this did not mean that rural society was egalitarian. Evidence from the 1930s and 1940s suggests that there were marked disparities in the quantity and quality of resources which households commanded. A handful of individuals, for example, had used funds accumulated through transport riding or the sale of substantial herds to buy land in their own right. In the Nebo district a total of 3 000 morgen had been bought by 16 individual African farmers.[39] In the Sekhukhuneland district, however, there were only a couple of examples of individual land purchases. One involved a man called Mantlanyane who had been living on crown land near the Steelpoort River:

> He found he could not get on with the headman in whose kraal he was living. He had all sorts of difficulties there and found the grazing was becoming more and more scarce. Furthermore, he realised he himself was unpopular down there … one day he had ninety of his cattle sold here in Lydenburg. He also sold his goats, his sheep, he sold his grain and every single thing he had there. Prices were high at that time and he sold at the top of the market. He did very well and one way and another he raised £800. So he bought 300 morgen in his own name … It was very good land.[40]

As this case suggests, accumulators could find themselves the objects of hostility and there were considerable variations in the size of individual herds. Abel Mosehle, for example, who was from a Christian family, recalled that by the time his father died in 1918 he had 100 head of cattle and 200 sheep although at that time many families did not have any cattle at all. Some men, particularly those close to the chiefs or able to offer them substantial 'gifts', could secure control over relatively large areas of arable land in the communal areas. But the overall tendency in the period was for a reduction in the size of land holdings and individual herds.

The residents of Sekhukhuneland faced a looming threat to their world and its core values: the creation of a permanently landless and/or stockless stratum. In the 1930s this spectre was held at bay through sub-division and by land and cattle loaning arrangements which prevented the creation of starkly defined rural classes. The slow haemorrhage of men to the towns on a permanent basis also acted as a pressure valve and, in some instances, allowed for the redistribution of resources. But just how long this elaborate balancing act could be maintained was open to question.[41]

Socio-economic factors were only one of a number forms of differentiation within the villages of Sekhukhuneland. The population of each chiefdom was divided into a number of distinct strata ranging from *bakgomana* (royals) who where members of the chiefly lineage, through *batala* (commoners) who did not have kinship links to the ruling core, to *mathupya* (descendants of captives). There was no simple relationship between rank, wealth and power, and relatively poor and powerless individuals were located at all levels of the society.[42] But *bakgomana* dominated political office and overall had larger herds and bigger and better lands. Elias Motsoaledi remembered, for example, being troubled as he grew up by the fact that, while his family depended on land loaned to them by his aunt,

> I saw the royal family had land and all the like, but I couldn't understand why [this was so], I had to ask exactly where is our land then? If this piece was given to us by our Aunt, where is our land?[43]

The most profound division that men and women remember in most villages in these decades was between the *baditšaba* (those of the community) and a small minority of *Bakristi* (Christians). Christians usually lived in distinct areas of villages known as *setaseneng* (derived from mission station).

According to John Phala, recalling his childhood in the 1930s, 'We can see that apartheid started there among the black people. There was a contradiction between … the *majakane* (Christians) and those they called *baheitene* (heathens).'[44] It is revealing that the term *majakane* was derived from the verb *jaka* meaning 'to live in a foreign country'.

There had been particularly bitter conflicts between missionaries from the Berlin Missionary Society and chiefs and commoners in the 1860s. It was widely believed – with good cause – that Christians had conspired with the Boers and the British to bring about the destruction of the Pedi Kingdom, and these perceptions and conflicts led to the withdrawal of missionaries and their converts to stations outside of the Pedi domain. But in the 1880s, missionaries established mission stations in the Pedi heartland once more and leading figures in the church came to be closely associated with Abel Erasmus and his clients.

Christianity was thus closely affiliated, in the minds of most Pedi, with colonial conquest and a broader assault on established values and practices. There were sporadic conflicts, especially between youths from the different religious camps. And while there was little difference in the overall standard of living of Christian and *baditšaba* segments of the villages, Christians constituted the overwhelming majority in the predominantly mission schools in the area. As a result, Christians dominated the small local educated elite of teachers and clerks.

Tensions between commoners and chiefs also flared from time to time in many communities. While the office of chieftainship was regarded as a vital buffer against white control, individual chiefs were by no means immune from popular criticism and challenge. These conflicts were most marked in those instances – for example, the cases of Abel Erasmus' clients – where chieftainship was blatantly the creation of colonial manipulation. In these situations commoners fought a long-drawn-out struggle to reduce the effective authority of the chief to the minimum possible, without invoking reprisals from white officialdom and, whenever they were able, to invoke the alternative authority of the *kgošikgolo*.[45]

But even in communities where the legitimacy of the chief was more securely grounded the nature of chiefly power was a point of ongoing contestation. The scarcity of resources meant that commoners were increasingly unable to employ the classic strategy of withdrawing from the areas of incompetent and/or capricious *dikgoši*, and chiefs could now look to white officials to confirm and maintain them in office in the face of challenge. The overall result was to make chiefs more authoritarian and remote from their subjects. Godfrey Pitje, who grew up in Sekhukhuneland and who returned in the 1940s to conduct anthropological research, observed that whereas in the past commoners had been able to speak in *pitso* (public meetings),

> Nowadays there is very little freedom of speech. Pedi chiefs are notorious for resenting remarks from commoners. After a commoner has aired his views it is not uncommon for the chief to ask 'Whose son is he?' ... It is a reflection of the mentality common amongst nobles ... that those lower than themselves are not capable of advising them ... Those who resent such treatment usually do so by reminding the chief that *Kgoshi ke kgoshi ka batho* (ie a chief is a chief by the grace of his people). This expression carries with it the threat that unless the chief rules by the will of the majority, his subjects may desert him. However, under European administration this threat cannot be carried out, at least not in the old sense.[46]

The imposition of special levies by the chiefs was a recurring source of con-flict. The most controversial of these charges involved Hunt's 'child' – the fund based on a land levy of £1 per taxpayer – which was initiated in 1923 and partly administered by the native commissioner. Although this fund con-siderably expanded the amount of land under the authority of the Paramount, it was far from universally supported. The payment of the levy ran counter to the long-standing popular conviction that 'the land belongs to us, we cannot buy our own ground'.[47] There was a deep-seated reluctance to buy back land that most people believed had been stolen by the whites.

The land that was acquired was often remote from the locations, already densely settled and did little to alleviate land hunger in the heart of Sekhuk-huneland. Some of the *dikgošana* also chafed against a system which expanded the power of the Paramount but did little to enhance their own po-sitions. Special collectors were appointed to gather the levy from groups of migrants on the Reef, and periodic raids were also conducted by the native commissioners' police in the reserves. Defaulters were sometimes manhan-dled and found themselves fined or even imprisoned. Conflict on this issue flared on a number of occasions from the 1930s onwards. In one instance a group of Pedi migrants working at Premier Mines formed an 'African Work-ers' Association' which protested to the chiefs that 'we do not refuse to pay levy but object to being chased like fowls'. They received short shrift, how-ever, being told that 'the children on the Reef are our children. They must take instruction from us.'[48]

Childhood and Education

The importance of chieftainship and commitment to rural society were in-stilled in children from early on in their lives. In the first decades of the twentieth century Pedi boys spent much of their time looking after livestock. Small boys herded calves, goats and sheep in the environs of the village. Older boys looked after cattle which where often kept at remote posts. They spent months away from their villages living in rough shelters, surviving on milk, the product of the hunt and grain they traded for dairy products. These youths became knowledgeable about the veld and the animals in their care. When not herding, milking or hunting they played musical instruments, sang, danced and fought.

Life at the cattle post could be harsh. It was bitterly cold in winter and food sometimes ran short. But most parents believed that only rough han-dling could turn boys into good citizens and that 'man is destined to live a tough life and therefore the boy must be hardened for it'.[49] These boys also had considerable freedom from the authority of elders and there were balmy summer days when food was abundant. Many men remember these as heady times when they 'rode cattle at a gallop' and 'drank milk like calves'.[50]

From an early age girls helped with child care in the *kgoro*. They also learned how to maintain the mud walls of the courtyards and the dung floors of the huts. They were taught to identify and gather wild foods. Girls spent long hours grinding corn, and fetching water and kindling wood. As they grew older they did more and more work in the fields, initially assisting with weeding but subsequently also helping with planting and harvesting. In those cases where fields were far from villages, mothers and their daughters lived in shelters at their lands for the most intensive parts of the agricultural season.[51] Taboos against women handling stock started to break down in the 1930s as a result of the labour shortages produced by widespread male migrancy, and there were examples where girls herded stock and assisted with ploughing. Hunt reported 'big girls herding the cattle and small girls herding the sheep'.[52] Girls from the village were also regularly called upon to work in the chief's fields and in the royal *kgoro*. Mma Malata, for example, recalled a typical day's labour:

> We went to hoe for the chief ... afterwards we put sorghum into a small dish and we started to grind. That was your job. When you had finished grinding we went to help the old women working with mud [walling]. Sometimes we went to cut reeds to build fences [and make baskets].[53]

But it would be wrong to imagine that girls were so burdened by labour that they had no time for play. Dorcas Phala, for example, remembered that 'we were enjoying ourselves playing and dancing'.[54] Women recall a rich repertoire of games and songs and the pleasures of eating the succulent maize and watermelons they picked while working in the fields.[55]

In the 1930s only a tiny minority of children attended the handful of mainly mission schools in the area, and these children were overwhelmingly from Christian communities. *Baditšaba* parents feared that schools were recruiting grounds for Christianity and were very reluctant to allow their children to attend. This fear was sometimes overcome in relation to their sons but was rarely suppressed in the case of girls. As Mma Malata recalled:

> We never attended school, we took care of the children, we the Basotho of Sekhukhune did not like school. We thought that those who go to schools are Christians (*majakane*) who have not been initiated. It was our custom that it will bring trouble, they said a girl should not be taught. A boy should [perhaps] be educated because he will go to town (*makgoweng*) and will have to talk to whites.[56]

Boys and girls spent a considerable amount of time in cohorts broadly based on age, and these played a vital part in their socialisation. As they approached adolescence these groupings became more formalised. Switch fighting competitions established clearly defined leaders amongst the boys. On the day of *mothibo* boys would go into the veld and cut bundles and bundles of switches from the long, slender shoots of moretlwa trees. Fighting would last all day with the switches whistling through the air and slicing through flesh. As the sun started to set, the youths would return singing to the village to present the overall champion – the *nkgwete* – to the chief who appointed him as leader of the youth. A leader – the *malokwane* – was also appointed from amongst the girls on the basis of her ability to sing and dance. Once these leaders were appointed, youths were no longer *bašemane* (boys) and *basetsana* (girls) but *mašoboro* and *mathumaša*.[57]

These adolescents formed a distinct sub-group. Their parents were not held responsible for their actions but they were also not full members of the community. They were summoned through their leaders to perform duties for the elders and especially the chief. But *mašoboro*, in particular, were also expected to be insubordinate and cheeky and were viewed 'as a lawless gang whose actions fall largely outside the pattern of tribal law'.[58] They established their own court and councillors and administered their own internal forms of – sometimes rough – justice. *Mašoboro* and *mathumaša* went through rituals of courtship and marriage and rehearsed many of the activities of married life. There was, however, a strong prohibition against full sexual intercourse.

The insubordination of these youths became particularly pronounced as the time for their initiation drew near. Their parents lamented their behaviour and their victims punished them vigorously when they got the chance. But it was also understood that this was a phase of generational assertion and antagonism which initiation was designed to harness and tether to the established order.

Initiation *(koma)* was held in the individual chiefdoms approximately every five years and its first phase (the *bodika*) preceded the second (the *bogwera*) by one to two years. Initiation marked the transition from youth to adulthood and was 'a cornerstone of the whole social and political organisation'.[59] It was compulsory for all youths of the appropriate age – from early teens to mid-twenties – to attend. They were secluded for three months at a time in lodges in the mountains. During the act of circumcision the youths were not supposed to show any sign of pain for: '*Monna ke nku, o llela teng*' (A man is like a sheep, he does not cry out aloud).[60]

This ordeal was merely one of many tests of courage and endurance which youths had to undergo. The instruction they received laid great empha-

sis on the office of chieftainship, and the authority of age, rank and patriar-
chy. Thenceforth these young men were to see themselves as a cut above
women and uninitiated men. But the leaders who had emerged through their
prowess as fighters now had to bow before the authority of the chief's son
whose seniority was repeatedly underscored during *koma*. Boys were
schooled in the history of the community, the arts of warfare and in the economic, political and sexual roles that they would assume as adults.

It was also compulsory for girls to attend initiation. Shortly after the
bogwera phase of male initiation the *byale* session for girls began. The *byale*
was held under the direction of the principal wife of the chief assisted by the
older women of the village and past initiates. They underwent a symbolic
process of circumcision:

> The girls are told that an operation is to be performed on them. A
> knife is sharpened in their presence and they are then taken, one by
> one, made to lie down, and covered with a blanket. The knife is then
> pressed between their legs. Although they are not injured at all, the
> girls cry out with fright when feeling the cold metal. As each girl is
> led away ... the women who perform the 'operation' emerge from the
> blanket with their hands reddened with plant-juices. The girls still
> waiting their turn, thinking that the hands of the women are covered
> in blood, must obviously be terrorised. Although they do not undergo
> the pain that boys do when circumcised, the fright and bewilderment
> of the girls must be equal to that of the boys.[61]

For a period of approximately one month the girls remained in seclusion in a
lodge. During this time they received formal instruction on the work and duties of a woman, on sexual matters and on their relationships with men. They
were also subjected to various endurance tests and had the importance of deference to their elders, to men and especially to the chief, drummed into them.

During initiation, and also more generally, young men were regularly reminded that their prime loyalty and responsibility lay in the countryside to
their chiefs, their parents and to the households they would one day establish
themselves. They were warned against the dangers and temptations of *makgoweng* and were told that locations, and especially urban women, were
dangerous, disease-ridden and degrading. And they had the example of
Christian youth – who it was believed simply abandoned their rural responsibilities – held up to them as an example of truly delinquent behaviour.[62]

Each initiation group was formed into a regiment led by a royal son, and
this process was designed to cement the loyalty of the members to the
chieftainship, reinforce the bonds between age-mates and create relationships
of solidarity and mutual co-operation that would last through life. After initiation, only marriage and the establishment of a household stood between

the young man and full adult status. John Kgoana Nkadimeng realised that, after his initiation at the village of Manganeng,

> From now on you are a man, you must think and behave like a man, you can now attend meetings ... you are responsible, you don't just go [around alone], you must be with the group, you must have discussions about the problems facing the village. It has a political element because it means that people come together to recognise that as one they can do nothing but together they can do something. [A man also retained] a special link with that group.[63]

Missionaries and converts viewed initiation as the bedrock of paganism and chiefly power and normally prohibited youths from attending. This deepened the cleavages between the groups still further, for non-initiated men could not be made privy to the affairs of initiates. Even in towns, when migrants held meetings, however educated a man might be, 'if you have not been to initiation school ... you are *nothing* man'.[64] This exclusion was something which many Christian youths felt deeply, and attempts were made within Christian communities to incorporate elements of traditional initiation. Confirmation was presented as an equivalent experience, and Godfrey Pitje remembers that informal age-sets were widely recognised amongst Christian youth.[65] But a yawning gulf remained.

When Christian youth were mocked for still being 'boys' by the graduates of the *koma* they responded with derision at their detractors' 'backwardness' and lack of 'civilisation'. Western education and notions of social 'advancement' played a central part in their self-definition, and Christian children were the dominant element in the schools in the region. The growth of these institutions was closely tied to the history of missionary endeavour although the state increasingly shouldered the burden of teachers' salaries and made some attempt to shape the curriculum.

In the 1930s the Berlin Missionary Society continued to play the central role but there was a significant Wesleyan presence and a handful of Catholic, Dutch Reformed and Anglican schools. The Lutheran schools only admitted those children who belonged to their church because they felt that 'pagan children would be a source of grave moral danger to their children'.[66] The other missions took a somewhat wider view of education and accepted the small numbers of *baditšaba* children who applied. The BMS schools, while obliged by state regulation to provide some training in English, nonetheless placed their emphasis on mother tongue instruction. Godfrey Pitje – who was a product of one of these schools – described how

> the Lutheran schools in Sekhukhuneland concentrated on religious training and manual work. Their boys recited chunks of passages

from the Old and the New Testament, Hymns and the Catechism. Just
as the pagan boys rendered free labour to the chief even so did their
boys to the missionaries. This manual labour was more in the nature
of forced labour than that of training in industrial habits.[67]

Almost all the schools were entirely staffed by African teachers, many of
whom were locals trained at one of a triumvirate of teacher training institutions – Botshabelo, Kilnerton and Grace Dieu. Teachers, being mainly
Christian and uninitiated, were viewed with some suspicion by *baditšaba*
communities but they had considerable standing and authority amongst converts. As Pitje recalls:

> The teacher and not the father becomes the symbol of discipline.
> When the boy is naughty his parents threaten to report him to the
> teachers. If they do the teacher punishes him without further
> investigation. Conversely when he is disobedient they accuse the
> teacher of not teaching him good manners and respect for elders.
> Home discipline is further weakened by the fact that the father is
> absent from home for most of the time thus leaving him to be
> disciplined by women whom he more often than not despises.[68]

Very few children continued beyond Standard Three. Those that remained in
school stayed until they were confirmed at the age of 16 or 17. One common
feature was that 'everywhere boys are more than girls, because most people
are prejudiced against the education of girls'.[69] The BMS schools in the main
only went up to Standard Four and children would languish at that level until
they reached the age for confirmation and left school. A number of schools of
the other denominations, however, expanded to include Standards Five and
Six and provided their pupils with rather more educational scope and somewhat greater prospects of securing clerical rather than manual employment.
In the 1930s the vast majority of school leavers, however, initially found un-
skilled employment and enjoyed little material advantage over their
'unschooled' counterparts.

While the forms of education that existed within *baditšaba* communities
were designed to bind the child to the social and political order which prevailed in the villages, in the case of a Christian child:

> From his mother's breast he is encouraged to look down on pagans
> (*baheitene*) and anything that savours of tribal traditionalism. The
> place of the head of the *kgoro* and that of the chief is taken by the
> evangelist or priest ... [the chief] is derisively referred to as 'the chief
> of the heathens'.[70]

At a time when recession, job reservation and segregation were eroding the
limited possibilities available to educated Africans, the images of modernity

'The approach to Schoonoord from the Magnet Heights road. [Showing] the office and the house and the police post, 1908.'

'Shooting cattle for East Coast Fever, Sekukuniland, 1909.' *(DR Hunt collection, original captions)*

'Tea time, tax tour camp, 1909.' [Hunt is seated in the middle].

'Tax tour camp, 1909.' *(DR Hunt collection, original captions)*

'Peace Celebrations 1919. Sekhukhune II is sitting in the middle.'

'View from Mohlaletse. An average Sekukuniland stad [village] built as usual close under the hills. Note huts surrounded by reed enclosed *lapa* (yards). Note *kgoro* or meeting place entrance beyond prickly pears in the centre of the picture.' [1920s?] *(DR Hunt collection, original captions)*

'Bodikane initiates on completion of school. Hair cut, bodies shining with grease.' [1920s]

'Bapedi girls selling chickens.' [Schoonoord 1922.] *(DR Hunt collection, original captions)*

'Women collecting water.'
[1950s.]
(PJ Quin, original caption)

Donald Rolfes Hunt,
31 May 1942.
(DR Hunt collection)

'Gathering *merogo*. Pedi mother and child gathering the first pot-herbs of the season.' [1950s]

'Girl grinding grain on a portable stone.' [1950s] *(PJ Quin, original caption)*

A *ngaka* (diviner/herbalist) surrounded by
his medicines and other paraphernalia,
early 1960s. *(HO Mönnig)*

Married woman making beer,
early 1960s. *(HO Mönnig)*

Pedi mother and her daughters enjoying a
watermelon. [1950s.] *(PJ Quin)*

A view from the *mošate* at the village of Mamone, early 1960s. The gathering place and the cattle kraal appear on the right. The extent to which mud walling has replaced the reed fencing shown in the picture of Mohlaletse in the 1920s is striking. *(HO Mönnig)*

and progress which were paraded before them by their teachers often proved to be mirages. All too often, in the words of Pitje, 'They are divorced from the old way of tribal living and yet cannot find their feet in the new.'[71]

By the 1930s there was, nonetheless, a growing recognition amongst some of the leaders of *baditšaba* communities that Western education was vital to negotiating the treacherous cross-currents of colonial society. Their main concern was to try and lessen the heavy cultural load conveyed by the mission schools. The chiefs who appeared before the Native Economic Commission in 1930 were unanimous in their plea for non-denominational education. 'Headman' Frank Maserumule pointed out that

> We have had denominational schools here for a long time but we do not see that we are making much progress ... Our people have the idea that if they send our children to the different churches ... the churches will absorb the children and they will live in those churches ... The missionaries object to the *lobola* [bridewealth] custom, and they object to the native circumcision schools. If a boy goes to circumcision school he will not be allowed back in the mission school. But if there is an undenominational school there will be no objection to the boy going to the circumcision school and then going back to the ordinary school.[72]

These anxieties had led to the establishment of 'tribal' schools in a couple of the larger villages. But the attendance at these schools remained low. Edward Mothubatse, who was the teacher at the school at Mohlaletse, pleaded before the Native Economic Commission: 'Why is our education not made compulsory? If the government were to look with a sharp eye at our education and tell our chiefs why there are so few children in schools, it would be a very good thing indeed.'[73] There was also considerable discontent that the central government refused to allow any of the local tax revenue to be spent on education in the region.

Marriage and Migrancy

Once girls had been to initiation school or had been confirmed, it was considered time for them to be married. In the 1930s some unions were the result of individual choices but in many cases – especially amongst the higher ranking strata of *baditšaba* society – marriages were arranged by the elders often long before the betrothed reached maturity. And in these social circles there was also a strong preference for marriage between cousins, which had the advantage of strengthening social bonds and establishing reciprocal flows of bridewealth goods. Men normally only married after they had spent some years as migrants and were able to contribute substantially to their *bogadi* (bridewealth). As a result, there tended to be a significant age difference between husbands and wives. This discrepancy was even more marked in the case of second or third wives. Most women who married in the 1920s and 1930s refer to their husbands as *mokgalabje* (old man), which is perhaps revealing of this age discrepancy as well as the language of deference.[74]

Young girls were expected to turn their backs on the relationships they had established prior to initiation and commit themselves to their ascribed partners. And while women looking back over their lives comment on this transition with considerable stoicism there are also undercurrents of distress. Reshoketswe Kgetsepe recalled that:

> We were having fun, the young men were proposing to us and we were accepting them but my family said no ... the marriage of that time was given to us by our parents. If you protest they will punish you, so we were just quiet, we were not like the children of modern times who beat their parents.[75]

Her experience was particularly difficult: her spouse was her father's brother's son who had been absent from the society for many years and had formed a relationship with a woman in town. It was hoped that their arranged marriage would re-establish his links to the countryside.

Marriages to migrant workers also involved periods of separation which usually lasted for months at a time and could easily stretch out for years. It is not surprising that husbands often emerge as rather remote figures in the accounts of women's lives. New wives usually stayed with their parents until the birth of the first child when they took up residence in their husbands' *lapa* (household). They now fell under the authority of their husbands' kin who they were expected to treat with considerable deference. Their husbands' mother, in particular, could make heavy demands on their time and their tolerance although these relationships were by no means always fraught with tension.

Remittances were the life-blood of the reserve economy but were often uncertain and sporadic components in the income of individual households. Before marriage, men sent or brought money home to their parents which was partly used to accumulate their bridewealth. Once they had married, this money did not automatically go directly or entirely to their wives, and some women recall protracted tussles – particularly with their mothers-in-law – over control of these funds. During these decades, tensions over remittances contributed to growing pressure from wives for the establishment of new and separate *lapa* and contributed to friction between households within polygamous marriages. A still more severe problem was that, while some men sent or brought money home on a regular and predictable basis, many did not. Mogwadi Tshesane, for example, felt it was inappropriate to send money to his wife but would bring her cloth or blankets when he returned home. He did, however, send money to his father to buy stock on his behalf. Other men failed to send money home but would give their wives lump sums when they came home on visits, which were sometimes sporadic. Yet others abandoned their responsibilites to their rural households entirely.[76]

The consequence of this erratic pattern of remittances was that many households were deeply dependent on the fruit of womens' labour in the fields not only for their food but also to meet their cash requirements. Women who ran out of provisions and money could turn to relatives for assistance or work in the fields of the more fortunate in exchange for small amounts of grain. Those who had sorghum to spare would take it to shops to sell or to exchange for salt, sugar, utensils, cloth and blankets.

Some women made and traded baskets and pots. But probably the most important local source of revenue for women at this time was the sale of beer. Women would brew sorghum beer and sell it to migrants who were at home, flush with money. Reshoketswe Kgetsepe recalls that, when she brewed at Mohlaletse, buyers were

> those that drink beer out of such a big village. The young men are going about looking for beer, they will compete with each other in buying it ... you will see a lot of money by the end of the day.[77]

In this way, the sale of beer, at least to some extent, redistributed the money that migrants brought into the villages. Groups of young men gathering to sample their brew also served, judging by the twinkle in the eyes of old women when they talk about such days, to enliven rural life considerably.

The income from beer brewing could also be important to men. Chief Kgoloko testified before the Native Economic Commission that:

> The brewing of beer has been helping our women to make money. In some cases you find that these women ... brew it to make money, so as to give it to their husbands, to enable them to pay their dipping fees or their taxes, whenever necessary.

On another occasion, he commented that 'our [tax] money does not so much come from labour centres as from beer'.[78]

Although it was considerably less common than brewing, some women also bought lengths of cloth from the shops and made clothes for sale. Dorcas Magomarele, for example, who came from a relatively prosperous Christian household, recalls making frocks and khaki shorts which she sold in her own and neighbouring villages for 'sorghum, money, chickens, everything. I did not discriminate.'[79] Cash could also be derived from seasonal labour on white farms; and while few women from the heartland of the reserves took advantage of this in the 1930s, it remained an option for those sufficiently desperate. Employment in agriculture was also more common in those communities which had white farms close at hand. Chief Sekwati Mampuru, for example, reported in 1930 that many women went out at harvest time to 'pick for the white man ... because there are farms close to my location'.[80]

Migrants were partly concerned to accumulate cattle to provide for their retirement. It was a commonplace observation that the Pedi 'look upon their stock as their bank' but it was also true that they regarded cattle as their pensions.[81] In the difficult conditions which prevailed in Sekhukhuneland, building up herds was a slow and risky process. Migrants also had to contribute towards their own bridewealth and then they were expected to contribute to the *bogadi* for their sons. Cattle were broadly defined as falling within a male domain but wives also asserted their rights to stock. Where a husband had more than one wife the cattle received in bridewealth payments for a daughter were seen as part of the 'house-property' of that wife and were expected to be used to provide *bogadi* for the son of that household. Hunt provided a crude but nonetheless revealing account of some of the dynamics which could result:

> An ordinary Mapedi likes to have three wives. Each have their own kraal or hut. Each of these huts has cattle assigned to it by the husband. The man finds it extremely difficult if he has to pay out cattle for any other purpose than for lobola for his son of that house. If he has to pay out cattle for any other purpose, for a fine, or anything else, he finds it extremely difficult to get a beast out of any of his wives. Supposing he should go to No. 2 hut and say, 'I want one of your beasts'. That wife will say to him, 'Why do you want one of mine; go to No. 1 or No. 3. Coming to me for one of my beasts shows that you are not liking me any more'. The Mapedi are very henpecked; at the same time he beats his wife, and quite right too! Yet, at the same time he is afraid of his wife.[82]

Cattle were not sold lightly in these decades, but migrants who succeeded in building up substantial herds had a source of milk, skins and meat and a store of value which could provide income in good years and partial insurance in bad. A good herd also provided ploughing teams which could be used to expand production on their own lands and which could be hired out to households which had insufficient stock to plough for themselves. But it was not only through stock or even the sale of grain that migrants were able to retire to the countryside. Some managed to sell their skills locally and, for example, earned modest amounts of money as builders and roofers.[83]

Rural retirement remained a key objective of most migrants in the 1930s and, while there where those who died or settled in the towns, many were able to spend at least the twilight of their lives at home and to assume the duties of elders in the *kgoro* and at *mošate*. The return home of husbands who had been away for much of their married lives was not always an easy experience for women who had grown accustomed to managing the household economy. And uncertainty over remittances was sometimes replaced by conflicts over the control of household income. But this phase of marriages was often short-lived. Retired migrants, usually significantly older than their wives, normally died well before their spouses. And the ranks of these widows were also swelled by those women whose husbands had been lost to, or in, *makgoweng*.

In theory, the positions of such widows was clear-cut in Pedi society:

> Normally a widow remains a minor occupying the same position in the family of her husband as she occupied during his life, and she remains under the tutelage either of his heir or of the guardian assigned by the relatives of her husband to continue enacting their powers in the marriage ...[T]he guardian ... is usually a younger brother of the deceased.[84]

In practice, however, in the 1930s and 1940s women who had spent a lifetime managing their own affairs and often effectively supporting themselves were disinclined to accept the authority of their husbands' relatives; and these kin in turn did not necessarily relish shouldering additional material burdens. In such cases, while women remained jural minors, in one description they 'behave like men, reject the services ... of their husband's agnates ... (and) become de facto homestead heads', although their positions remain 'fraught with ambiguity'.[85]

Migrant Associations

As women increasingly shouldered the burden of managing and maintaining the household economy, men found that they were forced to spend more and more of their lives away from home in alienating and harsh environments. But they did not allow themselves to be transformed into atomised economic units tossed to and fro in the swirling currents of market forces. Migrant workers crafted a variety of forms of association to provide themselves with succour and support.

From their earliest involvement in migrant labour, men from Sekhukhuneland stuck together both *en route* to work and, where possible, at their place of employment. Initially, this involved two dimensions. One was the exercise of chiefly power. Some of the first men who left Sekhukhuneland did so in regimental groups, and at royal behest. Elements of this form of organisation played a role well into the twentieth century. Chiefly representatives also travelled and lived with migrants. In the decades immediately after the Boer War chiefs made regular trips to mining centres to visit their subjects and – not least of all – to collect funds from them.[86]

The second element was the protection, comfort and sense of dignity that concentration and solidarity afforded young men living and working in grim circumstances far from home. In the nineteenth century a lone migrant was often prey to coercion and attack, whereas groups of Pedi migrants were able to defend themselves. As far as Pedi migrants on the gold mines in the early twentieth century were concerned,

> There is no doubt that they do not like being portioned out to the mines. In the first place they like to know before they leave the location to what mine they are going; and secondly a gang likes to go to the same place and not be divided up. [Indeed, if they are divided and allocated] they look upon themselves as being sold as slaves to the mines.[87]

The tendency of Pedi migrants to cluster around specific places of employment was also, of course, a response to variations in wages, conditions and proximity. Pedi experience of recruiters – *kalatšane* (cheats) – and long contracts persuaded men to avoid both wherever possible. Those who took this route were usually inexperienced, without money for transport, desperate for advances or instructed to do so by their parents or chiefs. An insistence on only taking contracts for specific mines and the predominantly 'voluntary' nature of most Pedi migrancy to the mines enabled men to maintain important elements of choice about where and with whom they worked.

The concentration of Pedi migrants at certain mines and the enforcement of ethnic divisions on the mines also allowed for some continuities in patterns of authority and organisation between countryside and compound.[88]

In the twentieth century it was not only through sporadic chiefly visits that rural hierarchies made themselves felt on the mines. Important additional dimensions were contributed by mine police and indunas who, at least in the Pedi case, were often older men of senior rank who acted as a link between men on the mines and their home villages. They also played a crucial role in recruitment, sending requests for workers to their communities and providing a focal point for men making their own way to the Rand. While operating within the constraints of their positions as the agents of compound control, these older men were able to offer migrants from their own home areas a degree of protection from some of the violence endemic to mine life, as well as a means to communicate grievances. They were also often called upon to arbitrate in disputes within the ranks of their countrymen. Marišane Phala, for example, captures some of the sense of continuity when he recalls that 'compound police were *bogoši*' (chieftainship).[89]

Some chiefs and independent recruiters insisted that each group of recruits be able to designate one of its number as a 'police boy'. In 1914, on the giant ModderBee mine – which was particularly popular amongst Pedi workers – there was an average of one 'native' policeman for every 20 workers. The compound manager complained that they 'want the highest wages; and those we give them to induce the native (sic) coming here'.[90] The exclusion of independent recruiters by the 1920s reduced this practice but it did not put an end to the central role of the mine police. Chiefs continued to play a part in influencing appointments. One tactic they used was to send letters of recommendation with migrants they deemed suitable for these positions.[91]

For much of the nineteenth century young men only undertook their first spell of migrancy once they had been initiated. A trip to the mines was to some extent incorporated as a stage in the transition to manhood. By the twentieth century, it was considered preferable to wait until *koma* before looking for work. But the reality was that many youths left for town before initiation. This did not mean that they missed initiation or the processes that surrounded it. The tendency of Pedi migrants to cluster at particular points of employment ensured that, while entire age grades seldom found work at one place, sections often did and could practise many of the activities – including singing, dancing and fighting – appropriate to *mašoboro*. Indeed, it seems to have been the practice for *mašoboro* to cluster at certain local mines partly for this reason. Penge and Premier Mines in the 1920s and the Anglo-French Colliery at Witbank in the 1930s were focal points for uninitiated youths.[92]

As soon as a decision was taken by the chief to establish an initiation group, word would be sent to youths working in mines and towns that they must return home. The network of mine police played a central role in communicating this information and ensuring that *mašoboro* returned home. Workers to replace the initiates were also sometimes sent from their villages. Lebike Mothubatse recalls:

> There, in the compounds, there were police from our place. They would call you there in the compound ... [They would say] you of this place, listen: at your place this year initiation is taking place ... the uninitiated that are working here can go home.[93]

They were assisted in this by members of the previously formed regiment and some of these men would also return to officiate at the initiation of their 'younger brothers'.[94]

After initiation, age-mates scattered more widely. But the existence of elements of chiefly authority in the compounds, the clustering of Pedi migrants and the enforcement of ethnic divisions on certain mines meant that standing by rank and regiment, and close bonds between age-mates, were not left behind in the countryside as workers journeyed to the towns and *mašoboro* became men. Migrants lived with workers from their home villages and districts, they discussed matters of home and they dealt with disputes that developed amongst themselves. Men also travelled between the different mines visiting their village- and age-mates and engaging in a range of activities with them from drinking to debate.[95]

At this time, Pedi migrants remained very wary of locations. Some went both there and to the town centres. But many liked little of what they saw. Sekgothe Makotanyane expressed an attitude that was fairly typical when he recalled:

> I just didn't like the location. I just wanted to work or come home if not working. I thought that the location people might mislead me and I didn't like them or their behaviour. I didn't like that it was easy for one to find a woman there and forget to come back home.[96]

Any man who became involved with an urban woman would be shunned by his fellows and the elders on the mines would deal with him severely. As Lebike Mothubatse recalls:

> Our elders were not permitting that you, a child having come to the town, should desire [urban women. They said] you will die soon. The women of the towns kill people. It was a binding regulation [and if you breached it] they would drive you out of the compound ... It was a disgrace ... they will just part ways with you.[97]

There was some homosexuality in the compounds but it does not seem to have played a central part in the world of Pedi migrants. Men were encouraged by their elders to go home if they could no longer stand compound conditions, and relatively short contracts and the proximity of Sekhukhuneland limited the role of homosexual relationships.[98]

In this world ties based on membership of specific villages remained vital but broader identities also played a part. Within Sekhukhuneland, the people thought of as being Pedi were primarily members of the dominant Marota chiefdoms. Other people would identify themselves by clan and chiefdom: as, say, Koni from Phokwane or Tau from Manganeng. In the world of the mines and towns, where rather cruder ethnic categories predominated, men both found themselves placed in wider groupings and realised that they needed to employ broader categories. The term 'Pedi' came to be widely used, and employers and officials often lumped all Transvaal Sotho together under this appellation. But migrants tended to group themselves into people from the south side of Pietersburg and those from the north: a division which in historical terms broadly coincided with the distinction between those groups which had been subject to the Pedi Kingdom and those which had not.[99]

Rurally based patterns of association were thus continued in modified form in the compounds but a variety of groupings more specific to the mines also developed. One was that close friends – usually from the same village – formed *megodišano* savings groups. These were rotating credit associations in which a number of migrants contributed every week or month and each would take turns in drawing the full amount. There were also larger, more heterogeneous and less stable associations called *mohlakana* which paid out a lump sum to men when they returned home. The latter were, however, regarded with some suspicion by migrants who feared for the security of their contributions.[100]

The most interesting form of association was too fluid to be called a group. One informant simply described it as 'the collection'.[101] If a man was injured, money would be collected primarily on a village or district basis to enable the victim to travel home. Some men might be delegated to accompany him. But the main role of 'the collection' came in the event of a worker's death. Although at that stage a man who died at work was buried in the mine cemetery, money would be gathered so that his personal effects could be taken home, and his wife and parents told of the circumstances of his death and sometimes given an amount of money.[102] It was strongly felt that his family should know his true fate and not be left wondering whether he had simply abandoned his rural responsibilities and been sucked into town life.

Despite all the barriers which they attempted to erect, rural communities nonetheless suffered a steady haemorrhage of men to the towns. Some families were left bereft of support and with the anguish of not knowing whether their sons or husbands were dead or alive. As one informant expressed it: 'There are some people who are just taken by the leg of the locust and vanish there in the towns.'[103]

Malaita

Pedi migrants outside of compounded employment also created a rich variety of associations. One of the most important and certainly one of the most visible of these involved the Malaita groups which gathered on Sundays and marched to the venues for their boxing contests. In Marabastad in the 1930s and 1940s the residents would gather

> to look at them in rival batches march up Barber street. They had on shorts, tennis caps, tennis shoes and handkerchiefs dangled from their pockets. They crouched, shook their fists in the air so that the bangles

round their wrists clanged. They moved with long strides like a black army ... they sprang and shouted.[104]

It was a sight that struck fear and sometimes loathing into urban black and white observers alike. But participants had a rather different self-image. Ngoanatsomane Sekhukhune remembers how, on the East Rand when they marched to their battle grounds on Sundays,

> We dressed well, we blew whistles, we could be seen by each and everyone. *We* were not hiding away in order to ambush people. [The implied contrast is with] the *tsotsis* who hide in the grass and kill people.[105]

Oral and documentary evidence for the decades before the Second World War suggest that the Malaita were mainly unschooled, non-Christian youths from the Northern and Eastern Transvaal. They were usually under the age of 21 and once they had passed through initiation and marriage their involvement in Malaita groups diminished. Although the majority were domestics in Pretoria and Johannesburg, a minority were in compounded employment and some were unemployed.[106]

Pedi youths usually headed for suburbs in which kinsmen and others from their village were already employed. Indeed, it was often through these networks – and especially with the assistance of older workers – that they secured employment. Individual suburbs could even become dominated by workers from particular districts and this may have contributed to the apparently suburban basis of some Malaita groups.[107] These youths were, however, divided between different households and lived and worked alongside servants of diverse origins. One former domestic recalled that in the 1930s: 'While during the week we were together with workers from other places on Sundays we [youths from Sekhukhuneland] separated ourselves and came together as one.'[108]

These adolescents were proud of their rural origins and looked askance at urban lifestyles. As Mogase Sekhukhune observed: 'Malaitas were people who boxed ... They were rural people who work in the town in the kitchens but they didn't go to the locations. They didn't like [urban] women.'[109]

Involvement in these groups helped youths to counteract the atomisation, degradation and drudgery of their working lives. They provided continuities with the rural worlds in which they had previously moved and assisted them to retain their distance from urban temptations in the crucial years of initiation and marriage during which their rural responsibilities were cemented.

Although these groups clearly drew some inspiration from previous forms of organisation on the Rand, much of what we know of them – their patterns of leadership, fighting, music, dancing, singing and even petty thieving –

shows strong affinities with *mašoboro* organisation and culture in the countryside. Many contemporary observers stressed the criminality of Malaita. But while some of these youths were drawn into criminal activity, it seems unlikely that crime was a central dynamic. Certainly, Pedi migrants distinguished sharply between Malaita activity as 'play for boys to show off their strength' and criminal behaviour.[110]

There is some evidence – especially in Pretoria – that gangs were based on specific suburbs. But the oral evidence stresses the regional and ethnic basis of the groups. Men from Sekhukhuneland would form one group and compete with other groups of men from 'north of Pietersburg' or groups described as 'the Venda' or the 'Lobedu'. But there was also an important multi-ethnic dimension: an overall champion would be recognised by all the groups and the men from one urban centre would compete against men from other towns.[111]

Aside from their bruising comradeship, Malaita groups provided their members with more concrete support. They pooled funds, kept each other informed about the availability of jobs and provided those who lost, or could not find, work with food and shelter. And the Malaita *nkgwete* or *ngwenya* (champions) received money from their followers. Although most men abandoned this rather rugged form of recreation by their early twenties, they did not sever their ties with rurally based networks. Older domestic workers kept an eye on the activities of the younger men from their home areas and they also clubbed together to assist one another in the event of death or disease.[112]

There were areas of broad similarity and even some overlap between the patterns of association which developed in the suburbs and those arising in the compounds. In both contexts, elements of *mašoboro* culture were maintained – albeit in modified form – and youths remained encapsulated in rural networks which in part shielded them from the allure of urban life. Once they were initiated, married and increasingly acquainted with the towns, the closeness of some of these bonds slackened. But linkages with other men from Sekhukhuneland continued to play a key role in the lives of migrants and were potentially crucial in the event of disaster.

The importance of these bonds did not preclude interaction with wider groups or forms of association which were not based on village or regional ties. Neither did it mean that men felt that it was appropriate for ethnic divisions contrived by the state and employers to be imposed as the central demarcations in the world in which they lived and worked. But migrant organisation, though widespread, tended to be informal and introverted. There is little evidence that non-Christian and unschooled migrants had contact with either wider political or labour movements in the decades before the Second World War.[113]

Elite Ethnic Associations

Pedi in the towns also created formal ethnic associations, and a Bapedi Union was established in the first decade of the century. In the late 1930s there are references to a newly formed Bapedi Union, a Bapedi Club, and a Bapedi National Society on the Rand. But what differentiated these groups from the associations described above is that they were dominated by Christians, those with some education, and those settled permanently in towns. In Johannesburg in the 1930s, for example, the main centres of activity for these sorts of associations were Sophiatown, Western Township and Alexandra.[114]

The Bapedi club was founded by J. Maketa Tema, who had primary school education and in 1931 opened 'the Sophiatown Plumbing Works'. The club's members were 'all Bapedi' and it was intended 'to keep people off the streets on Sundays and to keep them from drink. [It held] dances and concerts' and promoted sports.[115] Improvement and self-help seem to have been central themes in the activities of these organisations. In 1937, for example, the Bapedi Union proclaimed its objectives – significantly in English – as being to 'unite all Bapedi on the Rand and to make them know one another, to make some means to those who are homeless of getting jobs and to deal with matters which affect them'.[116] Exactly what assistance was actually given remains unclear.

Some of these organisations also collected funds to provide for a decent and Christian burial for members. It appears that the first 'Bantu Burial Society' was founded on the Rand in 1932 but there was a considerably longer history of such institutions amongst Afrikaners and coloureds.[117] Burial societies spread rapidly amongst the urban African population in the 1930s and were pervasive by the 1940s. In 1944, for example, some 65 per cent of households in Western Native Township subscribed to such societies.[118]

Unlike the *megodišano* and the Malaita, which were created in the context of a rurally focused migrant culture, these associations were moulded by the intersection of Christianity, education and urban life and were designed to provide their members with support in their struggles to fashion lives in the city. Thus, despite their elaboration of a 'Pedi' identity, they remained remote from most men from Sekhukhuneland who were working on the Rand.

Conclusion

In the 50 years since that fateful and bloody day in 1879 when the independence of the Pedi kingdom was snuffed out, profound changes had taken place in virtually every aspect of the lives of the population of Sekhukhuneland. A new political superstructure had been erected and an alien system of property had been entrenched. Tax and rent collectors stalked the land and white officials, missionaries and farmers had taken up residence in the Pedi heartland. But the most important transformation of all was that migrant labour had moved from being an important buttress for the economy of the region to providing its foundation. There was scarcely any aspect of the society which did not bear witness to this fact, and most men spent long stretches of their lives away from home.

But Pedi men and women had not simply surrendered to the imperatives of conquest and capitalism. They had struggled in a wide variety of ways to limit the intrusion of colonial power and market relationships and to fashion a world which allowed for continuities both between the past and the present, and between the countryside and the city. The elaboration of ideologies and associations which emphasised the importance of initiation, communal tenure, the possession of stock and chiefly rule was central to this endeavour. In practice, of course, rural society was neither egalitarian nor in equilibrium, and was shot through with divisions, tensions and debates. Christians often had a more ambiguous relationship to a rurally focused order even though the doors to colonial society were swinging closed against them. Migrants sometimes maintained no more than sporadic contact with their homes and there were significant numbers who failed to return to *Bopedi*. Nonetheless, Sekhukuneland in the 1930s, and especially the locations within it, was seen by many as a place of refuge – as a sanctuary from swaggering white officials and avaricious employers, from brutal policeman and the burden of passes, from wage labour and male barracks, from dangerous women and delinquent youth and from the rampant criminality which they believed infested urban society.

Notes

1   P. Delius, *Land*, p. 244. The term Pedi is used throughout this book as a shorthand way to indicate communities that lived in the heartland of the Pedi state. Although Sepedi was the language of the overwhelming majority and there were considerable cultural continuities, this was also a region which had experienced settlement by a variety of groups with initially distinct histories and cultures. This diversity had by no means been entirely extinguished and was continually reinforced by the arrival of new groups.

2   *Ibid*, p. 245.

3   Sir Garnet Wolseley (or Sir Woosle Garnet as he is recalled by some Pedi informants) was, of course, the model of the modern major-general immortalised in the Gilbert and Sullivan song.

4   Delius, *Land*, pp. 11-12.

5   The south-western portion only became known as Nebo in the twentieth century. The other locations were Pokwani's and Magalie's. Their names were also derived from mangled renditions of the names of chiefs and were allocated to chiefdoms which had previously fallen under Marota rule but which had broken away and had provided support to the Boers and the British against Sekhukhune in the 1870s. TA; SN177, Notulen Naturellen Locatie Commissie, 1882-1885; P. Delius, 'Abel Erasmus', in W.

Beinart, P. Delius and S. Trapido (eds.), *Putting a Plough to the Ground* (Johannesburg, 1986), pp. 184-94.

6   Delius, *Land*, p. 178.

7   D.R. Hunt, 'An Account of the Bapedi', *Bantu Studies,* 4, 1931, pp. 284 and 317; B.K. Hlakudi, 2. I use communal tenure as a shorthand term indicating systems in which married men derived rights to arable land from membership of kinship and political groups and these rights were not bought or sold. Grazing land was also open to all who possessed stock. But it is important to note that once rights were granted to arable land they were hereditary and could not easily be withdrawn. Part of the reason for the popular support for this form of land holding, which is a recurring theme in this study, lies precisely in the security of tenure that it offered. But it should also be pointed out that the term 'communal tenure' disguises great variations in actual patterns of tenure and control over land and that such systems were profoundly modified by colonial control and are far from static. For further discussion of these issues see Beinart, *Twentieth-Century South Africa*, p. 19; See also J. Bruce, 'Do Indigenous Tenure Systems Constrain Agricultural Development?', and S. Lawry, 'Transactions in Cropland Held Under Customary Tenure in Lesotho', in T.J. Bassett and D.E. Crummey (eds.), *Land in African Agrarian Systems* (Wisconsin, 1993).

8   H. van Coller, 'Mampoer in die Stryd om die Bapeditroon', *Historiese Studies*, III, 3, 4, 1942; A. Merensky, *Erinnerungen aus dem Missionleben in Transvaal, 1859-1882* (Berlin, 1899), pp. 400-4.

9   This section draws heavily on Delius, 'Abel Erasmus'.

10   S. Trapido, 'Landlord and Tenant in a Colonial Economy', *Journal of Southern African Studies,* 5, 1, 1978.

11   TA/SS3386/R7590/92-R977/92, Erasmus to S.N., 28/9/1892.

12   TA/SN40/R264/97, Erasmus Annual Report for 1896.

13   P. Warwick, *Black People and the South African War 1899-1902* (Cambridge, 1983), p. 101. This section draws heavily on this source and on Delius, 'Erasmus', pp. 207-9.

14   Warwick, *Black People*, p. 102.

15   Hunt, 'An Account', p. 316; TA/LBD/a975/5, Rhodesian Redwater in Sekukuniland, 31/8/1905.

16   S. Schirmer, 'The Struggle for Land in Lydenburg 1930-1970', unpublished Ph.D thesis, University of the Witwatersrand, 1994, p. 53. This section draws heavily on this source and on the D.R. Hunt Papers in the University of the Witwatersrand Historical Papers Library (UWHPL) A1655.

17   Berman and Lonsdale, *Unhappy Valley*, p. 237.

18   UWHPL/AD1438, *Native Economic Commission* (NEC), D.R Hunt, Lydenburg, 20/8/1930, p. 713.

19   Hunt, 'An Account'.

20   *Ibid*, pp. 314-17; and see enclosures in TA/NTS342/90/55(4).

21   TA/NTS342/90/55/(4), Hunt to the Under-Secretary of Native Affairs, 21 February 1911.

22   UWHPL/AD1438/*NEC*, D.R. Hunt, Lydenburg, 20/8/1930, p. 727.

23   TA/NTS6813/19/318/, *Pitso* minutes, 30/10/1931.

24   Hunt, 'An Account', p. 317.

25   *Ibid*, p. 318.

26   *Ibid*, p. 317.

27   This section draws heavily on Delius, *Land* pp. 48-61; C.L. Harries, *The Laws and Customs of the Bapedi and Cognate Tribes* (Pretoria, 1929), pp. 79-150; H. Mönnig, *The Pedi* (Pretoria, 1967), pp. 249-300; C.V. Bothma, 'The Political Structure of the Pedi of Sekhukhuneland', *African Studies*, 35, 1976; E. Mothubatse, 1-3; TA/NTS342/90/55, Chief Kgolokoe, 1910-1953.

28   E. Mothubatse, 4.

29   UWHPL/AD1438/ *NEC*, D.R. Hunt, 20/8/1930, pp. 715 and 717. See also E. Mothubatse, 4-5.

30   UWHPL/AD1438/ *NEC*, D.R. Hunt, 20/8/1930, pp. 661-3.

31   *Ibid*, p. 647.

32   Delius, *Land*, pp. 62-82; Delius, 'Abel Erasmus', pp. 202-9; R. Turrel, *Capital and Labour on the Kimberely Diamond Fields* (Cambridge, 1987), pp. 19-25, 92-4, 267; S. van der Horst, *Native Labour in South Africa* (Oxford, 1942), p. 230.

33   B.K. Hlakudi, 1; K.L. Manailane, 1.

34   *Ibid*; UG.10-13, *Union of Native Affairs Department Annual Report*, 1910-1911, p. 370; UWHPL/AD1438/ *NEC*, D.R. Hunt, 20/8/1930, pp. 657-8; and J.C. Yates, 22/8/1930, pp. 827-36; M. Kgagudi, 1; D. Lebopo, 2.

35   UWHPL/AD1438/ *NEC*, D.R. Hunt, 20/8/1930, pp. 657-8.

36   *Ibid*, p. 665 and J.C. Yates, 22/8/1930, p. 856. For comparative perspectives see 'Introduction' and P. Bonner, 'Russians on the Reef, 1947-1957', in P. Bonner, P. Delius and D. Posel (eds.) *Apartheid's Genesis 1935-1962* (Johannesburg, 1993), pp. 13-15 and 168-72; and B.Bozzoli, *Women of Phokeng* (Johannesburg, 1991), pp. 81-105.

37   See for example M. Kgaphola, 1; M. Mampuru, 1; R. Moetalo, 1; L. Mothubatse, 1; M. Phala, 2. See also the important insights provided by B. Sansom, 'Leadership and Authority in a Pedi Chiefdom', unpublished Ph.D thesis, University of Manchester, 1970, pp. 5-13.

38   *Most* and *ultimately* in the first sentence of the paragraph above are of course key qualifiers. There were households which were temporarily and less frequently permanently without these resources; UWHPL/AD1438/ *NEC*, D.R. Hunt, 20/8/1930, pp. 672-701; Chief Kgolokwe *et al.*, pp. 729-57, 20/8/1930; J.C. Yates, 22/8/1930, pp. 818-60; E. Motsoaledi, 1; P. Nkadimeng, 1; N. Sekhukhune, 1; D.P. Lebopo, 1; S. Morwamotshe, 1; M. Phala, 1; A. Mosehle, 1; M. Molepo, 'Peasants and or Proletarians', unpublished seminar paper, African Studies Institute, University of Witwatersrand, 26 September 1983; TA/NTS3519/353/307, Report SNC Sekukuniland, 1 August 1925.

39   UWHPL/AD/1438/ *NEC*, J.C. Yates, 22/8/1930, p. 830.

40   *Ibid*; D.R. Hunt, 20/8/1930, p. 699.

41   *Ibid*, pp. 672-701; J.C. Yates, 22/8/1930, pp. 818-60; A. Mosehle, 1; E. Motsoaledi, 1; D.L. Lebopo, 1-2; T. Lerutla, 1; N. Mabogwane, 1; E. Mothubatse, 4; M. Nchabeleng, 2; J.K. Nkadimeng, 1; P. Matjie, 1; L. Maredi, 1; TA/NTS/3519/353/307, Report SNC Sekukuniland, 1/8/1925; Harries, *Laws and Customs*, pp. 55 and 132; P.J. Quin *Food and Feeding Habits of the Pedi* (Johannesburg, 1959), p. 16. This precarious balance, rather like the liquidity of a bank, was maintained partly because not of all of those who could claim rights to land did so at any one time. The fact that most households could secure rights to land does not of course mean that all could, and there were families without land or cattle or both. The evidence does not – at present – permit any reliable quantification of the ratios involved or distinguishing between households which held reasonable hopes of securing rights to these resources in the future and those that did not.

42   G.M. Pitje, 'Traditional Systems of Male Education among the Pedi and Cognate Tribes', *African Studies,* IX, 2, 3, 4, 1950, pp. 57-8; Mönnig, *The Pedi*, pp. 268-9.

43   E. Motsoaledi, 1.

44   J. Phala, 1; E. Motsoaledi, 1; J.K. Nkadimeng, 1; G.M. Pitje, 1. Part of the depth of these divisions relates to the particular role played by missionaries in the nineteenth century. See Delius, *Land* and P. Delius, *The Conversion* (Johannesburg, 1984). One must of course also beware – even for this period – of overstating the starkness of the division. In some ways the concepts of *Baditšaba/Baheiteni* and *Bakristi/Majakane* represented contending ideal types – actual social relationships and practices

presented a considerably more blurred picture, and both categories of people shared
many day-to-day experiences both of life in the villages and of the world of migrant
labour. For example, a significant though still small amount of children from
baditšaba families were attending school in the 1930s and 1940s.

45   See for example TA/NTS342/90/55, Chief Kgolokoe, 1910-1953.
46   Pitje, 'Male Education', p. 47.
47   B.K. Hlakudi, 2.
48   TA/NTS6813/19/318, *Pitso* minutes, 30/10/1931.
49   Pitje, 'Male Education', p. 66.
50   See for example S. Mothubatse, 1; M. Mampuru, 1; K.L. Manailane, 1; J.K. Ntsoane, 1.
51   See for example D. Magomarele, 1; W.M. Moela, 1; L. Mampuru, 1; M. Malata, 1;
      Martha Phala, 1; D. Phala, 1; M. Raseomane, 1; R. Kgetsepe, 1.
52   UWHPL/AD1438/ *NEC*, D.R. Hunt, 20/8/1930, p. 669. See also Chief Sekoati,
      23/8/1930, pp. 917-18; J.C. Yates, 22/8/1930, p. 836; and Quin, *Food*, p. 15.
53   M. Malata, 1.
54   D. Phala, 1.
55   Martha Phala, 1.
56   M. Malata, 1; see also G.M. Pitje, 1.
57   The section that follows draws heavily on L. Mothubatse, 1-2; Pitje, 'Male
      Education', *passim*; Mönnig, *The Pedi*, pp. 107-28.
58   Mönnig, *The Pedi*, p. 111.
59   *Ibid*, p. 112.
60   Pitje, 'Male Education', p. 121.
61   Mönnig, *The Pedi*, p. 126. The accounts of female inititaion that exist are very thin as
      a result of the failure of a succession of male researchers, including myself, to
      persuade women to talk about these experiences.
62   K.L. Manailane, 2; M.J. Sekhukhune, 2.
63   J.K. Nkadimeng, 1.
64   *Ibid*.
65   G.M. Pitje, 1.
66   G.M. Pitje, 'Traditional and Modern Systems of Male Education among the Pedi and
      Cognate Tribes', unpublished MA dissertation, University of Fort Hare, 1948, p. 127.
      The section that follows draws heavily on this study and G.M. Pitje, interview 1.
67   Pitje, 'Traditional and Modern', p. 132.
68   *Ibid* p. 141.
69   *Ibid* p. 137.
70   *Ibid* p. 144.
71   *Ibid* p. 142.
72   UWHPL/AD1438/ *NEC*, Headman Frank Maserumule, 20/8/1930, p. 755.
73   *Ibid*; E. Mothubatse, 20 August 1930, p. 742; See also E. Mothubatse, 4-5.
74   J.K. Ntsoane, 1; W.M. Moadi, 1; D. Magomarele, 1; W.M. Moela, 1; L. Mampuru, 1;
      M. Malata, 1; Martha Phala, 1; D. Phala, 1; M. Raseomane, 1; R. Kgetsepe, 1;
      Mönnig, *The Pedi*, pp. 129-38 and 194-203. The section that follows draws heavily
      on these sources.
75   R. Kgetsepe, 1.
76   M. Tshesane, 1; L. Mampuru, 1; M. Moadi, 1; M. Malata, 1.
77   R. Kgetsepe, 1.
78   UWHPL/AD1438/ *NEC*, Chief Kgolokwe, 20/8/1930 p. 732; and TA/NTS
      6813/19/318, *Pitso*, 24/4/1930.
79   D. Magomarele, 1.
80   UWHPL/AD1438/ *NEC*, Chief Sekoati, 23/9/1930, p. 917.
81   *Ibid*; J.C. Yates, 22/9/1930, p. 824.
82   *Ibid*; D.R. Hunt, 20/9/1930, pp. 678-9.

83   E. Motsoaledi, 1; N. Mabogwane, 1; K.L. Manailane, 1; L. Mothubatse, 1; M. Phala, 1.
84   Mönnig *The Pedi*, p. 300.
85   Sansom, 'Leadership and Authority', pp. 144-5. Sansom is, of course, describing a later period but the issue of widows as a distinct social category surfaces in the documentary record from, at least, the 1940s. See TA/NTS10276/59/423/4, G. Ackron to CNC 18/5/49, and is referred to in interviews relating to the earlier period. See, for example, B.K. Hlakudi, 1-2.
86   Delius *Land*, pp. 62-82; A. Jeeves, *Migrant Labour in South Africa's Mining Economy* (Johannesburg, 1985), pp. 161-2; TA/SNA321/1385/06, C.L. Harries to SNA, 16/7/1906.
87   TA/SNA/124/03, W.F. Armstrong to Native Commissioner, Lydenburg, 25/2/1903.
88   UWHPL/AD/1438 *NEC*, J.C. Yates, 22/8/1930, pp. 827-36; D.P. Lebopo, 1-2.
89   Marišane Phala, 1; see also D. Radingoane, 1; L. Mothubatse, 1-2.
90   Jeeves, *Migrant Labour*, p. 182.
91   Marišane Phala, 1.
92   L. Mothubatse, 1-2; B.K. Hlakudi, 1; S. Motla, 1; C. Radingoane, 1; P.P. Matjie, 1; M. Kgagudi, 1.
93   L. Mothubatse, 2.
94   *Ibid*.
95   M. Kgagudi, 1; T.K. Morwamotshe, 1.
96   S. Makotanyane, 1.
97   L. Mothubatse, 2.
98   *Ibid*; M. Mampuru, 2; M.J. Sekhukhune, 2; M.M. Kgaphola, 1. Homosexual relationships appear to have played a more prominent role amongst Pondo and Shangaan migrants who came from more remote areas and who took relatively long and recurring contracts on the mines. For illuminating discussions of these issue see Harries, *Work, Culture and Identity*, pp. 200-8; and Moodie, *Going for Gold*, pp. 119-58.
99   M. Mampuru, 1; K.L. Manailane, 2; N.P. Sekhukhune, 1.
100   Mohube Phala, 1; D. Radingoane, 1.
101   C. Radingoane, 1.
102   *Ibid*; L. Mothubatse, 1-2; Mohube Phala, 2; M. Mampuru, 2-3.
103   M. Mampuru, 2.
104   E. Mphahlele, *Down Second Avenue* (London, 1959), pp. 100-1.
105   N.P. Sekhukhune, 1.
106   For a fuller discussion of the Malaita on the Rand and an attempt to periodise the development of these groups see P. Delius, '*Sebatakgomo:* Migrant Organization, the ANC and the Sekhukhuneland Revolt', unpublished seminar paper, African Studies Institute, University of the Witwatersrand, November 1988, pp. 8-12; See also UWHPL/AD1433, CJ/2/1/16, 'The Amalaita Menace by S.S. Thema', 18/7/1935; and AD843, 56/4/5, 'The Amalaita', J.R. Brent, 7/12/1939.
107   UWHPL. AD843, 56/4/5, 'The Amalaita', J.R. Brent, 7/12/1939.
108   K.L. Maredi, 1.
109   M. Sekhukhune, 1.
110   Mohube Phala, 1.
111   M. Mampuru, 1; M. Sekhukhune, 1; N. Sekhukhune, 1 ; K.L. Manailane, 2.
112   *Ibid*; J. Mashego, 2; J. Nkadimeng, 1.
113   *Ibid*; Mohube Phala, 1-2; Marišane Phala, 1.
114   A forerunner of the Bapedi National Society was the Eastern Transvaal African Association formed in 1932. See TA/NTS7219/93/326, H. Nkgaleng Nkadimeng to SNA, 2/7/1932 and GNLB.401/55/44, Assistant Native Commissioner Johannesburg (ANCJ) to Director of Native Labour (DNL) 19/7/1932, See also S. Trapido, 'A

Preliminary Study of the Development of African Political Opinion, 1884-1955' unpublished B.A. Honours dissertation, University of the Witwatersrand, 1959, p. 35; R. Phillips, *The Bantu in the City* (Lovedale, 1938), pp. 295, 420-21; P. Walshe, *The Rise of African Nationalism in South Africa* (London, 1970) p. 257; *Bantu World*, 23 January 1937; WU.CPL.ABX/410605c, H. Nkgaleng Nkadimeng to Dr A.B. Xuma, 5 June 1941; D. Magomarele, 1.

115   Phillips, *The Bantu*, p. 295.
116   *Bantu World*, 23 January 1937; see also TA.GNLB.401/55/44 ANCJ to DNL, 19/7/1932.
117   J. Iliffe, *The African Poor* (Cambridge, 1987), pp. 101, 119, 133-5.
118   *Ibid*; H. Kuper and S. Kaplan, 'Voluntary Associations in an African Township', *African Studies*, 3, 1944, p. 178.

2

'The Trust'

Rehabilitation and Resistance in the Northern Transvaal, 1936–48

They were coming into our homes ... even our own homes would be controlled by them ... Can you accept that if you marry a woman that another man just comes, throws you out of your house, climbs into your bed and sleeps in your blankets?[1]

The residual freedoms cherished by communities in the Northern Transvaal came under renewed assault during the 1930s and 1940s. This time, however, the threat came, not from Boer commandos or imperial artillery, but from officials clutching manuals on soil erosion who believed that they were the bearers of 'development'.

The villagers of Sekhukhuneland already had considerable exposure to one agenda for far-reaching social transformation – missionary Christianity. Missionaries had, after all, sought not only to save the souls of their converts but to remodel their temporal world. They challenged the role of chiefs and outlawed practices such as bridewealth, ancestor worship and rainmaking. But they went beyond these negative prescriptions to foster the ideal of autonomous communities of craftsmen and peasants bound together by bonds of faith and commitment to the market. While this image owed a great deal to profound processes of change in Europe during the nineteenth century, it also invoked the moral authority of the Scriptures. This bold vision bore little relationship to the bleak circumstances of most converts in the 1930s, and the evangelical zeal of missionaries had also been blunted by the passage of time.[2]

The officials who pursued rural reconstruction from the 1930s brought new certainties. They were convinced that their policies were scientifically grounded and the only alternative to ecological and economic disaster. And, like the missionaries before them, they were not easily swayed by a rising tide of popular resistance to their activities.

'The Problem Lies in the Reserves'

From the turn of the century onwards, concerns had been expressed over the capacity of the reserves to sustain a growing population. By the 1920s there was mounting anxiety over the deterioration of these areas. Mine-owners feared for the future of the migrant labour system, while officials and politicians were haunted by the spectre of rural impoverishment leading to mass urbanisation which would swamp white cities, scupper segregationist designs and nurture proletarian revolt.[3] The terms and intensity of this discussion were also increasingly shaped by a conservationist discourse focused on the issue of soil erosion. By the 1930s, this had become a dominant element in characterisations of the problems facing the reserves.

Concern over the destruction of natural resources by both African and settler farmers had a long history in South Africa. But, in the 1930s, African cultivators were singled out for special attention. This focus remains to be fully explained but appears to have had a number of causes. White farmers, alternatively insecure in slumps and expansionist in booms, railed against the 'destructive' methods of African producers. Droughts, dongas, demographic data, declining yields, 'rivers running brown with mud' and an imperfect understanding of African ecology all helped to fuel official concern.[4] And sensitivity to these issues was considerably enhanced by wider developments. American literature of the 1920s, highlighting the dangers of overtaxing the soil, circulated widely in English-speaking Africa. The warnings offered by these studies proved to be an 'horrific prophecy' as the story of the American 'Dust Bowl' unfolded in the early 1930s.[5]

> As the dust storms blew in from Nebraska to New York, and as broken farmers trudged and trucked to California, erosion and conservation were catapulted into the international arena. The new ideologists of conservation went even further than their predecessors in predictions of doom ... Hugh Bennett, appointed head of the [USA] Soil Conservation Service summed up the new position: 'The ultimate consequence of unchecked soil erosion ... must be national extinction'. A spate of books and articles elaborated on this apocalyptic vision ... These ideas were imbibed by increasingly receptive officials in the Colonial service and the settler states.[6]

Growing unease about conditions in the reserves, accelerating urbanisation and a context of heated debate about the 'Native Question' sparked by Hertzog's Native Bills and intensified by the Depression led to the appointment of a Native Economic Commission in 1930. The commissioners travelled the length and breadth of the country taking evidence before presenting their report in 1932. While the commission's impact on the final shape of Hertzog's legislation was limited, it underscored the seriousness of conditions in the reserves and argued that they were the core of both the problem and the solution to the 'Native economic question'.

The commission also provided a comprehensive formulation of the nature of the difficulties facing reserve society and a prescription for their solution which, although not accepted in its entirety, was to exercise a powerful influence on the official mind for decades to come. It enlisted the full weight of 'science' to support its conclusions and drew heavily on the testimony of 'expert' witnesses trained in the natural and social sciences. As Ashforth has pointed out, in practice the report's 'obeisance to science' took the form of 'a structure of metaphor mixing mechanical figures drawing on principles of Newtonian physics with organic metaphors drawing on principles of biological science'.[7] Within this discourse, the 'scientific facts' provided by the literature on soil conservation were given pride of place.

The central premise of the report was that a primitive subsistence economy co-existed with an advanced money economy in South Africa. While the latter was governed by economic rationality, the former languished in the 'grip of superstition and an anti-progressive social system'.[8] Growing human and stock population in the reserves – the result of benevolent colonial rule in combination with the irrational, uneconomic and unscientific nature of African society and agriculture – had dire consequences for the soil. At the 'root of the whole evil' was overstocking which was the consequence of the 'religious rather than economic way' in which Africans regarded their cattle.[9] In the near future these factors would lead to 'denudation, donga erosion, deleterious plant succession, destruction of springs, robbing the soil of its reproductive properties, in short the creation of desert conditions'.[10] If this impending crisis was not attended to promptly and effectively, the reserves would become wastelands menacing the future of the wider society.

In a fascinating intellectual sleight of hand, the commission laid responsibility for the plight of the reserves squarely on the shoulders of the inhabitants and brushed aside the effects of conquest, land alienation and segregation. Its solutions displayed equivalent mental dexterity. It rejected arguments that the conditions in the reserves demanded a retreat from segregationist policies and concluded that the prime solution involved effective measures to 'develop' these areas.[11] This prescription involved a comprehensive reorganisation of rural society which would include significant reductions of stock, the fencing of lands, concentrated settlements, improved seed and an expansion of agricultural education. The commissioners did concede that more land was required in order to relieve congestion in the existing areas and to allow scope for the introduction of better farming methods. But they also insisted that additional land should not 'allow the Native to remain in his backward state … [and] to put back the wheels of progress'.[12]

The scenario presented by the NEC report involved the gradual adaptation of African society together with 'progress grafted onto the well-rooted stock of Bantu institutions'. Chiefs were to play a central role.[13] But this stance did not include any serious consideration of whether African forms of production on the land were effective adaptations to the particular environments and might provide valuable perspectives for both policy makers and practitioners.

There were some flashes of insight into the importance attached to spreading risk and a grudging recognition of the 'hardiness of Native cattle'.[14] But the overwhelming emphasis was on the importance of shouldering aside 'primitive' practices and establishing 'modern' methods. The commission believed that such a shift would enable 'a large rural Native population to support itself on a reasonable basis of agricultural production'. But it also argued that the present system of 'one man one lot' constituted a brake on development and that limitations on the individual accumulation of land should be relaxed.[15] The commission failed to give guidance as to how both these objectives could be achieved within the restricted amounts of land available to Africans and, as will be explored further, it was left to increasingly exasperated officials to attempt to resolve this contradiction.

The report of the NEC caused an initial stir but public attention and debate was mainly focused on the progress of Hertzog's Native Bills. They inspired mixed emotions within African society. The main political groupings were hostile to the abolition of the Cape franchise but the proposal to provide Africans with additional land had considerably more appeal; and while it is difficult to gauge popular perceptions there does seem to have been clear support for this dimension within chiefly circles. There was, for example, the notorious telegram from Chief Maitse Moloi to General Hertzog which read 'Message from Transvaal and Free State Chiefs. Away with franchise. Give us Land'. But a more typical response was probably that expressed by Headman Frank Maserumule and supported by Chief Sekhukhune at a *pitso* in 1936. He argued that

> it is considered that in the interests of the Natives the bills should go through [and thus additional land made available but] the Cape vote should not be taken away [and] the Transvaal Natives should be allowed to send representatives to Parliament.[16]

There were high hopes that the implementation of the 1936 Native Trust and Land Act would bring relief to congested reserve areas, but Africans who welcomed its passage found that it carried a powerful sting in its tail. The Act vested all existing locations and reserves – some 10 500 000 morgen of land – in the South African Native Trust (SANT) and stipulated that 7 500 000 morgen of land should be added to this by the transfer of crown land to the Trust and through the purchase of land owned by 'non-natives'.

The bulk of this land – 5 028 000 morgen – was located in the Transvaal and much of the privately owned land comprised the enormous land company holdings in the northern and eastern regions of the province. The Native Affairs Department, however, endorsed the view of the NEC that the provision of additional lands was of little value unless effective measures were taken to combat soil erosion and overstocking. The long-term ambition was to restructure the existing locations and crown lands. It was proposed that detailed surveys be undertaken in order to define residential, arable and grazing areas, set stock levels and design measures to protect timber, and provide water.[17] In terms which were ominous for those who believed Trust land would help sustain elements of economic and political autonomy, it was spelled out that

> detailed and close supervision will have to be exercised to ensure compliance by people with the requirements of the Trust ... [T]hey must be prevented, for instance, from ploughing in residential areas, from constantly breaking up fresh patches of land for cultivation outside arable areas; from depasturing their cattle on reserved areas; from destroying fences, cutting down timber, burning veldt and malpractices of a similar nature.[18]

While the Native Affairs Department recognised that this transformation would be a slow process, it resolved that the lands purchased by the Trust should with immediate effect 'be allotted and occupied by natives in such a manner that it will not be ruined by malpractices but will be properly farmed without its carrying capacity being overtaxed'.[19]

The SANT produced a marked expansion in local-level bureaucracy. To ensure 'adequate supervision and control', a large and technically competent field staff was required. Qualified agricultural officers were appointed for districts, including Trust land, and under them were European agricultural field assistants. The bottom rung of this administrative ladder was made up of 'native rangers' who were expected 'to act as forest and fencing guards ... and generally to keep their superior officer in constant and close touch with occurrences and developments in the area'. The 'field assistants' were often drawn from the most marginal elements within white society and many relished the opportunity to exercise power over Africans.[20]

It took some time for these posts to be filled and after 1939 the enlistment of officials in the army resulted in serious staff shortages. But, overall, the Trust appointments considerably enlarged the role of the technical officers within the NAD and enhanced the influence of director of native agriculture. R.W. Thornton, who held this post until 1936, and whose evidence played an important part in shaping the conclusions of the NEC, was convinced that an ecological disaster causing a 'colossal permanent poor black problem' was a real possibility and threatened white South Africa with 'calamity'.[21] This bureaucratic restructuring underscored the importance of soil conservation within the NAD. The waning influence of paternalists like D.R. Hunt was partly supplanted by zealous young technocrats convinced that they had both science and urgency on their side. By the 1940s, native commissioners had to master the language and practice of conservation if they wished their careers to prosper.

The policy to be followed on Trust land was further amplified by a 1939 proclamation. To combat the 'evil of overstocking', powers were provided for the NAD – after consultation with the local population – to proclaim 'betterment areas' in which stock numbers would be assessed and 'surplus' animals culled. Detailed conditions which granted considerable powers of control to officials were also laid down for the occupation of Trust land. These strictly limited tenants' security of tenure and their ability to transfer or bequeath rights to land. 'Arable allotments' should not exceed five morgen which, in the case of second or third wives (or widows), was reduced to two-and-a-half morgen.[22] This formula reflected the injunction to maintain as large a population as possible in the rural areas both to stem the flow to the cities and to sustain a migrant labour system.

The NAD was sensitive to the NEC's urgings to begin to move away from the 'one man one lot' system but, as the department pointed out in a memorandum to J.H. Hofmeyr, the acting prime minister, in 1943,

> Rightly or wrongly the SA policy has been to give the native a little land, not sufficient to make him independent of the labour market but sufficient to enable wages to be fixed on the assumption that the natives' earnings are augmented by what he gets from the land. To change this policy is of course a matter of extreme difficulty and one somewhat beyond the scope of the Department of Native Affairs. The change can in any case only take place gradually. The department is nevertheless considering the establishment of closer settlements for industrialised natives and leaving the rest of the land to whole time native farmers. It would be appreciated however that the carrying out of this somewhat revolutionary scheme involves the establishment of satisfactory industries in the native areas and the payment of wages in these industries or in the towns and other employment which will

enable the native family to subsist without ownership of cattle and cultivation of the land.[23]

Trust and Tribulation

The implementation of the 1936 Native Trust and Land Act sent shock waves through the rural Transvaal and, while the residents of Sekhukhuneland were not initially heavily affected by the Trust, they watched with mounting alarm as the areas immediately to the north and to the south were convulsed by struggles caused by the implementation of the new law.

The first rumblings came not from the reserves or released areas but from neighbouring white farm lands. In 1938, in response to strong pressure from white farmers in the northern and eastern Transvaal, the state proclaimed Chapter Four of the Land Act in the Lydenburg district. This involved the registration of labour tenants, a minimum period of four months' free labour, and heavier taxes for landowners who rented land to Africans. Farmers hoped that these measures would solve the labour shortages they suffered. Instead it produced opposition involving nearly all the labour tenant families in Lydenburg. Tenants explaning their stance stressed that they objected to restrictions on their remaining independence. Resistance emerged out of a long-standing struggle amongst tenants to defend their households from white domination and to retain the maximum possible room for manoeuvre. Workers jealously guarded their ability to move from farm to farm to seek the best possible land and conditions of service.[24]

Tenants refused *en masse* to register and families started to leave the farms in significant numbers, with the majority moving to adjacent company and crown lands or reserves. Faced by such widespread and united resistance, farmers and the state were forced to retreat and the haemorrhage of tenants was stanched. But these events provided a first glimpse of the Act's fangs, which had previously been partially obscured by promises of land. The families who moved to the released areas to retain their 'freedom' were also unlikely to respond any more positively to the Trust's plans to regulate their new homes.

For the inhabitants of Sekhukhuneland, who had numerous historical and contemporary connections to the Lydenburg tenants, serious doubts were sown about the *real* purpose of the Act and questions started to be asked about whether this was not simply yet another disguised attempt at dispossession. These fears were soon fuelled by accounts of bitter battles just to the north in the early 1940s.[25]

As the 1930s drew to a close, there were few obvious warnings of the storms to come in the Pietersburg district. The Trust purchased 250 000 morgen of land from land companies and absentee landlords. The approximately

10 000 Africans who already resided on this land had resented the annual visits of rent and tax collectors and the fees they had to pay for their stock. But they had otherwise enjoyed considerable control over their own lives. 'They decided what crops they would plant and where they would plant them. They kept as many cattle, sheep and goats as they could afford.'[26] Some individuals had built up relatively large holdings of arable land (30 morgen or more) and sizeable herds.

This has led some observers to suggest that these communities were composed of 'independent peasants all their lives who live on a much higher standard of living than the tribes which go to the gold mines'.[27] But this characterisation ignores the high levels of differentiation both within these groups and amongst their neighbours in the locations, and the ample evidence that tenants on land company farms had a long and deep involvement in migrant labour. They had also recently suffered heavy blows from drought and pestilence. Land and cattle constituted important elements in the sets of resources which, in a variety of combinations, sustained households. Accumulating significant quantities of land and livestock remained general aspirations, although they were far from universal achievements.

Initially the Trust takeover of the farms went smoothly. The tenants welcomed the reduction of rents and stock fees that resulted. There was widespread anticipation that local administration would continue to rest on chiefs and heads of *kgoro*. As one official ruefully observed later, 'The locations had been under chiefs' control ... and natives at first thought that they would be left in supreme control of trust lands.'[28] Chiefs and headmen based in the reserves also looked forward to an expansion of their domains. This period of happy anticipation survived initial discussion with Trust officials over the division of the farms into residential, arable and grazing areas. But the tenants mood rapidly soured as the full extent of intended Trust control became apparent.

The first flickers of defiance started in 1940 when individuals were prosecuted for cutting down trees without obtaining permits from the Native Trust overseer. They intensified when officials broached the subject of stock culling in 1941. Fuel was added to the fire by the failure of officials to explain fully the nature of arrangements to individuals living on land abutting Moletzies location. Families which had been content in the belief that they were contributing to the purchase of farms to expand the location were outraged and embittered to discover that they were paying Trust rent.[29]

But the complaint that was voiced over and over again by tenants concerned the size of the plots allocated. Initially promised good land with high productivity, and somewhat in awe of 'the law', tenants went along with the new system. But the reality was often poor and even uncleared land; and the five and two-and-a-half morgen plots proved to be much smaller areas than most had expected to receive and many had previously cultivated. The division and demarcation of land also meant that families often had to move. The experience of living under the new regime proved intolerable to many. Hedged around by 'Trust' restrictions and afflicted by poor rains, families found that the size of their harvests plummeted. As one tenant commented, 'since the lands were allotted to us, we are buying mealies from other people'; another observed that 'we thought the government was sympathetic, now we think the government is death'.[30]

Discontent festered throughout 1941 and 1942. At meetings, tenants argued with officials that they had cultivated much larger areas in the past and could not survive on mere 'scraps' of land. And it appears that individuals who had previously accumulated large lands and sizeable herds played a leading part in the mounting protest. Trust officials, alarmed by the growing momentum of resistance, decided that the best way to prevent revolt was to make provision for additional land for those who could show that they had previously cultivated large fields. But the concession did not have the desired effect. This was partly because it was administered with such bureaucratic petty-mindedness that it had limited reach, but also because renewed calls for cattle culling from officials rubbed tenants' anxieties raw. By 1943 the resistance was also far more thoroughgoing than officials realised. Tenants, chiefs and headmen had originally welcomed the Trust because they believed it would bring more land and additional political and social breathing space. Instead, it brought hordes of officials, implementing a host of regulations and threatening further intervention – most ominously to cull stock. Tenants refused to apply for more land and increasingly asserted that 'the land belongs to them and they could plough where they liked and as much as they liked. They state that the land belongs to them and their grandfathers and they can do what they like.'[31]

Residents on some of the farms refused to register with the Trust, fences and trees were cut, beacons were moved or destroyed, land designated for grazing was ploughed, and there was widespread refusal to move to newly designated residential sites.

Headmen and chiefs saw that the practice rather than the promise of 'the Trust' was more likely to supplant their authority than to extend their control and were also amongst some of the larger land and stock holders. They provided local level leadership and were able to weld together a constituency which commanded diverse resources but which was united in its rejection of Trust control. An overarching leadership also emerged. It comprised, at first sight, a somewhat unlikely combination. The dominant figures were Mathews Molepo, who had been a principal of a local Dutch Reform School but had resigned after clashing with the inspectorate; and Sebantu Seboto, a 'Xhosa from the Ciskei' who had settled in Pietersburg in 1924 and had worked as an agricultural demonstrator until he was dismissed. They were, in one description, 'rising members of the African petty bourgeoisie whose paths of ascent had been blocked'.[32] Acting as crucial intermediaries for, and advisers to, the protesting tenants, they worked closely with the third key actor in these events – Hyman Basner.

Basner, an ex-communist, a native representative in the Senate and a lawyer with 'a happy knack of combining his public duties with his private practice' successfully defended (at below average rates, one must hasten to point out) a number of residents against legal proceedings instituted by the Trust.[33] These legal victories encouraged tenants to believe that they would be able to establish effective control over Trust land. The conflict came to a head in 1943 when officials attempted to enforce the removal of tenants on farms which had been designated as commonage. One resident retorted: 'We are glad to hear the native commissioner say this is the last word of the Government. Even today we are giving the final word to the Government, we are not going to leave the farms.'[34]

Open clashes developed after the rains fell, and police attempted to arrest individuals for illegal ploughing. When Jacobus Mashala was arrested on 9 November, fellow residents surrounded the police and forced them to release him. The native commissioner was mobbed and agricultural officers had assegais thrown at them.[35]

The following day it was reported that at least 500 Trust residents 'fully armed with assegais, battle axes and knobkerries' were 'hiding in the bush' and some 1 500 to 2 000 people were reportedly involved in open defiance. Many took to the bush. The episode was intense but relatively short-lived. A spotter plane was brought from the Pietersburg air school which was in radio contact with forces on the ground and helped to track and intimidate malcontents. The police arrested 'ringleaders' and individuals who breached Trust regulations. By the fifth day resistance was flagging. These events, which were dramatic enough in their own right, have been painted in still more lurid colours. The use of a plane, for example, has been transformed, by way of an academic version of Russian rumour, into a horror story in which 'peasants ... were literally bombed into submission'.[36]

In practice the state was able to re-establish control by rather more mundane and less bloody means. The NAD won significant victories in the courts after regulations were tightened up, and Basner's involvement also diminished. It served deportation orders on key 'agitators', including Molepo, and made concerted efforts to win the support of headmen and chiefs. While 'trouble makers' were threatened, 'well-behaved headmen were rewarded with retirement allowances and stipends'.[37] The NAD also offered some compensation to households which had suffered from removals. And it was able to exploit division amongst the residents – especially between long-standing tenants who had been in the forefront of resistance and new settlers who were relieved to get access to land even if it was under strict control. These tensions were intensified when protesting tenants began ploughing lands allocated by officials to others. And while women had played a role in the resistance, in part because of the inferior allotments provided to widows and wives, land controlled by women was targeted by the rebels. There were a number of instances reported in which 'widows have been robbed of their lands'. Officials acted swiftly to assist these individuals and won some support.[38]

These confrontations in neighbouring districts amongst communities closely linked by kinship, history and culture to the societies of Sekhukhuneland had the most immediate impact in *Bopedi*. But the arrival of 'the Trust' reverberated throughout the Northern Transvaal in the early 1940s. In the Zoutpansberg area, for example, the SANT set about transforming relationships on the farms that it had purchased. These measures also resulted in widespread resistance and the emergence of an organisation called the Zoutpansberg Balemi Association led by Alpheus Malivha, a Venda migrant worker. Although these events were more remote from Sekhukhuneland they were, in the slightly longer term and by means of the flow of information along migrant worker networks, also added to the store of popular understanding of the iniquities of 'the Trust.'[39]

But it was not only the experiences of near and distant neighbours that alerted the inhabitants of Sekhukhuneland to the dangers of the Trust. In the early 1940s, officials made a start on reshaping relationships on Trust land in Sekhukhuneland. Little was done in relation to the ex-crown farms close to the Geluks location. As the native commissioner pointed out in 1943, these

> have since the British occupation been under the control of various headmen acknowledging Sekukuni as their chief, who have had the rights to control grazing, arable and residential lands in so far as their followers are concerned. In cases of dispute matters are referred to Chief Sekukuni with the right of appeal to the native commissioner. The native occupiers have resided on these farms under these conditions since 1857 ... Further the residential and grazing rights are inherited from generation to generation and it will certainly lead to a great deal of discontent if they are interfered with.[40]

Broadly similar conditions prevailed on the small number of farms purchased by the Trust in the late 1930s. But the commissioner was more sanguine about the prospects for 'carrying out any restrictions or alterations that may be necessary' on the basis that 'the natives have been warned at the time of purchase that if they wish to remain on the farms they must comply with any demands that may be made by the Trust at any time'.[41] D.L. Smit, the secretary of the Native Affairs Department, was – despite the mounting furore in Pietersburg – determined that the department should 'not budge on the issue of control' and should push ahead with demarcating lands.[42] Heedless of the experiences to the north, even more meagre three-morgen plots were allocated. Worse still, it was proclaimed in 1943 that farms purchased by the Trust would automatically be proclaimed as betterment areas. The implementation of these policies, even if only initially on a handful of farms, created a local outcry.[43] From 1943, a newly formed and remarkably named organisation, the Sebataladi Motor Cottage Association (SMCA), denounced conditions on Trust farms where

> a state of oppression exists as the people are not allowed to plough on fertile ground ... [O]ne is only allowed to keep a certain number of cattle, goats or donkeys ... and elderly people, cripples and disabled people are not wanted on these farms.[44]

But Sebataladi's activities ranged far beyond the issues of 'the Trust' and shed light on other significant stirrings in Sekhukhuneland in the war years.

The Sebataladi Motor Cottage Association

The leaders of the SMCA came from Christian families in Sekhukhuneland who, after a few years of primary education, had found urban employment and then moved into trading. Lekati Maimela and his younger brother, Thomas, for example, grew up in Schoonoord where both attended the local Lutheran school until Standard Two. Lekati found employment with a law firm in Pretoria in the 1930s and, after a time, he also secured a job in the company for Thomas. The brothers were fascinated by their glimpses of the legal world. But the majesty of the law was not sufficient to stop them from supplementing their wages with trade in dagga and alcohol. They also established themselves as tailors making and selling trousers. Thomas secured a peddler's licence in Johannesburg and supplied 'medicine' to shops there.[45]

Pretoria in the 1930s also provided new political horizons. Naboth Mokgatle recalled how, shortly after his arrival in the city,

> walking westward through the old and famous location Marabastad ... I saw a large gathering of people ... [and] found four groups holding a joint open air meeting. They were the African National Congress, the ICU (the Industrial and Commercial Workers' Union of Africa) the Radicals and the Garveyites.[46]

While the Marabastad ICU was a fragment of a dying organisation its leader, Ishmael Moroe, was a powerful and courageous speaker and attracted a number of followers amongst migrant workers and petty traders. In 1939 his fiery oratory was silenced by an appointment as compound manager by the city council but the branch continued under the leadership of W.M. Malatje who styled himself the provincial secretary of the ICU.

In these years there was a running battle in Marabastad as the police attempted to close unlicensed shops in location houses. The harassed traders received some support and advice from the local office of the ICU and some paid the joining fee of two shillings and received cards. The Marabastad ICU also became involved in struggles in the countryside, partly through its migrant membership. The best documented episode involved the farm Kalkfontein which was adjacent to Sekhukhuneland. The tenants, who were threatened by a new landlord with eviction, brushed aside their supine chief and sought assistance from the ICU.

The Marabastad branch was idiosyncratic – even by the standards of the ICU – but did provide its members with some grounding in the history of the organisation. Oral informants recall that the ICU was an important model for the founders of Sebataladi. Many, indeed, describe the SMCA as the 'I See You' and it is probable that the activities of Moroe and Malatje in Pretoria were one influence on its founders. But it is also likely that the future leaders of Sebataladi were exposed to many other commercial and political currents which swirled in the testing world of the black lower middle classes during these decades. An important part of this context involved the co-operative and self-help societies which overlapped with a number of movements (including the ICU) and which mushroomed in the 1940s. And the leaders of Sebataladi, as we shall explore more fully later, also had substantial contacts with the ANC.

By the early 1940s, Thomas Maimela had left Pretoria and established himself as tailor serving the residents of the Witbank location and the nearby mine compounds. He became a close friend of Charlie Maluke Mashabela who was also from a Christian family in Sekhukhuneland and who owned a licensed general dealers store in the location. It was this combination which became the driving force behind the Sebataladi Motor Cottage Association, initially involving a core group of about 20 individuals with broadly similar backgrounds. Both Maimela and Mashabela were frustrated by the limited economic and political space afforded them in the towns and pondered the prospects for carving out additional room for manoeuvre in the reserves. They had also been able to use their income from trade to accumulate significant resources in their home areas. Maimela's interest in Sekhukhuneland, for example, was underscored by the fact that he had built up a large herd of cattle there. He and Mashabela imagined a future in which they could play a crucial part in bringing 'progress' to their compatriots at the same time as turning a nice profit.[47]

Misfortune proved to be the mother of invention. In 1942 Maimela sent six bags of mealies by railway truck from Witbank to his sister in Sekhukhuneland. But they never reached their destination. On making enquiries about his loss, he discovered there were widespread complaints that goods were disappearing from railway depots in the area. Railway lorries were the main means that migrants and others used to transport their purchases home and this predation threatened a vital lifeline. Thomas Maimela started to collect the consignment notes of individuals whose property had gone missing and launched his own investigations. He ultimately persuaded the Witbank police to take action. Charlie Kgarutle, who was in charge of one of the depots, was spotted wearing a pair of trousers which had been packed in a box which had been 'lost' in transit. Kgarutle was arrested and convicted and, after further theft was uncovered, there was considerable popular acclaim for Maimela.[48]

But Mashabela and Maimela did not rest on their laurels. In December 1942 they sent a letter to Chief Sekhukhune requesting his support

> to start an enterprise which will be of great benefit to you and the tribe as a whole. That is from chief to men, women and children. Our aim and objectives are to build sheds at every place where buses stop to off-load people's goods ... [W]omen and children are often bundled onto the buses as if they were bags and put off in the veldt in the rain and cold winds without any shelter ... Goods are put off in the rain and left to thieves.[49]

Mashabela signed as 'managing director' and Maimela as 'secretary and treasurer'.

These 'sheds' were the 'Motor Cottages' of the association's title, which also drew on elements in Pedi folklore captured in the proverb '*Sekhukhune se bonwa ke Sebataladi*' (broadly translated, this means that even a stealthy thief is seen by a watchful person).[50]

The SMCA constitution, which was sent to the native commissioner, stressed its intention

> to improve all African peoples who are members ... to carry on business and trade of any kind ... [and that it was] a purely Bantu enter price (sic) staffed by them.[51]

In 1943 Maimela, disenchanted with the prospects for a tailor in Witbank, returned to act as Sebataladi's organiser in Sekhukhuneland. He had high hopes for the future, confiding in his wife that all that I am doing will enable us to live decently. Here we are paying useless rent as pairs of trousers are finished ... I am going to be an Inspector of Depots and I will be paid out of the depots storage charges.[52]

Initially the SMCA set out to win the support of chiefs and the native commissioner, stressing its commitment to promoting education, modern agriculture and better health services. But the local authorities looked askance at the activities of these 'upstarts', who combined the political disabilities of being Christians and commoners. Receiving little encouragement from those quarters, Maimela focused his energies on organising public meetings where his complaints about the loss of goods enjoyed considerable support. At these meetings he also proclaimed Sebataladi's intention to build co-operative stores, schools and clinics. He sold SMCA membership cards and collected significant sums of money from people who longed to share in the rosy future he portrayed.[53]

Emboldened by this support and frustrated by the lack of response from the local rulers, the association started to elaborate a wide-ranging critique of local conditions in pamphlets and at public meetings. As noted above, these criticisms dealt with developments on Trust lands but ventured considerably further. Dipping fees, fines and the methods of tax and levy collection were denounced. It was argued that there was an urgent need for clinics to be built in the main villages because

Geluks location was infested with all sorts of diseases such as Malaria (which is very prevalent) Small Pox, Mumps, Tuberculosis, Chicken Pox, and Measles that can be cured or healed if medical attention was available ... and that a number of people (especially women and children) die without receiving medical attention.[54]

The association also raised the poor conditions of local roads and recent reductions in pay for road workers. It highlighted the inadequacy of the local provision of water, urging the construction of dams and access to piped supplies.

These issues were sensitive enough. But Maimela and the SMCA strayed onto treacherous ground when they raised questions about the role of the native commissioner, the chiefs and the local council.

Pamphlets issued early in 1944 proclaimed: 'The present native commissioner has no sympathy for the people' and that the 'Department of Native Affairs governs us as if we are prisoners ... very much like the Hitlerism we now see.'[55] The evidence provided to support this proposition ranged from the fact that visitors were required to leave their hats outside the commissioner's office to their authoritarian treatment of chiefs and their subjects. It

included accusations that the commissioner monopolised local water supplies
and that he had colluded in the theft of goods from the railway depots.

Initially in private, Maimela and other members of the SMCA argued that
chiefs were a barrier to progress. For example, in a letter sent to Maimela in
1943, his storekeeper cousin B.D. Lebetha wrote that

> nowadays chiefs are worthless because they still fail to enlighten the
> people with good advice ... [O]ur chiefs still say at public meetings, if
> one wants to give the people some good advice, whose son are you,
> who are you, what are you?[56]

Comments made in open meetings and documents also became increasingly
direct. A pamphlet issued by SMCA in 1944 stated that

> Chieftainship does not belong to the chiefs only, nor does the
> furtherance of the interests of the tribe. What is in the minds of our
> chiefs is the fear that the progress of the tribe will eventually bring
> about the loss of the powers of chiefs ... [T]hey feel that it should not
> be their duty to work for progress amongst their tribes. Our people die
> like mice, they are poor, they starve, they continually move out of the
> kraals, the chiefs do not want to face or know the cause of all these
> things ... What our chiefs do is to take or marry women without
> doing anything for them, they bear children but do nothing for these
> children. They like to drink beer and to eat and to collect our arrear
> taxes.[57]

The alternative to the existing order articulated by the SMCA focused on the
local council. Its leaders argued that the present council was 'powerless as the
members have to do as they are dictated to by the native commissioner' and
that it was inappropriate for chiefs to act as councillors for that is 'the position of a servant'. The SMCA suggested the commissioner and the chiefs
should resign and be replaced by elected representatives (presumably including some individuals drawn from the ranks of the association) whereupon
'control of the reserve' should be transferred to the council. It should be like
a town council and 'make laws and regulations for the reserve and be responsible to the Minister of Native Affairs'.[58]

The association's enthusiasm for the reform of local government met with
a chilly response from the chiefs and the commissioner who, by early 1944,
shared the conviction that stern measures were needed to silence the increasingly strident voices of Maimela and his associates. The leading chiefs –
probably with some official prompting – urged the commissioner to have
Thomas Maimela 'removed from our midst' to avoid the SMCA causing the
'secret destruction of our tribal control'. They argued that

he had stirred up trouble between the people, the chiefs and the council and [that] the young are always more in number than the older sections of the tribesman and the danger is that they are apt to trust that such a type of braggart and underminer of peace has some power over the Department ... There is world trouble in these times and we require no extra tribal strife.[59]

The first strategy was to use the courts to silence the SMCA. Maimela was arrested, charged with 13 counts of holding illegal meetings, held in a cell for nine days, and tried in the Lydenburg magistrates court on 29 May 1944. He was defended by Pixley ka Izaka Seme but was convicted on ten of the charges. However, the magistrate clearly found it difficult to take a serious view of meetings which appeared primarily concerned with goods missing in transit. To the considerable chagrin of both the commissioner and the chiefs, Maimela was cautioned and discharged. Undaunted, the commissioner pressed for a deportation order to be issued against him. In December of 1944 Maimela was banished, along with his wife and minor child, to a Trust farm in the Rustenburg district.[60]

Maimela turned to both the Transvaal African Congress and Basner for assistance. He was not, however, able to muster more than a handful of active supporters in Sekhukhuneland. There had been considerable popular sympathy for his actions in exposing theft from the depots and concern over many of the issues the SMCA had highlighted. But the association had massively overplayed its hand when it imagined that a small group of Christians and commoners could take on both the commissioner and the chiefs. When the inevitable confrontation developed, support for both Maimela and the association melted away. Banishment to a remote Trust farm where he would be unable to ply his trade or even run more than a handful of his cattle threatened utter disaster. His difficulties were further compounded by the cancellation of his exemption certificate. Thus, while he railed that 'Sekukuni is the owner of dogs and his dogs have bitten me', he was forced to plead ignominiously to be allowed to remain in Witbank.[61] Eventually, in 1946, after Basner had interceded with the Minister of Native Affairs and Maimela had given a written undertaking that he would no longer be involved in SMCA and promised to keep out of Sekhukhuneland, he was allowed to stay on in the Witbank location.

The Sebataladi Motor Cottage Association faded away almost as rapidly as it had burst on to the scene. Its history, though brief, opens a window on an emergent group of mainly Christian small traders who straddled town and countryside, chafed against the constraints in both arenas, and set out to find additional economic and political elbow room. They drew on Pedi folklore, elements of ICU and ANC organisation, their experiences in trade and ideas current in the co-operative movement of the day. Their activities probed the economic and political order for potential paths of advancement and provided a relief map of the stress points in the society. They challenged the dominant conception that chiefs and officials would marshal a slow march to modernity and offered themselves as leaders of a more rapid progress.

The rise and fall of the SMCA also provided a thought-provoking example for contemporary observers both of the political possibilities provided by a range of popular grievances and of the dangers of head-on confrontation with a combination of chiefly and official power.[62]

Thomas Maimela eventually returned to Sekhukhuneland in 1955. He earned an income through ploughing, transporting water and goods on his donkey cart and cutting and selling wood. He maintained a low political profile but by 1959 had become a staunch supporter of the Pan-Africanist Congress. His organisational energies were, however, mainly devoted to religion. In 1967 he was ordained as a minister in the Bapedi Lutheran Church. In 1973 he was killed in a car accident.[63]

The Sekhukhuneland Student Association

Other voices joined the debate over the implications of 'the Trust' and the importance of 'improvement' in the 1940s. A crucial forum for these discussions was the Sekhukhuneland Student Association, which was formed in the late 1930s. Its membership was also drawn overwhelmingly from Christian families but it comprised the upper crust of that world – individuals who had completed primary education and gone on to study at Botshabelo, Grace Dieu and Kilnerton. It was, in the words of one-time chairman Godfrey Pitje, 'a kind of umbrella organisation for the Sekhukhuneland elite – students, teachers, there were no doctors then – but whoever mattered in the field of education'.[64] It drew into its orbit the clusters of educated individuals who had formed 'improvement leagues' in the different villages in the 1930s and whose primary topic of discussion was how to bring 'progress' to the wider community. Students would return home during their vacations and give concerts to display the skills they had acquired and to 'spread the gospel' of education.[65]

These groupings also attempted to build relationships with the chiefs, envisaging a collaboration in which they could act in concert to 'uplift' their compatriots. But in the 1940s their relationships with the native commissioners were less happy. There were, by the 1940s, a number of young men in the area who had recently graduated from teacher training colleges which had directly or indirectly been affected by the wave of disturbances which swept through these institutions. These events were often dubbed 'food riots' but involved a much broader contestation of the racial structures of authority in the colleges.[66] Against this backdrop, and in the context of local and international political ferment, these college graduates were much more inclined than previous generations of students to question the local patterns of administration. 'The Trust', and especially cattle culling, was one recurring topic of debate. Despite some ambiguity – after all betterment, like these students, spoke a language of modernisation – the broad consensus within the SSA was that the shortage of land, not the surfeit of cattle, was the most pressing issue. And the 'young men' of the SSA were also prepared to challenge the native commissioner in open meetings in a way which would have been considered unthinkable even a few years earlier.

> They go to this meeting ... [T]he commissioner gets there in casual-wear, which they felt was the usual contempt of the white man for anything black ... [W]hen he gets to these meetings, somebody will automatically say rise. And these boys take offence at that. Who is he? He is a commoner, why must our chiefs, Sekwati you name them, why must they stand? ... [After speaking the commissioner] put his foot on the chair like this, and one of the boys said that's our furniture and we are not going to have it tainted by this man, and they gave him a very rough time, in fact so rough, that I am told that he went very near recommending the banning of the body.[67]

The old guard within the SSA were horrified by these tactics and a number went to the commissioner to 'apologise and to say, please don't think this is the general view'.[68] While officials toyed with the idea of acting against the organisation, its conservative ballast, its relatively low profile and its good relationships with the chiefs made it a less tempting target than Sebataladi. The SSA crumbled in the late 1940s but a number of the vocal young men involved went on to play prominent roles in the 'Youth League' and in the ANC.[69]

'A New Era of Reclamation'

The rash of resistance and the hubbub of debate in the early 1940s made little impression on official thinking. As the war drew to a close the NAD, fortified by a visit from Dr Hugh Bennett of the USA Soil Conservation Services, resolved to press ahead 'in much bolder form and on a much larger scale'.[70] D.L. Smit, Secretary for Native Affairs, announced 'A new era of reclamation'. This initiative was primarily a restatement of existing policy with some sabre-rattling on the issue of culling and a fuller discussion of soil conservation techniques. Where it diverged most markedly from earlier documents was in its detailed proposals for rural villages to provide suitable houses for the families of Natives regularly employed in industries and other services. Natives earning their living in this way cannot make efficient use of normal allotments and the establishment of healthy rural villages for their families is the best solution ... It must be accepted that there will never be enough land to enable every native in the reserves to become a full-time peasant farmer.[71]

Officials hoped that these villages, in the context of the large-scale industrial development that was anticipated after the war, would resolve the contradiction between rural restructuring and slowing the 'drift to the towns'. Exactly why families denied access to arable land and livestock should wish to remain in these villages was not a question that these rural planners chose to answer.

Despite the state's concern to press ahead, D.L. Smit maintained 'such a change cannot be enforced from above. The plan can be conceived above, but the change must come largely from the people themselves. They must adopt the plan as their own and work for it to come true.'[72] However, this commitment to 'consultation' was not based on the premise that rural inhabitants could make a contribution to evolving policy and practice but on the assumption that, given time, they would come to see the wisdom of official designs. Official exasperation mounted as communities remained sceptical of the new world on offer and in the late 1940s the NAD assumed ever larger powers to enforce rural restructuring. This combination of a rhetoric of participation with a reality of imposition set a style which found many imitators in the field of rural development in the decades that followed.

After 1945, 'the Trust' became an increasingly intrusive presence in Sekhukhuneland. Scores of farms were bought and residents on crown lands were also no longer immune from the ministrations of officials. Residents on Trust land were only allowed five free stock units and were informed that donkeys and goats, which were of particular importance to poorer households, would be radically reduced. Cattle culling also began to be enforced on a much wider scale than previously. Overall assessments of carrying capacity were undertaken and surplus stock was branded and sold at local auctions. By 1950, half the district had been affected. While individuals with large herds suffered particularly severely, all stock-owning households were at risk. The anger that these measures engendered was intensified by the fact that the stock sales produced a captive market for white farmers and speculators. There were also well-founded suspicions that white agricultural assistants were buying culled cattle or selling them to their friends at bargain-basement prices. The officials who engaged in these practices naturally had a strong interest in appropriating the most desirable cattle.[73]

Rapid progress was also made in the fencing of lands, the demarcation of plots and in laying out new settlements. But the issue of 'villagisation' remained a vexed question. There was a strong view that the process of rehabilitation should finalise the division between permanent industrial workers housed in villages and farmers with access to stock and land. However, the estimates provided of the numbers that would have to be moved off the land ranged from 40 to 60 per cent. These figures were a source of considerable alarm to officials whose brief included slowing the pace of urbanisation. There was also some scepticism about the potential economic viability of those left on the land. In consequence, while proposals for villages were put forward in a number of plans, the dominant practice was to allow individuals to retain access to land and stock. The result, in the context of intensifying land shortage, was that the plots allocated steadily diminished in size. Officials hoped, nonetheless, to weed out 'inefficient farmers' over time and to allocate their land to more productive individuals, thereby consolidating a farmer class.

There was little room in their vision of the future for female-headed households. Officials had no doubt that men would be the backbone of the permanent peasantry they hoped to create – a view which helped ensure that 'widows' were either excluded from the allocation of arable plots or granted plots a quarter – or less – of the size of those granted to males.[74]

In the Apjesboom block of Trust farms, for example, the native commissioner commented that 'the large number of widows who previously held lands in this group of farms, ... is a feature of all Trust farms in Sekhukhuneland. It is doubtful whether widows will make good farmers.' In this instance they were allocated one-morgen plots as opposed to the four morgen allocated to male household heads. This was despite the commissioner's somewhat rueful observation that 'widows' had 'in general discharged their financial obligations to the Trust more regularly than had male kraal heads ... and often had to support several minor children'.[75] He hoped, however, that the minimum rent payable for the land of £1 – whether the plot was large or small – would 'induce widows to move into a rural village as soon as it is established'.[76]

Conclusion

There were important rumblings in Sekhukhuneland during the war years. Individuals with a background of Christianity and some primary schooling crafted new associations, elaborated their own models of modernity and tested the political and economic constraints which held them fast. They focused on issues with wide-ranging popular resonances but were not able to mobilise a mass constituency; and they were brushed aside relatively easily by chiefs and officials who did not relish commoners and Christians with pretensions to local power.

But there was a topic of overriding popular concern in the 1940s – the advance of the SANT. People in virtually every village and household pondered the implications of this new order, which seemed determined to penetrate and dominate every nook and cranny of their world. In the name of 'development' and 'conservation' their cattle were culled, their lands diminished and demarcated. Communities found themselves hemmed in by a host of restrictions, ranging from a ban on cutting trees to prohibitions on keeping donkeys and goats. Households discovered that they had to pay fees for grazing stock and rents for residential sites. 'Widows' were informed that they were – at best – entitled to reduced amounts of arable land. New settlements were laid out in straight lines. But perhaps most ominous of all were the powers that SANT gave to white officials and their agents to interfere in the daily life of communities. Native commissioners and agricultural officers invaded communities with rolls of fencing wire, sheaves of regulations and lists of new charges. Chiefs and headmen who resided on land under control of the SANT found themselves functionaries in a tightly defined administrative system. These measures, popularly described as 'the Trust', were widely detested as intrusive, oppressive and inimical to the maintenance of even a residual political and economic autonomy. Mangope Phala's explanation of why he rejected 'the Trust' which opened this chapter gives vivid expression to the sense of violation of an inner domain and bears repeating:

> They were coming into our homes ... even our own homes would be controlled by them ... Can you accept that if you marry a woman that another man just comes, throws you out of your house, climbs into your bed and sleeps in your blankets?[77]

By the late 1940s 'the Trust' was making its presence felt across a broad swathe of Sekhukhuneland. It was only in the old locations that it had been held at bay. Officials were convinced that the time was right for a final campaign. But the last frontier was to be bitterly fought.

Notes

1 Mangope Phala, 1.
2 Delius, *Land*, pp. 108-26 and 158-81. N. Etherington, *Preachers, Peasants and Proletarians* (London, 1978).
3 A. Ashforth *The Politics of Official Discourse in Twentieth Century South Africa* (Oxford, 1990), pp. 90-3; S. Dubow, *Racial Segregation and the Origins of Apartheid in South Africa 1919-1936* (London, 1989), pp. 66-9.
4 W. Beinart, 'Soil Erosion, Conservationism and Ideas about Development, 1900-1960', *Journal of Southern African Studies*, 11, 1984, p. 3; See also W. Beinart, 'Introduction: the Politics of Colonial Conservation', *Journal of Southern African*

Studies, 15, 1989. Unfortunately, at present, the data is not available to attempt a detailed reconstruction of the ecological history of Sekhukhuneland. There is considerable comment in the official record from the 1930s on the ravages of soil erosion and dangers of overstocking but the perspectives that informed these reports did not include a close understanding either of the particular ecology of the district or of the agricultural and stock management strategies which had evolved within it. There was, however, a broad official consensus that an ecological crisis existed in the area. In 1941, for example, the director of native agriculture reported: 'I must urge the very great necessity for the improvement of conditions in Sekukuniland. The locations of Gelukwe and Mohlaletse are the worst denuded areas resulting from overstocking and erosion in the Union.' See TA/NTS7516/679/327, DNA to SNA 20/6/1941, for this quotation. See also NTS3648/1250/308(1) and NTS9535/138/400/81.

5   D. Anderson, 'Depression, Dust Bowl, Demography and Drought', *African Affairs* 83, 1984, pp. 326-7.

6   Beinart, 'Soil Erosion', p. 68.

7   Ashforth, *Politics*, pp. 75-7.

8   UG22-'32, *Report of the Native Economic Commission 1930-1932*, p. 3.

9   *Ibid*, p. 16.

10   *Ibid*, p. 11.

11   Ashforth, *Politics*, pp. 90-1.

12   UG22-'32, *Report of the Native Economic Commission 1930-1932*, pp. 29-30.

13   *Ibid*, p. 30.

14   *Ibid*, p. 47. This did not include any real attempts by officials to get to grips with local strategies for making the best use of agricultural and pastoral resources. In Sekhukhuneland, for example, little consideration was given to the role of cattle posts and/or to local models of grazing resources. For valuable comparative perspectives, see M. Drinkwater, *The State and Agrarian Change in Zimbabwe's Communal Areas* (London, 1991), esp. pp. 113-50.

15   *Ibid*, p. 30.

16   Dubow, *Segregation*, p. 152; see also pp. 149-57; TA/NTS6813/19/318, Pitso minutes, 28/1/1936.

17   D.L. Smit, *Statement of Policy Under the Native Trust and Land Act* (Pretoria, 1937), p. 7.

18   *Ibid*, p. 5.

19   *Ibid*, p. 7.

20   *Ibid*. Provision was also made for the expansion of the numbers of agricultural demonstrators.

21   UG22-'32, *Report of the Native Economic Commission 1930-1932*, p. 47.

22   *Government Gazette,* Proclamations 31 and 264, 1939.

23   TA/NTS3799/2567/308/(1), NAD commentary for J.H. Hofmeyr on memo from H. Basner dated 19/11/1943.

24   Schirmer, 'The Struggle', pp. 104-40.

25   *Ibid*, p. 124.

26   J. Bekker, 'We Will Plough Where We Like', unpublished Honours dissertation, University of the Witwatersrand 1989, p. 88.

27   *Ibid*, p. 11. This interpretation was most fully developed by Hyman Basner who, as is discussed further below, played an important role in these events both as a lawyer and as a senator.

28   Bekker, 'Plough', p. 17; TA/NTS3797/2548/308(2), Native Commissioner Pietersburg to SNA, 15/12/1943. The Trust charged its tenants an annual fee of 30 shillings per person which included the right to graze ten cattle free of charge. The

norm on company farms had been £2 per man and £1 per woman plus three shillings
per head for large stock and sixpence for small stock.

29   Bekker, 'Plough', p. 21.
30   TA/NTS3796/2530/308, meeting 19 January 1943; see also 2531/308 meeting,
      15 January 1943; 2532/308 meeting, 13 January 1943.
31   TA/NTS 3799/2567/308, Statement by temporary foreman at Vulcanus, 28/1/1943;
      See also Bekker, 'Plough', pp. 29-45.
32   Bekker, 'Plough', pp. 67-8.
33   TA/NTS3799/2567/308, Minister of Native Affairs reply to Basner's motion in the
      Senate, 5/5/1994; Bekker, 'Plough', pp. 61-9.
34   Bekker, 'Plough', p. 38.
35   *Ibid*, p. 40.
36   *Ibid*, pp. 40-5, for an overview of these events. See Lodge, *Black Politics*, p. 268 for
      the suggestion that villagers were bombed into submission.
37   Bekker, 'Plough', p. 73.
38   *Ibid*., pp. 74-5; see also pp. 47-59.
39   B. Hirson *Yours for the Union* (Johannesburg, 1989), pp. 126-34. See also Chapter 3,
      below.
40   TA/NTS3797/2541/308, Native Commissioner Sekhukhuneland to SNA, 24/4/1943.
41   *Ibid*.
42   TA/NTS1801/114/276, Meeting of Native Commissioners and SNA, 4/9/1942.
43   TA/NTS3797/2541/308, SNA to Native Commissioner Sekhukhuneland, 27/5/1943
      and 3/9/1943; SNA to Controller of Native Settlements, 31/8/1943. For Trust farms in
      Nebo see NTS3797/2542/308.
44   TA/NTS 7252/259/326, SMCA report on matters affecting the living conditions of
      the people of Sekukuniland, 19/3/1944.
45   TA/NTS 7252/259/326/ *passim*; N. Maimela, 1.
46   N. Mokgatle, *Autobiography of an Unknown South African* (London, 1971), pp.
      178-9. See also pp. 215 and 221-2. The following paragraphs draw on S. Mabilu, 1;
      J.K. Nkadimeng, 1; E. Mothubatse, 5; S. Kgoloko, 1; T. Mabogoane, 1; T. Lerutla, 1;
      H. Bradford, *A Taste of Freedom* (London, 1987), pp. 254-5; P. la Hausse, 'So who
      was Elias Kuzwayo? Nationalism, Collaboration and the Picaresque in Natal', in
      Bonner *et al.* (eds.), *Apartheid*, pp. 195-205; Schirmer, 'Struggle', pp. 232-40;
      TA/NTS348/183/55, W.M. Malatje to the Minister of Native Affairs, 2/3/1943.
47   TA/NTS725/259/326 *passim*; N. Maimela, 1; S. Mabilu, 1; M.J. Sekhukhune, 2.
48   TA/NTS725/259/326, M. Kuper to Major Jenner enclosing statement by Thomas
      Maimela, 11/5/1944; and covering letter from TAC and statement by Thomas
      Maimela, 9/1/1945.
49   TA/NTS725/259/326, C.M. Mashabela *et al.* to Honourable Chief, 8/12/1942.
50   S. Motla, 1.
51   TA/NTS725/259/326, SMCA to Native Commissioner Sekukuniland, 1943.
52   TA/NTS725/259/326/, T. Maimela to E. Maimela, 23/6/1943.
53   *Ibid*. See for example minutes of meetings, 17/2/1944, 27/3/1944 and reports of
      meeting by F. Maserumule.
54   *Ibid*; report on matters affecting the living conditions of the people of
      Sekhukhuneland 19/3/1944. See also SMCA to Department of Public Health,
      11/3/1944.
55   *Ibid*; and pamphlet 4/6/1944.
56   *Ibid*; and B. Lebethe to T. Maimela, 14/1/1943.
57   *Ibid*; and pamphlet 4/6/1944.
58   *Ibid*; Report on matters affecting the living condition of the people of Sekukuniland,
      19/3/1944; minutes of meeting 17/2/1944; and resolution, 17/3/1944.

59   *Ibid*; P. Moroamoche P. Kgoloko and F. Maserumule declaration, 12/6/1944; and
      letter to Chief Native Commissioner nd., 1944.
60   *Ibid*; and trial record 29/5/1944 and subsequent correspondence, 1944-6.
61   *Ibid*; Maimela to Chief Phetedi Kgoloko, 30/11/1945.
62   J.K. Nkadimeng, 1; G.M. Pitje, 2.
63   N. Maimela, 1.
64   G.M. Pitje, 2.
65   H.P. Maredi, 1.
66   J. Hyslop, 'Food, Authority and Politics, Student Riots in South Africa, 1945-1976',
      in S. Clingman (ed.) *Regions and Repertoires* (Johannesburg, 1991).
67   G.M. Pitje, 2.
68   *Ibid.*
69   G.M. Pitje, for example, played a prominent role in the Youth League.
70   D.L. Smit, *A New Era of Reclamation* (Pretoria, 1945), p. 2.
71   *Ibid*, pp. 3-4.
72   *Ibid*, p. 5.
73   D.P. Lebopo, 1-2; N.N. Lebopo, 1; M.J. Sekhukhune, 1-2; J. Yawitch, *Betterment –
      The Myth of Homeland Agriculture* (Johannesburg,1981), p. 12.; UWHPL,
      W. Ballinger Papers, Eiselen to Ballinger, 27/12/1950.
74   TA/NTS10276/59/423/4, Senior Assistant Director Agriculture to CNC Pietersburg,
      18/5/1949 and enclosures. NTS3775/2334/308/ General Circular 27/1948v and
      enclosures; and NTS2523/116/293a Proclamation 26/3/1949 and enclosures. Of
      course, 'widows' rights were not only at risk from officials but, as events in
      Pietersburg show, were also in danger of being overridden by some local men.
75   TA/NTS10248/38/423/3(a), Native Commissioner Sekhukhuneland to CNC
      Pietersburg, 9/10/1954.
76   *Ibid.*
77   Mangope Phala, 1.

3

Self-Rule and Sebatakgomo

The ANC, the Communist Party, Migrant Workers and the Reserves, 1939–55

When the news of the National Party's 1948 election victory filtered through to the villages of Sekhukhuneland, many recalled the last decades of the nineteenth century when they had been ruled by the 'Boers' and Abel Erasmus had installed puppet chiefs and exterminated their cattle. This analogy provided little comfort to communities concerned to halt the advance of 'the Trust'.[1]

The pre-1948 segregationist framework had admitted of a future, if remote, possibility of integration. But this was increasingly supplanted by the evolving dogma of apartheid, which stressed the need for perpetual political and cultural separation. Although the reserves enjoyed pride of place in this vision of the future, the new government initially departed very little from the broad policy paths laid down by the United Party. But in the early 1950s it began to introduce its own peculiar ingredients into 'the Trust's' noxious brew. From the perspective of communities in Sekhukhuneland, the most toxic of these was the Bantu Authorities Act of 1951, widely believed to be designed to breach their last lines of defence.

Attempts to establish Bantu Authorities in Sekhukhuneland produced a popular outcry. Officials trying to account for this response pointed to a shadowy organisation connected to the ANC, which they believed was manipulating mass sentiment. The sparse academic literature which subsequently touched on these events did little to clarify matters, referring to the role of 'real agitators and a shadowy organisation called 'Feta kgomo' or 'Sebata Kgomo'.[2]

76

At first glance these comments appeared to be yet another example of the agitator theory of conflict which has long provided a substitute for explanation in South Africa. But oral evidence gathered from the mid-1980s confirmed the existence and importance of an organisation called Sebatakgomo. Tracing the genesis of this movement took scores of interviews and an historical journey which traversed the changing nature of state intervention in the countryside, evolving patterns of migrant organisation and the connections to rural struggles of both the ANC and the Communist Party.

Boipušo – Self-Rule

One of the priorities of the new National Party government was to change the complexion of the Native Affairs Department. The NAD had altered considerably since the heyday of D.R. Hunt as native commissioner in the 1920s. There had been not only an infusion of agriculturalists; an ethnological section charged with gathering data and giving advice on 'tribal matters' had also been developed. NAD officers were increasingly expected to master conservationist discourses at the same time as studying ethnology and social anthropology. Native commissioners were no longer simply gifted amateurs, often with missionary or military backgrounds. They continued to be predominantly English-speaking, but were more and more the products of internal promotion and civil service courses run through the University of South Africa. They were also moved at regular intervals and few built up the depth of experience of a particular society achieved by some of their predecessors.[3]

Hendrik Verwoerd took control of the NAD in 1948, and ushered in a new era of change. He purged head office of its United Party-supporting leadership and replaced them with ideologically more-sympathetic appointees, often drawn from Afrikaans universities. In 1949 a leading Afrikaner nationalist educationalist and anthropologist, W.M. Eiselen, replaced D.L. Smit as Secretary of Native Affairs. Eiselen had grown up on a mission station in Sekhukhuneland, immersed in the Berlin Missionary Society creed that Africans should develop within their own cultures and should not be drawn into a 'European world'. He was merely the most prominent of a number of children of BMS families who helped provide a new breed of state officials, blending experience of African society with commitment to apartheid ideals.

Many of the new appointees had imbibed the formulations of both *Volkekunde* and the South African Bureau of Racial Affairs – the leading Afrikaner Nationalist think-tank on racial policy. It took somewhat longer for these changes to work their way down through the ranks, but by the mid-1950s a new order was well ensconced in the department. There had been a strong infusion of Afrikaans-speaking bureaucrats and the autonomy of local officials had been curtailed. In apparent confirmation of the worst fears prevailing in Sekhukhuneland, a spruced-up version of Abel Erasmus was paraded in the pages of the NAD journal *Bantu* as a model for native commissioners to emulate. And his resurrection was only one of a number of indications of important shifts in the ideological framework within which officials operated.[4]

The ideology of apartheid was not a predetermined and immutable master plan but 'a complex, changing and often contradictory mix of both short term pragmatism and general ideological thrust'.[5] Nonetheless, from the early 1950s the NAD placed greater stress on the ideal of long-term racial separation, especially in political and cultural spheres, and a number of axioms gained influence. Key assumptions were that cultural differences were divinely ordained and insurmountable and that chieftainship was the central and authentic institution within African culture, upon which an alternative and distinct domain could be constructed. The Bantu Authorities Act of 1951 defined an administrative system which dispensed with both local and national councils, and was based squarely on chiefs and tribal authorities. It also aimed to lay the foundations of a political and economic arena which would absorb the energies and aspirations of the African middle classes.

This Act was regarded as a crowning early achievement of positive apartheid legislation. But while it was a symptom of the arrival of the new regime it was also the outcome of long-standing debates over retribalisation within the NAD.[6]

From the 1920s the NAD had viewed chieftainship as a vital mechanism of administration and means of social control, and this perspective had been endorsed by the NEC. However, in the Transvaal the process of chiefly recognition was both partial and inconsistent. From the late 1930s the increasing emphasis placed on 'development' and the influence of 'the Trust' tended in practice to downgrade the role of chiefs. These contradictory tendencies, and the resistance engendered by 'rehabilitation', led to the emergence of a counter-lobby within the NAD which emphasised the need to co-opt chieftainship if community co-operation was to be achieved. This perspective found an eloquent spokesman in the person of the state ethnologist (and son of a BMS missionary) N.J. van Warmelo. In 1945 he argued that

> The one thing [the chiefs] have seen very clearly is that on Trust land, chiefs and all they stand for have been relegated to a position of minor importance. The inference obviously for them is that the Trust and all its works are not a good thing ... I can only urge the Department to make use of the only authority in existence amongst the natives. It is easy to destroy, but what do we put in its place? To hope that our few

officials, 'birds of passage' as they have been called, cut off from the people by barriers of language and social status, can take the place of the native aristocracy, is to me the complete utopia. Once natives become an amorphic mass, who will control them? It is hard enough in the towns, but in miles and miles of country it is impossible unless through some force amongst themselves.[7]

Van Warmelo concluded that a 'drop of honey attracts more flies than a barrel of vinegar' and urged that material advantages should be offered to secure the support of chiefs.[8] While these views did not win the day at the time, they provided a perspective which contributed to wider policy reformulations after 1948.

The policies implemented by the NAD in the early 1950s were a heady brew of betterment and Bantu Authorities. Officials believed that, once the new administrative system was in place, 'development' leading to self-sufficiency would proceed apace. After all, while elected office holders

> frequently find themselves in the invidious position that [when] they support a proposal from the government which they know is right they endanger their chances of being re-elected. By accepting Bantu Authorities this handicap will be removed and they will not be obliged to ask the people first whether a measure obviously in their interests should be enforced, nor need they tell them what they propose doing for them.[9]

The department was determined to achieve rapid and widespread acceptance of Tribal Authorities and rehabilitation. But it wished this to be on a voluntary basis lest 'our critics say that we are forcing it down their throats and putting the clock back'.[10] Officials looked for the opportunity for a breakthrough. The prestige and legitimacy of the Pedi Paramountcy which officials had long regarded with suspicion now held out the possibility of dramatic 'progress'. They noted that

> the influence of the Maroteng chiefly house stretches far beyond the present tribal area ... [In] the nineteenth century they were the recognised rulers of the Bantu who presently live in the ... area between Bosbokrand in the East, Pietersburg in the West and Pretoria in the South.[11]

The fact that the Pedi Paramount's authority had not previously been recognised by the state over the whole of the Geluks location, much less the broader region, was a stumbling block. But fate seemed to play into their hands. Chief Kgoloko, who in theory was in command of the southern part of the location, fell foul of officials in the early 1950s when, reluctant to antagonise his subjects further, he resisted initiating rehabilitation measures. The

Paramount Chief Morwamotše, in contrast, appeared to be sympathetic to these proposals. This turn of events set the native commissioner pondering 'if the tribe should be reunited under one chief ... a strong feeling of gratitude to the Department will grow up which will make for better reactions all round and for a spirit of co-operation in matters such as reclamation'.[12]

Kgoloko died in early 1953, aged 35, and the department had the choice of either installing a successor or re-establishing the paramountcy. The first option was made even less attractive because the likely successor, Kgolane Kgoloko, had 'been in the employ of the Canadian High Commission for about ten years' and it was believed that 'if he is not communistically inclined he has at least ideas which would make him unsuited to be appointed as the next chief'.[13] More importantly, Eiselen regarded this as a perfect opportunity to start Bantu Authorities rolling. He decided 'to reunite the tribe on the understanding that within three months it will agree to the establishment of a Bantu Authority if necessary with the powers of a regional authority'.[14]

On 20 August 1953, at Malegale in Sekhukhuneland, Morwamotše was installed as official paramount with considerable fanfare before an audience which included senior officials, chiefs and headmen. Speaker after speaker from the department urged upon the audience the importance of the speedy establishment of a Bantu Authority. But three months dragged by and no request was forthcoming. Thus began a cat and mouse game that was to drag on for years. In private meetings with officials, Morwamotše and his senior councillors gave assurances that they wanted to form a Bantu Authority. But in public gatherings, they deferred to angry and even bellicose popular sentiment and avoided any open commitment. The proposed system was dubbed *boipušo* in popular parlance, which in simple translation meant self-rule. But it also carried associations which derided the image of independence conjured by officials as a mask for anarchy and the destruction of properly constituted authority. Officials cast around for explanations for this apparently contradictory behaviour. Some settled on ANC influence as the most likely culprit.[15]

The ANC and Resistance in the Reserves

This interpretation was not completely implausible. The ANC was no stranger to Transvaal rural politics nor to Sekhukhuneland, having a rich history of connection stretching back to the first decades of the century. Chiefs played a key role in the foundation and early years of the organisation. Some of the most senior royals in Bopedi – Chief Sekhukhune II, Chief Tseke Masemola and Chief Sekwati Mampuru – maintained close connections with the ANC, and provided financial support. The latter two were members of the

ANC House of Chiefs from the 1920s. The members of the educated elite who pioneered political organisation often came from rural backgrounds and some had strong connections to chiefly families. S.M. Makgatho, for example, who was elected president of the ANC in 1917, and of its regional wing the Transvaal African Congress (TAC) in 1918, was the son of *Kgoši* Mphahlele, a senior Sekhukhuneland chief. In this period rural issues, in particular the 1913 Land Act, were of central concern to the ANC. Congress meetings were held at Mohlaletse under the aegis of the Pedi Paramount to denounce the act and to collect funds to support an ANC delegation which travelled to England in an attempt to secure British intervention.[16]

Most members of the ANC were drawn from the ranks of Christians (both the mainstream and independent churches) with some Western education and from the chiefly elite. But, in the years immediately after the First World War, the leadership of the TAC was 'swept away by an immensely powerful upsurge of working class agitation, being radicalised and fragmented at the same time'.[17] There is evidence that elements of this process spilled over into rural areas in the 1920s. The TAC made contact with Africans resisting the escalating labour demands of white farmers. And in the reserves, popular discontent over the levels of taxation, dipping and the actions of unsympathetic officials led to the formation of a number of branches. In the village of Matlala near Pietersburg, dramatic clashes took place between the chief and the local branch of the TAC. But as the 1920s wore on the rural activities of the TAC tailed off and were dwarfed by the campaigns of the ICU.[18]

By the 1930s the relative pull of the countryside had diminished. Remnants of rural branches kept Congress traditions alive but the principal connections of the TAC in the reserves remained the chiefs, whose role within the organisation had declined significantly. Many were disillusioned by the failure of Congress campaigns round the land issue and some questioned the purpose of their cash contributions. After the 1927 Native Administration Act, leading chiefs were also drawn into a tighter and alternative embrace by the NAD, a trend little affected by the renewed attempts of the ANC during the presidency of Pixley ka Izaka Seme to woo royals. The focus of concern of the TAC leadership also became increasingly urban in these decades.

This shift did not lead to a complete rupture, but there was only minimal organisation in the countryside, and by the early 1930s in Sekhukhuneland (and elsewhere) there was little evidence of ANC activity beyond intermittent contacts with senior chiefs.[19]

The fortunes of the ANC reached a more general nadir in the early 1930s and it was not until 1936, when the Rev. James Calata became secretary-general, and in reaction to the Hertzog Bills, that a gradual recovery took place which quickened in the 1940s under the leadership of Dr Xuma.[20] The beginnings of the revival of the ANC in the late 1930s brought yet another attempt to draw chiefs into Congress. But the House of Chiefs languished with no more than a handful of active supporters and provided an uncertain source of either political or financial support for the ANC. The revised 1943 ANC constitution finally abolished the Upper House but Xuma continued his attempts to mobilise the chiefs. While some showed a degree of renewed interest, many were fearful of the consequences of intensifying struggles for their own positions and most were wary of alienating an increasingly assertive NAD. The leading royals in Sekhukhuneland kept up sporadic contacts with the ANC but were careful to maintain a low political profile. And open chiefly political and financial support for the ANC remained the exception rather than the rule.[21]

Xuma's strategy did, however, involve an important shift. He stressed the incorporation of chiefs not as an end in itself but as a crucial element in a wider drive to establish branches and develop individual membership in rural, particularly reserve, areas. And there is, indeed, some evidence of organisational growth in the Transvaal countryside in the early 1940s. There were ANC connections amongst the Bakwena ba Mogopa and there is evidence of an ANC presence in Rustenburg. The Matlala branch had been relaunched in the 1930s and elsewhere in the Pietersburg area in the 1940s, and in the Duiwelskloof/Zoutpansberg area steps were undertaken to establish a local organisation. J.M. Nkosi established a branch at Witbank which made some attempt to penetrate the town's rural hinterland and made contacts both with Sekhukhuneland and labour tenants. He also had connections with Thomas Maimela and the Sebataladi Motor Cottage Association, and at least one joint meeting was held in Sekhukhuneland in 1944. But local Congress leaders were alarmed by the confrontational tone adopted by the SMCA and urged a more moderate approach.[22]

Connections to the rural areas were not only through the establishment of branches and visits by officials. Migrants joined the ANC in the urban areas in the 1930s and early 1940s. Although few in number and mainly from a Christian and relatively educated background, they nonetheless helped keep their home communities and chiefs informed of ANC activities and policies.[23] And there were prominent ANC leaders on the Rand who both acted as a focus for a migrant constituency and who maintained strong rural connections. Probably the most important of these – certainly in relation to Sekhukhuneland – was Elias Moretsele.

Born into a chiefly lineage in Sekhukhuneland in 1897, Moretsele had joined the ANC in 1917. He was a stalwart of ANC campaigns in the 1920s and 1930s and was appointed provincial treasurer in the early 1940s. Steeped in the history of Pedi dispossession and resistance, and despite having long lived in town, he maintained his links with the countryside.[24]

His cafe at 41 Pritchard Street in Johannesburg was an important meeting place. Basner described it as the 'centre of the radical element' in the 1940s and David Bopape recalls that 'Lembede, Mandela and Tambo, they would all take their lunch there'.[25] But less well-known figures like Thomas Maimela also stopped in there when they were in the city. And Pedi migrants working in town and living in the Johannesburg hostels ate there, for, 'you see, you know the type of porridge that people eat, mostly from Sekhukhuneland, Moretsele had that type of porridge, it was very good for the people'.[26] The 'old man' became something of a father figure for men from Sekhukhuneland and there seems to have been truth in the obituary comment in *New Age* that 'he was a centre of the Bapedi people of the towns. To him they came for advice on matters big and small.'[27]

There is thus some evidence of organisational growth in the 1940s and the existence of networks linking urban and rural areas. But the extent, effectiveness or durability of these developments should not be exaggerated for, by the end of the decade, there was little to show in terms of entrenched rural organisation. The TAC was deeply divided in the years 1941–3, in part over the importance to be attached to rural issues, and for a period split into two sections. Many of the rural branches established appear to have rested heavily on the initiatives and interests of individual founding members. They failed to gain momentum and collapsed within a couple of years amidst often acrimonious disputes about the failure of central organisation to provide financial or physical support, and counter accusations of the abuse of membership fees.[28]

But the most striking feature of these years was the failure of the central organs of the ANC to engage effectively with the major struggles that were being fought out in the Transvaal countryside. There is, for example, no evidence of concrete ANC support for the struggles of Lydenburg labour tenants against the proclamation of Chapter Four of the 1936 Land Act. Tenants' principal political connection was the liberal Senator Rheinallt Jones and his local election committee based on the African-owned farm of Boomplaats. A letter from Mrs Rheinallt Jones to the Rev. J. Calata, secretary-general of the ANC, requesting that his organisation should look into the trouble in Lydenburg, elicited a less-than-enthusiastic response. The correspondence took place in 1938, at the height of the confrontation, but produced no more than a commitment from Calata that the ANC intended to 'review the Land Act at a later stage'.[29]

The leadership of Xuma in the early 1940s, and the major struggles against the imposition of betterment planning and Trust control in Zoutpansberg and Pietersburg, generated little additional dynamism regarding the countryside. The evidence on this score is particularly skimpy for the Zout-pansberg, but there are no traces of systematic ANC engagement. The crucial organisational contact was between the Communist Party and Zoutpansberg Balemi Association, as explored below. In the case of the Pietersburg land disputes, the evidence is rather fuller. But the ANC connection emerges as equally tenuous. Long-standing local members of Congress – including those at Matlala – played a significant part in denouncing 'the Trust' but the ANC did not emerge as the organisation leading the resistance.

In 1942 M. Molepo, a leading figure in the struggle against 'the Trust' in the Pietersburg district, called a meeting to form a working committee of the ANC and there was some response from the ANC head office. In January 1943 Xuma attended a meeting in the Pietersburg municipal location at which the grievances of Trust tenants were aired and the meeting decided 'unanimously to support the ... ANC'.[30] But more than a year later, Molepo returned 118 unsold ANC tickets. And somewhat half-hearted attempts to ar-range a subsequent meeting for Xuma failed to yield fruit. Both Molepo and his ally Hyman Basner eventually abandoned attempts to engage ANC sup-port and were involved in breakaway groupings. Molepo headed the shadowy and short-lived African National Liberty Party while Basner helped to found the not very much more substantial African Democratic Party. With such un-certain support from local leaders and feeble intervention from central ANC leadership, it is unsurprising that a recent study of these events should have concluded that the 'resistance in Pietersburg never embraced or articulated the aims of the ANC or any other national goals'.[31]

The TAC petitioned on behalf of local leaders who clashed with the NAD, particularly those – like Maimela and Molepo – who fell victim to de-portation orders, which were the increasingly common state response to local 'agitators'. But, overall, there is little evidence of a concerted or coherent ANC response to local struggles. And the existing evidence supports Bas-ner's view that the leadership did not know how to respond to the intensity of struggles in the countryside. He recalled that 'Xuma wouldn't move when it came to anybody who resisted ... once it came to the stage of taking political action and not just presenting a petition to the government for redress ... Xuma wouldn't do more.'[32] There is also little evidence of sustained organis-ational growth in rural areas. The figures that do exist for 1946 – though incomplete – bear witness to this sorry state of affairs. Out of a total recorded provincial membership of 518, the only rural branch of any scale was Bethal, which had 14 members.[33]

In the latter half of the 1940s, the TAC once again initiated recruitment drives in rural areas. A key figure in these campaigns was the diminutive but driven Transvaal provincial secretary, David Bopape, who – though resident in Brakpan – had grown up in the Northern Transvaal. In 1947, for example, he undertook a trip to Sekhukhuneland and made contact with a local voluntary organiser and was able to draw on a local network of members and chiefly sympathisers. After securing the permission of the native affairs commissioner, he spent two weeks going from village to village holding meetings and recalls – perhaps with a degree of overstatement – that thousands of new members signed up as a result of his efforts. Bopape only made one trip to Sekhukhuneland, but he also travelled to the Zoutpansberg and elsewhere in the Transvaal.[34]

The recruitment drives launched by Bopape after the war may have changed this picture somewhat, but the impression remains of failure to follow up initial enthusiasm or to establish enduring structures. The message carried to the countryside sometimes showed a limited appreciation of the consciousness and context of these communities. For example, Bopape's attacks on the culling of cattle and the lack of land probably struck responsive chords, but his criticism of the migrant labour system was rather less-well received. After all, many saw migrancy as a defensive strategy with the alternative being the loss of children and/or husbands to the towns.

The continuing closeness of the ANC to chiefs also made for difficulties. Although general support for the office of chieftainship remained, there was also an accumulation of popular grievances against individual chiefs and widespread fears that the office had been corrupted by colonial control. In some instances, chiefs facing challenges from their subjects called on ANC leaders for assistance – a practice which did little to enhance the movement's popular standing.[35]

The late 1940s involved years of flux and struggle within the ANC, stemming in part from the activities of the ANC Youth League. Whether this grouping began to place rural issues and organisation on the agenda of the ANC remains a question. However, it seems unlikely, as the organisational base of the league was in urban areas and educational institutions, and its membership was comprised 'largely [of] intellectuals'.[36] According to Walter Sisulu, 'the issue of rural organisation was not on the [Youth League] agenda at all despite the fact that many of us had a rural upbringing'.[37]

In any case, as the decade drew to a close the scope for conventional ANC activity in the reserves diminished rapidly. The National Party victory of 1948 sounded the death-knell for open rural organisation. Under proclamations issued in 1939 and 1945, permission already had to be secured from chiefs and native commissioners for gatherings of more than ten people in the reserves. Powers also existed to prevent particular individuals from attending meetings, and allowing the NAD to remove troublesome individuals from specific areas of the Union. Prior to 1948, some individuals (like Thomas

Maimela) fell foul of these regulations. However, permission was given fairly frequently for meetings to be held. But after 1948 these repressive powers were given much fuller rein. Permission for meetings was routinely refused and pressure was intensified on chiefs to limit political activities in their areas. More robust rural organisation might have been able to weather these setbacks, but the frail and sparse formal rural presence of the ANC withered in these hostile conditions. By the end of the 1940s there appears to have been little in the way of a rural branch structure in the Northern or Eastern Transvaal outside of Bethal.[38]

What did exist was a loose network of broadly sympathetic, though often conservative, chiefs, which was increasingly constrained by the tightening embrace of the NAD. Chiefs were also, in many cases, nervous of the consequences of mass action for their own positions. ANC members were scattered across rural villages although, in some instances, they formed local clusters. The individuals involved were drawn mainly from chiefly, Christian and educated families. Migrant workers moving to and fro from the towns also provided an important link. And there were a number of individuals, like Elias Moretsele, who was elected to the ANC's national executive in the early 1950s, and who had strong links to the countryside.

Although these networks were not sufficient to root the ANC deeply in the countryside, they did ensure that the ANC was not entirely cut off from developments in the reserves, and some channels of communication and influence remained open. But, contrary to the fears and imaginings of exasperated officials, the ANC had limited capacity to mobilise a mass constituency able to challenge developments in rural areas. And its central organisational strategy – the use of chiefs and the establishment of local branches – seemed to have been effectively checkmated by the early 1950s.[39]

Migrant Organisation

While officials and prominent supporters of Bantu Authorities were searching in vain for evidence of a local ANC branch orchestrating the resistance, it gradually dawned upon them that the 'trouble ... came from the reef' and that migrant workers returning home from the cities were playing a vital role in sustaining the resistance.[40]

The changing patterns of migrant employment and association are a crucial element in explaining this dynamic. Significant shifts took place in the nature of Pedi employment on the Rand during the late 1930s and early 1940s. Since the turn of the century, some Pedi workers had found employment in the shops, hotels, offices and industry that developed on the Rand. But the overwhelming majority remained as mine-workers and domestics until the 1930s. The resumption of economic growth, in particular the expansion of secondary industry from the mid-1930s, was accompanied by an increasing tendency for Pedi migrants to seek more lucrative employment elsewhere. A fairly typical pattern seems to have been for workers with domestic experience to seek employment in the service sector or as messengers in the city, while men with mining experience tended to take work in the burgeoning factories of the Rand.[41]

Once they had a degree of familiarity with urban life and language, some migrants simply went from place to place until they found work. But they blazed paths which many others then followed, and village clusters developed at specific factories. Harry's Hat Factory in Doornfontein, for example, became a mecca for men from Manganeng.[42] South African Congress of Trade Unions (Sactu) activist John Nkadimeng recalls of the 1940s that many businesses had a policy of employing migrants:

> They didn't like the people who come from the townships – they liked people who came from outside. Many factories were like that at that time. You see [migrants] were not unionised, they were not conscious of this question. We didn't know anything about trade union rights and all these things, whereas the people in the townships ... knew a lot.[43]

Although some concentration of workers took place, the scale of these enterprises meant that the clustering of workers which had taken place in the mining industry gave way to a rather more atomised pattern. There were exceptions, however, and probably the most important of these was Iscor in Pretoria, which became an increasingly important focus of Pedi employment from the late 1930s.[44]

In the 1930s and especially in the 1940s and 1950s, a considerably smaller but nonetheless significant shift was also taking place into self-employment. As the example of the Maimela brothers suggests, a number of migrants initially supplemented their incomes through, and later turned fully to, activities like tailoring, hawking and taxi driving. Others set up unlicensed stores in locations or established shanty shops in Masakeng and other squatter camps. And while those who made this transition successfully were relatively few in number, their numbers included a growing group of men from *baditšaba* families who came to play an important role in the broader migrant world. They travelled widely, selling their wares and services, and carrying news and messages.[45]

Changes in the nature of employment also resulted in migrants finding new kinds of accommodation. Migrants left suburban backyards and the mine compounds. A number of their new employers, such as the parastatals and the municipalities, had their own compounds. But workers in offices and factories also had to find accommodation. One option became known as the 'locations in the sky', created by men moving into the servants quarters situated on the top of blocks of flats. Another possibility involved the hostels of the East Rand and Johannesburg, and a bed in one of these often came with the job. The Johannesburg City Council had established Wemmer Hostel in 1924, Wolhuter (known as Jeppe by migrants) Hostel in 1932, Mai Mai Hostel in 1940 and Denver Hostel in 1946. Jeppe and Denver hostels, in particular, housed increasing numbers of Pedi workers. After the war some migrants also secured houses in the locations.[46]

These new compounds and hostels showed some continuity with the mine compounds – not least of all in their unhygienic and cramped conditions. As Timothy Lerutla, who lived in Johannesburg in the 1940s, put it, 'Jeppe Hostel was ridiculous – life there, I don't even want to describe it, because we had to live like pigs.'[47]

But there were also a number of significant contrasts between these hostels and those on the mines. Importantly, ethnicity was not the official organising principle of this world. Clustering by village and district did take place in the hostels and compounds, but men from a variety of backgrounds could and did share rooms. While ethnic tensions existed, the 'faction fights' which bedevilled the mines were not a common feature of hostel life. The structures of control and authority which were so central to mine compounds were also nowhere near as pervasive in the hostels. All in all, the world of these hostel dwellers was much less-regimented and controlled than that of miners.[48]

Hostel dwellers were also less removed from a wider urban world than compounded migrants or suburban domestics. On the East Rand, hostels were often built in the locations, while the Johannesburg hostels were sited close to the city centre. This did not mean that tensions between migrants and urban Africans vanished. Indeed, the siting of hostels within locations in some instances exacerbated these tensions, but it lowered the barriers which had existed between migrants and city life. It was very much easier to gain access to, and hold meetings in, hostels than in mine compounds and they became centres of interaction for a far wider group of men than actually lived in them. The drab exteriors of Jeppe and Denver Hostels, which lay just to the east of Johannesburg's city centre, belied their importance as focal points where men from the mines, municipalities, kitchens, offices and factories could meet.[49]

These alterations in migrant employment and accommodation meshed with changes in the educational levels of Pedi migrants. As we have seen, there was considerable hostility to education amongst *baditšaba* communities in Sekhukhuneland and there was also miserly provision of educational resources. But in the 1920s, and particularly in the 1930s, this began to change.

The virtual stranglehold which the Berlin Missionary Society had on schooling in the area was loosened and a number of other missions, including the Anglicans and the Catholics, established primary schools. These churches did not insist that pupils were baptised and gave more attention to teaching English. Community schools were also founded in a handful of the larger villages and were partly sustained by government grants-in-aid. But the demand for the state to establish a system of non-denominational education fell on deaf ears until the end of the 1940s. Popular hostility to mission schools diminished somewhat during these decades. Migrant workers contemplating the changing circumstances in the cities started to tell their sons that they needed to go to school in order to secure reasonable employment. The continuing need for herders was partly met by boys alternating between one week with livestock and one week at school.[50]

In the absence of both missionary and state support, some communities set out to create their own schools. At Mafefe, for example, in the 1930s,

> We had one teacher who taught us under the mohlopi tree, he would lean his blackboard against it. [He] stayed in the village in a small thatched house which was built for him ... [H]e was hired by the community ... we paid him with chicken eggs.[51]

But this drive for education did not only take place in the rural areas. Many migrants on the mines and in the hostels became determined to learn to read and write. Often they would turn to literate fellow workers who, sometimes for a small fee, would assist them with basic literacy. Men from Sekhukhuneland also attended night schools either to upgrade their education or to acquire basic skills. The extent of this should not be exaggerated, for the majority of Pedi migrants had no experience of Western schooling by the 1940s. But many more men than before were now leaving for town with some primary school education. They were literate in Sepedi and often had some grasp of English which could expand rapidly with exposure to urban life. Some men became avid newspaper readers and they would tell their fellow workers the news of the day.[52]

The consciousness of migrants was, however, also significantly affected by a rather different set of experiences. Sekhukhuneland became one of the main centres of recruitment for military service in the Second World War. From the central magisterial district alone, 1 622 men enlisted and considerable numbers were recruited from adjoining areas. This high level of recruitment seems to have been the result of drought, continuing chiefly authority and coercion. Many men were also led to believe that they would receive substantial rewards. One man recalled that he thought 'I would get something splendid because I was fighting for the government.'[53] And there was a widespread belief that military service would be rewarded with land grants.

The military experience which ensued was a diverse one which deserves much fuller study. For some men it involved the grinding tedium and humiliation of standing guard armed only 'with an assegai. If you were approached you had to say "Halt" ... [I]f he refused to halt you would stab him with the assegai. [I]f he had a weapon I would use a whistle for help.'[54] Other recruits were trained as drivers, or medical orderlies. Some served in the North Africa campaigns and, while they finally were allowed to carry firearms, they also faced the perils of battle.[55]

Although the effects of this experience were not uniform, it considerably widened the horizons of many men. One common strand which runs through all the accounts is anger over the meagre rewards which the servicemen received on their discharge. This anger was partly directed towards the chiefs and local officials who had encouraged enlistment, and found expression in a deepened distrust of all they said. This scepticism, and the belief that they had been cheated of promised land, was to be a significant legacy for rural politics in the ensuing decades. It led, for example, to renewed anger over land levies which gave rise to marches in Sekhukhuneland led by ex-servicemen demanding that levies should be discontinued. But most of the demobilised soldiers had little option but to seek employment almost immediately in the towns, where they also played a part in the post-war political ferment.[56]

Migrant associations continued after 1945. Young men clustered in compounds and suburbs and Malaita champions continued to bludgeon one another – although they now usually did so under the approving gaze of the police and were seen more as an embarrassment than as a threat by educated Africans. But new forms of organisation appeared which were shaped by the changing circumstances of migrants. Burial societies were the most pervasive of these. In the late 1940s and the early 1950s, these societies ceased to be the preserve of mainly Christian and urbanised Africans, and a plethora of newly established societies claimed widespread migrant membership.[57]

The more diverse and atomised context in which migrants found themselves in these years did not lead to the abandonment of the village and district based networks which had sustained them in previous decades. But the solidarity of the compound and the suburb was replaced by more formal organisational structures which drew on the enhanced educational skills and earning power of migrants and used the centrally situated and relatively accessible hostels as their principal venues. In the first stage of development of these societies, clusters of migrants employed in one of the urban centres – for instance Johannesburg, Pretoria or Springs – would hold a collection in the event of one of their number dying to provide a proper burial in town. His belongings were also sent home with somebody from his community to inform the family of the circumstances of his death.[58]

In the 1940s there was an attempt, led by Marota royals, to create an overarching burial society called the Bapedi Advancement Society. Part of the impetus for this initiative came from the desire to maintain and even enhance the authority of the paramountcy and the chiefs in this changing context and also to ward off more radical claimants to the allegiance of Pedi migrants.[59] But this attempt to construct migrant organisation from the top down met with limited success. The main impetus for the rapid expansion of these societies was to come from below.

With the passage of time the loose local associations changed in several ways. Firstly, their structure became more and more village based. This evolution was made possible by the increasing numbers of men involved and bore witness to the centrality of local ties in migrant networks. They then became more formalised: chairmen and treasurers were elected and regular, rather than sporadic, contributions were elicited from members. But workers remained extremely wary of handing over their pay and insisted on a number of checks over the proper handling of the finances. By the mid-1950s many of these groups had opened bank and building society accounts, and developed special badges and membership cards. It became increasingly common for the bodies of workers who died to be transported back for burial in their home villages, with the members of the burial society also returning home for the funeral.[60]

Bringing home the bodies of migrants partly reflected a continuation of the earlier concern that communities and families should know precisely what had happened to men who were away in the towns. But burying men at home had other connotations. In communities where ancestors and their graves played a vital part in the life of the village and in the affairs of their close kin, bringing back the bodies of dead men was considered necessary to ensure a proper and harmonious relationship between the living and the dead. The practice of incinerating paupers which developed in the 1950s on the Rand was particularly horrifying to migrants. For while burial in the city was bad enough, the reduction of the dead to ashes seemed to make the establishment of any proper relationship with ancestors impossible. But the form of burial involving an elaborate funeral, the placing of the body in a coffin and, increasingly, internment in a separate cemetery, owed rather more to migrants' observation of Christian and urban forms than 'traditional' practices.[61]

Burial societies were not only concerned with ensuring a proper funeral. Equally importantly, they were welfare societies which offered a variety of forms of protection for their members and their families. Firstly, they provided for a lump sum payment to be made to the family of the dead migrant. Secondly, in the event of a migrant becoming ill or being injured, these societies provided funds and companions to ensure that the man reached home safely. Thirdly, if a man lost his job or his accommodation, members of the society often assisted him with money, food and lodgings and helped to find him alternative employment or housing.[62] In the 1950s these societies formalised the mutually supportive roles that looser migrant associations had long played and provided crucial protection against the capricious fates which presided over urban life.

Burial societies also provided a context in which the affairs of home could be mulled over and dissected in minute detail, and a channel of communication between migrants and chiefs. It seems to have been fairly common practice for special meetings to be convened to discuss specific issues which had come up in relation to home communities. By the mid-1950s, most migrants from Sekhukhuneland belonged to burial societies and these provided a central focus for migrant networks.[63]

Migrants, Unions and Politics

New opportunities opened up for migrants in the 1940s, but as the decade drew to a close they increasingly saw themselves as under threat in both the urban and rural dimensions of their lives.[64]

The most fundamental threat most migrants felt was to the rural world which played such a central part in their self-definition. For most migrants in these years, the towns remained *makgoweng* – the place of the whites. Despite their impoverishment, the rural areas and especially the reserves represented places of refuge from white authority and from the social corrosion of capitalist relationships. While the reserves were by no means immune to the effects of either of these phenomena, both access to land and chiefly rule provided barriers against total domination by white officials, employers and the market. 'The Trust' and Bantu Authorities were believed to be leading elements in a pincer movement designed to subvert this world.[65]

At the same time, migrants found their access to urban areas increasingly restricted. From 1945, after the brief and partial respite from pass controls of the war years, migrants confronted a growing battery of measures designed to monitor and control their movements and employment. These regulations impinged most directly on men who had, or sought, employment in secondary industry and in the towns. The issuing of a consolidated *dompas* (pass book) after 1952 symbolised this changing context for many and was keenly felt as yet another example of the state tightening its stranglehold on their lives. And the threat of being endorsed out of the towns to their homes, or worse still to the farms, loomed large in the lives of many workers.[66]

Migrants also found some of their accommodation niches in urban areas under attack. The state moved against the 'locations in the sky' established in blocks of flats. In Johannesburg in the mid-1950s migrants were removed from their inner-city sanctuaries and dumped into unfinished hostels in Soweto, far from their work. They had to try and reconstruct their lives in the midst of an often hostile population, while providing the favourite prey of juvenile gangsters.[67]

Many migrants felt themselves increasingly vulnerable in the towns during these years. They were haunted by possibility of arrest and incarceration in dank and dangerous prisons. Migrant reminiscences of this period repeatedly conjure up an image of being both outside of the law and yet increasingly victims of lawlessness. As Mogase Sekhukhune succinctly summed it up, 'As from 1948 [it] was *tsotsi* life.'[68] Mohube Phala recalled that 'when the government of the Boers of 1948 started it began with hardship [brought by passes] ... It changed many things because it cheated us ... It caused people to become *tsotsis.*'[69]

The increasing pressures in the towns led many migrants to place still heavier reliance on village and regional networks, and this may have been one important spur to the rapid proliferation of burial societies in these years. The existence of these supports played a vital part in assisting migrants to maintain their footholds in the urban areas.[70] But this onslaught also ensured that many were doubly determined to defend their remaining rural resources and autonomy.

The consequence of this was a growing political ferment amongst migrants on the Rand. In hostels and compounds, migrants discussed unfolding state strategies and information spread widely. In the early 1940s, men from Sekhukhuneland anxiously followed the advance of 'the Trust' and the battle to keep it at bay. The Nationalists' victory in 1948 deepened their sense of apprehension and the Bantu Authorities Act of 1951 fulfilled their worst fears. Chiefly autonomy was seen as a vital protection for rural communities but many migrants feared that chiefs would have little stomach to resist the threats and blandishments of the state. From the early 1950s, rumours that the Pedi Paramount Morwamotše Sekhukhune had agreed, or would agree, to the establishment of Bantu Authorities and that in consequence rehabilitation measures would be imposed in Sekhukhuneland sent regular alarms through the migrant community on the reef. Morwamotše's formal installation in 1953 and the homilies from officials on the virtues of Bantu Authorities delivered on that day fuelled these fears.[71]

In the turbulent and changing world of the 1940s and early 1950s, some workers from Sekhukhuneland became involved in trade unions and political organisations. The men who made these links usually had some common characteristics. They had primary school education and/or had attended night schools. Some had enlisted during the war. They lived in locations or hostels and were employed in factories, offices, hotels, restaurants and clubs as un-skilled or semi-skilled workers, messengers and waiters. Some had left formal employment and made a living as hawkers, tailors, traders or taxi drivers. Mine-workers and domestic workers do not seem to have forged wider links to anything like the same extent. But while the men who joined unions and/or political movements were a small minority of those from Sek-hukhuneland in towns, they came to include in their ranks significant numbers of men from *baditšaba* backgrounds who had undergone initiation. They also shared the same employment and accommodation as a growing section of their fellow migrants. And they joined and even initiated the burial societies which mushroomed in these decades. These men played a vital role as brokers between their fellow migrants and wider movements.[72]

Trade unions provided one vital channel into broader involvement. Contact with them was overwhelmingly the product of finding jobs in secondary industry. For some, the experience remained a remote one with unionists re-membered mainly as people who collected subs but had little wider impact. But for others, unions provided an entrance to a new world of organisation and politics. Elias Mathope Motsoaledi, for example, received a primary school education in Phokwane, worked as a domestic servant and then in 1943 found employment in a boot factory, led a strike and was dismissed. He subsequently found employment in a cosmetics factory and joined the Chemical Workers Union. John Kgoana Nkadimeng went as far as Standard Six at mission schools at his home village, Manganeng, and at Jane Furse. He also worked initially as a domestic but then found factory work in Johannes-burg. In the late 1940s, while working at the International Tobacco factory, he joined the African Tobacco Workers Union.[73]

The ANC remained generally remote from the world of migrant workers for much of the 1940s. The handful of men who joined the ANC in the urban areas in the 1930s and early 1940s were mainly from a Christian and rela-tively educated background. And while some individual leaders – like Moretsele – kept contact with a wider migrant world, many workers from Sekhukhuneland were alienated by the educated elite who dominated the ANC. The content and form of their politics seemed remote from their expe-riences and aspirations. Elias Motsoaledi, for example recalled that the ANC leadership didn't try to get to the grassroots level grievances of the people. Whenever you were in meetings they would listen to the articulation of the English language – they would encourage people to display their qualifications. They spoke in English ... but English was not the language of the masses.[74]

It was the Communist Party which made crucial inroads into the world of migrant workers in the 1940s and which showed most sensitivity to the rural dimensions of their lives. At first sight this is surprising, given the Party's grounding in urban working-class struggles. But it is important to recall that the Party had adopted a theoretical position which laid emphasis on the peasantry. In 1928, in the context of local rural turmoil and the prescriptions of the Communist International, the Communist Party adopted the slogan of an 'Independent South African Native Republic as a stage towards a Workers and Peasants Republic'.

This policy formulation emphasised that the 'black peasantry constitutes the basic moving force of the revolution in alliance with and under the leadership of the working class'.[75] Immediately after adopting this position, the Party made some attempts to penetrate the rural areas but these became increasingly feeble as the 1930s progressed. The CPSA was decimated and paralysed by internecine strife and by the end of the decade its remaining membership and activities were focused in the towns.

Rusty Bernstein, a leading member of the Communist Party at the time, recalls that, in the Transvaal in the late 1930s and early 1940s,

> we recognised in the Party, at least from the theoretical point of view, the importance of the countryside and the peasantry ... The practice of it was that in fact very little attention was paid to the countryside, partly because our links with the countryside, with rural people, were absolutely minimal. There were scarcely any links at all and the result was that rural questions almost didn't feature in the Party's ... discussions about work in the Transvaal.[76]

But Bernstein overlooks the fact that some members, often recruited via night schools, were migrant workers with strong rural connections.

There were differences of opinion within the Communist Party on the emphasis to be placed on rural issues. These probably broadly coincided with tensions over the relative emphasis to be placed on national or class struggle. But there is little evidence to support the suggestion that there was substantial principled opposition to organisation in the countryside. Nonetheless, there was little effort to flesh out the rather vague concept of the peasantry which informed Party policy, and the position of migrant workers did not receive systematic theoretical or organisational attention either. A combination of urban location, working-class roots and practical difficulties helped ensure that agrarian issues remained low on the CPSA's list of priorities for action.[77]

There were moments, such as elections for the Native Representative Council and for native representatives in the senate, when the Party's consciousness of rural issues was heightened, and there were individual members who argued for more vigorous rural engagement. One of the most important of these was Hyman Basner, who gained insights into rural society from his work as a lawyer and his experience of running – unsuccessfully – as a CPSA candidate in the 1936 senate elections. His emphasis on the need for rural mobilisation had a limited impact, and he also found himself increasingly at odds with central elements in Party policy. In 1939, following the Russian invasion of Finland, he resigned amidst considerable acrimony. In 1942 he stood successfully as an independent candidate for the senate and – as noted above – played a prominent role in assisting and highlighting rural struggles.[78]

The activities of a migrant worker from the Zoutpansberg – Alpheus Malivha – were ultimately more significant in terms of the Communist Party and the countryside. He was born in 1901 in Nzhelele in Venda and by the early 1930s, while working in a Johannesburg factory, had enrolled in a communist-run night school. He joined the Party in 1936 and from 1939 to 1950 served on its district committee.[79]

In 1939 Malivha, along with a number of fellow migrant workers from the Zoutpansberg – some of whom were also members of the Party – founded the Zoutpansberg Cultural Association. Its Johannesburg office was in Progress Buildings, also the headquarters of the CPSA, and the Party provided some organisational back-up – mainly in the form of transport, duplicating leaflets, legal assistance and occasional discussions of tactical issues. The ZCA was also given considerable prominence in the Venda section of the Party newspaper *Inkululeko*. The association was, however, seen very much as 'Malivha's baby'.[80] It was not considered as a subdivision of the Party but, as Bernstein recalls, 'we regarded the Party as having a role and what we would have classed loosely ... as mass organisations, as having a separate role, ... this was one of them'. And while Malivha was,

> in theory a disciplined member of the Party and subject to the Party's control and guidance at all times ... in practice because his base of operations was in the Zoutpansberg area which was a long way away and with which we had no direct contact or communications ourselves ... he was a law unto himself.[81]

The ZCA campaigned against forced conscription and made representations to the state to stop imposing penalties on late taxpayers. But, in response to mounting struggles in the Zoutpansberg, it increasingly focused on challenging the controls enforced on communities living on 'Trust Land'. Its initial tactics of petition and polite protest gave way by 1941 – in a context of mounting ferment in the area – to a call for open defiance of these regulations. Confronted by mass resistance, Communist Party-linked lawyers and a wartime context, local officials beat a retreat. These successes helped build a groundswell of support for Malivha and the organisation which, by 1943, had been renamed the Zoutpansberg Balemi (ploughmens) Association.[82]

After their initial successes, Malivha and the ZBA attracted mounting hostility from local police, officials and white citizens. As in the case of the Pietersburg resistance, the state began to use the courts more effectively. The earlier victories of the ZBA in assisting communities to flout 'Trust' regulations increasingly gave way to defeats. Officials intensified their efforts to exploit divisions in communities and to persuade chiefs that the ZBA was intent on usurping their positions.[83]

Many Communist Party members were also bemused and even a little uneasy about events in the Zoutpansberg. Bernstein recalls that: 'What we felt was that the Party couldn't possibly have a direct message to the peasants there' and also that there was 'an ecological side to it ... the Party certainly had some hesitation about insisting on the right to plough the river banks'.[84] George Findlay's view in 1944 was that

> the Platteland (rural) Africans are a secondary area – more propaganda is needed there, not peasant revolts. Intensify ideological work – don't water down to 'popular appeal' standards.[85]

It seems unlikely, therefore, that the Party wished to get drawn ever deeper into a spiralling conflict in the north – especially after the Soviet Union entered the war – or that, in the post-war world, it felt it appropriate to put these issues high on its list of priorities. In any event, by the late 1940s the ZBA had become a shadow of its former self. Malivha was banned from operating in the Zoutpansberg and his activities were mainly restricted to Johannesburg. He was, nonetheless, to continue to play a highly influential, although much less visible, role in relation to the countryside – one partly facilitated by the changing nature of the Communist Party.[86]

The Communist Party and Post-War Politics

The Party made considerable advances during the war years. Lodge has provided a striking outline of this transformation, pointing out that in 1939 the CPSA's

> following numbered less than three hundred, its influence in the trade unions was negligible, it was isolated from other political organisation among blacks ... Six years later the Party could count its adherents in

thousands rather than hundreds, it was capable of winning white local government elections, and its members presided over the largest-ever African trade union movement as well as contributing significantly to the leadership of the African and Indian Congresses.[87]

The 1940s also witnessed a considerable shift in the racial composition of the Communist Party in the Transvaal. Bernstein recalls that,

> numerically the Party just grew steadily from ... 1940/1 until 1946 and the black membership grew fastest and became the overwhelming majority. I mean that in 1940 the black and white membership must have been 50/50 or round about there but by 45/46 the white membership was a minority.[88]

This trend continued and was accentuated as white wariness of the Party re-surfaced as the Cold War set in. In these years the Party's main channels of recruitment were public meetings, the trade union movement and (though to a lesser extent than in the 1930s) night schools. It also established grassroots organisation in a number of townships, a development which has been most fully described in Brakpan. On the East Rand, the CP mobilised residents around immediate local concerns and issues, it contested advisory board elections and used elected positions to defend local interests.[89]

There had also been important developments in the Party's relationship with the ANC. In 1929, the CPSA had accepted a Comintern directive to work with the ANC. However, the ideological turmoil within the Party and the sorry state of Congress in the 1930s helped ensure it was not until the end of the decade that,

> for the first time in many years ... the Party's leading committees began to take seriously the question of developing the ANC, putting their strength or their muscle behind the development of a substantial ANC.[90]

A close relationship was established with the ANC, especially in the Trans-vaal, and in the 1940s a considerable overlap in membership and leadership developed. Leading communists like Moses Kotane, J.B. Marks, Edwin Mo-futsanyana and David Bopape played a central role in Congress and made an important contribution to rebuilding it. The leadership of the TAC after 1946 was dominated by Party members, and this was probably an important part of the backdrop to Bopape's recruitment drives in the countryside. But commu-nists' experiences within the ANC in turn helped to keep the 'national question' high on the Party's agenda.[91]

Probably most important of all in relation to subsequent rural organisation was the Party's post-war recruitment of a number of young migrant workers from the Northern Transvaal – for example, Elias Motsoaledi and Flag

Boshielo – who provided crucial entrées to wider migrant networks and who subsequently played a significant role. Some of these men came from families which faced a bleak future in the countryside. Elias Motsoaledi recalls that 'we had no land of our own ... this is part of what brought me into politics', while Boshielo came 'from a very poor family'.[92] But the most important common point amongst this group of migrants was that, after spells as domestic workers or miners, they found employment in secondary industry and then gained experience of trade union organisation and action. For example Motsoaledi, after joining the Chemical Workers Union, became a member of the Communist Party in 1945.[93]

The Communist Party was active in the world in which migrants moved – particularly the factories, the hostels and the unions. Moreover, the Party explained that world in ways which made sense of migrants' own experiences. Its stress, for example, on dispossession and a cheap labour system as lying at the heart of the South African political economy, its campaigns against the pass laws, and its emphasis on the position and role of workers had immediate resonances for migrants' own lives. There were also already migrant workers from the Northern Transvaal – men who were initiated, who spoke Venda and Pedi and alongside whom they lived and worked – who were members and even leaders within the Party. One particularly telling example of this political cross-fertilisation involves Flag Boshielo, who became a driving force in migrant political organisation. He had grown up along with Elias Motsoaledi in the village of Phokwane in Sekhukhuneland. In the mid-1940s he got a job in a bakery in Johannesburg in which a number of Party members had employment. One of his fellow workers was Alpheus Malivha who told vivid stories of the struggles he had led in the Zoutpansberg.[94]

Malivha became a crucial influence on Boshielo and other younger migrant workers within the Party. Boshielo, in turn, was active in Denver Hostel (one of the main municipal hostels which lay just east of central Johannesburg) and in the wider world of migrant associations, and he drew a number of his compatriots into formal politics. John Nkadimeng, for example – who was a unionist living in nearby Jeppe Hostel – recalls that 'he was the best man from my area'.[95] After they met at a burial society meeting, Boshielo played a critical role in Nkadimeng's political development and persuaded him to join the ANC in 1950 and the Communist Party in 1951.

Once these workers joined the Party, they were exposed to a programme of political education, starting with a new members' class which introduced them to basic elements of the CP's structure and policies. They were taught elements of the history and political economy of South Africa. Once they had completed this course, advanced classes dealt with a variety of topics – including trade union issues and the ANC. As Bernstein recalls,

> there was continuous political education going on in the Party ...
> there was always something going on and people were pressured by
> their unit, their groups ... [and] branches to participate in classes.

Just as importantly, the Party had 'really very high standards of practical
work'.[96] Members were expected to become actively involved in political
and union work and were guided through expanding responsibilities. Motsoaledi remembered that

> when they teach you politics they put you into the field, you were
> working ... the Party watches cadres developing – time and again
> they promote cadres, [eventually] they would say now as a developed
> cadre we are giving you this [George Goch] location and Denver
> hostel – they are both under you, yours is to plan and do everything –
> if you need leaflets tell us – but the planning is yours.[97]

There was also considerable emphasis on identifying and mobilising around
grassroots issues and grievances, and both policy and practice instilled this
approach as a basic political reflex in Party members.[98]

The Party at this time 'represented a rich composite of South African political traditions' and was not 'a Leninist vanguard of professional
revolutionaries'.[99] But the model of a vanguard Party to which some members aspired helped establish – at least in comparison with the ANC –
relatively high levels of political training and organisational dynamism
within the Party.

It was Party policy in these years to encourage its members to join the
ANC. But this view met some resistance amongst its migrant worker recruits
and others who viewed Congress as conservative and ineffective. From 1939
onwards,

> The Party really in the Transvaal did put a lot of muscle behind the
> ANC including pressurising its own black members to join ... and
> many of our members resisted it, they didn't want to, they regarded
> the ANC as being a sort of petty bourgeois organisation.[100]

But the CPSA's two-stage theory of transformation played an important part
in enabling some of its members to come to terms with their reservations
about the ANC. Motsoaledi, for example, remembered that,

> as a result of the education by the Party, I understood the long term
> programme of the Party and the short term programme of the ANC –
> then I came to understand the alliance – that when we achieve
> liberation the ANC struggle ceases and there is a continuation now
> with the class struggle. But I wasn't taught that therefore you must not
> continue with the class struggle [in the interim].[101]

In 1948, three years after having joined the Party, Motsoaledi joined the ANC and within six months was elected to the provincial executive.

There was not any substantial shift towards activism in the Party's formal thinking about the countryside in the late 1940s, nor was there a major rural initiative to follow on from the work of Malivha in the Zoutpansberg. But the older generation of migrants recruited in the 1930s – often via night schools – had been supplemented by a younger grouping rooted in factories, unions and hostels. These members were, unsurprisingly, more acutely aware of the political particularities and possibilities of migrant workers and rural villages than the leading Party ideologues. And they were certainly alive to any new threats to their position in both the urban areas *and* the reserves. Thus, the Party maintained a degree of sensitivity to rural questions – as Motsoaledi recalls – owing to 'the workers themselves – men who had come from the rural areas'.[102]

When, under threat from the Suppression of Communism Act in 1950, the CPSA formally disbanded amidst considerable confusion, the majority of African members of the Party threw themselves into building the ANC with reduced reservation and enhanced zeal. The organisational capacity and experience of these individuals thereby played an even greater role in Congress' development in the early 1950s. Reflecting on the 1940s and early 1950s, Bernstein suggests that this was a decisive contribution:

> The work content of a Party member's day was very considerable and they were used to working as an organised group, but the ANC was not, the ANC was a very loose organisation. You could join the ANC and pay five shillings and not ever attend a branch meeting ... our people brought into the ANC and for that matter into the trade unions a very particular style of work which wasn't indigenous to these organisations and I think that was our biggest contribution. Frankly, a lot of commentators write about the great theoretical contribution we made to these organisations. I think, in some ways, it's the other way round. They made a great theoretical contribution to us, but we made a really important organisational contribution to them and gave them what they lacked, which was a sort of organised disciplined core. The few spread out through the branches and through the various organisations, and this is what enabled them, I think, to grow as a great mass organisation.[103]

In the early 1950s the group of young workers from Sekhukhuneland, whose life histories we have touched on above, helped to rebuild the ANC. Motsoaledi, Boshielo and Nkadimeng all held senior positions within the Transvaal African Congress and played leading parts in the various campaigns launched by the ANC. Boshielo was the leader of one of the first Defiance Campaign volunteer units in Johannesburg on 26 June 1952. Nkadimeng was his deputy and returned from prison to find that he had been sacked from his job, whereupon he became a full-time organiser for the Council of Non-European Trade Unions.[104]

In these years, communists went through a process of re-evaluating their role in South African politics. Most members of the Party had supported its dissolution on the assumption that it was a ploy. But disquiet grew as little concrete appeared to be happening to reconstitute it. It was to be former members of the CPSA's Johannesburg district committee who took the decisive initiative in launching a new party. With new rules on recruitment and observation of strict security, the SACP was formed between 1951 and 1952 and its first national conference was held in 1953. By the time its second national conference took place in 1954, a solid core of members, and a structure of units, branches and district committees, was in place. After a period of debate, the ideology of the new party consolidated around the necessity for a close alliance with the ANC and the centrality of national democratic struggle.[105]

Sebatakgomo

It was against the backdrop of these major political changes that Flag Boshielo (now serving on the reconstituted Johannesburg district committee of the Party) initiated the idea of forming a movement to engage with rural issues. Strongly influenced by the example of the ZBA, by a period spent in the early 1950s in Sekhukhuneland training to be a herbalist, and by the ferment amongst migrants, he argued that rural struggles and the land question were vital. In 1954, after consulting closely with Alpheus Malivha, John Nkadimeng and more widely within the Party, he successfully sought CP approval for the establishment of a rural organisation. But it did not remain a purely Party initiative.[106] As Motsoaledi recalled:

> First of all it is organised by the Communist Party – but the Party realises that it is not within its sphere. In other words it realises that the important organisation to tackle this is the ANC. So it goes and organises and then gives it to the ANC ... and the members of the Party who are in the ANC prosecute it.[107]

The idea was floated in the Central Johannesburg Branch of the ANC, and in April 1955 a resolution was proposed by prominent unionists at the provincial conference of Congress 'to organise the farms and reserve natives into a trade union under the auspices of Sactu'.[108] In November the ANC national executive announced the formation of 'Sebatakgomo ... a peasants movement'.[109] The name chosen (literally translated as 'a predator amongst the cattle') had powerful resonances for men from Sekhukhuneland, for

Sebatakgomo in Sepedi is a call to war ... [W]hen you are attacked ... some one will take his horn and climb the mountain and blow and call Sebatakgomo ... it means there is war.[110]

Sebatakgomo's inaugural meeting was in Pretoria, at Bantu Hall in Lady Selbourne. Alpheus Malivha gave the keynote address, Boshielo was elected as chairman and Nkadimeng as secretary. The initial meetings were attended by individuals from disparate communities in the Northern and Eastern Transvaal. A core of communists rooted Sebatakgomo in an established history of rural mobilisation and placed considerable organisational drive and skills at its disposal.

The location of Sebatakgomo within the ANC both reflected Party policy and enabled the movement to draw in and consult with a network of senior individuals within Congress whose rural links and experience were vital to its growth. Prominent amongst these was Elias Moretsele. In the early 1950s there were also a growing number of workers and others with strong rural connections who were drawn into a more militant and mass-based ANC. These men were recruited rapidly into Sebatakgomo and it came to represent a thoroughgoing fusion of ANC and Communist Party networks and organisational experience.[111] It was, in the opinion of Walter Sisulu, 'the first well-organised [rural] movement in the history of the ANC'.[112]

Sebatakgomo was thus not a figment of a fevered official imagination. But it did not initiate popular rejection of Bantu Authorities, which clearly pre-dated its formation. At the time of its launch, it involved only a relatively small grouping of men with limited capacity to mobilise either migrants on the Rand or villagers in Sekhukhuneland. It was the state's determination to drive ahead with the establishment of Tribal Authorities and its attempts to co-opt the position and prestige of the Pedi Paramount that provided a powerful motor for the growth of the movement. And, while Sebatakgomo played an important catalytic role in intensifying resistance, the movement was also to be reconstituted in the context of mass-based politics.

Notes

1   Mothodi Nchabeleng, 1.
2   Mönnig, *The Pedi*, p. 40; Lodge, *Black Politics*, p. 290.
3   Ritchken, 'Leadership and Conflict', pp. 64-6, 89.
4   Schirmer, 'The Struggle', pp. 163-6.
5   J. Lazar, 'Verwoerd versus the Visionaries', in P. Bonner *et al.* (eds.), *Apartheid's Genesis*, p. 362.
6   *Ibid*, p. 368. See also P. Bonner *et al.*, 'Introduction', *Apartheid's Genesis*, p. 28.
7   Ritchken, 'Leadership and Conflict', pp. 106-7. This point contrasts with the view expressed by Professor Hammond-Tooke that 'whatever the subsequent activities and inputs of the Ethnological Section might have been, in the early days of the establishment of apartheid structures its role was minimal'. See W.D.

Hammond-Tooke, 'N.J. van Warmelo and the Ethnological Section; A Memoir' *African Studies* (forthcoming). This is not of course to suggest that the ethnological section drove policy but that views on the importance of propping up chieftainship expressed by Van Warmelo and other ethnologists contributed to evolving thinking on this subject within the Department. It is also clear that members of the ethnology section *did* play a vital part in intervening in local politics in order to advance the cause of Bantu Authorities and the fortunes of those sympathetic to them. See, for example, the discussion of the central role of C.V. Bothma in the struggle around the Paramountcy and Bantu Authorities in Sekhukhuneland in the 1950s described in Chapter 4. When I met N.J. van Warmelo in 1976 he explained to me at considerable length that apartheid was disliked elsewhere on the continent precisely because it dealt effectively with the issue of chieftainship and that as a result other governments feared that their own traditional leaders would rise up and demand an equivalent dispensation for themselves.

8 Ritchken, 'Leadership and Conflict', pp. 106-7.
9 TA/NTS1813/138/276/(4)1a, Minutes of Chief Native Affairs Commissioners Conference, 29-30/11/1955.
10 *Ibid.*
11 TA/NTS331/55/55, Minute from office of First Minister to Governor-General, nd., 1956.
12 TA/NTS342/90/55, M.A. Vermeulen to CNC, 19/5/1952.
13 *Ibid*, NC to CNC, 18/2/1953.
14 *Ibid*, Eiselen to CNC, 9/6/1953.
15 *Ibid*, Minutes of Installation, 20/8/1953.
16 E. Mothubatse, 5; P. Walshe, *The Rise of African Nationalism in South Africa* (London, 1970), pp. 1-37, 142-3, 227-8; A. Odendaal, *Vukani Bantu!* (Cape Town, 1984), pp. 1-23, 40-54, 72, 117, 258-85; T. Karis, G. Carter and G. Gerhart (eds.), *From Protest to Challenge,* vol. 4 (Stanford, 1977), pp. 68-9.
17 P. Bonner, 'The Transvaal Native Congress, 1917-20', in S. Marks and R. Rathbone (eds.), *Industrialization and Social Change in South Africa* (London, 1982), p. 305.
18 Sepuru, 'MaCongress and Rural resistance', pp. 25-6; TA/NTS 7661/23/332; Bradford, *A Taste of Freedom*, p. 148.
19 Bonner, 'The Transvaal Native Congress', pp. 305-6; E. Mothubatse, 5; Maredi, 1; Walshe, *The Rise*, pp. 210-13, 386.
20 Walshe, *The Rise*, pp. 239-54.
21 E. Mothubatse, 5; Walshe,*The Rise*, pp. 385-7.
22 *Ibid*; Hirson, *Yours For the Union*, chapter 10; (UWHPL), Xuma Papers ABX430112, T.R. Masethe to Xuma 12/1/1943; ABX430219, T.R. Masethe to Xuma, 14/2/1943; ABX430607c, T.R. Masethe to Xuma, 7/6/1943; ABX430823a, T.R. Masethe to Xuma, 23/8/1943; ABX, 430907c, Xuma to J.M. Nkosi, 7/9/1943; ABX430918a, J.M. Nkosi to Xuma, 18/9/1943; ABX43101b, T.R. Masethe to Xuma, 16/10/1943; ABX431021f, J.M. Nkosi to Xuma, 21/10/1941; ABX431122c, T.R. Masethe to Xuma, 22/11/1943; ABX40320a, J.M. Nkosi to Xuma, 20/3/1944; ABX440203b, J.M. Nkosi to Xuma, 3/2/1944; TA/NTS7252/259/326, Minutes meeting 17/2/1944.
23 K.L. Maredi, 1.
24 *Ibid*; J. Nkadimeng, 1, 3; Karis, Carter and Gerhart (eds.), *From Protest,* vol. 4, p. 97.
25 M. Basner, *Am I An African?* (Johannesburg, 1993), p. 113; D. Bopape, 1.
26 D. Bopape, 1.
27 H. Joseph, *If This Be Treason* (London, 1963), pp. 162-3.
28 See references in note 22 above. See also UWHPL, ABX460731b, Secretary Bookkeeper to Xuma and enclosures, 31/7/1944; ABX450727, Xuma to I. Chili, 27/7/1945; ABX460817b, T.R. Masethe to Xuma, 17/8/1946; ABX480615a,

Secretary Springbok Legion Witbank to Xuma, 15/6/1958. Institute of Commonwealth Studies (ICS), London University, South African Materials Project, (SAMP), No 99/100, interview H. Basner. See also Sepuru, 'MaCongress and Rural Resistance', pp. 64-6.

29   S. Schirmer, 'Freedom in Land and Work: Labour Tenancy and the Proclamation of Chapter 4 in Lydenburg', unpublished B.A. Honours dissertation, University of the Witwatersrand, 1989, pp. 43-4.

30   J. Bekker, 'Plough', p. 70.

31   *Ibid.*

32   ICS, SAMP,99/100, H. Basner, interview.

33   UWHPL, ABX460618, Bopape to Xuma, 18/6/1946.

34   D. Bopape, 1;

35   *Ibid*; G.M. Pitje, 2; E. Motsoaledi, 1-2; J. Nkadimeng, 1.

36   W. Sisulu, 1. See also Lodge, *Black Politics*, Chapter 1.

37   W. Sisulu, 1.

38   Walshe, *The Rise*, pp. 387-8; G.M. Pitje, 2; J. Nkadimeng, 1; W. Sisulu, 1; E. Motsoaledi, 1-2; D. Bopape, 1.

39   *Ibid.*

40   M.J. Sekhukhune, 1.

41   This observation is based on patterns emerging from life histories of Pedi migrants collected in Sekhukhuneland and on the Rand. See also TA/NTS.10276/59/423/4, W. Norton to Chief Native Commissioner, 11/7/1947.

42   J. Nkadimeng, 1.

43   *Ibid.*

44   M. Moreane, 1.

45   It is probable that migrants' desire to maintain a degree of autonomy from wage labour also found expression in these activities. M. Kgagudi, 1; J. Mashego, 1; K.L. Manailane, 2; K. Lerutla, 1; M.J. Sekhukhune, 2; S. Motla, 1.

46   M. Kgaphola, 1; M. Kgagudi, 1; J. Mashego, 1; J. Nkadimeng, 1; S. Mothubatse, 1-3; J. Nchabeleng, 1; K.L. Manailane, 2; G.H. Pirie and M. Da Silva, 'Hostels for African Migrants in Greater Johannesburg', *GeoJournal*, 12, 1986, pp. 173-82.

47   T. Lerutla, 1.

48   *Ibid*; J. Mashego, 1; K.L. Manailane, 1-2; N. Mabogwane, 1; M. Peskin and A. Spiegel, 'Migrant Labour Project: Urban Hostels in the Johannesburg Area', unpublished report, Institute of Social and Economic Research, Rhodes University, 1976.

49   D. Bopape, 1; J. Nkadimeng, 1; M. Ramokgadi, 1; K.L. Manailane, 1; J. Mashego, 1.

50   The Wesleyan Mission, though to a lesser extent than the BMS, also had an educational presence in the early period. Pitje, 'Traditional and Modern', pp. 123-47; Mothodi Nchabeleng, 1-2; B. Hlakudi, 1; E. Mothubatse, 4.

51   K.L. Manailane, 1.

52   S. Mothubatse, 1; S. Motla, 1; T. Lerutla, 1; K. Lerutla 1; M. Kgagudi, 1.

53   M. Mafiri, 1. See also T. Lerutla, 1; C. Radingoane, 1; L. Grundling, 'The Participation of South African Blacks in the Second World War', unpublished D.Litt. et Phil., Rand Afrikaans University, 1986, esp. Annexure E.

54   M. Mafiri, 1.

55   T. Lerutla, 1; C. Radingoane, 1.

56   B. Hlakudi, 1; Mothodi Nchabeleng, 1; T. Lerutla, 1.

57   M. Mampuru, 1-3; J. Ntsoane, 1; K.L. Manailane, 1 and 2; B. Hlakudi, 2; M. Kgagudi, 1-2; J. Thobejane, 1; Mohube Phala, 1-2.

58   *Ibid.*

59   J. Nkadimeng, 1; M. Mampuru, 2. The Bapedi Advancement Society was first established in 1922 to encourage the collection of a tribal levy for land purchase. But

     it seems that attempts were made to revive it in the 1940s. See TA/GNLB.380/5/326, D. Hunt to SNA, 28 November 1922. Part of the reason for the concern about radical influences in the 1940s stemmed from the activities of Sebataladi Motor Cottage Association in the 1940s. See Chapter 2.

60   M. Mampuru, 1-3; J. Ntsoane, 1; K.L. Manailane, 1-2; M. Kgagudi, 1-2; J. Thobejane, 1; B. Hlakudi, 2; T. Lerutla, 1; M. Mafiri, 1; J. Mashego, 1.

61   *Ibid.*

62   *Ibid.* The extent and range of assistance given varied significantly from society to society.

63   *Ibid.*

64   See Chapter 2 for a fuller discussion of some of the issues touched on here.

65   See, for example, B. Hlakudi, 1-2; M. Kgaphola, 1; M. Mampuru, 1; P. Matjie, 1; R. Moetalo, 1; S. Mothubatse, 1; J. Moukangwe, 1; J. Nchabeleng, 1; Mothodi Nchabeleng, 1; D. Bopape, 1. See also Sansom, 'Leadership and Authority', pp. 5-13.

66   M. Mampuru, 2; K L. Manailane, 1; L. Mothubatse, 2; J. Nchabeleng, 1; L. Maredi, 2; Mogase Sekhukhune, 2; M. Phala, 1.

67   J. Mashego, 2; Pirie and Da Silva, 'Hostels', pp. 173-5.

68   Mogase Sekhukhune, 2.

69   Mohube Phala, 2.

70   Migrant tenacity and networks also played an important part in the failure of attempts to entrench urban labour preference in the 1950s. See Bonner *et al.*, *Apartheid's Genesis*, pp. 1-42.

71   T. Lerutla, 1; J. Nkadimeng, 1.

72   This observation draws on a cross-section of interviews.

73   E. Mostoaledi, 1-3; J. Nkadimeng, 1-3.

74   E. Motsoaledi, 2; See also H .and L. Bernstein, 1; G. Ngake, 1.

75   Bundy, 'Land and Liberation', p. 260. See also B. Bunting, *Moses Kotane* (London, 1975), pp. 32-42.

76   H. and L. Bernstein, 1.

77   This is not to say of course that there were not individuals within the Party who were strongly opposed to effort being expended on the countryside. ICS, SAMP, No 99/100, interview with H. Basner; H. and L. Bernstein, 1; Motsoaledi, 3; B. Bunting, personal communication, London, 12 June 1990. See, for a more negative version of the role of the Party, B. Hirson, 'Rural Revolt in South Africa, 1937-1951', in *The Societies of Southern Africa in the 19th and 20th Centuries* (Collected Seminar Papers No. 22, ICS, University of London), p. 122; and B. Hirson, *Yours for the Union*, p. 133. It is difficult, however, on the basis of the evidence that he produces, to sustain the argument that a substantial section of the Party was actively hostile to rural work.

78   ICS, SMA, No. 99/100, interview with H. Basner; Hirson, 1; Bekker, 'Plough', *passim.*

79   Karis, Carter and Gerhart (eds.), *From Protest to Challenge,* vol. 4, p. 70. Malivha's early life history remains vague. There is, for example, fascinating but fragmentary evidence that Malivha, as early as 1932, was in contact with T.W. Thibedi and the Trotskyist Communist League of Africa. Hirson, 1; A. Drew, 'Events Were Breaking Above Their Heads', *Social Dynamics*, 17, 1991, p. 72. Oral research on Malivha's life and writing currently in progress should considerably clarify this picture. See, for example, T. Nemutanzhela, 'Pulling Out the Sticks and Removing the Stones from the Fields. Memory of Resistance to Betterment in the Zoutpansberg 1939-1944', History Workshop paper, 1994.

80   H. and L. Bernstein, 1. See also E. Motsoaledi, 3-4; J. Nkadimeng, 1, 3.

81   H. and L. Bernstein, 1.

82   A crucial source of additional information on Malivha and the ZCA/ZBA has been the Venda section of the Party newspaper, *Inkululeko*. I am grateful for the advice of

B. Hirson and L. Bernstein who directed me to this rich source and to T. Nemutanzhela who translated articles for me. See especially *Inkululeko*, December 1940, January 1941, April 1941, May 1941, June 1941, August 1941, November 1941, January 1942, February 1942, March 1942, May 1942, August 1942, September 1942, 6/2/1943, 20/2/1943, 27/3/1943, 20/6/1943, 20/11/1943, 4/3/1944, 15/4/1944, 10/6/1944, 22/7/1944, 14/7/1944, 26/8/1944, 30/9/1944, 7/10/1944, 25/11/1944, 9/12/1944. Hirson, 'Rural Revolts', pp. 115-32 and *Yours for the Union*, Chapter 10.

83   *Ibid*. The history of the ZBA and in particular its interaction with local struggles and consciousness clearly merits a full-scale study in its own right. Amongst the many issues such a study could explore further are the reasons for its decline after 1944. See Nemutanzhela, 'Pulling Up Sticks', which explores some of these questions.

84   H. and L. Bernstein, 1.

85   Hirson, *Yours for the Union*, p. 133.

86   J. Nkadimeng, 1, 3; E. Motsoaledi, 3-4.

87   T. Lodge, 'Class Conflict, Communal Struggle and Patriotic Unity', unpublished seminar paper, African Studies Institute, University of the Witwatersrand, 1985, p. 1.

88   H. and L. Bernstein, 1.

89   *Ibid*. H. Saphire, 'African Political Organisations in Brakpan in the 1950s', in P. Bonner *et al.* (eds.), *Apartheid's Genesis*; Lodge, *Black Politics*, pp. 97-8, 131-4.

90   H. and L. Bernstein, 1; Bunting, *Moses Kotane*, chapters 6 and 7; E. Motsoaledi, 2-3; ICS, SAMP, No. 99/100, H. Basner interview.

91   *Ibid*; Sepuru, 'MaCongress and Rural Resistance', p. 75.

92   E. Motsoaledi, 2.

93   E. Motsoaledi, 1-4.

94   *Ibid*; J. Nkadimeng, 1-3; G. Ngake, 1.

95   J. Nkadimeng, 1-3.

96   H. and L. Bernstein, 1.

97   E. Motsoaledi, 2; See also N. Mokgatle, *Autobiography of an Unknown South African* (California, 1971), pp. 239-42.

98   *Ibid*. H. and L. Bernstein, 1; J. Nkadimeng, 3.

99   Lodge, 'Class Conflict', p. 16.

100 H. and L. Bernstein, 1.

101 E. Motsoaledi, 2.

102 E. Motsoaledi, 3. See also J. Nkadimeng, 3.

103 H. and L. Bernstein, 1. See also E. Motsoaledi, 4.

104 Lodge, *Black Politics*, p. 302; J. Nkadimeng, 3; E. Motsoaledi, 2-4.

105 D. Everatt, 'The Politics of Nonracialism: White Opposition to Apartheid, 1945-1960', unpublished D. Phil. thesis, Oxford University 1990, pp. 49-118; E. Motsoaledi, 4; H. and L. Bernstein, 1.

106 J. Nkadimeng, 1-3; E. Motsoaledi, 3-4; Karis, Carter and Gerhart (eds.), *From Protest to Challenge*, vol. 4, p. 235.

107 E. Motsoaledi, 3. See also J. Nkadimeng, 3.

108 TA/NTS7694/443/332, Elekia Mamagase Nchabeleng, 23/1/1959.

109 Karis and Carter (eds.), *From Protest to Challenge*, vol. 3, p. 235.

110 J. Nkadimeng, 1, 3; see also E. Motsoaledi, 2-4.

111 *Ibid*. See also TA/NTS7694/443/332, Elekia Mamagase Nchabeleng, 23/1/1959.

112 W. Sisulu, 1.

4

The Tortoise and the Spear

The Sekhukhuneland Revolt of 1958

Early on the morning of 16 May 1958, 82-year-old Kgobolala Sekhukhune was roused from his sleep by a knock at the door of his hut. In the pitch dark, he responded. As the door swung open he was stabbed in the chest with a spear and hacked in the arm with an axe.

Within three days, nine men had been killed, many more had been grievously wounded and plumes of smoke from burning buildings and vehicles drifted into the pale winter skies. As convoys of police churned up complementary clouds of dust, men from the villages in the plains and the valleys scrambled up the steep slopes of the Leolo mountains to seek refuge in the caves and crevasses of this great natural fortress.[1]

The initial explanations officials and reporters offered for these events invoked history and terror in equal measure. A special correspondent for the *Rand Daily Mail* wrote:

> The Bapedi, tribesmen who were the once all powerful rulers of Sekukuniland, took up arms again last week for the first time in sixty years. They have reverted to guerilla-type tactics in an attempt to regain their lost power and past glory ... [Now] behind the brown clouds [of dust] in caves among the rocks the dreaded *'babolai'* [murderers] wait.[2]

Increasingly, however, a sinister, secret organisation was presented as the instigator and perpetrator of gruesome violence. It was not named Sebatakgomo, as might be anticipated from what appears in Chapter 3 of this work, but the Khuduthamaga (red and white tortoise). The tone of these interpretations owed a good deal to the fears of black conspiracy and atavistic revolt which flourished within colonial society, especially in the aftermath of the Mau Mau revolt in Kenya. But the police and state prosecutors were able to assemble evidence which, although fragmentary and even fanciful, suggested that the Khuduthamaga did exist and was centrally involved in the uprising.[3]

This chapter provides a more substantial reconstruction of the origins of the Khuduthamaga. It shows how its emergence was shaped by the interaction between Sebatakgomo and political forms and discourses associated with *bogoši* (chiefly rule). An attempt to reconstruct the chieftainship from below in order to prevent it from being captured by the system of Bantu Authorities lay at the heart of the matter. A core component of this initiative involved the endeavour to give new substance to the idea that *kgoši ke kgoši ka batho* (a chief is a chief by the people). As this struggle intensified, the question of how to deal with individuals perceived to favour *boipušo* (Bantu Authorities) was posed with growing urgency. The chapter traces how and why the conclusion was reached that they should be killed, and explores the consequences of this decision.

Migrants and Chiefs

The happy expectations that officials harboured after the installation of the paramount in 1953 gave way to mounting irritation as the months slipped by and still no request for the establishment of a tribal authority was forthcoming from Mohlaletse.

Towards the end of 1954, the Department of Bantu Affairs (BAD) rolled out its biggest guns. Dr Verwoerd, accompanied by Eiselen and senior officials, held an 'indaba' with senior chiefs from the Northern Transvaal at the Olifants River and urged them to accept both Bantu Authorities and Bantu Education. The ANC, forewarned of the meeting, managed to send an envoy to counsel the chiefs to resist Verwoerd's threats and blandishments. To Verwoerd's considerable annoyance, his audience remained largely non-committal. From 1955, Sebatakgomo also started to make its presence felt in the area, preparing pamphlets denouncing removals, culling and Bantu Authorities and establishing contact with the chiefs. Morwamotše Sekhukhune, the Pedi Paramount, found himself caught in a tug-of-war between officials and his senior advisers on the one hand, and the majority of his subjects in both town and countryside on the other.[4]

The scope for manipulation of the paramountcy was heightened by a prolonged partial interregnum. Sekhukhune II died after a long reign in 1943. His designated heir, Thulare Sekhukhune, had predeceased him in 1941 without producing an heir and the Maroteng *bakgomana* (royals) faced the problem of how to establish a legitimate successor. The immediate solution was to install Thulare's younger brother, Morwamotše, as acting chief with the responsibility of raising an heir for his brother. Morwamotše was a mild man of limited education. Reluctant to take a clear lead on any issue, he was content to delegate decisions to his councillors. In consequence, the affairs of the chiefdom were increasingly dominated by his more assertive brothers. The most senior of these was the tribal secretary, Mothodi Sekhukhune, but the most influential, and a man who later was viewed by many as the effective ruler at Mohlaletse, was Mabowe James Sekhukhune.[5]

Mabowe, a personable youth with a stocky frame and quick intelligence who enjoyed a warm relationship with his father, Sekhukhune II, was remote from the main line of succession. At the latter's suggestion, he left the local school and went to stay with a Lydenburg lawyer, 'Aapie' Roux, who had done work on behalf of the paramount. Mabowe attended the local mission school, where he completed Standard Six. During his stay in the Roux household, he also became well versed in the ways of the Afrikaner middle class.

In 1936 he went to the Rand and, after a brief spell as a mine clerk, found employment in the concession store at the Van Ryn Deep Mine where he worked for four years and mastered a range of the skills needed in commerce. During the 1940s he found employment in a number of other stores, dabbled in ANC politics, observed the 1946 mine-workers' strike and finally, in 1947, returned to Sekhukhuneland. His wish to marry an educated Christian woman was rejected by his family and he entered into an arranged marriage with a cousin whom he immediately dispatched to school.[6]

Trading in Sekhukhuneland in the late 1940s was dominated by a handful of white families. The strict enforcement of exclusion zones made it extremely difficult for new traders to gain licences. But Mabowe was able to use his connections to the paramountcy and 'Aapie' Roux to secure locations and licences for stores. The kinds of economic openings which Thomas Maimela had tried in vain to create a decade earlier started to present themselves in the early 1950s as the Nationalist administration lowered the obstacles to black traders in the reserves. Mabowe steadily expanded the number of shops under his control. He also developed close relations with a number of wholesalers based in Pietersburg and forged links with the family of Dr Naude, member of parliament for the town and Minister of Health, who was impressed by this shrewd and convivial Pedi royal.[7]

Mabowe believed that it was pointless to resist the Nationalist government and judged that both Bantu Authorities and Bantu Education would open up new avenues of opportunity and 'progress' within the reserves. He acted as a key link between the BAD officials based in Pietersburg and Morwamotše and his councillors. Morwamotše's closest advisers came to share

Mabowe's view that the paramountcy could derive considerable benefits from co-operating with the new dispensation.

Mabowe had close connections with other emergent black traders who also saw potential advantages in the proposed new order. In the early 1950s, after he was appointed by Morwamotše as chairman of the Sekhukhuneland school board, he threw himself into the task of refashioning local schooling. One of the obstacles to the expansion of schooling had long been popular hostility to missionary dominance. Mabowe saw Bantu Education as an opportunity to build community-based and locally-supported schools. When the only secondary school in the area was closed by the Anglican Church in protest against Bantu Education, Mabowe set about collecting a 'voluntary' contribution of ten shillings from each family in the location to build a new high school. He was also able to fashion a happy combination of his interests when he secured a trading licence for a prime spot adjacent to the new school.[8]

Mabowe was the most articulate and visible spokesman for a small minority within the reserve which supported Bantu Authorities. Aside from traders, this grouping included some senior royals and chiefs who were persuaded that the system would entrench and improve their positions. Some headmen also resented their positions in the old order and hoped for better out of the new. As Frans Marodi Nchabeleng complained in 1953, 'headmen have rendered long and good service and have many followers but they are still called headmen and they are not recognised by the government'.[9]

There were also clerks, policemen and agricultural rangers whose fortunes were closely tied to those of the local state. There was some division in the ranks of local teachers. The 'hotheads' of the Sekhukhuneland Student Association took a dim view of the new dispensation but most teachers came from conservative Christian backgrounds and were remote from the main currents of popular concern. While uneasy about the implications of National Party policies, they nonetheless tended, like Mabowe, to view resistance as hopeless and believed that, on balance, state intervention would bring 'progress'.

Broadly speaking, those whose life strategies revolved around migrancy and accumulating land and stock rejected Bantu Authorities, while those who were well placed to perceive opportunities in commerce, education and the local state took a rather more sanguine view. As Gad Sekhukhune observed, 'You know as a businessman or as a teacher you have got to visualise the coming land, they are a bit civilised unlike tribal people.'[10] But for many people the new order represented not civilisation but its reverse – a quantum advance of the world of the whites, the values of *majakane* and the storm-troopers of 'the Trust'.

Not all senior royals supported Bantu Authorities. Some believed that the new system would hamstring them politically and materially, while others feared for the popular legitimacy of the paramountcy. Godfrey Mogaramedi Sekhukhune, for example, argued that incorporation into these structures would defile the legacy of Sekhukhune I and sever the arteries of legitimacy and popular support for the paramountcy. He likened Bantu Authorities to a snake's egg that would hatch a viper in the heart of the polity. Speakers also derided the much-vaunted inducements of *boipušo*, saying that animals also ruled themselves.

Increasingly exasperated officials alternated between threats and promises. The paramount was reminded of the possibility of deposition. He was also offered additional powers, a larger salary and finally, in a frenzy of bribery at a public meeting on 10 December 1956, he was promised 'a railway bus, a secondary school, a clinic, a post office and a telephone'.[11] When Morwamotše agreed that he would like these facilities, Mr Prinsloo – the chief information officer of the Bantu Affairs Department – leapt up and shook him by the hand. An official photograph was taken and Mr Prinsloo announced that he was overjoyed that Morwamotše had accepted Bantu Authorities.

Delighted BAD officials began to prepare the proclamation of a regional authority with councillors nominated by the paramount and drawn from the Maroteng *bakgomana*, the more powerful headmen and a couple of teachers and shopkeepers.[12]

The Tortoise: Sebatakgomo and the Khuduthamaga

News of these meetings was carried to the Rand by migrant workers and men from Sekhukhuneland who gathered in compounds, hostels, factories and burial societies to debate and dissect events at home. They listened to the views of ANC and Communist Party members and were told grim stories by migrants from other areas about 'the Trust' and Bantu Authorities. Speculation about the intentions of the paramount and his advisers was rife.

This turmoil provided fertile ground for the growth of Sebatakgomo, which used meetings held in municipal hostels as its principal and most effective means of reaching a broader audience. The centrally situated Jeppe and Denver hostels were regular meeting places in Johannesburg. But gatherings were also held at Iscor in Pretoria, in Springs, Benoni, Germiston and Witbank. As 1956 progressed, and tension mounted in Sekhukhuneland and elsewhere, Sebatakgomo started to draw in a much wider constituency than existing ANC and CP members.[13]

Flag Boshielo was forced to withdraw from formal involvement in late 1955 when he – along with 41 other ANC and SACP activists – was banned from political activities. Nkadimeng took over as chairman but Boshielo continued to play a vital, if less-public, role. Committees composed of migrants from the same village were formed in each of the industrial areas. They elected a local branch which sent representatives to a central committee – the Khuduthamaga – based in Johannesburg. Nkadimeng recalls that migrants would have 'a village meeting to discuss their common problems at the village and they will bring the problems to the central committee'.[14] Thus, from its inception, Sebatakgomo tapped into the village-based networks and the diaspora of migrant workers which were so central to the lives of men from Sekhukhuneland working in the urban centres of the Transvaal.

Migrants travelling between the town and the countryside kept their home communities informed about urban activities and their fellow workers abreast of developments in Sekhukhuneland. Part of the strategy adopted was to press for open meetings – *pitso* – in the villages to discuss developments, and to remind chiefs and headmen of the intensity of their opposition to 'the Trust' in all its manifestations. Some Sebatakgomo meetings were held in the reserve, but permission to gather was routinely refused by the native commissioners, and this limited their scale. As the movement gathered momentum, members of the central committee made a point of visiting Sekhukhuneland and a wider circle of ANC activists also followed the long and dusty road north. Martin Ramokgadi, for example, who had been an important link to the struggles in Matlala, remembered that 'As a member of the ANC I had to go there and give moral support, try to organise, so I used to go there frequently to find out whether people are actually doing the job properly.'[15] And Kgaphedi Lerutla, who had previously often acted as a taxi driver for the ANC in Alexandra, recalls that he found his services increasingly in demand to drive activists to *Bopedi*.[16]

A number of individuals who had been politically active on the Rand, but subsequently settled in Sekhukhuneland, acted as key points of contact for the urban leadership of Sebatakgomo. One of the most important of these was Godfrey Mogaramedi Sekhukhune. A towering figure of a man, he combined considerable personal authority with great warmth and eloquence. A grandson of Sekhukhune I, he had attended school in the Mphahlele chiefdom. In 1939 he found employment as an orderly at Jane Furse hospital, but enlisted in the army in 1943. His wartime experiences intensified his anger at the subjugation and degradation of the Pedi Kingdom and the system of racial oppression which prevailed in South Africa. On his discharge, he took a job at Germiston hospital and made contact with the ANC. David Bopape recalls that 'He heard I was organising the ANC so he came to my place, then from there he attended meetings of the ANC and he became a member of the ANC and a very, very sensitive student he was.'[17]

At the end of 1950, Godfrey Sekhukhune returned to Sekhukhuneland and worked at the Jane Furse mission hospital once more. He became a key point of contact for both the leadership of the ANC and for Sebatakgomo. Nkadimeng, for example, recalls that when they visited the area, 'that was our station. We would first go to him. We would let him know that we are coming. He would make the arrangements.'[18] He also attended meetings at Mohlaletse and Mamone and monitored developments in these key communities.

The core of activists who initiated Sebatakgomo had intended to create a broadly based movement and made contacts with a wide range of rural communities and struggles – including groupings in the Zoutpansberg and Zeerust. But, from the outset, its main leadership was from *Bopedi*. A combination of their concerns and networks, and the intensifying struggle over the paramountcy, ensured that the membership came mainly 'from Sekhukhuneland because this is where we drew our strength'.[19]

The vast majority of these members were migrant workers from *baditšaba* communities in Sekhukhuneland and the movement was infused with Pedi history and symbolism. This provided a set of common values and shared experiences. However, there was also considerable diversity in the movement which can be conceptualised by means of a continuum.

At one end of this continuum, there were individuals with at least primary schooling, who had long histories of involvement in unions, the SACP and ANC, and who were familiar with the versions of democracy, nationalism and socialism propagated in these organisations. A number of these men played a key role in the leadership. At the other end of the continuum, there were migrants who had neither Western education nor involvement in unions or political parties, and whose primary commitment was to defending a residual rural autonomy. The latter, who probably comprised the majority of the membership, had models of organisation derived primarily from their experience of the political processes within chiefdoms, regiments and burial societies.

Some of these men were aware that many of the leaders of Sebatakgomo had wider political connections, but trusted them because they were from *Bopedi*. And when the leadership visited rural communities they stressed that they were from Sebatakgomo rather than emphasising their connections to the ANC.[20]

As the movement grew in strength, its 'Pedi' character became even more marked. In 1957, partly as a consequence of this shift, its name was changed to Fetakgomo. This was derived from the political maxim *'Feta kgomo o sware motho'* – (leave the cattle and take the people) – which was closely associated with the history of the Pedi Kingdom. This maxim also had more-immediate resonances, given the centrality of cattle culling to 'the Trust'.[21]

As state intervention in Sekhukhuneland intensified during 1957 and 1958, branches of Fetakgomo multiplied and membership soared on the Rand, in Pretoria and in Witbank. This growth was facilitated by the manner in which migrants grouped in burial societies joined *en masse* and, in some areas, branches of Fetakgomo and the local burial society became virtually indistinguishable in composition. The then-chairman of a Pretoria-based burial society, for example, recalls that 'Fetakgomo and this burial society were one thing'.[22]

The use of the term 'Fetakgomo', with its interplay of historical and contemporary allusions, highlights another of the reasons for the organisation's growth. An ideology focusing on key symbols with wide-ranging resonances was forged out of the interaction of its various components. Central to this ideology was a rejection of Bantu Authorities and 'the Trust'. This appealed to concerns both over the Nationalist government's denial of political rights to Africans within a common society, and to fears that the 'freedom of the chiefdoms' would finally be destroyed. As one office bearer remembered, 'we were pushing this thing behind the chieftainship … otherwise we were going to lose support'.[23] But while defence of *bogoši* was a crucial component in the aims of Fetakgomo, it was couched in terms which appealed to broadly based constituencies. The office of chieftainship – and especially that of the *kgošikgolo* – was celebrated, but it was also recognised that individual chiefs were incompetent and/or careless of their subjects' interests. The ideal that *kgoši ke kgoši ka batho* was stressed, and this resonated both with commoner concerns over the increasingly authoritarian and co-opted realities of chiefly rule and with the democratic discourse of the ANC.[24]

From late in 1956, Sebatakgomo set about bringing these ideals and the practice of chieftainship into closer alignment. As inconclusive meeting followed inconclusive meeting in Sekhukhuneland, fears grew amongst migrants that elements within the paramountcy were intent on doing a deal with the BAD.

In November 1956, messages reached the Rand that Morwamotše was about to capitulate. The leadership of Sebatakgomo dispatched a letter from *Sechaba sa Bapedi* (the Pedi community/nation) asking Morwamotše to convene a *pitso* at Mohlaletse to discuss the issue, and which would be attended by migrants and locals.[25] The letter was intercepted and ended up in the hands of the native commissioner. When the migrants, led by John Kgoana Nkadimeng, arrived on the appointed day, they found the police waiting for them with an order prohibiting the meeting. The large and angry crowd which had gathered was finally forced to disperse. But Morwamotše was clearly shaken by these events. Before the migrants returned to Johannesburg he told Nkadimeng, 'You go back and tell my people that I have not signed for the land [accepted Bantu Authorities].'[26]

The Sunday after their return from Sekhukhuneland, a meeting of Sebatakgomo was called. It was reported that police had prohibited the *pitso,* and members responded that the organisation was of little value if it could so easily be thwarted by the authorities. Nkadimeng suggested that in future Sebatakgomo should operate as far as possible in secret. They should find a secure means of conveying messages and only issue cards to trusted members. But it was also concluded that if the movement was to succeed, steps had to be taken against a more insidious enemy, and 'that all persons who proved to be renegades should be exposed and made known to members of the organisation'. Renegades were considered to be 'those working for the government or who are informers'.[27]

The fears of the migrants were intensified when news reached them that Morwamotše, within two weeks of giving them the assurance that he would not 'sign', had apparently publicly embraced both Mr Wessels and Bantu Authorities.

This turn of events persuaded the leadership of Sebatakgomo that drastic measures were required. But they still sought to avoid a head-on confrontation with Morwamotše, which could have both sown division in their own ranks and tarnished a vital symbol. It was therefore proposed that Mabowe Sekhukhune and others who formed the *Dihlogo tša Motse* (literally the heads of the village) – the inner circle of Morwamotše's administration – should be deposed and replaced by individuals who could be trusted by the migrants.

To this end, and after much debate, it was decided to send Phetedi Thulare (a senior royal) and Morewane Mothubatse to Mohlaletse to take matters in hand. These individuals, along with other migrants who were at home, started to contact influential villagers – amongst them Morwamotše's brother, Mosehla Sekhukhune – and to mobilise popular opposition to Mabowe, Mothodi and the other councillors. After some weeks, a series of meetings were held at Mohlaletse during which the existing advisers of the paramount were called to account. They were accused of secret dealings with officials, of withholding vital information and of misleading Morwamotše.

In these and subsequent meetings, the activities of Mabowe Sekhukhune came under particular scrutiny. He failed to attend them but, in his absence, was charged – amongst other things – with embezzling the funds for the new school and of misusing the chief's car. Most importantly of all, he was accused of conspiring to usurp the chieftainship. A reference to *Kgoši* James (Mabowe) Sekhukhune in the December 1956 issue of the BAD magazine,

Bantu, was seen as conclusive proof of the validity of these fears. Through all of these proceedings, however, care was taken to avoid direct criticism of Morwamotše.[28]

The upshot of these meetings was the replacement of the paramount's key advisers. Ntladi Mampuru was appointed as induna (*tona*) and Phetedi Thulare as secretary. A new inner council was constructed out of individuals who had a track record of opposition to Bantu Authorities. Mabowe – in the face of persistent rumours that an attempt would be made on his life – left the area and his shops were subject to an almost total popular boycott. Mothodi, and many of the other displaced advisers, sought refuge in the neighbouring village of Ntšabeleng.

These events constituted a major political coup. While appearing to operate within the conventions and forms of chiefly power, these meetings had in fact overturned long-established practices which restricted influence over these positions to a small group selected by the *kgošikgolo* and senior royals. Now a much broader constituency within the chiefdom had been actively involved, and the group installed in key positions also maintained close contact with Sebatakgomo's structures on the Rand.

One of the principal projects pursued by the new urban and rural leadership was to collect funds to provide Morwamotše with a new house and car. This was in part intended to remind the *kgošikgolo* that material rewards for loyalty were not the monopoly of the BAD.

In December 1956, Nkadimeng and Moretsele were arrested and were to spend the next five years embroiled in the interminable Treason Trial, during which the state attempted to prove that the leadership of the ANC was intent on fomenting violent revolution. But both continued to play a role behind the scenes, and another long-standing member of the Communist Party and the ANC – Lucas Kghapola – was elected chairman. As a result, the pressure from the Rand did not falter.[29]

Once again the BAD officials' hopes for the smooth establishment of a tribal authority were dashed. Morwamotše, flanked by his new advisers, denied that he had ever accepted *Boipušo*. In mid-March 1957, Dr Piet Koornhof was dispatched by Eiselen to investigate the situation. He was alarmed by what he found and argued that 'a setback ... will have repercussions throughout the Transvaal because Sekhukhuneland can be regarded as the heart of the Transvaal Bantu'. Koornhof recommended firm measures against the new advisers and continued support for Mabowe.[30]

Early in April, Phetedi Thulare and Godfrey Sekhukhune were arrested and deported to Matubatuba and Mtunzini respectively. Following these arrests, the urban leadership of Fetakgomo turned to lawyers for assistance. They received some advice from Mandela and Tambo but their most important and enduring source of legal support came from Shulamith Muller, whose under-resourced and over-stretched practice gave succour to scores of the victims of the apartheid state in the 1950s.

The *Dihlogo tša Motse* worked in close conjunction with Fetakgomo to raise money for the legal costs of contesting the deportations. The urban leadership made a number of visits to Sekhukhuneland in these months. A recurring refrain in their meetings was that it was 'time to win back the land but that they must now fight not with assegais but with money'.[31] They also reported on the rapid growth and activities of Fetakgomo in the urban areas and distributed membership cards. A number of major demonstrations were organised. The most dramatic of these occurred in July 1957, when 8 000 men donned ceremonial dress, gathered at Mohlaletse and handed officials petitions bearing 30 000 signatures demanding the return of the deportees.

The BAD response was two-pronged. On the one hand, repression was intensified. Over the following year there were further deportations, Morwamotše was deprived of his official authority to hear tribal cases, the school at Mohlaletse was closed, the ANC was banned in Sekhukhuneland and an effective local state of emergency was declared. On the other hand, overtures were made to a number of headmen to accept Bantu Authorities.

Partly influenced by the emphasis on culture and ethnicity within apartheid ideology, some individuals within the department had become increasingly uneasy about the elements of ethnic diversity within the Pedi state, and steps had already been taken to recognise a separate 'Koni tribe' under Frank Maserumule. As the assumed advantages of endorsing the paramountcy failed to materialise, this alternative perspective gained strength. C.V. Bothma, a young member of the ethnology division, became an increasingly influential figure and set about winning support for a multiplicity of tribal authorities based on the political and ethnic subdivisions which existed in the area. The principal inducement offered was that those 'headmen' who complied would be recognised as independent chiefs and head autonomous tribal authorities. While most *dikgošana* resisted these blandishments – not least of all for fear of the wrath of their followers – a minority responded positively. They were derided as *'dikgoši tša Bothma'* (Bothma's chiefs) by the supporters of the Khuduthamaga.[32]

These developments heightened tensions within the chiefdoms. The urban leadership of Fetakgomo urged that the organisation should be expanded in the rural area but Morwamotše and some members of the *Dihlogo tša Motse* resisted on grounds that existing political structures were adequate. A group of younger migrants – aged in their twenties and early thirties – who had participated in Fetakgomo activities in Johannesburg but had returned home, were not satisfied with this response. Led by Lebelike Mogase and

Mothubatse Mangope, they called a meeting of the *Dihlogo tša Motse*. They demanded to be allowed to participate in meetings of the council, as one member recalled, 'because they just saw us drink beer while they paid money and the banned men still had not returned. Therefore they wanted representation to put matters right.'[33] Morwamotše and some of the councillors resisted repeated demands along these lines, but eventually Kgetjepe Makotenyane and Nkopodi Rampelani said that 'they were our children and would help us with the work and a majority agreed to their involvement'.[34] These young workers were concerned to underscore the importance of the urban-based leadership. Once they were admitted, they urged that the name of the council should be changed to Khuduthamaga and that it should accept direction from its Johannesburg namesake – the executive committee of Fetakgomo.

The intervention of the young migrants saw yet another shift in the balance of power within the chiefdom. Now not only commoners, but also young men, had a decisive say in the inner councils of the paramountcy. Having secured unprecedented political leverage, these men helped build the Khuduthamaga into a major political force in the region. Office bearers were elected and regular meetings were held under a marula tree on the mountain slopes behind the royal *kgoro*. Branches were established in the major villages which sent two elected representatives to the central committee. Morwamotše was not present, except by special request, but was represented at meetings by his brother, Mosehla Sekhukhune. In practice, the Khuduthamaga became the effective focus of power and authority on the vital issues of the day.[35]

One of the most urgent issues it confronted involved strategies to deal with situations where subordinate chiefs might agree to the establishment of tribal authorities. While some of these rulers, such as the chiefs at Nkwana and Ntšabeleng, were well-entrenched, most were at loggerheads with the majority of their own villagers. And the fact that *dikgošana* who accepted Bantu Authorities were expected to make an immediate start on 'rehabilitation' further eroded their popular support. The strategy pursued in these instances was for their subjects to bring complaints against them to Mohlaletse where – after a hearing – they were deposed and replaced with individuals acceptable to the Khuduthamaga.

A number of headmen who suffered this fate appealed to local officials for support. The consequence in a handful of communities was the existence of two competing headmen or headwomen: one with minority support but with official recognition, the other supported by the Khuduthamaga and the majority of their villages.[36]

The Rangers

Within Sekhukhuneland, these events produced a profound polarisation between a small minority defined as supporters of Bantu Authorities and
dubbed *Marangera* (Rangers) and the overwhelming majority known as the
Makhuduthamaga – the people of the khuduthamaga. The term *Marangera*
was taken from the African agricultural rangers who served under white agricultural officers on 'Trust' farms. Rangers symbolised co-option by white
officialdom and the invasion and subversion of the inner domain of chiefdoms and homesteads. All those who publicly proclaimed themselves in
favour of tribal authorities and/or betterment earned this appellation. [37]

But the category also had broader connotations. It was coloured by the division between Christians and *baditšaba*. By no means all of the Rangers
were Christians but many were from *majakane* families and Christians had
long been viewed as a potential fifth column within the society. Black teachers were also closely associated in popular thinking both with Christianity
and, more broadly, with the intrusion of white power and values. The fact
that a number of teachers were prominent supporters of tribal authorities considerably strengthened these perceptions.

There was also deep suspicion of black traders. Epitomised in the person
of Mabowe Sekhukhune, traders were suspected of a willingness to betray
and subvert core values in the interests of securing their own material advantage. This perception was probably heightened by the failure of most black
traders to play the publicly redistributive roles that had helped legitimate previous patterns of accumulation within chiefdoms.

There was a widespread belief that the white officials' key informers were
to be found amongst the ranks of the Rangers, and a suspicion that some were
using the powers of witchcraft to defend and advance their cause. Rangers –
in short – came to symbolise not only Bantu Authorities and 'the Trust' but a
whole constellation of forces which threatened the 'freedom of the chiefdoms'.[38]

In 1959 Mothodi Nchabeleng – a teacher but nonetheless a staunch supporter of the Khuduthamaga – wrote a vivid account of these divisions:

> The Rangers were the spies of the system of Bantu Authorities. Their
> work was to go around arresting people and reporting those that spoke
> out against the system to the authorities ... Another word that caused
> fear was St Helena [deportation]. It came to the point that the ...
> Rangers refused to eat with the resisters and ... the people resolved no
> longer to accept food from the hands of the Rangers. Paying each
> other visits was now fraught with danger ... Fear of killing grew in
> the country of *Bopedi*. In the night people walked in dread of one
> another. The Rangers were always heard saying of the resisters, 'this

year they will go for ever'. Then it was often heard that so-and-so was picked up and sent to St Helena. Mockery and talking ill of one another grew night and day. As time went by it became evident that here in *Bopedi* would be no peace or reconciliation.[39]

This account highlights not only the depth of the divisions, but also conveys a sense of the role that witchcraft beliefs played in deepening polarisation. Belief in witchcraft was pervasive in both Christian and *baditšaba* communities, and the use of potions and poisons was regarded as the hallmark of the particularly feared category of day witches. Godfrey Pitje discovered, when he conducted research in the area in the late 1940s, that

> Everywhere I went, among pagans and Christians alike, I found people discussing the increase of witchcraft in the country and the spread of new diseases. Besides a sick man's bed sat men and women speculating on the possible witch responsible. Pedi teachers and ministers of religion are not immune and it was not an easy matter for one to maintain one's balance of mind in the face of these suggestions … Whereas it had been easy for me to detect the fallacy of magic and witchcraft while at College … it was a different thing to live among a people who were magic-ridden. Among them every happening has a magical explanation. When a man's livestock increases naturally while his neighbours' are not increasing at the same rate the former must be using magic to ensure the increases. When another's harvest has been good while … his neighbours' has been poor, it cannot but be that the former is using medicine. The selective element of lightning, which is much dreaded in the rainy season, cannot be explained in any other way than to ascribe it to witchcraft.[40]

Villagers had long contended with fears of the destructive power of witches. The conviction that witchcraft was on the increase may well have received some of its impetus from the growing ravages of malaria, tuberculosis, venereal and other diseases in these decades. But this belief was also probably one symptom of broader changes and cleavages. Classic analyses of upsurges of anxiety on this score within African societies have stressed the importance of 'underlying moral crises created for a group which sets a high value on its unity as its own development leads to a proliferation of conflicting interests within it' and a 'feeling that basic sentiments, values and interests are being endangered'.[41]

As we have seen, people had many reasons to believe that their way of life was in peril. And while individuals called on the services of *dingaka* (diviners) and used special medicines to protect them from evil forces, chiefs were prohibited from dealing with witchcraft cases. Many *magoši* circumvented this injunction but they risked severe official sanctions if they were seen to be too openly responding to their subjects' concerns about witchcraft. Thus, many believed that one vital element in communities' defences was decaying.

This climate of opinion infused perceptions of the conflicts in Sekhukhuneland. As Mothodi Nchabeleng recalled, 'they thought witches were poisoning people, mostly those who were strong speakers' [against Bantu Authorities].[42] The power to inflict disaster on one's enemies was another element in the armoury of witches which also appeared to some to be mirrored in the ability of Rangers to secure the deportation of their opponents. And one potent image of a witch is of 'the traitor within the gates' who has taken the wrong side in the 'basic social opposition between "us" and "them"'.[43] This does not suggest that there was a simple elision of witches and Rangers, but rather that forms of explanation which underpinned witchcraft beliefs shaded into the interpretation of these divisions and coloured the characterisation of Rangers.[44]

Feelings ran so high on these matters that the threat of violence was present in many meetings where Rangers faced their detractors. The experience of 72-year-old 'Ginger' Kambula at a meeting at Mohlaletse in September 1957 provides a vivid picture of one such encounter. Kambula, who was from a far-flung chiefdom but related to Morwamotše by marriage, had not attended a meeting at the paramountcy for some time and was not aware of how dangerous the political undercurrents had become. After having taken notes of the meeting on a piece of paper, he rose to argue that the paramountcy would be destroyed if the system of Bantu Authorities was rejected. The chairman of the meeting, Kgagudi Maredi, leapt to his feet and shouted 'take that paper on which he has been writing and tear it to pieces because he wants to give it to Mabowe. He is a Ranger.'[45] Then a group of men stormed down on him and beat him until Morwamotše and Mosehla Sekhukhune were able to stop them.

As the state intensified pressures in Sekhukhuneland, and succeeded in widening cleavages in the body politic, debates took an ominous new turn. Late in 1957, some of the younger migrants started to relay accounts of events at Zeerust and elsewhere where the houses of 'collaborators' had been burnt and some had been killed. It was argued in a meeting of the Khuduthamaga, with Morwamotše present, that 'it no longer is possible to live alongside people who caused our people to be arrested. They should be killed.' Morwamotše responded: 'If you want to practise witchcraft do it without my agreement. Why do you ask my permission to kill people?' He went on to say that he wanted no violence, and the Khuduthamaga as a whole supported him.[46]

By March 1958, it had become obvious to the BAD that neither threat nor promise could prise Morwamotše free of his new councillors. Officials decided on drastic measures. Morwamotše was suspended from office and 82-year-old Kgobalala Sekhukhune, a retired policeman remote from the main line of succession, was appointed in his stead. On 21 March, Morwamotše was deported to Cala in the Transkei, accompanied by his wife Mankopodi and their children.

The officials believed that they had provided a salutary display of their power. What they failed to understand at first was that by acting directly against Morwamotše they had delivered the most profound affront imaginable to popular political values. The shock waves of their ham-fisted action reverberated through the villages, compounds and hostels. In Johannesburg, John Nkadimeng addressed a mass meeting:

> I asked them, how can they be proud any more when their king has
> been taken away and they sit here with other people? What do they
> tell them, what do they say about their own life?[47]

These words also capture a sense of the importance of the paramount for migrants' own sense of identity.

Morwamotše's deportation came only two weeks after he had spoken out against the use of violence against Rangers. When the Khuduthamaga assembled in early April in the aftermath of his arrest, it was more receptive to militant voices. Mosehla Sekhukhune was the acting head. Stephen Zelwane Nkadimeng made an impassioned speech, proclaiming that the Rangers were the cause of Morwamotše's arrest and should be killed. He said that at the last meeting people warned that the chief might get involved if they fought with the Rangers. The chief had now been captured. Now was the time to kill the Rangers. A heated argument broke out in the meeting. Some shouted out that now was the time to kill them, while others argued that large amounts of money had been gathered to pay for lawyers which would be wasted if people took matters into their own hands. While a majority of the meeting remained reluctant, a vocal minority of younger men persisted in their demand for direct action. Finally, Mosehla Sekhukhune agreed that the Rangers should be killed because it was they who were responsible for the arrest of the paramount. Thereafter, individuals called out the names of people considered to be Rangers and lists of intended victims were compiled.[48]

In the weeks that followed, discussions continued amongst the group of younger men who described themselves as 'the soldiers of the Khuduthamaga'.[49] A plan was drawn up to attack Rangers simultaneously throughout the region on a set day. This action was to be executed by the 'youth'. Fears were expressed, however, that violence would widen and deepen cleavages within the villages, leaving the relatives of those killed embittered and intent on revenge. Such an outcome would have defeated a central part of the purpose of the planned attacks on the Rangers – which was to overcome internal disunity, restore community cohesion, and thereby strengthen defences against both misfortune and external intervention. In an attempt to combat the potential for division, relatives of the intended victims were urged to lead the attacks.[50]

On 13 May, men from the Reef and the reserve massed at the native commissioner's office at Schoonoord to demand the return of the paramount. Kgobolala – the acting chief – and Mosehla had a meeting with the commissioner during which Kgobolala pleaded, unsuccessfully, to be allowed to stand down. The commissioner then went out to speak to the crowd. He greeted them by saying 'Paramount Chief Kgobolala and the Bapedis' and then went on amidst mounting uproar to tell the assembly that Morwamotše would never be allowed to return. Members of the crowd shouted out:

> You are just here to collect our taxes not to appoint our chiefs. We will break down this building because it was built with our money, we will no longer pay taxes, and the police must no longer visit our villages.[51]

The crowd moved off to a nearby clump of marula trees. What happened then is shrouded in controversy. State witnesses later maintained that Mosehla and others made speeches giving explicit orders that 'Rangers should be killed'. But, notwithstanding the generalised outrage at what had transpired, it is improbable that they would so publicly have thrown all caution to the winds. More persuasive are the accounts that suggest that speakers laid the blame for this turn of events on the Rangers and that there were calls from within the crowd that 'the Rangers are known in every village and that they must be named and be kicked out of the villages. Others shouted out that they should be killed.'[52]

It was three days later (on 16 May) that Kgobolala was so rudely awakened as described at the beginning of this chapter. Another prominent Ranger at Mohlaletse, Thomas Mothabong Mabogoane, was also roused by a knock on his door before sunrise. He recalled that

> I heard voices outside the door and when I opened it I saw Mothubatse. I said 'what's wrong'? He then spoke in a soft voice so that I could not hear him. Then I realised what the whole village knows – they have come to kill me. I stepped outside and he stabbed me.[53]

Mabogoane, though seriously wounded, managed to flee, and both he and Kgobolala escaped with their lives. The fact that they survived, though heavily outnumbered, suggests that their attackers still lacked the resolve to murder. The assault was not only half-hearted, it was half-cocked as well; for the attacks at Mohlaletse took place in advance of the date set by the 'soldiers of the Khuduthamaga' for the eradication of the Rangers. Later on the same morning, police went to the village of Manganeng to arrest two of the more militant speakers at the Schoonoord meeting – Phaswane Nkadimeng who was heir to the office of local *kgoši*, and Stephen Zelwane Nkadimeng. The crowd that gathered blocked the police cars' exit route. The policemen panicked, opened fire, killed a man and a pregnant woman, and wounded several others before driving off at high speed with their captives. This episode snapped the final restraints and Rangers were attacked initially in Manganeng and then throughout Sekhukhuneland.[54]

When news of the shooting reached Mohlaletse early the next day, two regiments were mobilised to go to the assistance of the people at Manganeng but dispersed when they encountered a heavily-armed police column. Palane Matjie, recently returned from an abortive attempt to find and kill Mabowe Sekhukhune, joined the men *en route* to Manganeng. After the regiment's collision with the 'Boers', and now accompanied by Dihlare Masufi, he resumed the search for the second man on his list of targets – Dinakanyane Seroka – who was widely believed to be using witchcraft to assist the Rangers.

Eventually they found him, hiding in a donga.

> We said to him 'where are you from and where are you going?' He did not answer. Dihlare said to me 'Now what do we do with him?' I said 'he is our enemy we cannot just leave him, you are wasting time'. I hit him with a knobkerrie on his head then Dihlare stabbed him with a spear. It broke when it went into him … [H]e managed to pull it out … Then I stabbed him. I stabbed him. I finished him off.[55]

After they had killed him, they took his pass book which they delivered to the *mošate* (chief's place) saying, 'you don't have to worry any longer, we have killed him'.[56]

The next day, despite numerous warnings, a leading Ranger, Chief Kgolane, went back to his village of Madibong along with his induna, Makoropetje Maphiri. When they arrived, a crowd of 60 people – mainly men with assegais and axes but also some women with stones – stormed down upon them. They fled in separate directions. The chief took refuge in a house but was pulled out, beaten and stabbed to death. A millstone was placed on his battered head. Maphiri was also cornered and killed.[57]

Despite the spontaneous elements in the violence, the idea that its socially corrosive effects could be contained still seems to have played some part in shaping the pattern of events. At the village of Mphanama, Mangase Masha-

bela was identified as a Ranger, seized by an angry mob and taken to be executed. His life was spared, however, when four of his sons in turn refused to
strike the first blow.[58] At Manganeng, after the police shooting, the enraged
crowd surrounded the house of trader Motle Nkadimeng. It was led by a relative, Maseboto Ganatse. When he entered the house, he encountered the
daughter of his intended victim, Moseane. She said 'is it you?' He replied
'yes it is I, little niece'. She said 'is it really you that has come to kill my father?' He replied 'yes but if I kill your father you will not struggle or go
wanting.'[59] She begged to be allowed to stay with her father in his final moments but she was driven away before he was killed.

By 18 May, nine men had been killed, many more had been injured and
the property of Rangers had been put to the torch. Some of the victims were
publicly proclaimed supporters of Bantu Authorities; others – including traders and teachers – were attacked partly because they fell into the social
categories which were associated with the Rangers. But the violence was also
quite specific. While anger was vented on particular individuals, their families usually escaped serious physical injury.

Once this wave of killings was over, a war of attrition followed. Police
swarmed over Sekhukhuneland and many villagers took refuge in the mountains. There were further attacks – especially hut burnings – on Rangers, a
widespread refusal to pay taxes and an intensified boycott of Ranger traders.
Over 300 men and women were arrested and trials on charges ranging from
public violence to murder continued over the next two years.

But officials also realised that they had blundered by deporting Morwamotše and that little progress could be made until he was returned. After
officials received private assurances that he would be more co-operative in
future, Morwamotše was brought home in August 1958. His arrival was
greeted with jubilation and seen as a great victory by the majority of his subjects.[60]

Many of Morwamotše's followers, however, still languished in prison.
Twenty-one of them were on death row. The main activity of Fetakgomo
from May 1958 involved liaising with lawyers and raising the funds required
to pay the defence costs of the numerous cases. Migrants dug deep into their
pockets to foot this bill. Each member paid an annual fee of £7.10 shillings,
which must have been close to a month's wages for many, and additional
contributions were solicited.

Fetakgomo had to contend with intensified attempts by the police to infil-
trate and break the organisation. Meetings were increasingly held in secret, a
large donga near Denver Hostel providing one venue. While the police were
able to prise revealing statements from a number of individuals, the tight networks from which Fetakgomo was composed proved difficult for the police

to penetrate, and members weathered harassment and violence. When police arrived at meetings, or when individuals were arrested, they would simply declare themselves to be engaged in burial society activities and could produce burial society records to prove it.[61]

There were, however, some disagreements about strategy within the movement. The formation of the Pan-Africanist Congress in 1959 posed difficulties as some individuals attempted to draw Sebatakgomo into an Africanist orbit. Stress on the land issue had obvious potential appeal for members but the PAC's position in relation to court cases – 'no bail, no defence' – had little to commend itself to men whose main aim was to assist their imprisoned compatriots.[62] Some members countered the PAC challenge with the argument that it was important to make an open stand in support of the ANC, but this was resisted. As the then-chairman of the Pretoria branch of the Fetakgomo puts it, 'we said no, we are just fighting for our land, not on the side of the ANC, because they will involve us we don't know where, we said we are only talking about Sekhukhuneland that is our own place'.[63]

Other members, while clear in their support for the ANC, felt that Fetakgomo should not foster internal divisions or attract unnecessary publicity by proclaiming its political allegiances but should remain 'underground'.[64] These differences did not, however, develop into an open breach.

After a series of appeals, the number of individuals on death row was reduced to 14. Twelve men and two women, having been weighed and measured for the gallows, waited for month after month in Pretoria Central prison. They joined in the singing which rose to a crescendo on the night before victims of the hangman's noose met their fate. In the relative quiet of the day after the hangings, they had to collect the soiled clothing of those who had been executed and take it for cleaning. Once the judicial process had been exhausted, the leaders of Fetakgomo looked in mounting desperation for an alternative strategy to avoid executions. A campaign of petitions for clemency and letters of protest was mounted with the support of the ANC. John Nkadimeng recalls an inspired suggestion:

> It happened that Swart who was then Governor-General ... had to go to London. Then Walter Sisulu comes and says what we must do. We used to call him *mosohla* (the one who chews). When he was thinking he was chewing. He sat back ... and said write letters to six members of the Parliamentary Labour Party, one to the Archbishop of Canterbury, one to the Queen so that when this man goes there [he will know] that you can't hang people here and go there and shine.[65]

Swart relented in the face of this pressure, and in 1960 the sentences were commuted to long terms of imprisonment.

The Spear: Causes and Consequences

The preceding narrative contains elements of an explanation for the incidence and form of the violence. It grew out of a context of intensifying state intervention and repression in which core values of the society were placed under threat. Many people believed that their whole way of life faced destruction. The targets of the violence – the Rangers – were initially seen as agents of a malevolent enemy but, as the conflict intensified, they were increasingly believed to bear prime responsibility for the dangers that confronted the society. This depiction of their role was coloured by witchcraft beliefs, and the view gained ground that it was only by the removal of the 'enemy within', and the restoration of a cohesive community, that disaster could be averted.

The arrest and deportation of the paramount constituted the most profound affront imaginable to the social order which the *makhuduthamaga* sought to defend, and proved to be a trigger for violence. And the shootings by police at Manganeng helped to inject a more spontaneous and lethal element into the attacks.

But the question remains: why was it that Rangers were increasingly represented as bearing primary responsibility for arrests and deportations? It was, after all, visibly white officials and police who were the key actors, and few migrants or residents were under any misapprehensions about the relative power of the South African state. One part of an explanation is the widespread belief that, behind the scenes, Mabowe Sekhukhune and his allies were providing information to, and manipulating, officials in order to advance their own political ambitions. This view was also consistent with long-standing popular interpretations which placed internal divisions and conflicts at the forefront of explanations for profound setbacks such as the conquest of the polity by the Ndwandwe in the 1820s and by the British in the 1870s.

People also subscribed to the 'dual theory' of causation commonly contained within witchcraft beliefs, which sets out to explain the particularity of misfortune. Among the Azande, to cite a classic example, the question was posed as to 'why particular warriors, and not others, are killed by particular enemies in battle. Clearly those slain were killed by enemy spears; but an internal enemy, the witch, has caused this particular death.'[66] It seems plausible, in a context in which witchcraft accusations were rife, that the particularity of the misfortune of arrest and deportation was popularly accounted for by the witchcraft people believed the Rangers practised.

Another element of an explanation is highlighted by the mobilisation of the regiments at Mohlaletse and the centrality of the young 'soldiers of the Khuduthamaga'. The Pedi Kingdom had been defeated, disarmed and partially dismantled. But a military capacity and ethos had not been entirely

Chief Morwamotŝe sitting and Kgobolala Sekhukhune in the foreground. Photographed at Malegale in 1953 when the reunification of Sekhukhuneland was announced.

Chief Morwamotsê (left) and his councillors at Mohlaletse, early 1950s. *(PJ Quin)*

Flag Boshielo, 1955 (?)

John Kgoana Nkadimeng, 1955 (?)
(Bailey's African Photo Archives)

Chief Morwamotŝe alighting from his car at the opening of the Turfloop Agricultural College in 1956. Mabowe James Sekhukhune is holding open the door.
A reference in the accompanying text to 'Kgoŝi James Sekhukhune' caused an uproar. *(Bantu, 1956)*

Godfrey Mogaramedi Sekhukhune, 1970s.
(Mamatŝi Sekhukhune)

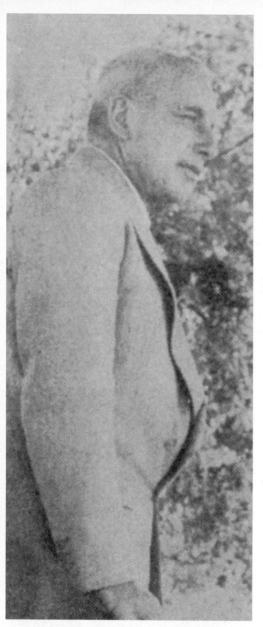

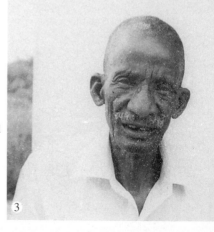

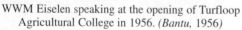

WWM Eiselen speaking at the opening of Turfloop
Agricultural College in 1956. *(Bantu, 1956)*

1. Elias Moretsele *(Mayibuye Centre)*.

2. Stephen Sekgothe Mothubatse; active in
Sebatakgomo and the ANC in the 1950s, photographed
at Mohlaletse, 1988.

3. Mothodi Nchabeleng, teacher at Mohlaletse in the
1950s, supporter of the Khuduthamaga and author of a
pioneering history of the 1958 revolt, photographed at
Ntŝabeleng, 1988. *(P Delius)*

extinguished. Accounts of the wars fought against the British and the Boers were told and retold, and the role of internal divisions in providing fatal chinks in the defensive armour of the state was recalled. The reality of defeat and control was acknowledged, but the legitimacy of the new rulers and especially their right to the land was far from recognised.

Within the villages, the socialisation of young men continued to hold up the ideal of the fearless warrior. Boys' principal form of recreation was stick fighting and young men learned to use rather more lethal assegais and battle axes. In towns, some participated in the 'bruising comradeship' of the Malaita. During initiation, youths' physical courage was repeatedly put to the test, they were steeped in military history and ultimately formed into regiments. One of the tasks entrusted to these regiments remained the defence of the community.[67]

Despite this schooling of young men in the military arts, Sekhukhuneland for much of the first half of the twentieth century was relatively free of serious violence. That was part of what differentiated it from the despised urban wilderness. But the young migrant 'soldiers of the Khuduthamaga' had also learnt to survive in the often-violent worlds of the compound, the hostel, the location and, increasingly in the 1950s, the prison.[68] They were, in varying degrees, exposed to the more militant mass-based politics of the period and became aware, through discussions with migrants from other districts, of violent resistance to state attempts at rural restructuring elsewhere. Armed with these experiences, the 'young men' were prepared to challenge the more cautious approach of many of the older generation in the villages.

This does not mean that these men relished violence or that murder came easily to them. Indeed, the botched attempts on both Kgobolala and Mabogoane suggest that the young men involved were partially paralysed by the sickening disjuncture that novices find between the theory and practice of war. But it is also true that young men steeped in this culture, and convinced that their communities faced mortal dangers, did not have to wrestle with Ghandian or Christian pacifism or a commitment to non-violent action that inhibited some of the leadership of the ANC when they pondered the choices open to them.[69]

Explanations which focus on the socialisation of young men, however, do not explain the role that women played in the violence. At Madibong, for example, women played a leading role in the resistance to, and ultimately the murder of, Chief Kgolane. Two women, Madinoge Pholokwe and Mapeetla Raseomane, were subsequently sentenced to death for their part in these events. Madinoge was the senior wife of Chief Kgoloko, and was two months pregnant when he died in 1953. Kgolane was appointed as regent on his brother's death and was entrusted with responsibility for Madinoge and the infant heir. He and Madinoge rapidly came into conflict, however, and she rejected his authority and established an alternative relationship with John Makopole Kgolane.

When Chief Kgolane indicated his support for a tribal authority and rehabilitation, and started erecting fences, Madinoge emerged as the leader of mounting popular hostility to his rule. The matter was taken to Mohlaletse, Kgolane was deposed and Madinoge appointed regent in his place. Kgolane did not accept this verdict and, to the fury of the villagers, continued to rule with the support of the native commissioner. When Kgolane returned to Madibong on that fateful day in May 1958, it was believed that during his absence he had conspired with white officials to have Madinoge and her key supporters 'thrown away to St Helena' (deported).

Although Madinoge was the effective leader of the opposition to Kgolane both in the preliminary hearings and in the supreme court trial that followed, the male officers of the court could not bring themselves to accept that a woman could have been the leader and it was her hapless lover, John Kgolane, who was portrayed as the villain of the piece.[70]

The story of Madinoge provides an example of the kind of role that the senior wives of chiefs could and did play in dynastic struggles. But as chief wife and potential regent she was hardly representative of women in general. However, while women played a less prominent part in leadership in other villages, or in assaults and in killings, they were at the forefront of the destruction of fences and other manifestations of 'the Trust'. And there is also evidence of women challenging men to take action. In 1954, at the village of Mafefe, Naphtali Lebopo was working with two other agricultural rangers demarcating fields, when suddenly a woman appeared and shouted: 'Men, you better bring me those trousers, we will wear them because you are cowards.'[71] Then men appeared, somewhat sheepishly, holding assegais. The rangers' truck was close at hand and they scrambled into it and sped off.

There were very few female migrant workers from Sekhukhuneland on the Rand in the 1940s and 1950s, and those who were in the towns were not represented in the urban structures of Sebatakgomo. Women were also excluded from the central political forums within the chiefdoms and did not participate in the meetings of the Khuduthamaga. But this exclusion did not prevent them from participating in the wider polarisation of communities or contributing to the growing conviction that Rangers should be removed from the villages. Songs composed and sung by women working in the fields and at *mošate* provided a running commentary on, and interpretation of, events.

This role was not simply a case of wives being swayed by the interests of their husbands. In the context of a migrant labour-based economy in which remittances were often sporadic and sometimes ceased altogether, many women depended on access to land and livestock to sustain their households. While formal control over both was vested in the hands of their husbands and brothers, *de facto* management of these resources had in many instances devolved to women by the 1940s and 1950s. 'The Trust', aided by its malevolent offspring *boipušo*, threatened to diminish or even deny the access of many families to these vital props to their livelihood and introduced definitions of rights to land and cattle which emphasised male control of these resources.

Widows and other female heads of households were anomalies in the minds of agricultural officials and were considered, at best, to have diminished claims to land and livestock. They were therefore faced with being forced into still-more dependent relations on male kin or even with outright dispossession. It is hardly surprising that women were numbered amongst the most militant opponents of 'the Trust' in all its guises.[72]

The Spear of the Nation

While the use of violence ran directly counter to the official policy of the ANC and SACP, there were undercurrents of discussion within both movements which may have contributed to these events and which were certainly affected by the Sekhukhuneland revolt.

In the aftermath of the 1952 defiance campaign, there was considerable debate about the viability of passive resistance, and some members, including migrant workers from Sekhukhuneland like Flag Boshielo and John Kgoana Nkadimeng,

> believed in the idea of fighting back. Now the question was if you fight back how would you do it. So people like Flag analysed this question especially after 1953 now with the Mau Mau revolt ... everybody was talking about it. And we had discussion groups where we were talking about this guerilla war, you know. We really cherished the idea that one day we would be able to fight back.[73]

Flag Boshielo – who, as we have seen, was a prominent member of both the underground SACP and the ANC, and the original driving force behind Sebatakgomo – was particularly taken up with this issue and devoured all the material he could find on Mau Mau. He went to Sekhukhuneland in the early 1950s to train as a herbalist and explore the possibilities of rural guerilla warfare. On his return, he argued still more strongly for serious consideration of armed struggle.

The grouping of migrant workers from Sekhukhuneland who formed the inner circle of the leadership of Sebatakgomo formed an important context within which he expressed his views. Boshielo was banned in 1955 and restricted to Johannesburg, but remained an influential figure. It is not possible to establish conclusively what influence – if any – these views had on the thinking of the 'soldiers of the Khuduthamaga'. But Stephen Zelwane Nkadimeng, who led the demand for violence against the Rangers within the Khudhuthamaga, was also a member of the ANC and the SACP and probably well-versed in these early debates about armed struggle.[74]

Whether or not they were influenced by discussions within the ANC and the SACP, these events certainly played a part in fuelling the debate about armed struggle within sections of the national movements. The willingness of communities to take up arms, the fact that the mountains and caves of Sekhukhuneland had once again given rebels shelter and that the state had been forced to return the paramount, all gave food for thought to men from Sekhukhuneland like Boshielo, Nkadimeng, John Phala and Elias Motsoaledi, who were ultimately to play significant roles in Umkhonto we Sizwe (MK)

The revolt also provided Boshielo with additional ammunition in his campaign to put armed struggle on the political agenda. The question may have cropped up in the regular discussions he held with Nelson Mandela, then a rising leader in the ANC, and Michael Harmel, an influential figure within the Communist Party. The law firm established by Oliver Tambo and Mandela also played a part, along with Shulamith Muller, in challenging the deportations and organising the defence of the rebels. And the ANC and SACP leadership, embroiled in the interminable Treason Trial, had ample opportunity to reflect on the significance of these events. Not least of all, they were confronted by requests from militants from Sekhukhuneland and subsequently from Pondoland for guns to pursue their struggles more effectively. And while they were not yet able to meet that demand, they did put emissaries from Pondoland, whose own struggles were just beginning, into contact with veterans of the 1958 revolt.[75]

One must be careful not to overstate the role of either Boshielo or the Sekhukhuneland revolt in the shift to armed struggle. Both were no more than pieces in a much larger puzzle.[76] But this evidence does illuminate Mandela's references to the role played by the rural revolts in prompting the decision to take up arms in his statement from the dock at the Rivonia trial. It also helps explain why Elias Motsoaledi, when asked in 1993 to describe the formation of Umkhonto we Sizwe, began his account with the battle against 'the Trust' in the Northern Transvaal. For him, at least, the Sekhukhuneland revolt was the opening skirmish in the war of liberation. And interviews with other key activists confirm that the violence in the Northern Transvaal, followed by the Pondoland revolt, made an important contribution to the decision to take up arms in both the ANC and the Communist Party.[77]

Once MK was formed, Sebatakgomo networks provided a rich source of recruits. Godfrey Sekhukhune, back in Sekhukhuneland after his banishment to Natal, became the key contact and recruiter for MK. John Phala recalls of the early days that

> Organising the volunteers to go to MK was simple and easy because Sebatakgomo was strong … In the Sekhukhune area we would just call the people [in the village] in a mass meeting and say 'The ANC wants soldiers, the ANC wants soldiers.' Then everybody was rushing to call his or her son to come and join MK. Here in the [Jane Furse] hospital was the headquarters of recruiting for the ANC. Godfrey Sekhukhune was a male nurse in this hospital. So when we organise the volunteers to join MK we used the ambulance. So Motsoaledi was coming to collect people here at the hospital because they have been collected in an ambulance from all over our villages.[78]

Just what the somewhat staid collection of doctors at the hospital in 1962 would have said if they had discovered the purpose to which their ambulance service was being put beggars the imagination!

Conclusion

Policemen and prosecutors were right to suggest that the Khuduthamaga played a significant part in the Sekhukhuneland revolt. But the picture of a sinister conspiracy bent on violence, which they painted in the courts in an attempt to secure the conviction and execution of its members, obscures as much as it reveals. As we have seen, the organisation emerged out of popular concern – especially among migrant workers – that chieftainship would become an instrument of Bantu Authorities and the hated 'Trust'. It was part of a remarkable attempt to make real the ideal that *kgoši ke kgoši ka batho*, which resonated both with the democratic values articulated within the ANC and with commoner conceptions of chieftainship.

Sebatakgomo and the Khuduthamaga were able to mobilise a very broad following and to effect significant changes in the nature of chiefly rule partly because of a strategy and ideology which celebrated chieftainship – especially the paramountcy – at the same time as it set about transforming it. But it is also important to recall that the attempt to democratise the institution never challenged a second fundamental proposition, *kgoši ke kgoši ka madi a bogoši* (a chief is a chief by the blood of chieftainship) which stressed the hereditary basis of chiefly rule. And the exclusion of women and uninitiated men from key political forums and processes went unquestioned.

Equally, while the Khuduthamaga mustered widespread popular support and participation, it was also a forum in which dissent was viewed with mounting hostility and in which the eradication of cleavages within the community became an overriding value. The perception of individuals stigmatised as Rangers evolved from one which portrayed them as agents of the system to one in which they bore primary responsibility for its actions. They were first shouted down, then driven from the villages and finally assaulted and even killed. These were extreme circumstances in which communities faced a fundamental assault from state structures commanding very little legitimacy and providing almost no meaningful channels for the representation of popular sentiment. Nonetheless, it must also be said that aspects of the popular political culture which evolved in this bleak environment, in which division, dissent and disaster were seen as intimately interconnected, provided a blighted legacy for subsequent generations.[79]

Notes

1   *Rand Daily Mail*, 30/7/1958; UWHPL, A410/C2-9, Sekhukhuneland, 16 June 1958; Supreme Court (SC), Circuit Court (CC), 1959/13/188/1, evidence of Kgobolala Sekhukhune, 29/7/1958.

2   *Rand Daily Mail*, 24/5/1958 and 22/5/1958.

3   *Rand Daily Mail*, 30/7/1958. Khuduthamaga is now widely used as the term for executive committee but this usage may not have developed until the 1950s and may be partly grounded in these events. See, for example, the contrast between the definitions provided in succeeding editions of T.J. Kriel, *The New Sesotho-English Dictionary* (Johannesburg, 1950 and Johannesburg, 1967). Under police interrogation, one of the key members explained 'Kudu Thamaga means a secret, it is just like a tortoise, a person cannot establish where its head or legs are. It is not easy to kill because its head is not prominent. The only way you can kill it is to throw it in the fire.' TA/ NTS 7694/443/332/ *Onrus in Sekhukhuneland en Stamsake, 1925-1960*, Seraki Kgoloko, 6/10/58; see also CNC Pietersburg to SNA, 26/5/1958; and S. Kgoloko, 1.

4   J. Phala, 1-3; E. Motsoaledi, 1-3; J. Phala, unpublished manuscript, nd, Robben Island.

5   TA/NTS3331/55/55 Chief Sekhukhune Bapedi, 1920-57; M. Nchabeleng, '*Boipušo*', unpublished manuscript, 1959; G. Sekhukhune, 1; T. Mabogoane, 1; B.K. Hlakudi, 2; S. Mothubatse, 2.

6   M.J. Sekhukhune, 1; B.K. Hlakudi, 1-2; G. Sekhukhune, 1.

7   *Ibid*; see also TA/ NTS 7694/443/332/, pp. 37, 46, 56, 72, 75, 76, 77, 119-20, 124, 243-9.

8   M.J. Sekhukhune, 1; G. Sekhukhune, 1; B.K. Hlakudi, 1-2; Nchabeleng, '*Boipušo*'.

9   TA/NTS342/90/55, Minutes of meeting at Malegale, 20/8/1953.

10   G. Sekhukhune, 1.

11   TA/NTS/342/90/55, W. Eiselen to CNC, 9/6/1953.

12   UWHPL,A410/C2-9, Sekhukhuneland, 16 June 1958.

13   J. Nkadimeng, 1; J. Phala, 2; K. Manailane, 1-2; J. Mashego 1-2.

14   J. Nkadimeng, 1. See also J. Phala, 2.

15   M. Ramokgadi, 1.

16   K. Lerutla, 1.

17   D. Bopape, 1.

18   J. Nkadimeng, 1; also Mamatši Sekhukhune, personal communication, 1988.

19   J. Nkadimeng, 1. See also J. Phala, 2.

20   M. Ramokgadi, 1; J. Mashego,1-2.

21 N. Sekhukhune, 1-3; J. Nkadimeng, 1; Mothodi Nchabeleng 1-2 and '*Boipušo*'; TA/NTS 7694/443/332, Elekia Mamagase Nchabeleng, 23/1/1959; Monnig, *The Pedi*, p. 40.

22 M. Mampuru, 1; see also J. Mashego, 1-2 and K. Manailane, 1.

23 J. Mashego, 1; see also J. Nkadimeng, 1; M. Ramokgadi, 1.

24 *Ibid*; N. Mabogwane, 1; M. Phala, 2; Nchabeleng, '*Boipušo*'; TA/NTS7694/443/332, Elekia Mamgase Nchabeleng, 23/1/1959.

25 TA/NTS/7694/443/332, *Sechaba Sa Bapedi* to Morwamotše, November 1956.

26 J. Nkadimeng, 1; see also TA/NTS 7694/443/332, Elekia Mamagase Nchabeleng, 23/1/1959; NTS8977/198/326, Bapedi Tribal Authority, 1957-8.

27 TA/NTS7694/443/332, Elekia Mamagase Nchabeleng, 23/1/1959; J. Nchabeleng, 1. Both Nkadimeng and Boshielo were active in the underground structures of the SACP and this may well have had some influence on the quest for secrecy.

28 *Ibid*; see also Seraki Kgoloko, 12/9/1958; M. Nchabeleng, '*Boipušo*'; J. Nkadimeng, 1; N. Sekhukhune, 1-2; Mohube Phala, 1; UW, CPL, A410/c2-9 Sekhukhuneland, 16 June 1958; *Bantu*, December 1956, p. 18.

29 *Ibid*.

30 TA/NTS8977/189/326, Bapedi Tribal Authority, 1957-8, P. Koornhof to SBA, 30/3/57.

31 TA/NTS7694/443/332, Seraki Kgoloko, 12/9/58; J. Nkadimeng, 1; J. Nchabeleng, 1; N. Sekhukhune, 1.

32 Nchabeleng, '*Boipušo*'; TA/NTS8977/189/326, Bapedi Tribal Authority, 1957-8; N. Sekhukhune, 1; J. Nchabeleng, 1-2.

33 TA/NTS7694/443/332, Seraki Kgoloko, 12/9/58; Phala, unpublished manuscript.

34 *Ibid*.

35 *Ibid*; see also N. Sekhukhune, 1-2; J. Nchabeleng, 1-2; M. Phala, 1-2; M. Nchabeleng, '*Boipušo*'; S. Motla, 1.

36 TA/NTS8977/189/326, Bapedi Tribal Authority, 1957-8; SS/CC/13/1/3/9/58, see, for example, the evidence of Madinoge Kgoloko, Phetedi Kgoloko, Morewane Mashabani, Phaswane Mashabela and Johannes Mashabela.

37 Sansom, 'Leadership', pp. 35, 64; Nchabeleng, '*Boipušo*'; N. Sekhukhune, 1 and 2. The term '*voortrekker*' appears in court records and in Sansom's account as an alternative to '*Makhuduthamaga*'. But it is now rarely used and, while there are speculative accounts of its derivation and meaning, I have not through interviews been able to clarify the issue. I have, therefore, utilised the more widely used and understood term, '*Makhuduthamaga*'.

38 *Ibid*. These terms also harked back to the bitter and costly struggle between the allies of Abel Erasmus and the supporters of Sekhukhune II in the 1890s. See also G. Sekhukhune, 1; M.J. Sekhukhune, 1-2; P. Matjie, 1; J. Nchabeleng, 1-2; Mothodi Nchabeleng, 1; K.L. Manailane, 1-2; D. Radingoane, 1. These perceptions, as we will see below, also influenced the choice of targets for attack when violence broke out in 1958.

39 Nchabeleng, '*Boipušo*'. The use of the term 'St Helena' to indicate deportation was probably shaped by its role as a destination for deposed chiefs in the nineteenth century.

40 Pitje, 'Traditional and Modern', pp. vii and xii.

41 This is inevitably a speculative discussion, for the material is not available to explore in depth why people believed witchcraft to be on the increase at this time or even to be sure that the anxiety about witchcraft being on *the increase* was new.

   For an account of changing disease patterns in the region, which argues that the incidence of malaria, venereal disease and tuberculosis probably increased significantly in the first decades of the twentieth century, see J. Rees, 'Health Patterns in the Northern Transvaal, 1900-1932', unpublished M.A. dissertation, University of

Witwatersrand, 1992. The leadership of the Sebataladi Motor Cottage Association certainly shared the view that these and other diseases were on the increase (see Chapter 2). For valuable comparative perspectives on witchcraft in Africa see M. Gluckman (ed.), *The Allocation of Responsibility* (Manchester, 1972), pp. 24-5; see also M. Warwick (ed.), *Witchcraft and Sorcery* (London, 1970). This issue is also discussed further and more fully in Chapters 5 and 6.

42   Mothodi Nchabeleng, 2.
43   'Witch hunting, then, goes together with a feeling that basic sentiments, values and interests are being endangered. A society in order to feel secure must feel that not only its material interests but also its way of life, its fundamental values are safe. Witch hunting may increase whenever either of these elements seem gravely threatened.' A witch is 'the traitor within the gates ... is on the wrong side of the moral line ... He has secretly taken the wrong side in the basic social opposition between "us" and "them".' P. Mayer, 'Witches', in Warwick (ed.), *Witchcraft and Sorcery*, pp. 60-3.
44   Mothodi Nchabeleng, 1; G. Pitje, 1; Pitje, 'Male Education', pp. 76, 107; Monnig, *The Pedi*, pp. 76-7: M. Mampuru, 3; P. Matjie, 1.
45   TA/NTS8977/198/326, Ginger Kambula, ? September 1957.
46   TA/NTS7694/443/332, Seraki Kgoloko, 6/10/1958; see also P. Matjie, 1; and L. Mothubatse, 1-2.
47   J. Nkadimeng, 1; Nchabeleng, '*Boipušo*'; M. Phala, 1-2.
48   TA/NTS7694/443/332, Seraki Kgoloko, 6/10/1958; G. Sekhukhune, 1; P. Matjie, 1; L. Motubatse, 2.
49   *Ibid*; Phala, unpublished manuscript.
50   Mothodi Nchabeleng, 1; J. Nchabeleng, 1-2; SS/CC/14/2, Mangase Mashabela, 30/9/58.
51   TA/NTS7694/443/332, Elekia Mamagase Nchabeleng, 23/1/1959; Seraki Kgoloko, 6/10/1958; N. Sekhukhune, 1-2.
52   *Ibid*; SC/CC/1959/13/185/1, evidence, Stephen Sekhukhune 29/7/58, Charlie Sekhukhune, 31/7/1958; SS/CC/185/14/2, evidence, Legane Mashigwane, Nkopodi Ramphelane, 8/10/1958; Malekutu Thulare, 9/10/1958; SS/185/15/3, Mabatani Marutani; P. Nkadimeng, 1.
53   T. Mabogoane, 1.
54   P. Nkadimeng, 1; Phala, unpublished manuscript; SC/CC/1959/13/185/1, evidence Major W. Kokot.
55   P. Matjie, 1; see also SS/CC111/1959/ *Crown vs Pelane Matjie*; Mogase Sekuhkune, 1; L. Mothubatse, 1.
56   P. Matjie, 1.
57   SC/CC/1959/13/185/1, evidence of D. Kgoloko, P. Segobodi, J.H. van Rooyen; R. Moetalo, 1; M. Raseomane, 1.
58   SC/CC/185/14/2, evidence of Mangase Mashabela, 20/9/58.
59   SC/SS/185/13/1, evidence of Kabule Motle, 11/9/1958.
60   Nchabeleng, '*Boipušo*'; TA/NTS7694/443/332; G. Sekhukhune, 1; N. Sekhukhune, 1; M. Sekhukhune, 1; UWHPL410/C2-9, Sekhukhuneland, 16 June 1958.
61   M. Mampuru, 1-3; J. Mashego, 1-2; K. Manailane 1-2.
62   Phala, unpublished manuscript; J.S. Thobejane, 1.
63   B. Hlakudi, 2; M. Kghapola, 1.
64   J. Nchabeleng, 1.
65   J. Nkadimeng, 2.
66   Gluckman, *The Allocation,* p. 7; see also Hunt, 'The Bapedi', pp. 284-5, and P. Delius, 'The Pedi Polity under Sekwati and Sekhukhune', Ph.D. thesis, London University, 1980, pp. 354-6; *Berliner Missions-berichte*, 1862, p. 331; J. Winter, 'The

Tradition of Ra'lolo', *South African Journal of Science*, IX, 1912, pp. 97-8; Nchabeleng, '*Boipušo*'; Mothodi Nchabeleng, 2.

67   Delius, *The Land*, pp. 181-246; G. Pitje, 'Male Education', pp. 105-99; Mönnig, *The Pedi*, pp. 117-20; M. Mampuru, 1; K. Manailane, 1-2; E. Mothubatse, 1-3; J. Nkadimeng, 1.

68   E. Motsoaledi, 1-2; J. Nkadimeng, 1-3; T.M. Sekhukhune, 1-2; N.P. Sekhukhune, 1-2. See also W. Beinart, 'Political and Collective Violence in Southern African Historiography', *Journal of Southern African Studies*, 18, 1992, esp. pp. 473-86; P. Bonner, 'The Russians on the Reef', in P. Bonner *et al.* (eds.), *Apartheid's Genesis* (Johannesburg, 1993).

69   Lodge, *Black Politics* pp. 106, 232-4.

70   M. Raseomane, 1; R. Moetalo, 1; K. Lerutla, 1; M. Lerutla, 1; L. Mampuru, 1; TA/NTS342/90/55, Chief Kgoloko, 1907-53; SC/CC/185/13/1, evidence Madinogo Kgoloko, Phetedi Kgoloko, Morewane Mashabani. See also SS/CC/185/15/3, evidence of Phetedi Kgoloko, John Makopole Kgolane, Madinoge Pholokwe.

71   N. Lebopo, 1.

72   B. Hlakudi, 1-2; M. Raseomane, 1; L. Mampuru, 1; M. Lerutla, 1; R. Moetalo, 1; R. Kgetsepe, 1; N. Lebopo, 1; D.P. Lebopo, 1-2; D. Magomarele, 1; TA/NTS 10276/59/423/4, G. Ackron to CNC, 18/5/49. As we have seen in Chapters 1 and 2, the category of 'widow', which runs through both official and oral accounts, probably refers to a range of households which for a variety of reasons (of which the death of a spouse was only one) were effectively female-headed. Plans for trust farms adjoining the Sekhukhuneland reserves in the early 1950s included large rural villages comprising of individuals who had been deprived of rights to land or stock. As to the result, 'large numbers of widows who previously held lands in this group of farms ... which is a feature of all Trust farms in Sekukuniland ... it is doubtful whether widows will make good farmers ... [T]hey should get one morgen [instead of four morgen] ... [T]he fact that the minimum rental payable for land is £1 whether it is one or five morgen in extent is a factor which may induce widows to move into a rural village as soon as it is established.' (NTS10248/38/423/3, Aapiesboom Trust Farms, 16/1/1954.) See also NTS10248/423/2 and A-C, Mutsi *Groep Trust Plase*.

This paints a somewhat different picture to the one drawn of processes in the Ciskei and Border region in the same period. The contrast is partly accounted for by the difference between women without rights to land who were able to secure some access to land through 'the Trust' and women in the Sekhukhuneland case who had access to land and who confronted the danger of this being significantly reduced or even denied. That is not to say that there were not some women in the broader region for whom 'Trust land' was considerably better than no land. See A. Mager, 'The People Get Fenced', *Journal of Southern African Studies*, 18, 1992, esp. pp. 778-82.

Another vital issue in this period involved passes for women which was a crucial issue in the Zeerust revolt and were a source of conflict just to the north of Sekhukhuneland. No attempt was made by officials to introduce this issue in the already volatile context of Sekhukhuneland in this period, but news of these struggles travelled on migrant networks and was presumably interpreted as yet another threat both to the 'freedom of the chiefdoms' and to the position of women. See C. Hooper, *Brief Authority* (London, 1960) and D.M.C. Sepuru, 'Succession Disputes, MaCongress and Rural Resistance at GaMatlala, 1919-1980', unpublished B.A. Honours dissertation, University of the Witwatersrand, 1992, pp. 107-8.

73   J. Nkadimeng and J. Phala, 1. Another indication of how long-standing these discussions had been is Mandela's recollection that 'I had first discussed armed struggle as far back as 1952 with Walter Sisulu.' See N. Mandela, *Long Walk To Freedom* (Johannesburg, 1994), p. 258.

74   *Ibid*; J. Nkadimeng, 3; Motsoaledi, 1-3. See also P. Delius, 'Sebatakgomo and the
      Zoutpansberg Balemi Association', *Journal of African History*, 34, 1993, pp. 306-13.
75   J. Nkadimeng, 1-3; E. Motsoaledi, 1-2 and especially 5; J. Nkadimeng and J. Phala, 1;
      L. Mdingi, 1; Mandela, *No Easy Walk to Freedom* (London, 1973), p. 168;
      D. Goldberg, 1; B. Hirson, 2; L. Bernstein, 2.
76   P. Bonner, B. Harmel and I have been engaged on an Albert Einstein
      Institute-supported oral history project to try to put the elements of the puzzle together.
77   E. Motsoaledi, 5.
78   J. Nkadimeng and J. Phala, 1.
79   See Chapter 6.

5

'The Cattle are Gone'

Transformations, 1960–85

Morwamotše and his wife Mankopodi returned to Mohlaletse on 8 August 1958, amidst scenes of great jubilation and rejoicing. Horns were sounded and men, women and children streamed from all corners of Sekhukhuneland to welcome them home. The people's joy at the restoration of the *kgošikgolo* was tempered by concern for those who languished in prison, but there was widespread relief that the forces of the 'Trust' and *Boipušo* had been defeated. Few people realised that they were watching the death throes of the social and political order they cherished, and that over the next two decades their world would be utterly transformed.[1]

A War of Attrition

At first, there seemed little to fear. Morwamotše and his councillors resumed their previous pattern of reassuring officials of their good intentions in private while remaining intransigent on the issue of *boipušo* in public and in fact. This strategy was not without cost. While a number of the exiles were allowed to return home, the BAD insisted that the banishment of the most intransigent would continue until the paramountcy established a tribal authority. But the department soft-pedalled in other areas. Attempts to introduce rehabilitation measures in the reserves were abandoned, the culling of cattle was suspended, and, while planning proceeded on Trust lands, it was agreed that all those who had previously had access to land should receive allocations. This did not put an end either to land shortage or discriminatory practices and merely led to the apportionment of ever-smaller plots. But it did prevent the official creation of starkly defined rural classes.[2]

139

The BAD had not given up the struggle to redesign rural society, but its priorities had shifted. The Nationalist government had appointed the Tomlinson Commission to investigate the possibility of the development of the reserves within an apartheid framework. Its final diagnosis showed considerable continuities with formulations harking back to the Native Economic Commission and beyond. The Tomlinson report, presented in 1956, proposed the creation of a small farmer class, the uniform imposition of betterment and the relegation of the remaining 49 per cent of the rural population to industrial villages. To overcome the danger of mass urbanisation which had scuppered previous designs, it suggested massive state investment in reserve areas to create local employment. But this was not a price that Verwoerd or the cabinet was prepared to pay and their rejection of this element of the report sounded the death knell for plans for the radical restructuring of reserve economies.

The new dispensation did not spare communities from the models and ministrations of 'development' planners. But the 'new era of reclamation' increasingly gave way to the cynicism of 'stabilisation ... loose planning and rapid resettlement'.[3]

Other aspects of the Tomlinson report were more in tune with official thinking and helped to provide 'scientific' justification for them. There were, for example, strong echoes in the Bantu Self-Government Act of 1959 of the commission's stress on 'clearly distinguished ethnic groups' amongst 'the Bantu' and the importance of the development of separate 'Bantu States'.[4] The Act specified eight national units or 'bantustans' with a form of government built on the basis of the Bantu Authorities system.[5] While the fantasy of economic self-sufficiency for the reserves faded, the dream that the bantustans could provide an effective alternative arena for Afriçans' political and social aspirations grew ever more vivid as the 'decade of defiance' drew to a close.

This shift in policy placed even greater pressure on local officials to establish tribal authorities in their areas and so lay the foundations for the new order. In 1962, the Lebowa Territorial Authority, which incorporated Sekhukhuneland, was established. Officials despaired of securing the participation of the Pedi paramountcy and concentrated instead on trying to break its power and undermine the unity of opposition they faced. Headmen were tempted with the promise of chiefly appointments if they accepted Tribal Authorities but, while a handful did so, the overwhelming majority remained obdurate.

The leadership of Fetakgomo monitored developments and when they saw danger signs acted quickly to stiffen chiefly resolve. They also participated in 1960 in the launch of Transvaal-wide movement Lekwebepe (meaning between the Vaal and the Limpopo) which was intended to mobilise a broader constituency to resist the state's evolving plans for rural reconstruction.

But this resolute opposition was undermined in the early 1960s. The banning of the ANC and the PAC, the destruction of Umkhonto we Sizwe networks and the intense police harassment of those activists who remained in the country, made it increasingly difficult for either Fetakgomo or Lekwebepe to operate effectively. In the climate of repression and fear which prevailed, the balance of persuasion swung in favour of the Bantu Affairs Department. By the mid-1960s, 26 'independent' chiefs and Tribal Authorities had been established in Sekhukhuneland and the paramountcy was in danger of complete collapse.

Morwamotše died in 1965. After a fierce tussle which gave rise to accusations of witchcraft and ended with the departure of rival contenders from the village, Morwamotše's wife Mankopodi assumed office as regent for her minor son, Rhyne. From the royal lineage of Manganeng village, she had a forceful personality. In the declining years of her husband's life, she had played an increasingly prominent political role. Once she assumed office, she promoted the view that the only way to save the paramountcy was to reach an accommodation with the BAD. In 1968 she agreed to establish a Tribal Authority at Mohlaletse and was rewarded with the chairmanship of the regional authority and recognition as paramount. She insisted that headmen who had remained loyal to Mohlaletse should also enjoy recognition as chiefs and this led to the establishment of a further 29 chiefs and Tribal Authorities.

By 1970 the district of Sekhukhuneland, which, 15 years previously had three recognised chiefs, boasted 54 *magoši*. Many of the chiefs who had been appointed before 1968 were reluctant to submit to the authority of Mohlaletse, and this caused conflicts in the heart of the polity which fester to this day. The urban leadership of Fetakgomo was appalled by what it saw as Mankopodi's capitulation, and its relationship with Mohlaletse ruptured. But there was little Fetakgomo could do to prevent this turn of events.[6]

The remaining deportees who were finally allowed to return home experienced a similar sense of betrayal. Many came back heavy-hearted, feeling that their struggles and sacrifices had been in vain. Kgagudi Maredi, for example, returned to his family after 11 years in King William's Town, amidst praises for being a man prepared 'to die for the land' only to find 'that they have accepted it, I found that they have accepted it, *that* is what broke my heart.'[7]

For many migrants and villagers, the establishment of Bantu Authorities sounded the death knell of chieftainship. But some of the worst fears were allayed when 'the Trust' was not extended to the old locations. Most initially resigned themselves to the new system as yet another symptom of the colonial degradation of an institution which they still valued highly. And, despite its ultimate surrender, the fact that the paramountcy had held out for so long helped to ensure that it retained a degree of popular legitimacy. While suspicions of the motives of individual chiefs reached new heights, chieftainship was still seen as central to the maintenance of cherished rights and values. But there was also a widespread awareness of the changes which were being wrought in the institution. And the BAD's interventions in succession disputes to ensure that sympathetic candidates achieved office further eroded confidence in chiefs and led to a rash of intractable local-level disputes.[8]

A substructure of headmen, which had not previously enjoyed state recognition or material support, and which in consequence had needed to maintain significant levels of local legitimacy, now enjoyed both state recognition as chiefs and received salaries. Councillors began to be appointed by the chiefs and some were salaried. They also increasingly enjoyed office as a result of connections to the chief rather than, as in the past, representing a significant segment – usually a *kgoro* (ward) – of the community. Chiefs also exploited their position in new bureaucratic structures to buttress their power. For example, chiefs began to be entrusted with registering work-seekers through the newly established tribal labour bureaux which formed the first line in the increasingly elaborate system of influx control. It became common practice amongst chiefs to refuse to register recalcitrant subjects, thus jeopardising their possibility of employment.

The cumulative effect of these and other changes was to deepen the gulf between chiefs and their subjects and to make *magoši* even less responsive or beholden to the communities they ruled. This was a process which was far from uniform, and there were individual office holders who ruled with some care for their subjects and maintained significant levels of support. But few doubted that the ideal that *kgoši ke kgoši ka batho*, which had been such an important rallying point for Sebatakgomo, was becoming ever more remote from the realities of rural life. [9]

The Knot Tightens

This political restructuring had major ramifications for the residual freedoms of the inhabitants of Sekhukhuneland. It was accompanied by changes which, although less visible, had even more profound consequences for the future of the society. Penned in by tightening influx control and swelled by large-scale immigration, the population of Sekhukhuneland soared. It rose rapidly in the 1960s, virtually doubled between 1970 and 1980 and maintained high levels of growth in the early 1980s.[10] The trickle of people moving into Sekhukhuneland from the white farms turned into a torrent as the struggles over labour tenancy reached a new climax. During the 1960s, the heady days of high apartheid and economic growth, 'separate development' was pursued with renewed zeal, and officials and farmers moved decisively to put an end to African families' access to land in 'white' farming areas. Although there were sometimes disagreements between male household heads and their wives and children over how to respond to these pressures, many tenant families did not wait to be given their marching orders. Egged on by their children, tired of racism on the farms, restrictions on access to urban employment, and the miserly provision of education, they *trekked* to neighbouring reserve areas. While some were able to take advantage of connections to villages in the old locations, most had little choice but to head for 'Trust' land. As Daniel Mnisi put it,

> We came to the Trusts as we were tired of working on the farms. We were told that at the Trusts one could own a piece of land ... Conditions are slightly better ... compared to the farms. One can wake up at his own time in the morning.[11]

And Mr Malapo recalled having heard that, in Sekhukhuneland, 'people are free, children can go to school and they could work wherever they wanted'.[12]

The 'Trust', which had seemed so restrictive and intrusive from the perspective of the inhabitants of the old locations in the 1950s, appeared for labour tenants on white farms by the 1960s to be a relative haven which offered them at least some autonomy from white control and room for economic manoeuvre.

The 1960s also brought an intensified onslaught against settlements described in the grotesque language of the times as 'black spots'. These blemishes on officially defined white landscapes consisted of rent tenants, residents of mission stations and communities which had purchased farms. The support for apartheid policies from the leaders of the Berlin Missionary Society (BMS) bore bitter fruit for their followers when mission stations which had been built up over almost a century were closed down. Not even Botshabelo near Middelburg, which had once rivalled the power of ZAR and the Pedi Kingdom and had become a regional economic and educational dynamo, was spared. And, in a final tragic act in a long history of dispute over rights to land on these stations, the residents were defined as mere tenants. They were therefore compensated only – and inadequately – for their houses and not for the fields they lost.

Starting in the 1870s, a number of groups had left the mission stations in an attempt to gain independent access to land. Some succeeded in purchasing farms – such as Boomplaats in Lydenburg and Doornkop in Middelburg – before the 1913 Land Act prohibited this practice. Many of these communities, along with other groups which secured land outside the reserves, flourished on the basis of a combination of migrancy and market production in the early decades of the twentieth century. But, from the 1940s, they became increasingly congested and a tenant class expanded as a result of immigration from the surrounding farms and barriers to further land purchases. State pressure on these communities mounted from the late 1940s and gave rise to protracted resistance involving Sebatakgomo as well as national political movements in the 1950s. However, in a general climate of deepening political repression, most communities were eventually defeated by a combination of tactics of divide and rule and naked coercion.

Mary Pule recalled the end of protracted resistance at Doornkop when in 1974, in the middle of winter, the peace of the settlement was shattered by the roar of government trucks. 'Small boys of soldiers came with everything to kill us.' Heavily armed police moved through the town breaking windows and throwing sections of roofing to the ground. People gathered in small frightened groups. Others locked themselves into their houses. The police started shooting the locks off the doors. They kept shouting: 'Where are your things? Get your things!' Bundles of belongings were slung on to the waiting trucks. This destruction went on for four days. When Mary saw the mangled remnants of her house being unloaded in a resettlement camp in Lebowa, she remembers that 'I felt sick, and I cried until I didn't have tears any more.'[13]

Landowners who accepted resettlement received some compensatory land in Trust areas but this was of poorer quality and more remote from markets. Farmers who had spent years developing their agricultural enterprises and who had built dams and irrigation canals had to start all over again. As in the case of the mission stations, tenants were not entitled to compensation for the access to land which they forfeited.[14]

Labour tenants, rent tenants and landowners all found themselves consigned to 'Trust' lands. Those who moved in the 1940s and 1950s were subject to betterment controls and could retain only limited amounts of stock, but were often able to secure access to fields. However, as the movement of people gathered momentum, 'planning' came to involve the squeezing of more and more people on to smaller and smaller plots of land. By the mid-1960s, officials abandoned attempts to provide agricultural land. New settlers on Trust land could only hope to secure quarter acre building plots and had to dispose of their stock before they assumed residence. This trend also affected individuals who had owned land prior to their removal. By 1972, only those who had at least 40 acres were given compensatory Trust land.[15]

Resettlement and rehabilitation refashioned the villages of Sekhukhuneland. The established villages, which had nestled in the foothills with a core of interconnected *kgoro*, frayed at the edges as processes of change and pressure on space led to more fragmented and expansive building patterns. Unplanned towns sprawled outwards from key centres like Jane Furse hospital. But the Trust lands witnessed even more radical transformations. From the 1950s, betterment villages mushroomed across the veld. Distinct residential stands were laid out on grids and set boldly upon the plains amidst fenced fields. These settlements were dubbed *malaeneng* (the place of lines) by their inhabitants in recognition of their dreadful symmetry.

From the 1960s, closer settlements were established to cater for individuals who were endorsed out of towns, or who came from farms and mission stations and were denied land rights. The families consigned to these villages were required to dispose of all livestock, except their poultry. The popular designation of these villages was *tickylaene* (three-penny lines) which signified both symmetry and the complete dependence on cash for survival within these villages. The 'industrial villages' which had so excited policy makers since the 1930s had finally come into being. But they had done so on the basis not of a newly created farmer class and local industry, but of mass resettlement and draconian control over movement.[16]

While households without land and livestock were most starkly corralled within closer settlements, they became an increasingly important aspect of all communities in the area from the 1960s.

This development was least acute in the established villages in old reserve areas which experienced relatively low levels of immigration. But the capacity of even these villages to juggle land allocations was exhausted. In a context of intensifying land shortage, chiefs asserted their control over the allocation of any land that was available and expected payment to secure sympathetic consideration of requests for plots. And the fragmentation of fields and landlessness mounted with each succeeding generation.

By the 1980s, better and larger lands were dominated by the ruling strata within chiefdoms while longer-established members of the villages also retained access to land. Between 20 and 40 per cent of households were completely landless, with recent settlers being the least likely to enjoy land rights. But the apparently stark division between landed and landless was blurred by the fact that some landless families were able to borrow unused land while other landholders were unable to muster the resources to put their land under production.

The position was even bleaker in most betterment villages, where it was common for more than half the population to lack land rights. In this situation, inheritance was often vital to securing rights in land. The ideal was that sons inherited a portion of the land allocated to their parents. But over time, middle sons and then even the eldest son were excluded and inheritance was concentrated on youngest sons who were expected, in return, to take care of their parents in their declining years.[17]

The decades after 1960 also witnessed a radical reduction in the importance of cattle in the local economy. The diminution of cattle numbers was an integral part of 'the Trust' and, as noted above, settlers on these lands from the 1960s were increasingly prohibited from bringing any livestock with them. But even in old reserve areas, where state controls were considerably less exacting, cattle declined in significance. Recurrent drought and encroachment on grazing land through settlement and cultivation took their toll. Also crucial was the expansion of schooling, which diminished the availability of youths for extended periods of herding. This led in the 1960s to the collapse of the cattle post system which had allowed for flexible exploitation of grazing resources. Cattle were instead kraaled in villages, and this led to the exhaustion of the local veld, with animals having to be moved long distances to water and grazing every day.

It also increased the probability of erosion and of damage being done to crops. The responsibility of herding cattle fell more and more on retired migrants who typically managed the stock of a group of relatives. Animals, weakened by this combination of circumstances, were ill-equipped to withstand either drought or disease. Every year in the spring, large numbers of cows and calves died before the first summer rains provided relief. Cattle were concentrated in fewer and fewer hands and many families faced mounting obstacles in securing the use of a span for ploughing at the appropriate time.

From the 1960s onwards, tractors became the dominant means of working the land. Each community that accepted the establishment of a Tribal Authority was given a tractor and, while these rarely survived more than a couple of seasons, they considerably widened the appreciation of the speed and range of this form of traction. As the Tribal Authority tractors collapsed, private tractor owners – usually shopkeepers – found a considerably enlarged market for their services. And it was often easier for migrants to send back cash for the hire of a tractor than to attempt to ensure that a span could be procured at the right time. The increasing use of tractors and the lack of herders led many families to sell off cattle or not to replace those that died. Cattle theft also flourished in the context of inadequately supervised stock. Stolen cattle were either sold to local butchers or slaughtered immediately and the meat sold at knock-down prices.

By the 1980s, only a minority of households in the region still had stock and the herds that remained were dominated by goats and sheep. In previous generations, eldest sons had expected to inherit the custodianship of family herds, but this aspect of inheritance now dwindled in significance. And a span of oxen drawing a plough, already a rare sight in 1976, is virtually unheard of in contemporary Sekhukhuneland.

It was not only draught power which was forfeited. The vital contributions that milk had made to the diet of households and manure had made to fertilising of fields were also lost. And the celebration of cattle which had once been such a central element in – especially male – Pedi culture now had a hollow ring.[18]

Migrants and Households

Transformations within the migrant labour system were less visible but equally important for the changing face of Sekhukhuneland. As the 1950s progressed, influx control started to bite, particularly after the system of labour bureaux had been fully established. Some migrants managed to slip through the ever-finer mesh of this net but increasing numbers of men found themselves with little option but to follow formal channels of recruitment and accept the extended contracts which they had previously shunned. They were also faced with heightened obstacles to their escape from the most unattractive and lowly paid jobs in industry. After 1970, the slump in the growth of employment in the South African economy meant that the number of work-seekers from Sekhukhuneland raced ahead of the creation of new jobs. By 1976, labour bureau day at the magistrates offices was a chilling sight as crowds of desperate men crowded round the handful of recruiters hoping to be amongst the tiny minority who would secure work.

This context, and real increases in the level of mine wages after 1973, also resulted in some men returning to mine labour which had thought they had left far behind them. But, while the period of economic growth in the late 1970s brought some relief, the sharp downturn after 1983 had dire consequences for Sekhukhuneland.[19]

Isaac Sekhukhune recalled how,

> in the late '70s and early '80s business was good. People were working and sending money home until [after] 1983 when I realised that most of my customers in the shop were blue card people, waiting for unemployment insurance claims at Schoonoord. They had been laid off and had to come back and wait for claims. It was all over, people working in the firms, factory workers were retrenched.[20]

This was not a temporary setback. Retrenched migrants and new work-seekers battled to find work for the rest of the decade as employment opportunities stagnated.

Migrant associations also changed in form and focus. The various village-based burial societies continued to function but many were subject to processes of fission and regionalisation. By the 1980s, a range of societies was present in most local and migrant communities. The benefits offered by these groups tended to be more limited than had been the case in the 1950s, and migrants had started to join more than one group to compensate for this.

Although burial societies continued to provide opportunities for workers to discuss their concerns about developments at home, their fragmented nature meant that they were less inclusive and influential arenas for discussion than they had been. But these societies did continue to offer a channel of communication between migrants and chiefs, and to be used for debates about community issues and the collection of funds for community projects.

There was often, however, an uneasy relationship as chiefs attempted to use burial societies to assert controls over migrants while the latter at times attempted to curb abuses of chiefly power. Considerable disquiet was expressed by workers over the changing nature of chieftainship and the behaviour of individual chiefs. But the pressure that migrants could bring to bear was intermittent and it was usually only over the Christmas period, when large numbers of men returned to the villages, that they could exercise real influence. Chiefs and councillors who feared challenges to their authority went out of their way to avoid convening meetings at this time of year.[21]

Migrant workers, under threat both at home and at work, were receptive to organisation by the independent trade union movement, which started to expand rapidly from the late 1970s. Migrant networks were mobilised through the hostels on the Rand once again, but this organisational drive focused on pay and conditions in the towns and not on rural transformations. In the 1980s, many unions did become increasingly sensitive to 'community' issues, but the problems with which they concerned themselves were in urban townships. The difficulties facing migrants in their home villages were rarely given attention.

As unions grew, they also attracted larger numbers of young educated workers from the townships who often came to dominate leadership positions. Their manner and concerns did not sit easily with older men from the countryside. But unions did not only make their presence felt in distant cities. In the late 1960s and 1970s the Steelpoort River Valley, which lies on the southern boundary of Sekhukhuneland, saw a surge in mining, especially of chrome, vanadium and platinum. While many of the mines were carefully situated to the south of Steelpoort and thus beyond the borders of Lebowa, the workers were accommodated in industrial townships and hostels within the 'homeland's' boundaries. In the early 1980s, the Metal and Allied Workers Union began to recruit members in the area, and came to play an important role on both sides of the river.[22]

But the most important change of all involved the beginnings of large-scale female labour migrancy from the early 1960s. Some women had participated in migrant labour from the 1930s but they were relatively few in number and mainly from Christian families. The radical transformation of the rural economy, which took place from the late 1950s, saw increasing numbers of families without land or livestock and almost entirely reliant on cash. The dwindling availability of these resources also reduced incentives for male migrants to remit part of their income. Some men responded by encouraging their wives to seek work in town, a rather larger number became even more erratic in the dispatch of money and sent a still-smaller proportion of their incomes home. Others established alternative relationships in the towns and stopped remitting at all.

In these circumstances, even households that still retained land rights were often not able to plough because of lack of cash. Some support could be derived from networks of kin and neighbours, but there was little long-term option for households which did not benefit from money remitted by fathers, husbands, brothers or sons but for some female members to seek wage labour.[23]

The end of the labour tenancy system on neighbouring white farms brought a considerably expanded demand for seasonal labour. By the 1970s, it was widespread practice for white farmers to travel to the villages to recruit. After payment to the chief to secure his blessing, women were called together at the *mošate* and offered work. Farmers' bakkies and trucks crammed full of women careering along the rutted and potholed roads at breakneck speed became a common sight. While seasonal labour was a vital source of cash for some households, it was an intermittent and badly paid form of employment. Increasingly more attractive – especially to women who had some schooling – was domestic work. But they had to run the gauntlet to find employment. It was illegal for them to travel to urban areas to look for work, and the paltry offering of labour contracts at the local labour bureaux were for men only.[24]

Women were often initially assisted to find employment and accommodation by kin or migrants from their home villages. Their first jobs were usually in the most poorly paid reaches of domestic service – in the nearby towns or in Indian and white working-class suburbs – but as they gained experience they looked for work in the better-paying white middle-class residential areas.

Female migrants also participated in a range of migrant associations. They initially joined burial societies and independent churches frequented by men from their own home areas. But some women also formed groups independently of their male compatriots. They established *megodišano* – rotating saving clubs – in which they took turns as recipients of pooled cash or goods. These *megodišano* helped women maintain the discipline of saving and periodically provided them with significant resources to send home.[25]

The range and nature of women's associations remains to be explored fully, but there is a rich account of the how women from Lebowa formed *Kiba* 'music groups'. These were started by mainly single or divorced women who, after a period of performing with male groups, established independent groups and crafted their own version of this musical form. Their associations also provided for a variety of forms of mutual support and were one element of the elaboration of a 'Sotho' identity which, while couched in the language of tradition, was also grounded in the profound upheavals which had marked participants' lives.[26]

The songs and reflections of members of the *Kiba* groups vividly illustrate that the accelerated processes of change since the late 1950s have often not been conceptualised within the society in terms which are readily captured in crude modernist discourses. Male migrants, for example, lamented the loss of land, cattle and the co-option of chiefly power, and some joined trade unions. But they did not necessarily see themselves simply or even primarily as 'workers'. Many men – including individuals who lacked land and livestock – continued to elaborate a vision in which chiefs would once again rule 'by the people'. And the image of Sekhukhuneland as a refuge from the disorderly and dangerous world of *makgoweng* remained potent.

Bopedi was still regarded as a place were *koma* (initiation), *'molao'* (law) and *'setšo'* (tradition) might prevail. Many men saw it as a far better place to build a household, raise children and ultimately retire. And women who entered urban employment because of the absence of male remittances did not simply couch their decisions in terms of the collapse of established practices. They instead spoke of the appropriate performance of duties within the family. Helen Matilja, for example, explained her decision to take work as a domestic servant by the fact that: 'In *Sotho* the oldest child should support the younger ones.'[27] She thus invoked the obligation placed upon an oldest son to act as a custodian of family assets as a way of legitimating her role as a wage-earning daughter. This 'discourse … operates to endorse the substitution of a daughter for a son while retaining notions of duty and proper behaviour intact'.[28]

Despite the searing transformations being experienced, the households, villages and chiefdoms of Sekhukhuneland remained as vivid reference points in conceptions of home and in an imagined world of continuity which sustained both male and female migrants in often harsh and lonely lives in the city.

While the flow of remittances into households faltered, there was another source of family income which grew in importance from the 1960s – pensions. Urban Africans received pensions after 1943, but the state concluded that rural Africans should not be provided with benefits which would 'conflict with or break down their tribal food sharing habits'.[29] It was not until the mid-1960s, in the context of official resolve to prevent urbanisation, that men and women in the countryside, of 65 years and over, were granted pensions. In Sekhukhuneland, the registration of pensioners coincided closely with the spread of Tribal Authorities and became a crucial source of patronage for newly elevated chiefs. Chiefs summoned people from appropriate initiation groups to the *mošate* for registration and countersigned completed forms. As a local official at the time recalls, 'that strengthened the position of the chief in his community. [I]f you were not law abiding, surely you would not expect him to be helpful when it comes to pension applications.' In the 1960s, supporters of the Khuduthamaga 'even if they qualified they wouldn't get it, they just wouldn't get it ... while some would get pensions even if they didn't conform in terms of their age because their chief had embraced *Boipušo'*.[30] Pensions in the 1970s were manipulated in similar fashion to reward supporters of the ruling party in Lebowa and punish its opponents.

As other sources of income withered, the significance of pensions to household economies increased. While they started from a very low base, average African pensions nonetheless rose in real (1975) terms from R67 per annum in 1970 to R162 in 1981.[31] In many villages in the early 1980s, pensions which amounted to R30 a month were second only to remittances in overall significance for household income, while land and livestock lagged ever further behind.[32] But by no means all the individuals who were entitled to pensions actually received them. While political discrimination played a part, the main culprits were bureaucratic red tape, corruption and incompetence. Many old people waited in poverty and in vain for months and years. Agnes Mohlatsi, from Bothashoek closer settlement, commented in 1981 that

> people in this place have been waiting for four to six years. This is what happens if you can't sign your name, if you print with your thumb. Then they say: 'No, we will send the papers to Pretoria.' We think that once we have printed with our thumb, the officials at the magistrates office take the money for themselves. If this is not so, then why do we never receive the money? ... And some people can't prove their age since they have no birth certificate ... then the official says 'You are still young, go off and get married again so that your husband can support you.'[33]

Nonetheless, when the Lebowa pension van visited villages every second month, the payouts provided a major cash injection into the local economy. And a colourful cross-section of hawkers and petty traders followed the van from village to village. Pension day was also market day when people who had been eking out an existence for weeks could for once again spend a little.

Excluding a tiny minority of salaried individuals and beneficiaries of established businesses, households which benefited from regular remittances were the most economically secure. They were also more likely to be able to invest in crop production and sustain a herd. At the other end of the spectrum were the most vulnerable households, which lacked income from either remittances or pensions.

Even households which retained land rights often did not have the cash required to plough and plant. But some were able to take advantage of a local form of sharecropping which evolved in the 1970s called *tema ka tema*. This system allowed a plot holder to have a portion of his or her land ploughed in return for an equivalent piece of land which the tractor owner could use for his own benefit. But, in most cases, members of households who did not receive remittances or pensions had little option but to seek some cash income from informal activities such as washing, building, cleaning, hoeing, harvesting, hawking and brewing, which provided sporadic and often minuscule amounts of money. A women described how, in 1981,

> When I have money I buy fruit from a lorry which comes from Groblersdal. Then I sell it to people. This is because I haven't found proper work since I came here. This is not real work, it gives only money to buy a small packet of sugar, tea, some bread. Some women here start doing this fruit selling and then stop because there are so many doing it that not all of them get customers. Sometimes if you are selling fruit in the street, you get arrested by the police, because you have no licence. The licence costs R10.[34]

If income from these kinds of activities proved elusive or insufficient, assistance from kin or neighbours provided a lifeline. But if this help was not reciprocated, it diminished sharply. And in the difficult circumstances of contemporary Sekhukhuneland, there is an increasingly narrow range of kin who can legitimately be approached for help.

In Sekhukhuneland, in common with other reserve areas, the dominant tendency in the twentieth century has been for the importance of larger kinship/residential groupings within villages, and especially settlements, to diminish. This process was far from uniform, but the view expressed in 1961 that 'there is no *kgoro*. In the old days everyone lived together and we had cattle. But now we are like Christians, each man's home is a *kgoro*,' would have had powerful resonances in most communities.[35]

Recent analysis has tended to place much greater attention on the role and composition of individual households. But it would be wrong to imagine – as some have – that the consequence of the process of fragmentation for households has been a simple transition from extended to nuclear families. In practice, a wide variety of differing and constantly shifting forms of household exist, very few of which meet the definition of a nuclear family. The absence of both male and female migrants and the presence of – variously – siblings, grandparents and grandchildren makes for a vast array of household forms.

Despite this complexity, it is possible for an imprudent historian to venture a number of bald generalisations about the changing forms and dynamics of households. One change involved the significant increase in the proportion of female-headed households, albeit it in a wide variety of forms. This was hardly a new phenomenon, and probably the most distinctive development involved an increase in the number of female-*linked* extended households composed of a woman, her daughters and her daughters' children. These households suffered from the absence of male remittances but could pool other kinds of resources.

The most economically vulnerable households of all often consisted of lone women and their children, lacking access to either remittance or pension income. The declining commitment of some migrants to their rural households also led to a greater reliance being placed on assistance between brothers and sisters. In these cases, the 'traditional' cattle linkage of siblings from the same household was invoked in explanation and in support of evolving practices. The contending claims made on migrants by their wives and sisters which sometimes resulted made for deeply distressing conflicts. It also became increasingly common for children to be left in the care of grandmothers, sisters or in a wide variety of other fostering arrangements while their parents worked in the cities and on the farms. Thus grandparents and aunts, who had conventionally been indulgent figures one step removed from battles over domestic authority, were transformed into frontline troops in struggles for control in the household.[36]

While crumbling mud huts with rusting iron roofs held in place by boulders bore mute testimony to desperate circumstances, houses with brick walls, glistening windows, pitched roofs and ample garages, also became an increasingly common sight from the 1960s. This symbolised the fact that by no means all fortunes were in decline. Some of these homes were built with migrant savings and remittances but most bore witness to the expansion of local bureaucracy and business. From the 1960s, and especially after Lebowa achieved self-governing status in 1972, there was a steady increase in the numbers of black civil servants, teachers and nurses. Many of these were concentrated in Lebowakgomo and other administrative centres in the region, but the handful of salaried individuals – including chiefs – who lived or maintained houses in the villages and settlements constituted the wealthiest stratum of local society. Their ranks were swelled by African clergy in the employ of mainstream churches and leaders of independent churches with substantial followings.[37]

Alongside chiefly homes and tribal offices, the most elaborate buildings belonged to local businessmen. Mabowe James Sekhukhune and others blazed a trail in the 1950s which many were to follow in the ensuing decades as white traders were forced out of the area, and large commercial concerns were prohibited from setting up shop. But business licences remained far from easy to obtain in the 1960s and 1970s. Aspirant shopowners had to show that they had adequate capital, and restrictions were placed on new shops being opened within a specified radius of existing stores. They also had to win approval from chiefs and councillors, which could be an expensive process. And civil servants – including teachers – were prohibited from applying for licences.

Successful applicants came from a variety of backgrounds. They included men who had experience of working in stores either in Sekhukhuneland or on the Rand, and migrants who invested their savings, and their hopes for a secure retirement, in shops. Some were individuals who had been frustrated by the difficulties in securing licences in urban townships and turned instead to the villages of their birth. Despite the formal prohibitions on government employees holding licences, many were civil servants who used their salaries, experience and the opportunities presented by office to establish businesses. They secured licences in the names of close relatives and transferred them into their own names when they were sufficiently well-established to allow them to retire from public service.[38]

The example of K provides an insight into many of the processes at work. His father was a relative of a prominent businessman and had worked as a shop assistant. After matriculating, K secured a job as a clerk in the magistrates offices and gained wide experience of different administrative divisions and local postings. In 1972, he became aware that Lebowa was planning to introduce citizenship cards. K bought a passport photo camera and managed, using a nominee, to secure a local contract to take pictures for the new cards. This proved to be a very profitable venture and within a matter of months he had secured the R1 800 capital required to apply for a business licence. This was initially issued in his father's name.

By 1973, there was already a surfeit of general dealers in the area and K was only able to obtain a licence for a hardware store. But this proved to be fortunate, as he was able to take advantage of rapidly growing local demand for building materials and his business prospered. By 1980, he was in a position to buy nine tractors and made extensive use of the *tema ka tema* system to secure access to land. In good years, he cultivated up to 50 hectares on his own account. He also ploughed for cash and was eventually able to hire a piece of land from a local hospital on which he established a piggery and a market garden. The recession after 1983, however, found him seriously overextended and, with a mounting cash-flow crisis, his business came close to complete collapse. He battled to keep his shop and farm going at the same time as maintaining his children at private schools.[39]

This history both suggests the importance of bureaucratic connections and also hints at other wider trends. The small pockets of commercial farming that emerged in Lebowa in these years were much more likely to be the by-product of success in commerce or the underpinnings of a significant salary than an outgrowth of production on the land. Equally, while K's business ventures had their own very particular trajectory, the timing of their rise and fall had much wider resonances. Rising population and the economic upswing of the late 1970s meant that, while unemployment continued to be an issue, there was healthy inflow of remittances into the local economy and a wide variety of businesses prospered.

One of the most dramatic increases was reflected in liquor stores and 'bar lounges', where those with money could immerse themselves in bottled beer. This had a tragic consequence, in that the income from home brewing, which had long provided a vital lifeline for local women, plummeted. The apparently easy pickings in commerce led to growing pressure for the easing of licensing controls. In 1978, the Lebowa Peoples Party, which controlled the homeland government, loosened the regulations in an attempt to shore up its support base and because of the kickbacks to its members who were involved in the allocation of licences. The consequence was a flood of new shops which soon began to outstrip the levels of local demand.

The recession after 1983 sent shock waves through a commercial world built on sand. But the granting of new licences and overtrading barely abated as retrenched workers used their redundancy cheques to enter into a wide variety of trading ventures. While some businesses continued to prosper, many floundered. And a question posed with increasing insistence in Sekhukhuneland was 'why do some succeed where so many fail?'[40]

Education and Youth Culture

In this context of dwindling herds and diminishing fields, the experience of growing up in Sekhukhuneland was transformed. The most significant development in these decades involved the establishment of mass education. By the 1950s primary schools, mainly located in the largest villages, were scattered across the region and there was one local secondary school at Jane Furse. Closed in the mid-1950s by the Anglican Church in protest against the introduction of Bantu Education, its place was initially taken by two junior secondary schools. But from the 1960s onwards, there was a rapid proliferation of schools in Sekhukhuneland.

Migrants, particularly those working in 'the firms' (factories), became increasingly convinced of the importance of schooling in obtaining better pay and conditions, and their commitment to securing an education for their children increased. Although Bantu Education was viewed with considerable suspicion, it nonetheless appeared to offer education which was not church controlled, and resources to expand rural schooling.

The proliferation of Tribal Authorities also encouraged the spread of schools. Many of the newly appointed chiefs and their supporters felt that their recently defined autonomy should find expression in the establishment of separate educational institutions. The provision of school buildings in rural areas was a responsibility which fell on local communities. The state in theory contributed on a Rand for Rand basis once classrooms had been completed but in practice found a wide variety of ways to minimise its obligations. Villagers and migrants carried the burden of fundraising and construction and achieved impressive results. By the end of the 1960s, most villages in Sekhukhuneland boasted a primary school, and the early 1970s witnessed the proliferation of junior secondary schools. In the late 1970s and the early 1980s senior secondary schools – with classes up to matric – were widely established. In a surge of activity between 1977 and 1982, the number of senior secondary schools in Lebowa almost quadrupled, increasing from 38 to 146.[41]

But the resources of time and money which communities invested in erecting schools in the hope of securing a better future for their children brought disappointing returns. For, while buildings blossomed in the veld, the quality of education provided within their walls withered. Until the 1950s, the training of black teachers from and for Sekhukhuneland was dominated by missionary-run colleges. Institutions like Botshabelo, Pax, Kilnerton, Grace Dieu, Bethesda and others had been – in varying degree – under-resourced, authoritarian in their methods and milieu, and racist in their treatment of black staff and students. Nonetheless, they had boasted relatively well-qualified and committed educators and had produced teachers who were thoroughly trained in their chosen fields and displayed considerable dedication to their professions.[42]

These teacher training colleges, already weakened by financial woes and wracked by student unrest, were a prime target in Verwoerd's campaign to entrench Bantu Education. What, after all, could be more important in moulding the hearts and minds of the next generations of 'Bantu' children than getting a firm grip on the training of their teachers? Verwoerd also declared his intention to keep institutions for advanced education away from the urban environment and to establish them, as far as possible, in the reserves.

Of the 38 colleges in existence in the country as a whole in 1948, 26 were closed down in the ten years after 1956, with the first effects being felt in the Transvaal. In the institutions that survived, Afrikaans-speaking principals were appointed, debate was discouraged, fundamental pedagogics entrenched and white, English-speaking staff phased out. The colleges were tethered to

Afrikaans tertiary institutions which determined their curriculum and pro-vided a model of stifling and sterile methods of instruction. The colleges were increasingly staffed by black lecturers but the new appointees by and large 'simply copied the authoritarian methods they had learned from their Afrikaner mentors'.[43]

At first, these changes had little effect at school level as the majority of teachers had received their training in mission institutions. Some educators were bitterly opposed to Bantu Education and a handful of teachers resigned, but most were reluctant to mount any open challenge to the new system. In-stead, they devoted their energies to overcoming the considerable challenges involved in switching to teaching in the vernacular without appropriate re-sources.[44]

But as schools started to multiply, this picture changed. Many of the older teachers retired or were promoted out of the classroom and their places were taken by the products of the new colleges. The growing demand for teachers and local political pressure led to the establishment of new colleges and rapid expansion of college places. The number of training colleges serving Lebowa increased from three to seven. But few staff with appropriate qualifications were available and even those who had formal training lacked relevant expe-rience. Recent graduates from the University of the North, for example, who had never worked in a school were increasingly set to work training teachers. The demand for teachers, particularly for high schools, soon far outran the capacity of the colleges to provide them. Teachers with primary teaching cer-tificates and diplomas were entrusted with secondary school classes. Increasingly, private teachers who lacked any formal teaching qualification but had junior or senior certificates were pressed into service at all levels. Many of the teachers, fresh out of college or school, were little older than the bulk of their charges. While teachers of North Sotho or biblical studies were soon in plentiful supply, there was a desperate shortage of competence in maths and science. Levels of proficiency in English declined. As an older teacher observed somewhat caustically, 'when the missionaries left, I don't know whether they left with their English or what. But English broke down just there.'[45]

By the 1970s and 1980s, education was seen by a cross-section of the so-ciety as being fundamental to survival and essential to any kind of advance. But rapid, poorly planned and resourced expansion had dismaying results. On the one hand, despite communities' herculean efforts, the capacity of schools had been easily outstripped by the growth in numbers of pupils. The demand for staff and equipment for the schools, on the other hand, far exceeded the supply of teachers and resources. The consequence was a proliferation of schools with massively congested classrooms, often lacking doors, blackboards, desks and windows, which froze in winter and baked (and leaked) in summer.

Many classes, particularly in primary schools but also in secondary schools, were conducted outdoors. Most schools lacked libraries and even the most rudimentary scientific and technical equipment. Textbooks were in very short supply and pupils had to purchase their own books, stationery and uniforms from intermittent and expensive local supplies. Students who failed to pay their fees could be excluded from schools and those who came to school improperly dressed ran the risk of a similar fate.[46]

Teachers, often young, poorly trained and underqualified, faced massive classes with pathetic resources and many veered between cynicism and despair. There were, of course, teachers who were both gifted and committed, but the overall picture, painted by students and older teachers, of conditions in the schools by the early 1980s is bleak. Teachers often failed to come to classes or, if they did, arrived unprepared or even drunk. Students were taught by rote and discouraged from asking questions. The sexual harassment of female students was a recurring problem. Tiny Mankge recalled, for example, that:

> There was this teacher and he wanted me ... But I didn't like that. I told him straight out that I won't do that thing. So the following day we were all wearing caps to school. He came and said 'why are you wearing a cap?' I said 'no, it is a uniform'. He said 'I see you are growing up, this is why you do these things.' So he called me and beat me for that and I mean I could not do anything![47]

If a girl fell pregnant in this or any other way she was excluded from the school. But Tiny's experience points to another feature of school life. Some teachers, deeply alienated by the impossible context in which they worked, uncertain of their subjects and fearing for the collapse of their authority, literally hit out. While corporal punishment had long been a feature of both Pedi society and local educational institutions, the recent products of teachers' training colleges took its use to new heights. Boys and girls alike were variously slapped, beaten with canes and lashed with sjamboks for offences which included not having full school uniforms, being unable to pay school fees on time, arriving late, asking difficult questions or failing tests. Children from families which struggled to maintain them at school thus suffered additional punishment and humiliation. And the sjambok tucked under some teachers' arms became the ever-present symbol and source of their authority.[48]

The creation of a rather more uniform youth culture was a significant consequence of the expansion of schools. Changing circumstances lessened the reluctance to educate females, and the sex ratios in the schools had tilted very slightly in favour of girls by the early 1980s. The previous pattern in which the cattle post, agricultural and domestic labour, and initiation were the central shaping experiences in most youths' lives, while a minority of mainly Christian children attended schools and lived largely separate lives, was steadily eroded. More and more, school came to be the central focus of, and education a dominant value in, the lives of Christian and non-Christian alike. While initiation remained an important institution in most communities, the proportion of boys and girls who did not attend *koma* grew.

This did not, of course, mean that cleavages amongst the youth vanished: indeed, tensions and conflicts continued both in and out of school. Initiated youth snubbed their uninitiated fellows and mocked them as *majakane*, while the latter derided the 'backwardness' of the *maheitene*. And patterns of association also tended to form along these lines. Nonetheless, this common context did serve to multiply contacts and friendships across this divide and the growing enthusiasm for Western sport – particularly football – provided additional common experiences. School was also the forum in which children of recent immigrants were initially integrated into the wider society. The rapid growth of Zionist and other independent churches broadened popular participation in Christianity and contributed to the blurring of divisions. Elements of Christian ritual – prayers to open and close public meetings, for example – became a common feature of community life.[49]

From the 1960s, then, some divisions among rural youth started to narrow. A deep gulf remained, however, between the experiences of pupils in Sekhukhuneland and those who lived in the cities of the Transvaal. More than 300 kilometres of often-dreadful road with infrequent, slow and expensive transport, and an almost total absence of newspapers, coupled with Radio Lebowa's fanciful and partial version of events, ensured that most young people at schools in Sekhukhuneland secured only glimpses of the lifestyles of their urban counterparts. In the 1960s and early 1970s, it was young migrant workers who brought news of what was happening in the towns and their worlds – centred on the compound, the hostel and the factory – were remote from, if not in actual conflict with, those of urban youth.

The 1976 student-led revolt which seared its way through township after township did not find a counterpart in Sekhukhuneland. Pupils certainly were aware of what was happening. Heightened police activity and the circulation of some pamphlets helped to ensure a tense atmosphere in the area for much of the latter half of 1976. And there were isolated acts of arson and brief class boycotts. But, in the main the students stayed in school, wrote their exams and there was little in the way of open confrontation with local authorities.[50]

It was precisely this relative tranquillity in 1976 which was to reinforce a process which brought urban and rural youth into closer contact. Many migrant and even immigrant Pedi parents, confronted by a paucity of urban schools and fearing for the future of their children growing up amidst the *tsotsis* and the turbulence in the townships, chose to send their children back to Sekhukhuneland to be educated. Female domestic workers also had little choice but to send their children home. The bloodshed in 1976, the disruption of township schools and the spread of secondary schools in Lebowa strengthened this tendency. Some families actually moved back to *Bopedi* but the more common pattern was for children to be sent there to stay with grandparents, other kin or foster parents, and for their parents to send back money for their support. Sometimes they would occupy homes which their parents built in the hope of eventual retirement in Sekhukhuneland, while in other instances their parents hired accommodation for them in the villages.

There were often tensions between these pupils and local children who believed that these 'outsiders' gave themselves airs and graces. But these children, some of whom returned to the cities during the holidays, provided a vital link between evolving urban and rural youth cultures. Their urban experience provided them with a certain cachet. They, along with local children who visited relatives in the townships, relayed information about the latest forms of language, music and dress in the townships and brought records, magazines and newspapers with them to Sekhukhuneland. Youths who spent time in the city also carried news of urban politics and ultimately, as we shall explore further, brought accounts of the growth of youth organisation in the townships.[51]

But changes in youth experiences and culture were by no means confined to the schools. There was a considerable drop-out rate, particularly at secondary level. This was as much the result of financial difficulties as failure, for the policy within schools was to push students up to the next standard. Some students left school for periods to wait for, or earn, additional funds. Others repeated matric in the hope of passing. Both processes ensured a wide age-range in the schools with students in their early or mid-twenties a common feature. As external employment opportunities dwindled and the local economy atrophied, school leavers – even those who had passed matric – faced a mounting struggle to secure employment. This resulted in a growing number of unemployed youths in each village.[52]

Unable to find work, marry or establish households, many young people were trapped in social limbo. They were no longer children, and some had been initiated, but they could not make the transition to full adult status. Young men who lacked resources to pay bridewealth fathered children they could not support and the families of the young women concerned were forced to shoulder additional burdens. Youths lived in a world ruled by money but depended on begging, badgering or bullying for a share of the re-

Sekhukhuneland landscape near Glen Cowie mission station, 1987. The picture shows both the density and atomisation of settlement and the wide array of forms of housing. (*Struan Robertson*)

Women selling fruit and vegetables in Jane Furse, 1987. The produce sold was mainly bought from white farmers.

School near Ngwabe, Sekhukhuneland, 1986 *(Struan Robertson)*

Outdoor class, Moretsele School, Sekhukhuneland, 1987. *(Struan Robertson)*

Shop near Ngwabe, Sekhukhuneland, 1987. This is typical of stores in the region. Note also the youths congregated at the entrance and the stall outside.

Youths bringing home firewood from the barren hills near Mohlaletse, 1993. *(Struan Robertson)*

mittances received by their mothers or of the pensions paid to their grandparents.

Some young people battled to find avenues of escape from this predicament. But many, overwhelmed by the odds stacked against them, strapped for cash and deeply bored, congregated at local stores and were dubbed *maparkshops* as a result. The ubiquitous 'bar lounges' became a favoured venue and quickly absorbed any cash that youths secured. Some found that dagga (marijuana) helped to kill time or dabbled in trading it to the towns. A number facing a choice between taking work on nearby white farms or embarking on a life of crime took the latter option. The most common strategy was to travel to urban areas, break into houses and return home to sell the stolen goods. But some of these youths also found local victims. As a result, villagers who had long taken satisfaction in the relative absence of the disorders they saw in urban areas found that marginalised youths contributed to a marked increase in violence and theft in the countryside.[53]

Conflict, Explanation and Action

By the 1980s, the struggle to defend residual elements of economic and political autonomy which had shaped resistance in the 1950s was in disarray. The last local economic props for many households had crumbled while headmen and chiefs were sucked ever deeper into homeland structures. There was a decisive increase in dependence on remittances and mounting unemployment threatened the urban lifelines of local society. The rapid expansion of education considerably broadened youths' horizons, but recession consigned them to economic and social limbo.

Beset by these difficulties, most households also had to do daily battle to secure water and fuel. These necessities had been in short supply in the 1950s but the rapid expansion of population from the 1960s, which intensified pressures on local resources, left women and children spending long hours each day finding firewood and fetching and carrying water. With dwindling and irregular cash incomes and limited access to crops, milk and meat, the quality of diet of households suffered. Nutritional surveys carried out from the late 1980s revealed distressingly high levels of chronic malnutrition amongst children. These statistics led to fears that the potential of many youngsters was being blighted by undernutrition in the first years of life. This threat was compounded by the paucity of primary health care, by the lack of access to safe and secure sources of water and by inadequate nutritional and health education.[54]

Multiple processes of change stretched and strained the fabric of local society. Old conflicts intensified and new disputes gained momentum in both domestic and public domains. Many households survived by pooling resources, but these co-operative ventures could also be threatened by a wide variety of internal struggles. Husbands and wives, youths and their parents, wives and their mothers-in-law, brothers and sisters, grandparents and grand-children often provided vital mutual support but they could also be drawn into bitter conflicts over control of the remittances and pensions which were so vital to survival. Feelings of guilt, anger and jealousy between neighbours were heightened by rapid resettlement, disparities in material circumstances and by the growing inability or unwillingness of some households to respond to repeated requests for assistance.

Profound processes of change were often expressed in an idiom of continuity, but the disjuncture between norms and practices could become acute. For example, while villages and settlements were composed of growing numbers of female-headed and female-linked households, women were barred from formally inheriting land and livestock. As a result, they could find themselves dispossessed of resources which they had long commanded by errant husbands or sons acting with chiefly support in terms of 'customary' law. And migrants who had ceded effective authority within the household to their wives while they were in the towns sometimes encountered determined resistance when they sought to establish domestic control on their retrenchment or retirement.

It was not only gender relations that seemed topsy turvy. The authority of age was also far from secure as some youths left in the care of their mothers or grandmothers flouted the authority of elders and menaced them for money.[55]

While myriad forms of conflict – some trivial and some severe – played themselves out within households and families, the nature of chiefly power and practice were also subject to intensified criticism and debate. Despite the popular belief that chiefs should 'rule by the people', they were increasingly recast as state functionaries, manipulating bureaucratic power while resting on the active support of a fragment of their communities. And the vastly expanded number of recognised chiefs vied with one another to sustain lifestyles which displayed ostentatious levels of comfort. In this changing context, a number of recurring points of friction developed within chiefdoms. The level of chiefly exactions and their abuse of community funds became a festering issue. Families had to meet a range of levies. There was an annual 'traditional' levy which, in the 1960s, replaced the payment to the chief which every migrant had long been expected to make on his return to the village. All families now had to pay whether migrants were present or not, and the amount was steadily increased.

A second important annual levy in most villages was for the school building fund. But, beyond these payments, communities had to meet a series of specific requests. Chiefs expected their subjects to raise money to buy them cars, to build them houses and to pay the bridewealth of – at least – the *mohumagadi* (chief wife). They were also expected to deliver a variety of traditional tributes, including a portion of all beer brewed and cattle slaughtered, as well as rendering labour on the chief's lands and in the royal *kgoro*. Women living in the villages who had alternative employment were not spared from these demands on their time and school children found their studies disrupted by summonses from the *mošate* to work. And parents had to pay very stiff fees when their children attended initiation school.[56]

These demands placed a heavy burden on subjects already struggling in a context of mounting unemployment and growing numbers of households without remittances or pensions. They were also particularly resented by those families who had no access to arable land. Demands for tribute labour also caused resentment. Some women argued that 'people don't want to go and work for nothing. People know that Lebowa pays the chief ... [I]f he wants women to work for him he must pay them.'[57]

It was not only the existence or magnitude of these demands which caused discontent. The greatest anger was caused by the regularity of major misappropriation of community funds by the local elite. This was particularly marked in relation to the school building funds which communities discovered, with depressing regularity, were pitifully small or non-existent despite years of heavy payments which should have swelled the coffers to bursting. Chiefs and headmasters were often – with good grounds – believed to have colluded in the theft of this money. These accusations were an important source of acrimony in the villages and also placed considerable strain on migrants' relationship with chiefs. By the early 1980s, while few risked open criticism of chiefly rule, many gave vent to their anger about chiefly exaction and corruption behind closed doors.

The growing sense of the erosion of core relationships and values is captured from the perspective of a young man in a poem written by Mokibe Sydney Ramushu in the early 1980s.

> There is confusion between father and mother; there is confusion.
> There is confusion between parents and daughters; there is confusion.
> There is confusion between parents and sons; there is confusion.
> There is confusion between teachers and students; there is confusion.
> There is confusion between the tribal authority and the community; there is confusion.
> There is confusion between the principal and the teachers; there is confusion.
> There is confusion between teachers and students; there is confusion.
> There is confusion amongst students; there is confusion.
> There is confusion between employer and employee; there is

confusion.
There is confusion between rich and poor; there is confusion.[58]

It is not surprising, in this climate of conflict and change, that the popular perception of witchcraft being on the increase remained pervasive. As in earlier decades, people found evidence for this interpretation in the incidence of misfortune, including the sudden onset of physical or mental illness. Sickness was not understood to be merely a consequence of chance infection or stress but was viewed as a result of the displeasure of the ancestors, the jealousy of witches or the breach of taboos. The confidence of communities in the capacity of a system of chieftainship, which had been co-opted and partly discredited, to fulfil its duty in organising their defences against supernatural hazards had also been further undermined.

Both men and women were believed to practise witchcraft. The conventional view was that men were most likely to be day witches, working with magic and medicines, while women were considered to dominate the ranks of night witches and be able to pass their power on to their daughters. Suspicions of witchcraft flourished in a number of contexts but quarrels between neighbours, within households and amongst close kin provided particularly fertile seedbeds for the germination of charges of witchcraft. Husbands who wished to divorce their wives with the minimum of costs and complications found suggestions of witchcraft to be perfectly tuned instruments of severance. And while individuals thought to practise witchcraft could suffer social isolation, such a designation could be a source of some power.

People treated those thought to be witches with considerable caution. An older woman, for example, who lacked support or protection from male kin, could ensure enhanced respect by hinting that she possessed witchcraft powers. And there is also little doubt that some individuals sought to harness magical powers for their own purposes.[59]

But it was not only illness, conflict and misfortune that fed into the ongoing discussions of witchcraft within the society. It was believed that people consumed by jealousy were particularly prone to using witchcraft against the objects of their envy. And the good fortune some individuals basked in also fuelled this debate. The question posed above, as to why some succeeded where so many failed, was often at least partly answered in terms of witchcraft. Business people, in particular, were believed to rely heavily on medicines to ensure the success of their ventures. The body parts of young children were held to be an especially potent source of medicine. As one informant noted, 'businessmen, business people ... if they can get this [medicine] especially from a youngster *then* they are free to prosper'.[60]

It was also generally believed that businessmen used witchcraft to harm their competitors, and most traders sought reciprocal protection against such threats. But another source of wealth and power was believed to be control over *ditlotolwane* (zombies). Witches were believed to be able to capture the spirit of their victims before they killed them. At night they were resurrected and sent out to steal those things the witch needed. They were also used as

> the worker of the witches. They send them at night to plough the lands, to thresh the corn and bring it home, to fetch firewood and water ... You see the *baloi* (witches) are always rich and have lots of food, but you seldom see them working.[61]

Witches also prospered because they captured and tamed wild animals such as baboons and snakes or even changed people into animals and sent them out to work and to steal.

Belief in witchcraft was pervasive and provided a powerful and often-used repertoire of explanations for a wide range of processes and events. But, prior to the mid-1970s, formal accusations of witchcraft and direct action against witches were far from commonplace. The incidents that took place in the context of the Sekhukhuneland revolt represented desperate measures in extreme circumstances. In the main, individuals and households sought protection by means of magic, ritual and medicine. While other forms of employment stagnated, the numbers of *dingaka* (diviners) expanded rapidly in these decades. A wide variety of individuals adopted this calling but they had a common theme:

> his or her bones will always refer to part of your problem as being because of witchcraft. And I think that around [my village] 80% of the people are still going for that. It means that once in maybe every three months, when a person dies, you hear the same old story. And when you go to the *sangoma* (diviner) you don't allow your neighbours to see you because then they would know where your protection comes from. So the people allegedly know who are the creators of their problems, but because of the nature of the secrecy around the issue, people nurse their anger all the time. They have learned to live with their anger at the people the bones describe as witches.[62]

Zionist churches – especially the Zionist Christian Church (ZCC) which grew rapidly in these decades – also provided a sanctuary which offered measures for healing and to ward off witchcraft. These churches emphasised the reintegration of matter and spirit. For Zionists, 'the state of the body is a vital indicator of being, providing a discourse upon their location in the social material and spiritual world'.[63] They acknowledged the role of ancestors and witches in physical disorder and personal disaster, and offered the countervailing power of 'the Spirit', the cleansing properties of 'holy water' and a cohesive community. The main office bearers in these churches were men but the majority of their followers were women – often drawn from the most economically vulnerable households. In a world which appeared to be falling apart, church membership offered networks of mutual support and a sense of community which embraced men, women, ancestors and 'the Spirit'.[64]

Prior to 1976, when villagers believed that protective measures against witchcraft were proving ineffective, a complaint would be made to the chief and his councillors. If they considered the circumstances to be sufficiently serious, they called on the services of a *ngaka* from a distant place, and who was therefore presumed to be impartial, to establish who was responsible. Once identified, these individuals suffered a variety of fates. Some had their heads partially shaved and were paraded through the village. Others were fined, beaten or expelled from the community, but men and women found guilty of witchcraft were rarely killed.

The whole process had to be undertaken with considerable circumspection, as it was illegal either to accuse or punish witches. Chiefs and headmen had to weigh pressure from their subjects against the danger of official reprisal. But native commissioners were usually prepared to turn a blind eye if the process remained low key.[65]

From late in 1976, this pattern started to be redrawn into a considerably more menacing form. A wave of witch killings swept through Lebowa and, by the end of January 1977, at least 14 people had been executed. There were individual episodes of the killing of witches in the region in most of the following years. In 1984, there was another wave of executions. At least 20 individuals were killed in Lebowa and executions continued into 1985. Newspaper reports suggest that pressure for these actions came from below and that chiefs were either swept along by popular outrage or by-passed. Communities collected money to consult *dingaka*. Once they had identified the witches, the accused men and women were killed by a wide variety of means ranging through stoning, clubbing, hanging and burning, with the last method becoming increasingly common. From 1981, there are examples of tyres being used in burnings, and it is possible that the infamous 'necklace' (placement of a burning tyre around the victim's neck) drew some of its inspiration from these witch killings.

Lists of defendants in subsequent trials suggest that the majority of killers were men of a wide age-range.[66] Most of these incidents were precipitated by lightning strikes. Death by lightning was widely attributed to witchcraft. After all, what could be more awesome and apparently directed than an individual or group of people being struck down by a bolt from the heavens? This area of the Transvaal is particularly prone to violent electrical storms, and increasing population densities heightened the probability of fatalities.

The witch killings, from 1977 onwards, all flared up in the period of peak thunderstorm activity. The major waves of killings in 1976/7 and from 1984 also coincided with drought years. This conjuncture was not only because barren lands and dying livestock were additional tortures for societies already on the wrack. Drought was also seen as a symptom of witchcraft and the alienation of ancestors. The meagre rains provided additional evidence of the declining ability of chiefs either to limit the depredations of witches or to mount effective rainmaking ceremonies. With grim irony the clouds that failed to deliver drenching rain nonetheless unleashed a deadly cargo on the communities below. Witches, with their fearsome armoury, seemed to revel in dry conditions![67]

Notes

1 Nchabeleng, *Boipušo.*
2 TA/NTS7694/443/332, minutes of meeting 10/11/1958; see also pp. 82-154 of this file.
3 F. Hendricks, 'Loose Planning and Rapid Resettlement', *Journal of Southern African Studies*, 15, 1989, p. 322; H.F. Verwoerd, *Development and Progress in Bantu Communities* (Pretoria, 1955).
4 Ashforth, *Politics*, pp. 168, 179.
5 *Ibid*, pp. 178-9.
6 TA/NTS7694/443/332/ pp. 82-154, 366-77; Phala, unpublished manuscript ; J. Phala, 2; J. Mashego, 1; Lebowa, Director Social Planning to Director Constitutional Activation, 10/7/84; Bothma, 'Political Structure', pp. 177-95; I.S. Sekhukhune, 3-4; P. Nkadimeng, 1.
7 K.L. Maredi, 1.
8 This observation is distilled from numerous unrecorded discussions in Sekhukhuneland. There is enormous variation in the views expressed but few adults are prepared unequivocally to condemn the institution of chieftainship. See also M. Phala, 2; J. Nchabeleng, 1-3; Mothodi Nchabeleng, 1-2; I.S. Sekhukune, 1-4; J.K. Ntsoane, 1; L.K. Manailane, 1-2.
9 M. Molepo, 'Peasants and/or Proletariat? A Case Study of Group of Migrant Workers at Haggie Rand Limited from Molepo Village', African Studies Institute Seminar paper, 26/7/1993; I.S. Sekhukhune, 1-4; E. Nchabeleng, 1-3; J.K. Ntsoane, 1.
10 The official population of the district of Sekhukhuneland in 1970 was 162 889, comprising 43,8% males and 56,2% females. By 1980 this had risen to 298 667, with 44,7% male and 55,3% female. The total population in 1985 was 377 140. The equivalent figures for Nebo are 1970, 133 284, 42,2%, 57,8%; and 1980, 204 714, 43,2%, 56,8%; 1985 264 304. By 1980, 52,7% of the Sekhukhuneland population was between one and 14 years, while the equivalent figure for Nebo was 52,3%. For these and other statistics, see the Development Bank of South Africa, *Report on Lebowa 1986* and *Regional Poverty Profile: eastern and northern Transvaal 1993*. See also Appendix 2.
11 Schirmer, 'The Struggle', p. 308
12 *Ibid.*
13 Transvaal Rural Action Committee, *Newsletter,* 30/1/1995.
14 Schirmer, 'The Struggle', pp. 219-55; D. James, *The Road from Doornkop* (Johannesburg, 1983); E. Letsoalo, 'Survival Strategies in Rural Lebowa; A Study in

the Geography of Poverty' unpublished M.A. dissertation, University of the
Witwatersrand, 1982, pp. 1-81.

15   *Ibid.*
16   A 'ticky' was the popular term for a threepenny coin. Letsoalo, 'Survival', pp. 43-81.
17   Reliable statistics on the issue of land rights for this period and region are not
      available but there are a number of sources which give a broad sense of what was
      happening. See Letsoalo, 'Survival', pp. 43-81; Molepo, 'Peasants', pp. 1-18; I.S.
      Sekhukhune, 1-4; P.P. Matjie, 1; D. James, 'Kinship and Land in an Inter-Ethnic
      Rural Community', unpublished M.A. dissertation, University of the Witwatersrand,
      1987, pp. 132-52; James, *Doornkop*, pp. 3-42; F. D'Souza *et al.*, *Operation Hunger:*
      First Report on Estimating Rural Vulnerability in Black Rural Communities in South
      Africa (Johannesburg, 1987), pp. 8-12; B. Sansom, 'Leadership', pp. 128-30.
18   Molepo, 'Peasants', pp. 1-18; I.S. Sekhukhune, 3; S. Morwamotshe, 1; James,
      'Kinship', p. 139; James, *Doornkop*, pp. 24-6; Operation Hunger, *Northern*
      Transvaal. Assessment and Planning at Riba (Johannesburg, 1995). The fact that
      increasing number of families were without stock did not mean, however, that
      overstocking in terms of the local ecology ceased to be a problem. The available
      statistics suggest that actual stock levels continued massively to exceed the assumed
      carrying capacity of the veld. See DBSA, *Regional Poverty Profile*, p. 109.
19   Mogase Sekhukhune, 2; N.P. Sekhukhune, 1; J.K. Ntsoane, 1; J. Nchabeleng, 1;
      P. Mphela, 1; S. Morwamotshe, 1; K.L. Manailane, 1; Molepo, 'Peasants' pp. 1-18.
      Ritchken suggests that, between 1982 and 1984, the number of registered migrant
      workers from Lebowa 'virtually halved' and oral sources recall the early 1980s as a
      period of significant retrenchments. But other sources paint a rather less dramatic
      picture. See, for example, Ritchken, 'Leadership and Conflict', p. 344; and DBSA,
      Lebowa 1986, Table 5-28. These figures are aggregated and far from reliable.
20   I.S. Sekhukhune, 3. The available statistics suggest that in the Northern Transvaal the
      unemployment rate rose from 20,3% in 1980 to 39,7% in 1990. DBSA, *Regional*
      Poverty Profile, p. 90.
21   J.K. Ntsoane, 1; J. Nchabeleng, 2.
22   E. Nchabeleng, 2; I.S. Sekhukhune, 2; A. Sitas, 'African Worker Responses on the
      East Rand to Changes in the Metal industry, 1960-1980', unpublished Ph.D. thesis,
      University of the Witwatersrand, 1983, pp. 302, 312, 400-44; B. Fanaroff, personal
      communication, December 1988; *Weekly Mail*, 28 April 1989.
23   D. Riba, 1; R. Kgetsepe, 1; W.M. Moadi, 1; L. Mampuru, 1; James, 'Kinship', pp.
      116, 157-9; James, '*Mmino wa Setšo*: Songs of Town and Country and the
      Experience of Migrancy by Men and Women of the Northern Transvaal' unpublished
      Ph.D. thesis, University of the Witwatersrand, 1993, pp. 73-90, 219-22. Available
      figures suggest that migrants remitted between 1% and 10% of their income by the
      end of the 1980s and that this proportion had fallen considerably since 1970, perhaps
      from as much as 30%. DBSA, *Regional Poverty Profile*, p. 11. See also J. Yawitch,
      'The Relation between African Female Employment and Influx Control in South
      Africa, 1950-1983', unpublished M.A. dissertation, University of the Witwatersrand,
      1984, pp. 285-98; and Operation Hunger, *Northern Transvaal*.
24   *Ibid.* See also S. Schirmer, 'Struggles', p. 289. By the end of 1980s, casual workers
      on farms in the Northern Transvaal earned on average R555 per annum. In 1986,
      daily workers on farms in the Steelpoort Valley were earning R2 per day.
25   James, '*Mmino*', pp. 91-5; A. Maponya, unrecorded discussion, 1995.
26   James, '*Mmino*', *passim.*
27   D. James, '*Bagagešu*/Those of My Home: Migrancy, Gender and Ethnicity',
      unpublished Institute for Advanced Social Research seminar paper, University of the
      Witwatersrand, 13/3/1995, p. 12. See note 8 above for attitudes to chieftainship.
28   *Ibid*, pp. 12-13.

29   F. Wilson and M. Ramphele, *Uprooting Poverty* (Cape Town, 1989), p. 64.

30   I.S. Sekhukhune, 4. The number of old age pensions granted rose from 32 967 in 1970/71 to 56 506 in 1975/6. The amount involved increased from R1 727 956 to R6 134 600. Benbo, *Lebowa – Economic Revue 1976* (Pretoria, 1976), p. 57.

31   Wilson and Ramphele, *Uprooting Poverty*, p. 64.

32   Letsoalo, 'Survival', pp. 107-9; Yawitch, 'African Female Employment', p. 288. Recent village-level research showed 57,1% of households primarily dependent on remittances, with 20,6% primarily dependent on pensions. Operation Hunger, *Northern Transvaal*.

33   James, *Doornkop*, p. 31. See also Yawitch, 'African Female Employment', p. 289.

34   Quotation from James, *Doornkop*, p. 57. Households which enjoyed remittances from more than one member or could draw on both remittance and pension income were particularly well placed. See, for a general picture of household income, James, *Doornkop*, pp. 28-31; James, 'Kinship', pp. 15-16; Letsoalo, 'Survival', pp. 43-81; I. Sekhukhune, 2-4; D'Souza,*Vulnerability*, pp. 8-12.

35   Sansom, 'Leadership', p. 126. See also W. Beinart and P. Delius, 'The Family and Early Migrancy in Southern Africa', unpublished seminar paper, African History Seminar, University of London, May 1979.

36   Deborah James has made a major contribution to the study of kinship and households in this region. See James, 'Kinship', pp. 95-158 and James, '*Mmino*', pp. 142-58, 219-25. The rest of the paragraph is heavily dependent on this work. See also Sansom, 'Leadership', pp. 144-5, which indicates lower ratios of female-headed households in the early 1960s. His data shows 43 out of a total of 174 homesteads (approx 25%) to be women, while James found in 'Morotse' that 56% of households surveyed contained members whose link to each other is traced through females and 33% were female-headed. James, 'Kinship', p. 108. These fragments of information based on different communities are, of course, insufficient to sustain systematic and secure comparison across time. See Chapters 1, 2 and 4 of this work for a fuller discussion of some of these issues.

37   James, 'Kinship', pp. 7-8; Benso, *Lebowa Economic Revue*, pp. 50-5.

38   K. Lerutla, 1; M.K. Phokoago, 1; S.M. Nchabeleng, 1; G. Sekhukhune, 1; I.S. Sekhukhune, 1-4; M.J. Sekhukhune, 1-2.

39   K. Interviews, 2-5.

40   K. Lerutla, 1; M.K. Phokaogo, 1; S.M. Nchabeleng, 1; G. Sekhukhune, 1; I.S. Sekhukhune, 1-5; J.M. Sekhukhune, 1-2; M.B. Molaba, 1.

41   I.S. Sekhukhune, 3; L. Manyike, 1; P.M. Rachidi, 1; S.P. Lekgoathi, 'Reconstructing the History of Educational Transformation in a Rural Transvaal Chiefdom: The Radicalisation of Teachers in Zebediela from the early 1950s to the early 1990s', unpublished M.A. dissertation, University of the Witwatersrand 1995, chapter 4; Benso, *Lebowa Economic Revue*, pp. 46-8; and annual reports of the Lebowa Department of Education, 1975-1985. See also DBSA, *Lebowa* 1986, which provides a range of statistical material on education in Lebowa. One important estimate it contains is in table 10.1.3, which suggests that by 1985 approximately 72,2% of the age group 15-19 in the region was attending secondary schools.

42   T. Tau, 1; L. Manyike, 1; S.P. Lekgoathi, 'Reconstructing' pp. 121-54.

43   Lekgoathi, 'Reconstructing', p. 134.

44   P.M. Rachidi, 1; L. Manyike, 1.

45   Lekgoathi, 'Reconstructing', p. 141; see also P.M. Rachidi, 1; L. Manyike, 1. The available statistics suggest that, in 1986, 14,73% of teachers were unqualified and 74,59% were not adequately qualified, DBSA, *Regional Poverty Profile*, p. 151.

46   These observations are based in part on my own visits to schools in Sekhukhuneland in the late 1980s. See also Thušanang group interview, 1.

47   T. Mankge, 1.

48   These are issues and themes running through dozens of interviews and discussions.
      Older teachers and some students argued that male teachers were more likely than
      female teachers to be violent, drunk and sexually aggressive and also pointed out the
      problems of sexual relationships existing between staff and students were
      compounded by the fact that young teachers and some of their older pupils differed
      very little, if at all, in terms of age. See for example L. Manyike, 1; T. Tau, 1; M.B.
      Molaba, 1; M. Moagi, 1; P. Sebapu, 1; S. Matlala, 1; M. Mbuyane, 1; P. Magodi, 1;
      E. Nchabeleng, 2-3; Morris Nchabeleng, 1; T. Mankge, 1; P. Mbiba, 1; M.B. Molaba,
      1; Thušanang group discussion. See also Lekgoathi, 'Reconstructing', chapters 3 and
      4, and 'Assessing the Political and Cultural influence Originating from the Urban
      Areas; Students' and Teachers' Responses to Political Mobilisation – The Case of
      Zebedielia, 1976-1994', unpublished seminar paper, Education Department,
      University of the Witwatersrand, 1994.
49   *Ibid.*
50   *Ibid.*
51   *Ibid.*
52   *Ibid.*
53   *Ibid.*
54   Quin, *Food and Feeding Habits, passim*; D'Souza, *Vulnerability*, pp. 8-12;
      N. Breslin, *Operation Hunger National Nutritional Survey* (Johannesburg, 1994).
55   J. Small, 'Women's Land Rights. Case Study in Lebowa', *TRAC Occasional
      Publication, Johannesburg*, 1994; James, 'Kinship', pp. 153-60; J. Nchabeleng, 1;
      M. Puane, 1; M. Malata, 1; James, '*Mmino*', pp. 142-52. See also Ritchken,
      'Leadership and Conflict', Chapter 7; Yawitch, 'African Female Employment', pp.
      284-8.
56   These points are derived from dozens of interviews and discussions. See, for example,
      E. Nchabeleng, 2-3; Morris Nchabeleng, 1; I.S. Sekhukhune, 3; M. Mbuyane, 1;
      P. Magodi, 1; S. Matlala, 1; M. Moagi, 1; N.A, 1; S. Moganedi, 1; M. Puane, 1.
57   *Ibid.* Quotation is drawn from Small, 'Women's', p. 6.
58   Quoted in I. van Kessel, 'From Confusion to Lusaka', *Journal of Southern African
      Studies*, 19, 1993, p. 594.
59   By the 1980s the distinction between night and day witches appears to have eroded to
      some extent. There also appears to have been a general view in Sekhukhuneland that
      women predominated in the ranks of witches although they were not necessarily
      regarded as the most dangerous practitioners of these dark arts. Pitje, 'Traditional and
      Modern', pp. vii, xii; M. Puane, 1; J. Nchabeleng, 3; S. Matlala, 1; M. Raseomane, 1;
      W.M. Moadi, 1; Small, 'Womens', p. 4; R.L. Anderson, 'Keeping the Myth Alive:
      Justice, Witches and the Law in the 1986 Sekhukhune killings', unpublished B.A.
      Hons dissertation, 1990; Monnig, *The Pedi*, pp. 71-8. For important case studies
      within the broader region see Ritchken, 'Leadership and Conflict', Chapter 7;
      I.A. Niehaus, 'Witch-Hunting and Political Legitimacy: Continuity and Change in
      Green Valley Lebowa, 1930-1991', *Africa*, 63, 4, 1993, pp. 498-527; and J. Stadler,
      'Witches and Witch-hunters: Witchcraft, Generational Relations and the Life Cycle in
      a Lowveld Village', forthcoming in *African Studies*. I have also benefited from
      numerous unrecorded discussions on this issue with – amongst others – P. Mbiba,
      P. Mnisi, C. Rachidi, A. Maponya and I. Sekhukhune.
60   M.B. Molaba, 1.
61   Monnig, *The Pedi*, p. 74.
62   M.Z. Mabiletša, 1.
63   J. Comaroff, *Body of Power, Spirit of Resistance* (Chicago, 1985), p. 211. On the
      issue of the form and incidence of accusations, see Niehaus, 'Witch-hunting' and
      B. Sansom, 'When witches are not named', in M. Gluckman (ed.), *The Allocation of
      Responsibility* (Manchester, 1972).

64   Comaroff, *Body of Power*, especially Chapters 6 and 7; I.S. Sekhukhune, 3-4;
     P.P. Matjie, 1-2; J.P. Kiernan, 'Where Zionists Draw the Line', *African Studies*, 33,
     1974, pp. 80-90; J.P. Kiernan, 'Poor and Puritan', *African Studies*, 36, 1977, pp.
     31-43; James, *'Mmino'*, pp. 225-8. These comments partly grow out of personal
     observation over the last two decades but are really no more than an agenda for the
     major programme of research which the history of Zionism in this region clearly
     merits.
65   J. Nchabeleng, 3; I.S. Sekhukhune, 2-5; M.Z. Mabiletša, 1; Mönnig, *The Pedi*, pp.
     71-8.
66   Anderson, 'The Myth', pp. 23-5.
67   *Ibid*, pp. 28-30. In 1985 the weather bureau reported that despite the drought lightning
     was more common than usual owing to the high amounts of static electricity created
     by the dry climatic conditions. See *SASPU State of the Nation* February/March 1985.
     While detailed research has not been done on incidents in which witches were killed
     in central Lebowa in the mid-1970s, there are rich accounts of witchhunts in the
     lowveld in this period that stopped short of killings. See Niehaus, 'Witch-Hunting and
     Political Legitimacy' and Stadler, 'Witches and Witch-Hunters'. These stress the
     effects of Betterment, the influx of population and collapsing agricultural production
     which resulted in new and denser residential patterns and had important effects on
     both gender and generational relationships. These issues are explored further in
     relation to Sekhukhuneland in the 1980s in Chapter 6 of this work.

6

Cadres, Comrades and Witches

The Sekhukhuneland Revolt of 1986

'Fear and loathing stalks Lebowa', proclaimed the headline. In April of 1986, Sekhukhuneland, as the centre of the most significant rural uprising in three decades, was front-page news once more. The 1986 revolt showed some important continuities with the struggles of the 1950s. But the profound changes in the nature of the society in the intervening years ensured that the composition, actions and aspirations of the rebels bore little resemblance to earlier patterns. This chapter charts the shifting configuration of politics in the region from the early 1970s to the 1986 revolt and, in closing, sketches the run-up to the 1994 election in this part of the Northern Transvaal.

Lebowa

Apartheid ideology and practice continued its grim progress during the 1970s. The National Party had classified Africans as citizens of 'homelands', thus justifying their economic subordination and exclusion from the centres of power. It now determined that these distinctly unseaworthy hulks should be set adrift on international waters. In 1972 Lebowa – including Sekhukhuneland and areas to the north of Pietersburg – was granted self-governing status. Pretoria harboured the hope that this region would follow the Transkei over the horizon into independence. But this renewed and extended version of *Boipušo* proved far from simple to effect. Once again, Sekhukhuneland was a reef which tore a hole in the government's plans.

The constitution of Lebowa stipulated that its legislative assembly should consist of 60 chiefs nominated by the various regional authorities, and 40

172

members elected by public vote. It was anticipated that this constellation of representatives would prove conservative and amenable to central government's designs.

Kgoši M.N. Matlala, who had been a leading supporter and beneficiary of Bantu Authorities in the 1950s, was groomed to be chief minister. In 1973, the first elections were held. The candidates were drawn mainly from the established educated and commercial elite. The dominant figure was Dr C.N. Phatudi who, from the 1940s, had risen through the ranks of the education system to a senior position in the inspectorate. But it also included a handful of individuals whose primary allegiance lay with the ANC but who believed that the homeland system was a political terrain which should not be surrendered entirely. Godfrey Sekhukhune, for example, stood as candidate. He had endured detention and torture in the 1960s but decided, after soundings with the ANC in exile, that the overriding issue was to block independence. After the election, which drew a 35 per cent turnout, he helped broker an alliance between Dr Phatudi, the bulk of the elected representatives, and the Sekhukhuneland chiefs. This grouping was united in opposition to Kgoši Matlala and independence. Phatudi promised to press for extra land and to grant the Pedi Paramountcy greater powers. He was elected chief minister by 45 votes to 40 in the legislative assembly and formed the Lebowa Peoples Party. *Kgoši* Matlala, who was reluctant to be denied the spoils of office, joined forces with the governing party in 1974.[1]

Formal independence was thus held at bay. But as Lebowa's administrative machinery expanded, becoming the principal conduit for funds from central government and the dominant source of local employment, its political and economic shadow lengthened across the countryside. Access to services and opportunities increasingly depended on individuals' capacity to pick their way through the burgeoning bureaucracy and to secure a sympathetic hearing from relevant officials. And only the most foolhardy or courageous risked alienating the chiefs and councillors who operated their own toll gates on the road to central resources. The sizable funds and subsidies managed by the Lebowan government amidst inadequate financial controls provided an inducement to a variety of forms of corruption which made their appearance in the 1970s, and which gathered considerable momentum in the ensuing decade. In this context, networks of economic and political patronage came to constitute the sinews of government.[2]

Chiefs remained the cornerstone of local government and a dominant element in the central administration. The overlap between their areas of control and those of the various departments of state contributed to the fog that shrouded the administrative system. But the Lebowa government also enjoyed considerable formal authority over traditional rulers as it had been granted the powers previously vested in the central government to appoint and dismiss chiefs. In the first decade of its existence, the Lebowa cabinet exercised these responsibilities with considerable caution for fear of the potential political fallout. But, from early on, an uneasy relationship developed between the central government and the Pedi Paramountcy. Phatudi failed to make good on his promise of enhanced powers for the paramountcy and the irritation this provoked compounded the deep scepticism at Mohlaletse over the legitimacy of this recently engineered political structure. These circumstances led to fears amongst the Lebowa leadership that the Pedi Kingdom might yet rise up to haunt them. But the troubled relationship was also the result of a protracted and corrosive conflict within the paramountcy.[3]

Acting Paramount Mankopodi's dealings with her senior councillors soured in the early 1970s. This was partly the result of disquiet over the decision to accept Bantu Authorities, but it was also the outcome of her reluctance to take their advice on a range of issues. In 1974, the *bakgomana* decided that it was time for her son, Rhyne, to come home and assume office. He was 28 years old, had completed matric and was working for the Lebowa government. When Mankopodi was informed of this decision she was outraged and refused to abdicate, asserting that it was her prerogative to decide on this issue, not that of the *bakgomana*. A deadlock ensued and charges of witchcraft were traded.

Rhyne, placed under considerable pressure from both his mother and the *bakgomana*, wilted. He argued that Mankopodi should be reinstated and refused to assume office. In response, the councillors sent his mother back to her natal village of Manganeng and in September 1975 approached another of Morwamotše's sons – Kenneth Kgagudi Sekhukhune – to become paramount. This appointment had, however, to be ratified by the Lebowa government. Phatudi and his cabinet were placed in a quandary. Rhyne was well known within Lebowa government circles and Mankopodi both was owed political debts and received strong support from a political network focused on her brother, Phaswane Nkadimeng, the chief at Manganeng. But Kenneth was championed by Godfrey Sekhukhune and the cabinet was reluctant to go against the wishes of the *bakgomana*. While Phatudi prevaricated, violence erupted at Mohlaletse. On the nights of 21 and 22 February 1976, the huts of eight supporters of Mankopodi and Rhyne and a shop were burnt down and the individuals targeted fled from the village. In August 1976, Kenneth was finally confirmed as acting chief at Mohlaletse but was not given effective recognition as paramount. The relationship between Mohlaletse and Phatudi deteriorated further.[4]

In the years following, the discontent which festered at Mohlaletse merged with wider criticism of Phatudi's administration. After the Transkei was granted independence in 1976, there was mounting anxiety that Phatudi was planning to go the same route. There was also a growing conviction in Sekhukhuneland that the area was being discriminated against in the allocation of the resources commanded by the Lebowa government. It was widely believed that these benefits were being monopolised by a political and economic network situated to the north and rooted in the Mphahlele chiefdom – the area close to the new capital of Lebowakgomo in which Phatudi had grown up. Late in 1977, four MPs from Sekhukhuneland led by Godfrey Sekhukhune broke away from the Lebowa Peoples Party and formed the Black Peoples Party. Its title reflected the dominant rhetoric of the times rather than any direct connection to the Black Consciousness Movement, and its main – largely indirect – external political influences were Inkatha and the ANC.[5]

The BPP recruited active supporters amongst chiefs and young businessmen and tried to capitalise on a wide range of grievances. It urged opposition to independence, recognition of the Pedi Paramount, an enhanced role for chiefs, a clampdown on nepotism and corruption and a relaxation of controls on business licences. The election saw a considerably increased turnout in Sekhukhuneland and Godfrey Sekhukhune topped the local poll. But the BPP had a limited presence in some of the other constituencies and failed by four votes in its attempt to oust Phatudi. Denied office, the coalition began to crumble. As one member put it, 'our people couldn't remain in opposition, especially not the chiefs, they feared that the rulers will deny them facilities'.[6] The members of the BPP drifted back to the LPP. A low poll in the 1982 election saw many of its former supporters, including Godfrey Sekhukhune, lose their seats as voters took their revenge for dashed hopes and broken promises. The politics of patronage and sustained opposition proved incompatible, and there was not to be another serious electoral challenge to the LPP. But the founders of the BPP argued that their intervention had, at very least, played a vital role in stiffening the resolve to resist independence.[7]

The ANC and MK in Bopedi during the 1970s

While Lebowa politicians debated the patterns of patronage, the ANC began to re-establish a presence in Sekhukhuneland. This development was initially, however, rather more the result of official malice than organisational design. During the early 1970s, a number of individuals who had been involved in the first MK sabotage campaign completed their prison sentences. In 1972, Peter Nchabeleng returned home after eight years on Robben Island. In the 1950s he had lived in Pretoria and had been active in the Office Workers Union, Sactu, the ANC and Sebatakgomo. On his release in 1972, he was banished to Sekhukhuneland and returned to the village of Apel in which he had last resided 25 years before. He could not find employment and was regarded with considerable caution by villagers who had been told that he was a 'dangerous terrorist'. But he was reunited with his family. His son Elleck recalled that

> all the time when I was still young I wanted to know where my father is, my mother told us he was in jail, she was somewhat reluctant to tell us why he was locked up ... When he came back he briefed us about why he was in jail ... He explained that he didn't kill anyone, steal from anyone and that he did all this for the people, not for personal gain.[8]

Peter Nchabeleng introduced his children to political debates and encouraged them to read and take an interest in current affairs. Elleck remembers that 'we ended up establishing a very strong relationship with him ... we were friends'.[9]

Nelson Diale was also released in 1972. He had grown up in the village of Masemola and had found employment as a waiter in Pretoria. He joined the ANC and the Domestic Workers Union in the 1950s and he was recruited into MK during 1962. When his eight-year prison sentence was over he was also banned for four years and restricted to his old village. He was informed that:

> We must not go to gatherings, we must not meet more than three people, and you must not go to schools, universities ... Well, I decided to plough. I went to the chief and said, 'Chief, I want a piece of land to plough, the government has banned me.' He did not refuse, he gave me a piece of land and family friends provided donkeys. When the rainy season came I ploughed beans, maize, corn and all that ... That is how I lived. The South African Council of Churches was also giving grants to ex-political prisoners. We were getting R25 per month, it was better than nothing.[10]

In the repressive climate of the mid-1970s, and under the watchful and vindictive eye of the local security force, these two men remained somewhat isolated. But they did provide a focal point for a handful of local Congress supporters who were brave enough to risk contact. They formed small discussion groups which, amongst other matters, raised the issue of people leaving the country for military training under MK's auspices. As 1976 ran its bloody course, Nchabeleng and Diale also became a vital source of information for the growing numbers of young people who wanted to find out more about the ANC. But the most remarkable visit they had in the course of that year was from an MK unit led by a young commander, Mosima Gabriel – better known as Tokyo – Sexwale.[11]

After its destruction within South Africa in 1963, MK attempted to re-build in exile. It was argued within the ANC/SACP that it was vital to launch an armed struggle in order to stimulate the process of political regeneration.[12] In 1967, at the ANC's request, MK guerillas were sent into Rhodesia in the company of fighters from ZAPU, with the objective of building a bridgehead for military infiltration into South Africa. The campaign was a military disaster. No guerillas made it back to South Africa in a condition to fight and scores were killed, arrested or fled into neighbouring Botswana. Heavy emphasis continued to be placed on military action with the dominant model being rural guerilla warfare, but few initiatives were taken and frustration mounted in the camps over the lack of action. In 1970, Flag Boshielo – the founder of Sebatakgomo and now an MK commissar – persuaded a reluctant leadership to allow him to attempt to lead a group back to South Africa.[13] The contingent was ambushed as they crossed the Zambezi River and Boshielo was killed. In the early 1970s, guerillas were infiltrated into South Africa from Botswana but none were able to establish themselves securely.

After 1974, the tide began to turn. The defeat of Portuguese colonialism and the rise of both worker organisations and the Black Consciousness Movement within South Africa created new possibilities. Released political prisoners also played a vital role in reinvigorating the frail ANC underground. In 1973, Martin Ramokgadi was released from jail. He had been active in the ANC, the SACP and Sebatakgomo in the 1950s, and had channelled recruits to MK in the early 1960s. In 1975, Joe Gqabi completed his sentence. He had been one of the first MK members to receive military training in China. Ramokgadi and Gqabi made contact with John Nkadimeng, who had remained under banning orders in Soweto. In 1975, having established a command committee chaired by Nkadimeng, they recruited members in the embryonic trade union leadership, made contacts with student groups and got in touch with old comrades from Sebatakgomo and the ANC.[14]

The Soweto uprising of 1976 caught the ANC offguard. Joe Slovo recalled that the leadership saw it as

> an indication of serious failure that against the background of the biggest massacre in our modern history, we could count only two policemen killed in the six-odd weeks after the rising started. Fifteen years after our commitment to armed struggle, we could mount no organised retaliation by armed struggle using modern techniques.[15]

In the ANC's view, the revolt demanded an armed response to sustain whatever confidence and support it enjoyed inside the country. It also led to a rethink of the importance of urban as opposed to rural guerilla warfare. The ANC now saw military activities in town and countryside as mutually reinforcing in the context of a protracted 'people's war'. But in the months after June

1976, and before the organisational implications of these conclusions could be fully digested, a number of MK cadres led by Naledi Tsiki and Mosima Sexwale were infiltrated from Swaziland into the Transvaal. Their brief was to mount immediate combat actions and to accelerate the process of building internal MK structures. They linked up with the Transvaal committee established by the released Robben Island prisoners, although the lines of overall authority remained unclear.[16]

In this context, Peter Nchabeleng and Nelson Diale were contacted by Martin Ramokgadi. He made several trips to Sekhukhuneland from September 1976 onwards, and held discussions with them about forming local MK structures. Elleck Nchabeleng, who was then 18 years old, was recruited into the scheme and his father set about mobilising old connections from Sebatakgomo and the Khuduthamaga to provide volunteers for military training. In December, Mosima Sexwale and Charles Ramusi arrived at Apel. Elleck Nchabeleng recalled his excitement at meeting

> the first guerillas. They came with some equipment, AKs, scorpions, Tokerov pistols, and an F-1. With two others from our discussion group, we organised a meeting place on the banks of the Olifants River. We held discussions explaining the history of South Africa, why is there a need for the armed struggle and why people should take up arms and fight. Then they asked us whether we were interested in joining MK ... so we joined MK on the banks of the Olifants River.[17]

One unit was established at Apel and another under Diale at Masemola. The plan was to provide internal political and military training while sending individuals out for short periods for additional instruction, and so to build up a web of units spanning the villages in the region. In this way, an underground structure would be formed which would be capable of sustaining a 'people's war'. But this bold vision was never to be realised.[18]

The unit led by Tsiki and Sexwale worked at breakneck speed providing political and military instruction in Soweto and elsewhere on the Rand, as well as setting up units in the Northern and Western Transvaal. It also launched the first MK attack inside South Africa since the 1960s when it blew up a section of railway line near Pietersburg with plastic explosives. The beginning of the end came when a group led by Sexwale encountered police after having crossed from Swaziland at the end of November 1976. Sexwale threw a hand grenade and seriously wounded two constables, so spilling the first blood in MK's new campaign.

But this episode provided several clues to the security services. Once the first individuals were taken into custody and tortured, security police were rapidly able to uncover the entire Transvaal network. Over 163 individuals were detained and a number, after long periods of solitary confinement, agreed to give evidence for the state. Sexwale and 11 others – including Tsiki, Ramokgadi, Diale, Nchabeleng and Gqabi – were put on trial for their lives. But the fates for once were kind to them. The original judge who was assigned to the trial died before it was completed and a new trial had to be staged. Arthur Chaskalson and other defence lawyers skillfully exploited discrepancies between the testimony given in the two trials. Ramokgadi, Tsiki, Sexwale and others nonetheless received long sentences.[19] But Peter Nchabeleng, Diale and Gqabi were acquitted. This was partly because Elleck Nchabeleng, despite beatings and months in solitary confinement, refused to testify and thus broke a vital link in the chain of evidence. As Nelson Diale observed, 'the person who saved us from death was Elleck Nchabeleng ... he refused to give evidence throughout the year [1977] until 1978'.[20]

As a result, less than five years after having been reunited with his father, Elleck found himself *en route* to Robben Island to begin a six-year sentence.

This episode provided welcome evidence to many South Africans that MK was active and would and could strike back. But this was achieved at enormous organisational and personal cost. Rather than building the underground, its consequence was the destruction of fledgling structures of considerable potential. While awaiting trial, Gqabi and Ramokgadi wrote a document outlining the lessons they drew from this experience. They argued that armed action should not be attempted until a well-developed underground and organised domestic political base had been established. Gqabi took this document with him when he went into exile after his acquittal.

In Sekhukhuneland, networks which could have contributed to organisational growth were decimated and even the staunchest ANC supporters were wary of further involvement in political and military adventures. The result was that, while the area was still seen as a potential base for operations by the MK command, little in the way of an underground movement had been established by the beginning of the 1980s.[21] Peter Nchabeleng and Nelson Diale languished in their villages under renewed banning orders and amidst neighbours who regarded them with considerable apprehension.

The Comrades Take Command

The tempo of popular struggle in urban South Africa quickened in the early 1980s. The independent trade union movement, having survived the chill winds of the 1970s, started to grow more rapidly. The Congress of South African Students (Cosas) became a major force in schools and launched youth congresses in many centres which incorporated the young unemployed. A wide variety of civic organisations also sprang up in the townships. In all of these contexts, returned Robben Island prisoners and activists fought with considerable effect to assert the pre-eminence of a 'Congress' political tradition. In 1983, against the backdrop of this organisational upsurge and the reforms initiated by the Botha government, the United Democratic Front (UDF) was launched. Although it did not endorse armed struggle, the UDF draped itself in the colours of the ANC. The first campaigns of the UDF were against elections to new ethnic parliaments and local councils. By the mid-1980s, a pattern of insurrection and repression based around schools, universities and townships had risen to a peak.[22] These struggles, travelling by a wide variety of routes, also breached some of the barriers between town and countryside.

Workers from Sekhukhuneland numbered amongst the migrants recruited into the union movement. While these organisations had a primarily urban focus, migrants' experiences within unions nonetheless had an impact in rural areas. For example, the ideas of accountability and financial control which were fostered in the more effective unions fed into concerns about chiefly abuses of power and community funds and helped to stimulate migrant associations' challenges to the practice of chiefly rule.

But migrants were initially wary of proclaiming their union affiliations within their home communities, and it was only in the Steelpoort mining area that trade unions became an open force in local politics. The Metal and Allied Workers Union recruited members with some assistance from Chief Mampuru – a former member of Sebatakgomo and the Khuduthamaga – who allowed them to establish an office in his village and warded off unwelcome attentions from the security police. Unionists not only organised on the mines but also pioneered community structures in the neighbouring villages and townships. In 1984, Mawu split partly because of divisions over support for the UDF. The Steelpoort branch followed the local organiser, Tom Flatela, into a new union (the United Metal and Motor Workers of South Africa) and later in the year the Steelpoort Youth Congress (Steyco) – the first grouping of its kind in Sekhukhuneland – was founded. Its president was a shop steward and branches were established in various villages along the river. But while Steyco had contacts with youth elsewhere in Sekhukhuneland, the organisation's wider impact was limited. It was too closely tied to a sub-regional mine-based political economy to be easily exported to communities further afield.[23]

There were, however, stirrings amongst the youth in other villages. News of events in the urban areas filtered in through the media. Migrant workers, urban youths who attended local schools and boys who visited family and friends in the townships, or who found temporary employment in the cities, told of their experiences as observers of, or participants in, township revolt. Students from a range of tertiary institutions also returned home with accounts of campus action and politics. The Turfloop campus of the University of the North, in particular, started to provide organisational impetus throughout the region. In the 1970s, despite their relative proximity and role as the crucible of the Black Consciousness Movement, students at the university had rarely been politically active in their rural hinterland, although they did have some impact in the immediate environs of the campus and in nearby townships. In the 1980s, the main student grouping, the Azanian Students Organisation (Azaso), shuffled off its Black Consciousness origins and adopted the principles of the ANC's Freedom Charter. It also managed to gain control of the SRC at the University of the North and thus unlocked a treasure trove of organisational resources ranging from cash to cars. The campus soon became known as 'Lusaka' (after the headquarters of the ANC) in activist and police circles alike.[24]

Early in 1984, students at the University of the North from Sekhukhuneland came together and committed themselves to promoting organisation in their home villages. Nico Matlawa recalls that they set themselves the task

> that as the university closes, you must go and organise in your areas and we are going to do a follow up. When you come back you must come and give us a report back. And you must never give us a false report because we shall move and study around and see as to whether you really did something at home.[25]

From 1983, small informal discussion groups comprising of school and college students gathered in many villages. They discussed Cosas and the UDF, and aired their concerns about conditions in the schools and abuses of chiefly power. While there was no general disruption of schooling at this time, there were loud rumblings of discontent and sporadic class boycotts. Tiny Mankge recalls that, at Jane Furse,

> there were students who were already knowing about politics and I remember in 1983 we had a meeting ... it was clear that the things that were happening in the schools did not satisfy them. And they didn't really know what to do about those things. So when they heard about Cosas meeting students' demands and things they became motivated even when they did not really know what Cosas was. But they had a light.[26]

Some students made contacts with Cosas in the urban areas, and from 1984 onwards there were occasional visits from Cosas activists from the Rand who outlined their struggles and demands to local pupils. And from 1985, as struggles intensified in the Middelburg and Witbank townships, and under the cloud of the first state of emergency, some young activists took refuge in the homes of relatives in Sekhukhuneland and added to the political ferment in the villages. They carried the message that whites enjoyed free education and free books in properly equipped schools and that black students should get the same. They condemned corporal punishment and called for elected Student Representative Councils to give pupils a voice in running the schools. These demands resonated with local experiences and grievances. But while Cosas was an important model and source of influence, very little formal organisation was established under its banner and, until the end of 1985, only a handful of youth in each village were politically active.[27]

A more concerted organisational drive emanated from the village of Apel and, in particular, from the household of Peter Nchabeleng. After his surprise acquittal in 1978, he was served yet another banning order which finally expired in 1983. He was an obvious contact point for the UDF and in early 1986, when the Northern Transvaal region of the organisation was launched, he was made president. But while the UDF proclaimed its intention of organising in rural areas, in practice its energies were absorbed by the tumult in townships and very little attention was paid to the Transvaal countryside. Peter Nchabeleng's younger son Morris recalls that:

> Organisations like the UDF were not very familiar to us. We were close to the UDF because my father became president, but we were having problems because you would find that maybe a member of the UDF would only come after some months.[28]

Peter Nchabeleng provided a powerful symbol of a local Congress tradition, a rich source of political history and advice, and access to wider political networks. But it was his sons who played the catalytic role in the spread of youth organisation in Sekhukhuneland.[29] In June 1984, Elleck Nchabeleng was released from Robben Island. In his years in prison he had undergone intensive political education. He recalled that 'I learned a lot. I had known things as slogans, I now understood more deeply.'[30] He left the island under instruction to become involved in a range of organisational activities. On his return to Apel, he found that while no formal structure had been established there was considerably greater political interest amongst the youth than had existed in the mid-1970s.

In August, at a welcome home party that was held in his honour, he explained 'why I went to prison and that it is not the end, and that I may end up being locked up again'.[31] By the end of the month the Sekhukhuneland Youth Committee was formed, primarily composed of school students living in the neighbouring villages of Apel and Nkwana. Nine youths set out in a combi to attend the first UDF rally in the Northern Transvaal at Seshego. They returned home with the papers for the million signature campaign which was a central UDF initiative at the time and which echoed a 1950s

ANC campaign. While they youth were happy to sign, if a little perplexed at the point of the exercise, older people were considerably more cautious:

> As one old man said, 'no, this thing has long expired – we had a one million signature campaign in the 1950s, now you guys are really taking chances.' We didn't know about the earlier campaign – we said, 'no, this is new'. He said 'no, it is not. I signed my name in 1955 ... and I am not going to sign again.'[32]

At the end of 1984, Elleck found employment with the Community Resource and Information Centre (Cric) in Johannesburg, which had been established by white activists who had graduated from the National Union of South African Students. Cric both provided him with resources and gave him free rein to undertake organisational work. Although he was engaged on a number of fronts, he made regular trips home, taking with him newspapers and pamphlets, and providing money to support the political activities of the youth. His younger brother, Morris, who was 20 years old and still at school, began to play a leadership role and the Nchabeleng household became a hive of activity. 'It was open for everybody. People would stay overnight, others will come at 11.30 ... and stay till the next day. They felt at home at my place. My father gave them a chance.'[33]

The youths who gathered there discussed the contents of the Freedom Charter, the latest news, local issues and wrestled with the – for many – unfamiliar concepts and language of class analysis. One particularly protracted debate was over whether or not the women who sold vegetables by the roadside formed part of the bourgeoisie.[34]

But, for much of 1985, this activity – while intense – remained restricted to a relatively small group. Morris remembers that:

> There were initially three of us going around looking for some people who were interested. We were not really organising them, just calling them. Freedom songs were very interesting to them and because of lack of political education we were just going up and down singing and people were joining us. We used to hold some meetings and discuss the situation in our villages, talking about the crisis in the schools and the crisis in the village caused by the chief and the principal.[35]

This was the situation that Richard Magerule Sekonya found when he returned home to Nkwana in September of 1985. He was studying at Tompizeleka Agricultural College and had played a leading role in the SRC and in protests against the presence of national servicemen and underqualified and incompetent individuals amongst the staff. Early in September, the students took matters into their own hands. They seized a truck and a tractor, packed up two of the offending staff members' possessions, and ordered them to leave the campus. The police arrived, shot and injured two of the students, and the college was closed.

On his arrival in Sekhukhuneland, Richard made contact with Morris. The two of them agreed on the need for renewed organisational effort and decided to establish a youth structure encompassing their neighbouring villages. With a core group of scholars and students, and with the assistance of money, materials and workshops from Elleck and others from Cric, they organised firstly in their own villages and then fanned out across Sekhukhuneland. They worked at breakneck speed, contacting individuals and encouraging the formation of youth structures. In many villages, they found that youths were already on the move and by the end of 1985 an umbrella body named the Sekhukhuneland Youth Organisation (Seyo) was established.[36]

Richard Sekonya recalls that

> the first big, big meeting which we had was on New Years' Eve 1985. We started singing and chanting from Apel to Nkwana and back again. We were assembling and discussing, showing other people the reasons why we are on the street. We were chanting freedom songs – some people were not aware of what they were. To us, it was successful. Many people were coming and it was a new thing in this area – but it was good.[37]

In early 1986, the youth movement grew at an enormous rate. The original core of intellectuals and activists was joined by a mass following consisting of school pupils and, increasingly, unemployed youth, for whom these activities provided a welcome relief from social limbo and the grinding tedium of village life. Rapid expansion was facilitated by the fact that there were no formal membership requirements and all youth were automatically considered to be members of the youth congresses. Groups were also established in villages which had not been visited by the core group of activists or previously shown much sign of political life. As Elleck puts it,

> they got the UDF from newspapers and heard about the formation of youth congresses, so they just got together and called themselves *macomrades* without any politics at all – saying, 'no, the Boers are mad – *Amandla Awetu'*.[38]

A wide variety of local leaders emerged in this context, including young unionists, scholars, students and unemployed school leavers.[39] The case of Steve Moganedi, who achieved prominence at Jane Furse in 1986, provides an illustration of the range of influences at play. He was born in Soweto in 1960, became a rastafarian, was caught up in the 1976 revolt and detained for three weeks. His parents felt that life in the township was becoming too dangerous and brought him to Jane Furse. There he spent some time at local schools but then dropped out because of lack of funds, found work but was fired after a strike. In the early 1980s, he returned to school for a time and also became involved in local discussion groups. When asked how he had become a leader he replied:

> It started in this way, before the soldiers cut my dread-locks, I already had a strong following, people were very much in support of me, in fact they liked my dread-locks and as such I realised that I have a good relationship with the people ... One day I sat down and thought, how can I make myself successful since I was not working. And then, during that particular night, I had a dream and in that dream I saw myself speaking in front of a crowd.[40]

In early 1986, the Nkwana/Apel leadership looked for ways to put their new-found strength to use. There was a long-standing dispute over land with the neighbouring chiefdom at Masha. This community had been the victim of re-settlement in the 1960s. They had been relocated to land where the cattle posts of both the Apel and Nkwana villages were situated and where some families had established permanent settlements. After their arrival, the Masha community attempted to enforce its control over the land and other local resources. This produced a simmering conflict which flared up once more in February 1986, and the youth leadership decided to march on Masha. They were, however, met by police gunfire and a disabled boy – Solomon Maditsi – was killed and several youths arrested.

Heavy-handed police action fanned the flames of revolt and set in motion a corrosive cycle of death and defiance. Shootings and arrests gave rise to heightened anger and action amongst the youth, which led to renewed confrontation with the police and more deaths. The youth took up the UDF campaign to 'isolate the police'. Individuals who were believed to be informers were assaulted. Girls with lovers in the police force were 'severely disciplined'. Shebeen owners and shopkeepers were ordered to stop serving members of the security services. Increasingly, police were attacked when they entered the villages. Some parts of Sekhukhuneland, including Apel/Nkwana, became in effect no-go areas for the security forces. Funerals, especially the night vigils which preceded burial, became central forums of mobilisation and education, with activists leading the youth in chants, slogans and political songs celebrating the ANC and MK. The speakers exhorted their youthful audience to still-greater bravery and sacrifice. School boycotts started in the Apel region, although schools elsewhere continued to operate until the end of February.[41]

In early March, police shot a youth at a meeting near Schoonoord. At his funeral, it was decided that the time had come to close down those schools that remained open and stage a mass demonstration of youth power. On 3 March, taxis and buses were hijacked all over Sekhukhuneland and driven to the schools. Mandla Mbuyane, who had previously not been politically involved, told how early that morning at Matsebong school near Jane Furse,

> We were surprised to see a lot of buses [and people] coming to collect us at school. Some were marching, singing, raising their arms. We nearly ran away but at last we went with the buses. We didn't know where we were going so we just marched on. When we reached the bus stop, they were singing. It was the first time that we heard freedom songs. As time went by I found myself singing with my hand raised. I was interested. I heard someone say 'free books for all'. I knew I didn't have books. I wanted free books. I heard someone say 'we need water'. I knew that our village was suffering from a shortage of water. I wanted water as well. I heard someone singing *panzi ya magoši* [down with the chiefs] and I knew that they were oppressing our mothers and our fathers. So I knew they were talking of things which I had been feeling the weight of all along, but did not have the power to do anything about, because I was too young.[42]

The convoy set out for Lebowakgomo, gathering more and more pupils as it proceeded. But about halfway to its destination, the crowd was stopped by a contingent of armed Lebowa police. In the ensuing confrontation, youths were beaten, shot and finally scattered. A week later, eight youths were shot by police at Motetema near Groblersdal. In response, 'war' was declared on the Lebowa government and police. Property belonging to the 'enemy', and those believed to be in sympathy with it, was targeted. Buses, cars, government buildings, shops and some schools were burnt. Trucks and vans making deliveries to local shops also came under attack and consumer boycotts were launched against selected black businesses and white stores situated on the borders. More broadly, it was believed that 'the white man was the enemy, especially the Boers'.[43]

Farmers who ventured into the area were stopped at improvised road blocks. The more fortunate were allowed to proceed after paying a stiff fee for 'an ANC permit' issued by the youth. Farm workers living within Lebowa were prevented from crossing the border to work. The Steelpoort Valley, which had been a bitterly contested boundary of the Pedi Kingdom for much of the nineteenth century, once again echoed with bloodcurdling threats and accusations. Under cover of night, youths and some workers crossed the river and torched crops and farm buildings. Farmers were up in arms and the far right-wing *Afrikaaner Weerstand Beweging* started to gather support in the valley and to dispense rough justice to those unfortunate enough to cross its path. But for the next two months, while farmers fumed on the borders and the army and police made sporadic raids and arrests, the comrades were in command of Sekhukhuneland.[44]

A Brave New World

While 'the comrades' were often portrayed in the press as being a cohesive grouping with a uniform political purpose, it is clear that this was far from the case. In Sekhukhuneland, by the middle of 1986, a cross-section of youth were involved, ranging from seasoned activists to individuals who had not previously shown any interest in politics. Processes of political education were at best rudimentary and for the vast majority of participants rarely extended beyond learning songs and slogans. In consequence, the understanding of the objectives of organisation and action was almost as diverse as the membership and evolved according to local experience and circumstance. And a particular danger for analysts in this instance – as in many others – is to attempt to read off popular consciousness from the pronouncements and subsequent reflections of the most articulate leaders.[45]

With this caveat in place, it is possible to make some broad observations about who the comrades were in this area and what they sought to achieve. The loose youth groupings which mushroomed in 1986 were primarily composed of pupils, students and unemployed secondary school leavers ranging in age from early teens to mid-twenties. They were – in short – the beneficiaries of the rapid expansion of senior schools in the area since the mid-1970s. Youths who had not attended school or who had only received primary education tended to remain outside of their ranks. Girls participated in many of the meetings and activities but were very sparsely represented amongst those who assumed leadership positions or who raised their voices in internal debates. As the movement grew, and clashes with the security services intensified, there was widespread agreement that the Lebowa government and police and their allies were the central targets. Lebowa represented the local face of apartheid and a corrupt and repressive order which intruded on people's lives at both village and regional level. Elected and chiefly members of the Lebowa Legislative Assembly were urged to step down and, at the height of the revolt, a handful announced their intention to do so. But once the police had been driven from the villages and local property belonging to the government had been destroyed, there were few obvious targets to attack. Urban campaigns of boycotting rents and service charges could not readily be translated into a rural context.[46]

Youth groupings decided that the time was ripe to reform the schooling system. Buildings erected with the money and sweat of their parents remained largely undamaged. Some schools shut down entirely but many continued to function, although SRCs elected by the pupils assumed effective control. Unpopular principals and teachers were driven away. Corporal punishment was outlawed. And

> teachers and principals were forced to work with the SRCs which meant that morning assemblies were used to make announcements about meetings or rallies and to sing the anthem *Nkosi Sikel'i Afrika*. Some students challenged teachers in the classroom to provide 'people's education' and criticised the syllabus ... School opening and closing times were changed to make allowance for students who had to walk far to school – who previously had faced beatings for coming to school late.[47]

But pupils lacked the resources or skills to launch alternative programmes and teachers resisted any active involvement. Even in the schools that remained open, education ground to a halt. In some schools, the new leadership became as intolerant of dissent as had been the old and imposed corporal punishment or menial labour on any who dared flout their authority or who failed to attend meetings regularly and punctually. Tensions also surfaced between unemployed school leavers who had little to lose from the disruption of classes and pupils whose thoughts began to turn to end-of-year exams.

The sway of the youth extended well beyond the school yard. Young people had long listened to their parents lamenting chiefly abuse of power but

> while parents saw those abuses, they were afraid to do anything about it. But when they were at home the parents talked about them and the children heard their parents' complaints. Now as their organisation grew in strength they were able to take up those issues.[48]

The youth both heard and they observed:

> The chief is doing nothing for the people ... but he makes our mothers contribute a lot of money whilst the government is paying him. He robs them by saying it is the money for this and the money for that but they are not telling us what the money is being used for. The people here are crying because the community's money is being stolen.[49]

In many villages, the initial campaign launched by the youth was for a proper accounting for community funds and, in this demand, they enjoyed considerable support from their parents. In some villages in late 1985 and early 1986, youth and migrant groups acted in concert on this issue. But the youth were far from clear or united about what role chiefs should play in future. At first, the dominant impulse was to insist that chiefs should rule 'by the people'. But when these demands were not met, and some chiefs received assistance from the army and the police, a call for chiefs to be swept aside gathered force. In the village of Madibong, where particularly bitter clashes took place, the comrades sang as they marched on the *mošate*:

> *Nako e fedile.* The time is over
> *Nako ya magoši.* The time of the chiefs
> *Re a le tšea a lefase le.* We will take this land.[50]

Some chiefs adopted a low profile and avoided open confrontation wherever possible. Others remained under armed guard or fled the district.

While parents were sympathetic to some of the demands made by the youth, they became increasingly alarmed by their patterns of behaviour. Groups of singing, chanting, *toyi toying* youths paraded around the villages by day, while at night meetings were held in the surrounding hills. At dusk, bands of youths would go from house to house to ensure attendance – especially of the girls. Kerina Sekonya describes how

> they would sing the songs of the comrades whenever they were coming to call us. They would come into the house and tell us we should go. They didn't ask your mother they just said 'come let's go'. You would just have to go with them. They would threaten you with their belts and ultimately you would think that if you refused, they would beat you. Our parents were afraid of them ... [they dare not refuse] but you could see that they were against it.[51]

The anxieties of parents were intensified when news filtered out that some comrades had declared that it was the duty of the youth to father more 'soldiers' to replace those that had fallen in battle and that girls should abandon contraception. As Johannes Makgolane recalls,

> we explained to them that we are being reduced by the police and they should not use contraception and so prevent the soldiers who might come and help us in the future ... [Some girls] just listened, others were against it but [in the end] they agreed as there was no one kneeling down to ask them to agree to it, no one was [being] soft about it during that time.[52]

As the power of the comrades grew, patterns of generational revolt and male assertion intertwined. Groups led by young men enforced their power in relation to their parents and grandparents, and their dominance over girls.

Businessmen in the villages were particularly aggrieved and threatened by the actions of the youth. They were subjected to regular demands for food and money, and their persons and property were threatened if they refused. Shopkeepers could not go to town to buy stock and companies dare not deliver. Buses, cars and taxis were regularly hijacked so that youths could attend rallies and funerals or simply move between villages. Criminal elements also joined in the free-for-all. And an ominous debate reached traders' ears as to whether or not they were part of the 'enemy'. These pressures galvanised them into action. Isaac Sekhukhune recalls how

> the Sekhukhuneland Chamber of Commerce called a meeting of traders. A few members with higher political consciousness advised the chamber to disarm the youth by giving them advice from closer range. We came up with the idea of forming a Parents' Crisis Committee ... to take on the task of educating the people in a struggle spirit.[53]

The committee was duly formed. Although it remained dominated by business people, it also included Peter Nchabeleng and unionists from the Steelpoort area. Some time passed, however, before it had much effect.

The behaviour of the comrades sent shock waves through the villages. But while some simply revelled in their new-found freedom and power, others saw themselves as agents of reconstruction who would rid villages of conflict and oppression and create new and cohesive communities. In some villages the youth set up 'people's courts' in the form either of mass meetings or disciplinary committees:

> A woman would take a complaint to the youth. You would have small boys 15-20 years old presiding over family problems, telling the husband you will be home before 7, if you are late we will sjambok you ... even the rate of drinking went down in the villages. So they were very popular with some old ladies but not so popular with the old men with drinking problems.[54]

Divorce was also frowned upon and discontented couples were ordered to stay together. In the imagined community of the comrades, families remained united. But these courts did not only handle domestic disputes. They also dealt with political offences such as 'speaking ill of the organisation' and serious crimes, like theft and rape, in effect usurping the role of chiefs' and magistrates' courts. Migrant workers and parents who sympathised with complaints about corruption and maladministration did not take kindly to youths taking control of the villages, defying, judging and threatening their elders and denouncing the institution of chieftainship. Many of the stalwarts of the Khuduthamaga and Sebatakgomo, who had been the militant young men of their day, were appalled by the behaviour of the comrades and incredulous that they could invoke the authority of the ANC.[55]

There was, however, another element in the comrades' diagnosis of problems confronting the community which both owed a great deal to the concerns and conversation of their parents and which initially elicited broad-based support: concern over the plague of witches which many believed to be gnawing at the foundations of society. Youths had grown up in households which had resonated with complaints about the disasters and diseases inflicted by witches. Many of these witches had been named during visits to *dingaka* and most were neighbours or kinsmen. While their identities and deeds were mulled over behind closed doors, and protective magic was deployed, many families continued to live cheek by jowl with people whom they believed to be their cruellest tormentors.

The rise of the comrades took place against the backdrop of the renewed wave of witchcraft killings which swept through the Northern Transvaal from 1984 and which had claimed victims in Sekhukhuneland late in 1985. On 19 October, Betty Mahlo was stoned to death by a group led by her neighbours because:

> During this year my father passed away, mysteriously. When our father was buried our neighbours did not attend the funeral. About two weeks later my brother was knocked down by a car and he was buried Saturday last. My friends and brothers came together and decided to kill the [neighbour Betty Mahlo] because she is the one bewitching the family.[56]

In every village, the issue of witchcraft was raised amongst the comrades. In Steve Moganedi's dream, for example, which had placed him on a platform addressing a crowd, what he was telling his audience was 'how I was suffering and how I had been bewitched. How [witchcraft] had made me lose interest in my studies.'[57] Youths debated what to do about witches. Some argued that they should be persuaded – if necessary forced – to put their powers to beneficial use by rendering the police powerless or by 'providing muti to kill the Boers', and some 'witches' were approached for help.[58]

Others argued that witches deserved to die as they were now causing comrades to be arrested and killed.[59] At one workshop, Elleck Nchabeleng recalls one youth saying:

> No comrades, here is a serious problem. They are talking about things we don't even know. But we are having our own problems here at home that have to be faced. A member of your committee was struck by lightning last month ... now we say an injury to one is an injury to all. What should be our position? On this side we have got the police, the army and the witches against us and of course our position with the army and the police is clear. But now with the witches, what should be our line?[60]

This debate was resolved differently in different villages. In most, 'witches' were not attacked or killed although in some instances there was a precarious balance of forces. James Nchabeleng, an ANC/SACP activist in the 1950s, recalls that in the village of Ntšabeleng the comrades drew up a long list of witches and informed the chief and his councillors that they intended to kill them. In the argument that ensued,

> I told them about politics. That the people whose names you are using, Mandela and the others, I was going about with them. I know well that he never said burn the people. Now if you burn the people you must know that you are not following him. You are doing your own things. You will belittle yourselves and demean his name.[61]

In the end, the threat was not carried out at Ntšabeleng, partly because of divisions amongst the youth leadership and the intervention of security forces. But in some villages, the youth decided to act. In the Apel/Nkwana area, the cradle of youth organisation and the home of Peter Nchabeleng, 32 people accused of witchcraft were killed over a two-month period from February to April 1986.

'African Television'

When the news of these killings broke, Sekhukhuneland was catapulted on to the front page of the national press. The last time that the media had paid any attention to the area was during the 1958 revolt and, although some journalists tried to form an understanding of both the place and the events, many reached for the same clichés about primordial Africa that had sustained reporters three decades earlier. *The Star* lamented the fact that 'superstition and violence in response to alleged witchcraft are old features of tribal life'.[62] Under the headline 'Savagery', the *Pretoria News* editorialised that these deaths 'are sobering reminders that savagery lies shallow in Africa'.[63] Others, partly out of concern to distance political organisations from these events, joined in the chorus. Peter Mokaba, a youth leader and UDF official, denied that 'political agitation' had played a role and said that 'superstition was rife in Lebowa ... the victims had been killed on the instruction of witchdoctors'.[64] Progressive lawyers initially adopted a similar tack, arguing that the killings were not the work of youth organisations but had been orchestrated by 'conservative ... tribal elders'.[65] After a week, despite the fact that most of the questions remained unresolved, the story had run its course and the media moved on to fresh horrors.

A fuller understanding of these events requires an exploration both of the context in which they took place and the processes which led up to them. The villages of Apel and Nkwana lie in the arid northern section of the old Geluks location, close to the Olifants River. Over the decades they had sprawled out alongside the foothills of the Leolo Mountains and had grown together. As the settlements expanded, they had developed distinct named subsections ranging in size from scores to hundreds of people. These usually included a number of clusters of kin but the old *kgoro* structure of settlement had long since been overwhelmed by the pressure on space, and neighbours were by no means necessarily relatives.

Although the settlements had intertwined, the politics of the two villages had taken distinct paths. The chief at Nkwana, Stephen Potlake Pasha, had been one of the first in the area to accept Bantu Authorities and to break with the paramountcy, while the smaller Apel village ruled by Peter Nchabeleng's cousin, Molokwe Nchabeleng, remained resolutely opposed to *boipušo*. Tensions flared between the groups from time to time and were reflected in songs mocking the 'Rangers' of Nkwana that were sung at Apel. However, these communities shared a harsh environment in which the rains failed with even greater regularity than elsewhere in the region. And the cumulus clouds that piled up against the mountains, raising hopes of rain, often delivered only thunder and lightning. The local perception was that this was a place particularly prone to lightning strikes. It was also an area which was believed to be especially troubled by witchcraft.[66]

By 1986, the tension between the two communities was at a relatively low level. The divisions of the 1950s had been partly overlaid by the anger they shared over the land dispute with Masha, and the youth leadership had deliberately bracketed the two villages in one branch of Seyo. But relations between Stephen Pasha and his subjects at Nkwana were particularly strained. The chief had a girlfriend at Lebowakgomo and was rarely seen in the village. There was also a dispute about his alleged misuse of school funds, and a group within the village, predominantly consisting of migrant workers, was demanding a full accounting and pressing for Potlake's replacement by his half-brother. When the youth started to mobilise in the area, one of the first steps they took was to

> call him back home. They said that if he was interested to be chief in
> that area, he must stay at home. If he wants to stay in Lebowakgomo
> … he must stay but he must forget that he is actually the chief.[67]

Stephen Pasha returned to Nkwana. But he was under attack on two fronts and was in no position to assert his authority. His main concern was for his own survival and to ensure that the youth and migrants did not form a common front against him.

In the preceding decades, recurring anxieties about witchcraft in these villages had usually been resolved by consulting outside diviners and banishing offenders. But in 1976 an event took place which remained deeply etched on the memories of all who witnessed it. A girl was killed by lightning and her father suspected of responsibility. Richard Sekonya recalls that:

> He had some goats and his herd was growing quite tremendously. He
> had taught his goats and he was communicating with them. People
> were strongly suspecting that it was witchcraft because when he saw
> them on the mountains he would just call *Dipudi tla gae* [goats come
> home]. They would say 'baa' and they would actually come down and
> that was associated with witchcraft.[68]

The man had two wives. He had children by his first wife but spent much of
his time, and committed most of his resources, to his second wife, who was
childless. As a result, there was considerable tension between the two households. His eldest son found it impossible to hold down a job and 'people were
saying "he doesn't work, his father has bewitched him"'.[69] When his daughter was killed, it was seen as decisive proof of his guilt. He was hung from a
tree and tortured until he confessed and then he and his second wife were
placed in their hut and burned to death. The crowd gave 'the first son to the
first wife, the matches to set fire to the house'.[70]

During 1986, with the Seyo leadership concentrated on getting the youth
movement going in the region, youth organisation spread rapidly within the
villages. Soon every subsection had its own group of comrades, who were
left to their own devices for much of the time and who pondered appropriate
forms of action and 'legitimate targets'. The issue of witchcraft soon surfaced. It was couched in terms which drew both on long-established
discourses and the new language of youth politics. Discussions about class,
community and witchcraft intertwined:

> We realised that those witches kill innocent people ... [T]he poor
> people, they [the witches] just play with them ... just kill them
> miserably because no one can take action against them. But they are
> scared of rich men because they will take further steps against them.
> So as the youth we realised that even the poor people, we must not
> just ignore or neglect them, we must help them. They are members of
> the community. We must save the community.[71]

The issue of witchcraft had considerable political appeal. There was, after all,
widespread agreement amongst youth and their parents that witches were the
bane of the community. And few disputed that, if they could be eradicated, a
new era of cohesion and harmony would dawn. It was also a dimension in
which Potlake Pasha had conspicuously failed to fulfil his responsibility to
protect his subjects. But these discussions might have remained theoretical
had the fates not intervened.

On 8 February, the day of the funeral of Solomon Maditsi, who had been
shot during the excursion to Masha, a young 'comrade' named Mamphakashe
Kupa was killed by lightning. The youth were in an uproar as a result, and rumours circulated that an old woman had been heard to say that all comrades

should be killed. Members of the dead boy's family and others, both young and old, were adamant that steps should be taken against the witches. The next morning, the local Seyo leadership convened a meeting at Morokalebole school where the matter was debated. Some of the leaders advocated caution, but the mood favoured decisive action. The meeting decided to consult a diviner and money was collected from those present, and more broadly in the community, to cover the costs. Three elderly people who were suspected of complicity in the killing, and a number of youths elected by the meeting, were sent to visit a diviner – Ramaredi Mamoratwa Shoba – who lived in the Pelangwe subsection of the Nkwana chiefdom. However, one of the suspects – Mpakhana Kupa – protested against using a local *ngaka* and urged instead that they followed the normal practice of consulting a specialist who lived further afield. The youths saw this as a ploy to evade identification and the trip was aborted. The following day a youth delegation – including prominent figures from Seyo – went to Pelangwe to consult with Shoba, the local *ngaka*.[72]

Ramaredi Shoba was in her thirties, the aunt of one of the comrades and a full-time *ngaka*. But she did not 'throw bones' or manipulate objects like most other diviners. Instead, she hung a white sheet on the wall in a darkened room and gave small groups 'green muti' to drink, which made them feel intoxicated. They would then stare at the wall and call out:

> 'you who are responsible for the death of this man *come* we want to see you'. So then that particular person will appear, so when he appears on the screen you must ask the person if he is really the one. But it is impossible for that person to talk. He just nods.[73]

The viewers would call out the names of the individuals they knew, and the identity of the witches would be relayed to the crowd waiting outside. Youths also reported seeing witches at work and zombies labouring in fields and houses.

Shoba is often described as the '*spieel* (mirror) woman'; mirrors have a long history as instruments of witch detection in Africa and elsewhere. But other terms are also used by the youth in describing the technique she used. 'The screen' is one that recurs, as is 'the video' and – often said with a half-laugh – 'African television'.[74] Part of Shoba's appeal for the youth was that they saw her methods, like their politics, as being modern. By the 1980s, even in the villages of Sekhukhuneland, youth culture was influenced by film, television and video. Many adolescents only had the most intermittent contact with these forms of media, but they were seen as core elements in a world they caught glimpses of, and longed to share.

Shoba's procedure synthesised the pressing everyday concerns of village life with a yearning for a new order.

It also, in practice, placed the identification of witches squarely in the hands of the youth and it is not surprising that on this first visit to the screen – as on subsequent visits – their suspicions were confirmed. Mphakana Kupa, his wife Kgolane Kupa, and Moditi Johannes Moraswi were seized and forced into a hut which was doused with petrol: 'We locked them in, tied the door with wires so that they could not escape ... We set it alight and that was the end of them.'[75]

This episode ensured that the issue of witchcraft was high on the youth groups' agenda for action. On 19 February, at nearby Pelangwe, a pregnant woman was killed by lightning. The youth gathered and elected representatives from each *kgoro* to 'go to the mirror'. They returned with the names of two men and two women. Makibela Makgolane testified later how youths approached her mother, who was carrying a table, and said 'come along, you witch, we are going to burn you'. Matilda Ngake pleaded in vain with the crowd to spare the life of her mother. But those accused of being witches were 'driven like beasts' to a hut, locked in and burnt.[76]

A month passed with no schooling or effective policing in the villages, while comrades did battle throughout the region. In this capricious context, the chief at Apel went out of his way to avoid a confrontation with the comrades while Potlake Pasha manoeuvred adroitly to prevent the youth from challenging his position, and to focus their attention elsewhere. Many of the comrades believed that he tacitly supported their campaign against witches, and few doubted his delight when one of his leading opponents fell under suspicion.

Peter Nchabeleng and some of the original youth leadership attempted to deflect attention from the issue of witchcraft but had little success. A gulf started to open up between the youth and the older generations on the methods employed. While some adults believed that fiery execution was a witch's just dessert, many felt that more moderate forms of punishment – like banishment – were sufficient reprisal. And every killing left a grief-stricken and angry cluster of relatives and friends who disputed both the verdict and the authority of the comrades. But the youths were not prepared to compromise. An activist recalled that: 'There was this suggestion by the parents that these people should be evicted from the community ... We refused to accept this suggestion.'[77]

The comrades pointed out that milder punishment had not previously been conspicuously successful in eliminating witchcraft, and that

> these people have done terrible things ... so they must receive a
> double terrible punishment which is not familiar ... [B]urning

somebody alive is a severe punishment so ... [other witches] when
they think to do another thing, they will think no, the fire, you will die
terribly.[78]

Many also believed that it was only by the complete destruction of a witch's
person and medicines that he or she could be prevented from striking back
from beyond the grave. And 'if you just ordinarily kill a witch, there will be
someone who is responsible for the death and the family of that witch will
use their magic to take revenge'.[79]

Youth also pointed out that, in pre-colonial times, witches had been put to
death and that only ten years previously adults had also seen fit to burn
witches at Nkwana.

In late March a new cycle of burnings began. There was a lightning strike
at Apel on 25 March which injured a woman. A meeting was called and a
delegation dispatched to Ramaredi Shoba. It returned with the names of two
women who were interrogated and then executed. On 1 April a meeting was
held by the youth in the Maisela subsection of Nkwana to discuss a lightning
strike close to the home of one of the comrades. Once again a deputation was
sent to Shoba, and once again it returned with a list of names. Two women
and a man were taken to a nearby hill. The sons of the two women were ordered by the crowd to give their mothers petrol to drink and place tyres
around their necks. They were then forced to pour petrol over them and set
them alight. The logic of this horrifying act, presumably, was that it would
reduce the probability of reprisals against the comrades.[80]

As the movement gathered momentum, the direct connection between
death by lightning and reprisal loosened. Near misses and a wide variety of
episodes believed to be manifestations of witchcraft – reported sightings of
animals thought to be witches' familiars, of zombies, of naked men and inex-
plicable nocturnal disturbances – now spurred the youth on to action. On
9 April, a meeting was called to discuss the apparent epidemic of witches.
Shoba was brought from Pelangwe. She set up her screen and a couple of
suspects were identified.

But the assembled youth believed that the time for half-measures had
passed and the only solution was to deal with all of those believed to be
witches, regardless of whether they had been seen on the screen. On 9 and
10 April, youths from the different subsections of Nkwana rounded up the individuals they judged to be witches in the various neighbourhoods. Their
captives were interrogated about their practices and ordered to bring their
medicines. Many were then taken to a hill called Thaba Nchu (Black Mountain) where they were doused with petrol or, when supplies started to run
low, with paraffin. The terrified victims were covered with tyres and wood

and sometimes forced to light the matches which set them ablaze. Twenty people were burned alive.[81]

Individuals recall how, for two days, bands of youth moved through the villages searching for victims, singing

> *Re tlile re tlo go tšea* We have come to take you
> *O kare re tlo go tšhuma* It may be that we will burn you.[82]

And how the plumes of heavy black smoke rising from Thaba Nchu twisted in the air over the village.

Comrades and Witches

While the preceding narrative provides a number of clues regarding underlying social patterns, many questions remain incompletely answered. Not least off these involves who the killers were, and who they killed.

Witchcraft was a cause for concern for the vast majority of members of these villages. But the active participants in the movement were overwhelmingly drawn from the youth. In the early stages of the killings, some adults attended meetings and even egged the youth on to action. But as the burnings gathered momentum, the complexion of the crowd grew ever younger. The average age of those involved was 19, with the majority still at school although secondary school leavers who had remained in the villages also played an important part. Girls were present throughout, but remained on the edges of the crowd, and rarely played a central role in the interrogation or execution of suspects. They were, however, expected to collect wood to fuel the fires.[83]

The composition of these groups was, in short, identical to that of the comrades. The evidence does not support the view that those involved in killing witches were a distinct group. Some of the original core members of Seyo distanced themselves from these events. But others did not, and while they may not have been always, or even often, at the forefront of the crowd, they visited Shoba's screen and were present at burnings. As the youth movement grew and developed a mass following, the issues raised by the initial leadership were reformulated in terms which made sense to local level leaders and their supporters.

In the specific circumstances of Apel/Nkwana, witchcraft emerged as a dominant concern, and no leader could stand against it and hope to retain his position. Ramaredi Shoba facilitated action. She did not instigate or even direct it. And the issue of witchcraft was not an alternative to a political programme. Rather, the eradication of witches was seen as a fundamental part of the creation of a new community freed of the oppression, iniquity and misfortune which had dogged village life under apartheid. The young men who undertook the task brought to it the certainty and energy of adolescence, and the conviction that radical action could triumph where their parents' cautious measures had failed.[84]

These observations bring the crowd into somewhat sharper focus. But they do not explain who the victims were, or illuminate their relationship to their accusers and executioners. It is clear that the fires did not consume strangers or abstract sociological categories, they destroyed neighbours and relatives. In every instance, youths from the various subsections of Nkwana and Apel sought out the witches in their own immediate communities. It was often individuals closely connected to the families that had experienced misfortune who went to the mirror and took the lead in identifying witches. They brought to the screen their own genealogies of conflict within and between families, and lifetimes of listening to complaints about witchcraft and hearing witches named. In some instances, youths named their own parents or grandparents. In others, nephews named uncles and aunts. In one particularly well-documented case, the son of a first wife took the lead in naming and killing his father's second wife. And long-standing disputes between neighbours also played their part.[85]

Many also believed that groups of witches with powerful leaders existed and that witches passed on their skills – mainly to their daughters. The consequence of this was that the friends, spouses and especially daughters and sisters of individuals named as witches also came under suspicion and ran a high risk of being named and killed. As the movement gathered momentum, and the link between specific disasters and executions weakened, the victims increasingly became individuals 'generally known to be witches' within neighbourhoods.

There is also evidence of youths exploiting the events to take revenge over specific grievances. One youth who had made a girl pregnant had been angered when her mother reported the matter to his parents. He took the lead in naming her as a witch and in her subsequent murder. Another individual who had clashed with his storekeeper employer identified him as a witch, and helped to burn him.[86]

The accusers and the accused were bound together by ties of locality and kinship. But they were separated by age and gender. The average age of the executioners was 19 or less. The average age of their victims exceeded 60. Of 24 victims whose age can be broadly specified, 19 were over 50 years of age and many of those were in their sixties and seventies. Equally, while the vast majority of active participants in the identification and killing of witches were boys, two-thirds of their victims were women. Twenty-one of the 31 victims whose sex can be established were female. But while these numbers suggest some patterns which will be pursued below, they also run the risk of desecrating the charred remnants of the dead by converting them into lifeless statistics. A fuller account of the lives and local perceptions of some of the men and women who died is as important to comprehending the nature of these events.[87]

Mphakana Kupa and Kgolane Kupa, who were amongst the first three burned on 10 February, were respectively grand-uncle and aunt to the boy Mamphakashe Kupa, who was killed by lightning. Mphakana was an elderly man who served on the school committee and

> who had donkeys and a cart which he used to harvest firewood for selling and he was fetching and selling water. He was also commonly known to be a witch. They were saying he was having zombies on top of the mountain. People thought that zombies were helping him get the firewood [because] he was making many loads. He was an old but active person.[88]

His wife, Kgolane, was suspected both because of her husband and because she came from 'a family of witches'. Her brother, Selelepe Thobejane, who was burned on 10 April,

> was known to be a witch. He had a field near to a river. Even when there is so much drought he was still getting a crop and as a result he was suspected. But before that there was this man called Setlogo Sekonya. That man just went missing ... In the community it was known that he [Selelepe] is responsible for that man. He is his zombie. Some people even said that, behind the mountain where he was staying, if you could go at midday you could still see the man in the clothes in which he had gone missing ... [Long ago] when his family consulted a *ngaka* they found this man [Selelepe] was responsible.[89]

Some hours after Selelepe died, the youth returned to the spot where he had been burned only to find

> that everything was cleared up, there were no bones left, nothing. They said 'it's his wife, she is going to do something'. So they went to [his wife Raisebe] and they said 'bring those things out.' She got those bones out. They said 'what were you going to do with them?' She said, 'No, I was going to bury them.' They said 'why didn't you ask our permission? We know ... what you were going to do.'[90]

On the assumption that she was planning reprisals against the comrades, Raisebe was also killed.

Makgwale Pasha was burnt along with her daughter, Mpate Pasha, in Nkwana on 9 April. Makgwale, who was in her late sixties, was 'commonly known to be a bad person and a witch'.[91] A variety of allegations were made about her. It was said, for example, that she bewitched her brother's son many years before, had been identified by a *ngaka* and had been paraded through the village with her head shaved. Her daughter, Mpate, was in her early forties. She was an unmarried woman with two children who made a living by making and selling clothes and curtains. She died partly because 'there is this belief that if the granny is close to one child in the family, then that granny will dedicate all her secrets and everything that is valuable to that person'.[92]

More crudely put, she died because 'a witch's daughter is also a witch'.[93]

But by no means all the individuals who died were commonly suspected of being witches. Magdeline Ngake, who was in her forties, and was burned at Pelangwe on 20 February, was a staunch Methodist and a storekeeper. Many people were surprised when she was identified in the mirror. It is not possible to establish her relationship to her accusers, but the fact that her father was one of the more prosperous businessmen in the area may have played a part in shaping her fate. Another suspect – Matlabane Thobejane – was a businessman who had achieved rapid success and thereby incurred popular suspicion. He also resisted demands for food and money from the comrades. He lost his mother to the flames and his girlfriend, who was a nurse, narrowly escaped with her life. There is also a suggestion that some members of the business community attempted to direct the anger of the youth against their rivals, but it is not possible to test this proposition against the existing evidence.[94]

Mashakwane Sekonya, who died at Nkwana on 10 April, was an 'old woman' who was believed to have turned her husband's brother into a zombie. Her elderly sister, Rampati Pasha, who lived alone, was also burned along with her friend and neighbour Ramatsimele Pasha, who had a growth on her knee which people believed was caused by magic used to counter her witchcraft. Manyake Talane, who lived with her husband and her granddaughter, was in her seventies and could no longer walk. She was dragged away by the comrades during the generalised killing of witches at Nkwana.[95]

A number of local *dingaka* were also attacked. Selejane Ben Mathebe, for example, was a pensioner who sold medicines and potions. A number of young children had died in quick succession in his neighbourhood in the early 1980s and suspicion had fallen upon him. When the youth went to his house on 9 April, they made him bring out all his medicines and explain their composition and purpose before they took him away and burned him.[96]

The youth were the primary actors in these tragic events and in some instances played a leading role in identifying witches. But in many cases the individuals who were targeted had long attracted suspicion within the community. They had been defined as witches through complex processes of family and neighbourhood conflicts and visits to *dingaka* over many years.

Youths had grown up listening to accounts of their evil deeds, of the disasters they had caused and the zombies they commanded. They had also noted the failure of their elders to do anything decisive about these nefarious acts. And they added their own personal ingredients to this potent cocktail of suspicion and accusation.

The fact that the majority of the victims were women reflected broader attitudes within the community. The division between day witches, who were mainly male, and night witches, who were mainly female, had eroded by the 1980s and it was widely believed that the ranks of witches were dominated by women. One activist, when asked to explain this, commented:

> That is our own tradition. All the time linking women to witchcraft. It is how we grew up. Bad things are actually associated with women. Most men are migrant workers and as a result are not at home. In any family, if one of the children is not doing good things, the father will always associate that child with the mother. This is your child ... You see bad things are associated with women ... Men don't trust women.[97]

Witchcraft powers were also believed to be passed on in the female line:

> It is very rare that if, as your mother, I am a witch and you are my son, and I am having a daughter, that I can chose to give my heritage to a male.[98]

The attacks on the daughter of a prosperous local entrepreneur and on the female associates of another shopkeeper may also have been indicative of the belief that the power of female witchcraft had been one motor of economic success. It was regarded as essential to a properly ordered society that women should remain under male authority, partly because they were believed to harbour the potentially anarchic forces of nature. Here, as elsewhere, women were said 'to bewitch out of innate capacity, as a function of ambiguous values, the ambivalences naturalised in their very substance'.[99] And the ambiguity of women's positions within the villages had been intensified by the processes of change at work which had not altered their formal status and had increased their dependence on cash income, but had also extended their control over households and their centrality within village life.

The sex ratio amongst the adult and elderly population in these villages was significantly tilted towards females, and substantial numbers of households were female-linked or female-headed. To a considerable extent, local disputes were therefore played out between women. But there was another important context: young men, who had been raised to expect to exercise control over women, instead found themselves trapped in social limbo and unable to assert either male or adult authority. They depended on or collided with the women who controlled pensions, remittances and households. And they heard their fathers and uncles complain that women were insubordinate. Youths also had strained relationships with the oldest generations in most villages, who deplored their unruly and precocious behaviour and could often barely conceal their distaste for their politics. The youth in turn stigmatised the elderly as custodians of a reactionary order. They also believed that older men and women envied their educational achievements and expanded possibilities, and that this jealousy spurred some of them on to witchcraft.

These tensions were compounded by the implicit or open threats of witchcraft which were one of the last weapons available to some older villagers. This context ensured that some of the youths rounding up witches revelled in the exercise of power and the opportunity to enforce both respect from their elders and authority over women.[100]

Much of what happened in Sekhukhuneland in 1986 comes as no surprise to those familiar with the study of witchcraft in Africa. Witchcraft accusations are often a currency of conflict between neighbours and within families, but as this episode confirms, 'witchcraft is not simply an imaginative "idiom". It is chillingly concrete, its micropolitics all too real.'[101] The element of generational revolt also echoes processes in witchcraft eradication movements which have been described by social anthropologists in Central and East Africa since the 1930s. For example, what happened in the early 1960s when the Kamcape movement in Tanzania

> takes over a village in a 'cleansing' operation has certain resemblances to a miniature revolution. The abrupt assumption of authority by young men and young women ... seems to suggest that the old order has been overturned ... But this reversal of social roles and values exists only for the hour or two that the Kamcape operation lasts.[102]

But what took place in Sekhukhuneland went well beyond a symbolic and temporary reversal of social roles. In a context of the collapse of the legitimacy of local forms of authority and national revolt, the youth took control in the villages. They also went well beyond a ritual drama of identifying and then reintegrating witches into a healed and reunified community. Against a backdrop of witchkillings in the Northern Transvaal since the mid-1970s and the necklacing of *impimpis* (informers) who were held responsible for undermining community solidarity in the townships, the youth were determined to deal with the problem once and for all by utterly destroying the culprits and their powers.

Had there been periodic symbolic witchcraft eradication movements in the Northern Transvaal to provide relief and to create reimagined communities, these killings may never have come to pass. But in the context of colonial prohibitions against punishing witches, the crumbling credibility of chieftainship and intensifying processes of conflict and change, communities believed they were bereft of effective defences and had become infested with witches. The comrades came to the rescue.

Repression and Reform

On 10 April, while the comrades were executing witches, other members of the community contacted the police to tell them what was happening. That evening, a strong force of Lebowa police arrived at Nkwana. Smarting from their pariah status in this and other villages, shocked by what they found, and convinced that these deeds could only be the work of the comrades and their patrons in the UDF, they arrested Peter Nchabeleng. As they took him from his home, they told his wife that she would never see him alive again. True to their word, they took him to Schoonoord police station and beat him until he signed a confession and until he was so grievously battered that he died.

The next day they returned to round up the comrades. Morris Nchabeleng was arrested as he attempted to flee to Turfloop. The policeman who hauled him from a taxi told him: 'we have killed your father and now we are going to kill you'.[103] Peter Nchabeleng was given a hero's funeral and more than twenty thousand people made their way to Apel to honour him and mourn his passing amidst 'home-made ANC and Communist flags held aloft on poles roughly hewn from local thorn trees'.[104]

The comrades continued to hold sway in other villages until early in June but then the army and police, under the cloak of a second, still more draconian, state of emergency, launched a major onslaught against the youth. They were assisted by vigilante groups which were usually made up of close associates of the chiefs and unemployed older men. The vulnerability of the comrades to counter-attack was increased by the fact that their unruly and violent behaviour had alienated significant sections of most communities. By mid-1987, after months of shootings, beatings, detentions, torture and the reconstruction of networks of informers, the youth movement had collapsed.

Eighty-two youths from Apel/Nkwana appeared in seven murder trials during 1987 and 1988. In the first trial, the defendants pleaded not guilty but, in the face of damning evidence, received heavy sentences. Two youths identified as leaders were sentenced to death. Thereafter, defence lawyers adopted a strategy of entering guilty pleas with a deep-seated belief in witchcraft offered in mitigation. If youths under 18 pleaded guilty they were usually sentenced to no more than a caning and the lawyers negotiated with the prosecution that, if juvenile offenders admitted culpability, charges would be dropped against many of the older accused who risked more severe sentences.[105]

A semblance of normality returned to the villages. But graffiti painted on rocks and walls, the rumble of armoured vehicles, roadblocks and clusters of green army tents told a different tale. Pupils and teachers returned to classes in the latter half of 1986 but in many schools education barely resumed. The authority of principals and their staff had been profoundly undermined and alternative structures such as SRCs had collapsed. A deep-seated malaise set in. Teachers, faced with unruly and unwilling classes, became still more demoralised while pupils arrived at school late and spent the day hanging around the yard or left early. Class boycotts were endemic and the matric pass rate plummeted to below 40 per cent and continued downward. Already bulging classes became still more bloated as thousands of failed students, unable to find employment or gain access to teacher training colleges, returned to school. Some dedicated teachers and committed students battled on, but the overall picture was bleak.[106]

Many chiefs breathed a sigh of relief as the security services cracked down and some who had fled the area returned to their villages under army protection. At Mohlaletse, Kenneth and his councillors had avoided a direct clash with the comrades but relations had been extremely strained. The retired migrants and stalwarts of the Khuduthamaga who formed the inner circle of advisers had been appalled by the behaviour of the youth and – especially – their denigration of *bogoši*. The youth in turn saw these 'old men' as unsympathetic to their cause and were angered that they had not done more to assist them when they had been under attack from the army and police. But no sooner had this tension eased than a new and even more dangerous threat to the position of *kgošikgolo* loomed on the horizon.[107]

In 1982 Rhyne, who had declined to assume office in 1975, had written to the magistrate in Sekhukhuneland saying that he wanted his chieftainship back, but was informed that the matter was closed. In 1984, however, a group of younger men led by Makotanyane Morwamoche and Kgetsepe Makotanyane, who felt excluded by the old guard at Mohlaletse, started a campaign to have Rhyne reinstated. They alleged, amongst other things, that there had been mismanagement of tribal funds. For several years their efforts came to nothing, although they did muster some support in the village and the region. But in 1987 the Chief Minister of Lebowa, C.N. Phatudi, died. In the manoeuvrings which surrounded the succession, the Mohlaletse dispute emerged as a bargaining counter. Nelson Ramodike, who eventually if narrowly emerged as victorious, did so partly with the assistance of Phaswane Nkadimeng, Mankopodi's brother and Rhyne's uncle, who was appointed as a minister. In January of 1989, despite intense opposition at Mohlaletse, Kenneth was deposed by order of the Lebowa cabinet. Rhyne was proclaimed to be the 'born *kgoši*' and reinstated.

The logic which underpinned this decision was that rank alone determined succession to office, however unpopular or incompetent the individual might be. This view was, of course, a far cry from the conception that *'kgoši ke kgoši ka batho'* and from historical precedents in which power and popularity had often trumped genealogical position in contests for high office.[108]

Shortly after this decision was announced, Rhyne and his mother attempted to return to Mohlaletse but were prevented by the majority of the village from assuming effective control. He and Mankopodi remained under police protection in a mobile home parked in the premises of the tribal office, while Kenneth's supporters challenged Ramodike's action in the supreme court and set about collecting money from villagers and migrants to meet the very considerable legal costs involved. Rhyne made several attempts to enforce his authority with the backing of the Lebowa police – notably by prohibiting all who did not recognise his authority from cultivating their lands – which intensified popular anger. On 23 December 1989, Rhyne's armed guards opened fire on a demonstration against his heavy-handed measures, which was led by migrants who had returned home for Christmas. When the shooting stopped, three men lay dead and many more had been wounded.[109]

As this grim decade drew to a close, the political pendulum swung from repression to reform. In February 1990, the unbanning of the ANC and the SACP transformed political possibilities in Sekhukhuneland as elsewhere in South Africa. From late in 1989, initiatives had been taken to rebuild UDF structures in the region and to get civics off the ground in the villages. But now, playing a high stakes' political poker game with the National Party, the ANC needed to muster support in both town and countryside and to construct as broadly-based an alliance as possible.

In Sekhukhuneland, and more widely in the Northern Transvaal, the events of the mid-1980s had left a somewhat ambiguous legacy. A broad cross-section of rural society had been exposed to the symbols and slogans of the ANC. But the anarchic behaviour of some of the comrades had left deep political scars. Migrants and chiefs who had played a central role in ANC-linked politics in the 1950s viewed the youth, who were now the most vocal source of support for the movement, with considerable unease – a perspective which was shared by many local businessmen.

The ANC also confronted the problem of how to deal with homeland-based politicians and parties which had long been locked in conflict with both migrant associations and youth congresses, but which in an era of multi-party negotiations might prove important allies. And some of the leadership of the ANC was also haunted by the example of devastation wrought by

Renamo and Unita in neighbouring countries and determined not to provide hostages to reactionary fortune.[110]

There was an initial upsurge of organisation in 1990, with youth groupings at the forefront. Rallies were held to welcome 'returning heroes'. John Nkadimeng, Elias Motsoaledi and others visited the land of their birth for the first time in three decades. At meetings they recalled the history of the 1950s, the vital role of the Communist Party, the struggles of Sebatakgomo and the campaigns of MK. Stalwarts of this history of struggle were able, at long last, to reclaim their political heritage publicly.

But there were aspects of the message which the ANC leadership preached which many of their supporters found less than palatable. Efforts were made to allay the anxieties of local businessmen, and leading figures in the ANC appeared to embrace precisely the chiefs and homeland leaders whom the youth and some migrants regarded as principal foes. Mandela made clear his view that chiefs had a long and proud history of association with the ANC and had an important role to play in their communities. In rallies in the Northern Transvaal, he insisted that prominent chiefs share the platform with him. Nkadimeng and others involved in Sebatakgomo recalled the positive role played by chiefs in the fight against *Boipušo*. They tended, however, to gloss over the extent to which this had been the result of intense popular pressure and the profound transformations in the nature of *bogoši* which had taken place in the intervening years.[111]

Many chiefs in the regions remained apprehensive about the ANC, but some of the more prescient were quick to grasp the hand of friendship that was being offered to them. They hurried to join the ranks of the ANC-aligned Congress of Traditional Leaders of South Africa (Contralesa). Their numbers included some of the more popular chiefs in the region as well as individuals detested by the majority of their subjects and most closely associated with the crackdown by the army and the police in the 1980s. The latter group now proclaimed themselves as supporters of the ANC and denounced attempts by the youth and migrants to raise issues of corruption and maladministration in the villages as 'uncomradely behaviour', appealing to the ANC leadership for support. Many chiefs also saw the somewhat belated attempts to establish civic organisations as a threat to their positions. Their anxieties were heightened by the prominent role played by organised youth and workers in some of these initiatives. They complained to both the Lebowa authorities and the ANC that civics were malignant growths and threatened to activate vigilante groups to cauterise them. It was also made very clear to members of civics that they were on a collision course with local rulers. Partly as a result of this, civic structures in Sekhukhuneland remained sparse and weak.[112]

The majority of the chiefs retained close links with Nelson Ramodike and the Lebowa Peoples Party – renamed the United Peoples Front in 1991 in line with the spirit of the times. Ramodike's administration was principally distinguished by incompetence and corruption on an epic scale. Long-standing Congress supporters were dismayed by the persistent courtship of Ramodike by the national ANC leadership. The logic behind these advances appears to have been the importance of multi-party alliances in the negotiations process and the misguided belief that Ramodike commanded a political machine which controlled a significant rural vote. The chief minister saw in these approaches the possibility of steering his foundering administration into calmer waters and launching a new political career.

In October 1990, a senior delegation from the ANC national executive committee met with the Lebowa cabinet. Ramodike denounced civics, argued that there was little effective ANC organisation in Lebowa and intimated that he could fill this gap. *Kgoši* Matlala suggested that 'the ANC does not need to crack its head about organising, the chiefs are there to do the job'.[113] These comments struck a chord with the ANC leaders whose own relationship with civic structures was less than easy and who were insecure about their own organisational capacity in rural areas. During the meeting, it was agreed that 'a communality of interest had developed between the ANC and the Lebowa government' and that there was a need to 'redirect the activities of structures on the ground'.[114]

Thereafter, Ramodike continued in his position as effective leader of the UPF but also joined the ANC. He was rewarded for his political agility by being invited to share a platform with Mandela at a June 16 Rally in Soweto in 1991. But while he promised the national leadership his organisational support, he and his followers actively discouraged the establishment of civics and branches of the ANC, while repeatedly calling on head office to curb local members. The consequence was an increasingly strained relationship between local and national leadership, with bitter complaints voiced in Sekhukhuneland and elsewhere that Ramodike had considerably greater access to ANC headquarters and received a much more sympathetic hearing than did members of ANC branches.

The Mohlaletse branch was particularly aggrieved. It included some of the leadership of Fetakgomo and was chaired by the white-haired and imposing figure of Kgagudi Maredi, who had been one of the first deportees in 1957 and had been banished for more than ten years. The branch, which was one of the biggest in the region, was strongly in support of the deposed chief, Kenneth Kgagudi, and looked on in mounting horror at the blossoming relationship between Ramodike and the ANC leadership. Old men, who for years had cherished the hope that the ANC would be able to operate openly once

Youth on the move at Manganeng in the late 1980s. The banners refer to Cosas, display the hammer and sickle and carry the slogan 'each one teach one'. *(Titus Nkadimeng)*

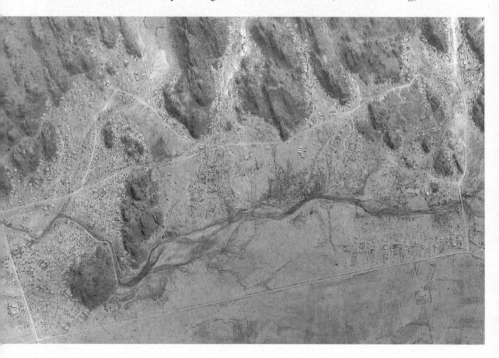

Aerial photograph showing the thousands of households of Apel *(to the left)* and Nkwana *(to the right)* alongside the foothills of the Leolo Mountains.

Relatives gather the charred remnants of a victim of the witch burnings in the region in 1986.
(The Star)

COMRADE

PETER NCHABELENG

PRESIDENT ~ UDF N. TRANSVAAL

A COMBATANT FOR LIFE

A PATRIOT TO THE END

Globe.

Issued by UDF, Khotso House, Johannesburg.

Poster produced by the UDF after the murder of Peter Nchabeleng by the Lebowa police in 1986.
(Mayibuye Centre)

Political graffiti, Jane Furse, Sekhukhuneland, 1988. *(Struan Robertson)*

Youth marching with ANC and Communist Party flags to the 'welcome home' rally for John Nkadimeng at Manganeng in 1990. *(P Mbiba)*

Elias Motsoaledi speaking at his 'welcome home' rally at Phokwane in 1990.

Nelson Diale speaking at the same rally, 1990. *(Tony Harding)*

Kgošikgolo KK Sekhukhune outside his palace, Mohlaletse, 1992. *(Struan Robertson)*

Kgagudi Lot Maredi speaking at a meeting at Mohlaletse, 1993. He was a leading figure in the resistance in Sekhukhuneland in the 1950s and was banished to the Eastern Cape for over ten years. He was the first chairman of the ANC branch established at Mohlaletse in 1990. He died in 1994. *(Struan Robertson)*

Nelson Mandela arriving in Jane Furse, Sekhukhuneland, 30 November 1992. *(Struan Robertson)*

more, could barely believe that it would endorse the leader of Lebowa who – alongside many other vices – appeared to them to be hell-bent on the destruction of the paramountcy. And while local ANC structures attempted to avoid getting drawn into the dispute, Mohlaletse members were amazed to hear some senior members of the ANC echo the Lebowa cabinet's view that Rhyne was the 'born chief', and that was all that mattered.

In June 1991, the supreme court set aside the appointment of Rhyne, concluding that 'there is no basis in customary law or history or logic for the contention that a *kgoši* who ... renounced or repudiated his chieftainship can reclaim it later'.[115] Kenneth was reinstated but this judgment did not put an end to the matter. Both the Lebowa cabinet and some individuals within the ANC with connections to Rhyne repeatedly attempted to reopen the question.

The Mohlaletse branch was not only remarkable in the continuity of its leadership with earlier phases of struggle, but also in having a significant component of older members. The more usual pattern in the region was for local organisation to be dominated by young men. Despite the evaporation of the initial euphoria that followed the unbanning of the ANC, there was a steady spread of ANC branches and the relaunched ANC Youth League established a solid core of support. But active members of the ANC remained a small and youthful minority in most communities. By far the most dramatic upsurge in organisation in the early 1990s came from amongst civil servants and teachers who had not been in the forefront of political activity in either the 1950s or the 1980s but who now joined ANC branches in significant numbers, some becoming leading figures.[116]

But the ANC was not the only, or even the primary, focus of this organisational awakening. There was a rapid expansion of trade union membership and increase in industrial action which both was caused by, and in turn contributed to, the collapse of the Lebowa administration and the deepening educational malaise. Sekhukhuneland felt the backwash from these developments most powerfully in its schools. In 1990, the Sekhukhuneland Progressive Teachers Union was founded. Towards the end of the year, it was incorporated into the South African Democratic Teachers Union (Sadtu).

Sadtu provided a liferaft to teachers trapped in the rapidly deteriorating conditions which had prevailed in Lebowa schools since the mid-1980s. It also gave them a place and a voice in the process of making a new order. While older teachers and most headmasters were suspicious of this initiative, their younger colleagues joined in large numbers. In Lebowa, Sadtu raised a host of deep-seated grievances ranging from inadequate facilities, through corruption and nepotism in the education department, to pay and conditions of service. It also initially called for the resignation of Ramodike.[117]

Steadily deteriorating relations between the administration and teachers led to protracted strikes in 1991, 1992 and 1993. Teachers also launched 'defiance campaigns' and resisted inspectors' and headmasters' attempts to monitor or evaluate their performance. These struggles caused considerable strain in their relations with both pupils and parents who, although they had sympathy with many of the teachers' grievances, were distressed by the disruption of schooling. Particularly galling were 'chalk downs' in the lead-up time to end-of-year exams, and the fact that for some teachers defying the authorities meant spending still less time preparing lessons or in the classroom. Some youths were also rather sceptical about the new-found militancy of their instructors and recalled their rather less progressive position in earlier years. Complaints about sexual harassment and neglect of teaching duties surfaced once more in a number of schools and colleges. And the question of whether corporal punishment should be used in schools continued to divide teachers and their pupils.[118]

Notwithstanding these differences, regional ANC structures, which had strong teacher representation, routinely supported the action of Sadtu, as did the leadership of youth organisations. There were, however, complaints in these quarters about lack of consultation and there was also growing concern that the collapse of authority over teachers and other government employees would return to haunt any future administration.

Despite the turmoil in Lebowa, and steadily mounting evidence of corruption and maladministration, the ANC leadership persisted in its relationship with Ramodike. Fresh storms burst in 1994 when he was placed high on the ANC election list in recognition of the part he had played in the Patriotic Front. A senior ANC spokesman justified his selection with the comment that 'when people become ... too clean they make mistakes they regret later'.[119] However, during the run-up to the election, a chorus of protest from local structures, protracted strikes by teachers and civil servants and renewed allegations of improper conduct, finally persuaded ANC headquarters to relent and remove Ramodike from the list.

At the beginning of 1994, the ANC still had a long way to go in terms of establishing broadly based grassroots organisation, but it also did not confront any serious challenge at a local level. The United Peoples Front was widely discredited and disliked and had also suffered as a result of Ramodike's fling with the ANC. The PAC had slogans which at first sight were designed to appeal to a rural constituency, but it had little historical connection to the region and failed to establish effective organisation there in the 1990s.

The ANC, in contrast, had prominent leaders who hailed from Sekhukhuneland and had long-standing supporters amongst both migrant workers and the youth who remained loyal, despite elements of disenchantment.

Chiefs, teachers and civil servants were all able to identify with Congress and to see their own interests being advanced by an ANC victory at the polls. As importantly, Nelson Mandela commanded respect and support from an enormously wide constituency, ranging from conservative chiefs to militant youth.

The ANC election campaign in the Northern Transvaal focused on the provision of basic services, employment and housing. Little was said about land. In Mandela's election rallies in the region, he managed both to show deference to local chiefs and insist on a better deal for rural women.

But, as processes of mobilisation gathered momentum, the issue of witchcraft – which had been festering since 1986 – reared its head once more. In the first four months of 1994, elements within the youth, usually acting with wider support in their communities, accused more than 70 people of witchcraft and killed them. These youths promised to bring 'real freedom ... saying that there would be no witches left in the new South Africa'.[120]

In the end, despite the appalling levels of disorganisation on the part of the Northern Transvaal operation of the Independent Electoral Commission, which left young and old alike queuing for up to three days in the merciless sun, the people of Sekhukhuneland and elsewhere in the Northern Transvaal voted overwhelmingly for the ANC. Congress achieved its most massive victory in this region, winning 92 per cent of the vote and all but two seats in the legislature.

But the ANC administration now faces the daunting task of delivering on its promises to make a material difference to the lives of ordinary people in a region burdened with the rotting hulks of three homelands and the highest levels of poverty in South Africa. Its supporters are divided amongst themselves about the appropriate forms of economic and political intervention and the long march that lies ahead is bound to test the limits of loyalty of some followers and to set others at their comrades' throats. Finally, after decades of courting resistance, the ANC faces the formidable challenge of leading reconstruction.

Notes

1   M. Horrel, *African Homelands* (Johannesburg, 1973), p. 59; W. Breytenbach, *Tuislande: Selfregering en Politieke Partye* (Pretoria, 1975), p. 75; unrecorded discussions with G.M. Sekhukhune in 1976 and 1982.

2   W. Beinart, *Twentieth Century*, p. 210; Ritchken, 'Leadership and Conflict', pp. 148-55; The Commission of Inquiry into the Appropriation of the Lebowa Revenue Fund and Alleged Mismanagement, which was appointed in 1989 and reported in 1992, found that 'gross financial mismanagement and corruption was rife in the Lebowa administration', and this view certainly accorded with popular perceptions: see South African Institute of Race Relations, *Survey of Race Relations, 1992/3*, p. 26.

3   G.M. Sekhukhune, unrecorded discussions, 1976 and 1982; I. Sekhukhune, 1-5.

4   P. Nkadimeng, 1; I. Sekhukhune, 5; SC *K.K. Sekhukhune vs N. Ramodike and others*, Pretoria, 20/6/1991.

5   I. Sekhukhune, 2; G.M. Sekhukhune, unrecorded discussions, 1976 and 1982; South African Institute of Race Relations, *A Survey of Race Relations, 1977*, pp. 356-7 and *1978*, pp. 294-5. *Rand Daily Mail*, 15/2/1978, 15/3/1978, 10/8/1978.

6   I. Sekhukhune, 2.

7   *Ibid*; and G.M. Sekhukhune, unrecorded discussions, 1976 and 1982. It is unclear whether or not Phatudi seriously considered the independence option. He certainly never indicated in his public pronouncements that he was contemplating independence.

8   E. Nchabeleng, 1.

9   *Ibid.*

10   N. Diale, 1.

11   *Ibid*; and E. Nchabeleng, 1.

12   The brief history of ANC/MK strategy and action which follows draws heavily on H. Barrell, 'Conscripts to their Age: African National Congress Operational Strategy, 1976-1980', unpublished D.Phil. thesis, Oxford University, 1993, pp. 73-127. See also L. Phokanoka, 1.

13   Lodge, *Black Politics*, p. 302; M. Ramokgadi, 1; E. Motsoaledi, 1-2. Boshielo's family in Sekhukhuneland were not fully aware of his fate until the unbanning of the ANC in the 1990s.

14   Barrell, 'Conscripts', pp. 92-3. E. Nchabeleng, 1; J. Phala, 1 and 2.

15   Barrell, 'Conscripts', p. 129.

16   *Ibid*, pp. 128-51.

17   E. Nchabeleng, 1.

18   *Ibid.* See also N. Diale, 1; M. Ramokgadi, 1; UWHPL, AD1901, SC, *State vs Mosima Gabriel Sexwale and eleven others*, Pretoria 16 January 1978, especially the evidence of E. Matsimela; M. Maleka; M.L. Sepleu; M.J. Sibeyi; S.M. Lekgoro; T. Thangalani; M.F. Matati; A. Debiela; and statements in mitigation of sentence by M. Sexwale and N. Tsiki.

19   *Ibid*; J. Phala, 1 and 2; and Barrell, 'Conscripts', pp. 144-51.

20   N. Diale, 1.

21   Barrell, 'Conscripts', pp. 148-51; N. Diale, 1; E. Nchabeleng, 1; J. Nkadimeng and J. Phala, 1. It is probable that some arms caches were established there in the 1980s and some MK guerillas based themselves there for periods of time. The army, concerned that this was the case, took to sealing caves in the Leolo Mountains which had long provided places of refuge to those who sought to challenge colonial power.

22   Beinart, *Twentieth Century*, pp. 225-35.

23   E. Nchabeleng, 2; R. Sekonya, 1; S. Moganedi, 1 and 2; T. Mankge, 1.

24   *Ibid*; N.A., 1; Thušanang group, interview, 1; P. Sebapu, 1-3; P. Mbiba, 1; N. Matlawa, 1; Van Kessel, 'Confusion', p. 603.

25   N. Matlawa, 1.

26   T. Mankge, 1; see also P. Mbiba, 1; S. Moganedi, 1-2; M.Z. Mabiletša, 1.

27   *Ibid*; T. Harding, 'Resistance and Development in Rural Areas', unpublished paper, 1990, pp. 1-2; P. Magodi, 1.

28   Morris Nchabeleng, 1; see also Van Kessel, 'Confusion', pp. 598-600.

29   E. Nchabeleng, 2.

30   *Ibid.*

31   *Ibid.*

32   *Ibid.*

33   *Ibid*; R. Sekonya, 1.

34   *Ibid.*

35   Morris Nchabeleng, 1.

36   R. Sekonya, 1; Morris Nchabeleng, 1; M. Mabiletša, 1; M. Puane, 1.

37   R. Sekonya, 1.

38 E. Nchabeleng, 2; see also Morris Nchabeleng, 1; M. Mabiletša, 1; R. Sekonya, 1; P. Sebapu, 1-3; S. Mokadi, 1; P. Mogadi, 1.

39 *Ibid.*

40 S. Moganedi, 2; see also interview 1.

41 *Ibid*; R. Sekonya, 1; Morris Nchabeleng, 1; E. Nchabeleng, 2-3; J. Makgolane, 1; S. Mokadi, 1.

42 M. Mbuyane, 1; see also P. Mbiba, 1; S. Moganedi 1 and 2; N. Matlawa, 1; Harding, 'Resistance', pp. 1-6.

43 P. Magodi, 1; see also M. Mbuyane, 1; J. Nchabeleng, 3.

44 *Ibid*; see also Harding, 'Resistance', pp. 1-6; *The Star* 5/5/1986, 11/5/1986, 26/5/1986 and 27/5/1986; and pamphlets circulated calling for an increase in daily wages for farm labourers from R2 to R5.

45 While the evidence of local-level leaders is obviously very important both to what has gone before and what follows, I have also tried to tap the views and memories of individuals who witnessed or were caught up in these events, but who did not play leadership roles across a range of villages – including Madibong, Marulaneng, Mohlaletse, Schoonoord, Ntšabeleng, Apel, Nkwana, Phasha and Jane Furse. But even this sample still leaves out of the picture the specific experiences of scores of villages.

46 These observations are based on a wide range of interviews and on trial records which are discussed more fully below, as well as unrecorded discussions with P. Mbiba, P. Mnisi and C. Rachidi. See also E. Nchabeleng, 2-3; Morris Nchabeleng, 1; P. Sebapu, 1-3; T. Mankge, 1; K.J. Sekonya, 1; P. Magodi, 1; M. Mbyuane, 1; Morokalebole group interview, 1; Thušanang group interview, 1.

47 Harding, 'Resistance', pp. 2-3.

48 J. Nchabeleng, 3.

49 M. Puane, 1. See also E. Nchabeleng, 2-3 and T. Mankge, 1, on relations between youth and migrants.

50 P. Magodi, 1.

51 K.J. Sekonya, 1. See also Morokalebole group interview, 1, in which boys and girls expressed contrasting views of events. The fact that some girls were coerced does not, of course, mean that all were. Some young females also relished their new-found freedom from parental control.

52 J. Makgolane, 1; see also Morokalebole group interview, 1.

53 I. Sekhukhune, 2. See also E. Nchabeleng, 2-3; M. Makotanyane, 1.

54 E. Nchabeleng, 3. See also Van Kessel, 'Confusion', pp. 605-6.

55 See, for example, K.L. Maredi, 1; J. Nchabeleng, 3.

56 SC32/88 Lydenburg, *State vs P. Maile and seven others*, 2/2/1988. Quotation drawn from statement made by P. Maile, foming part of court record, 21/10/85.

57 S. Moganedi, 2.

58 N. Aphane, 1; S. Matlala, 1.

59 M. Mbuyane, 1.

60 E. Nchabeleng, 2.

61 J. Nchabeleng, 3; see also M. Puane, 1.

62 *The Star*, 17/4/1986. *The Star, The Sunday Times, The Weekly Mail* and the *Sowetan* all also carried considerably more informative reports.

63 *Pretoria News*, 16/4/1986.

64 *Sowetan*, 17/4/1986.

65 'Memorandum re *State vs Morris Nchabeleng and others* and eight other matters' prepared by Cheadle, Thompson and Haysom, nd, 1986.

66 E. Nchabeleng, 2-3; I. Sekhukhune, 1 and 5; M. Puane, 1. Also unrecorded discussions with P. Mnisi.

67 R. Sekonya, 1.

68   *Ibid*; see also P. Talane, 1 and 2.
69   *Ibid.*
70   *Ibid.*
71   T.P., 1.
72   *Ibid*, 1 and 2; R. Sekonya, 1; Morokalebole group interview, 1; P. Sebapu, 1-3;
      J. Makgolane, 1; M. Mabotha and others, SC White River, 11-13/11/1987.
73   T.P., 1.
74   E. Nchabeleng, 2 and 3; P. Talane, 1 and 2; J. Makgolane, 1; P. Sebapu, 1-3; Morris
      Nchabeleng and others, SC 25-27/11/1987.
75   M.J., 1.
76   R. Sekonya, 1; P. Talane, 2; K.R. Makgolane and others, SC White River,
      9-10/11/1987.
77   M.J., 1; see also R. Sekonya, 1; P. Talane, 1 and 2; P. Sebapu, 1-3; Morokalebole
      group interview, 1.
78   T.P., 1.
79   Morokalebole group interview, 1.
80   R. Sekonya, 1; P. Talane, 1-2; Morris Nchabeleng and others, SC 22-27/11/1987; G.
      Pelebese and others, SC33/38/ Lydenburg, 4/2/1988.
81   R. Sekonya, 1; P. Talane, 1 and 2; J. Makgolane, 1; Morokalebole group interview, 1;
      P. Sebapu, 1-3; Morris Nchabeleng, 1; B. Molaba, 1; M. Puane, 1; K. Sekonya, 1;
      M. Sekonya and others, SC Lydenburg 9-10/5/1988; A.T. Kupa and others, SC35/88/
      Lydenburg 9/2/1988.
82   E. Nchabeleng, 3.
83   Apart from interview material these observation are drawn from an analysis of the
      information available in the legal records on all the youths who were charged. If the
      average age was calculated on the basis of those convicted, it would be even younger.
      But such a calculation would ignore the fact that the lawyers fairly rapidly adopted a
      strategy of allowing minors to plead guilty because they received relatively light
      sentences – usually caning – in return for charges being dropped against the older
      youths and known political activists.
84   Morris Nchabeleng, 1; E. Nchabeleng, 2-3; P. Sebapu, 1-3; R. Sekonya, 1; P. Talane,
      1-2; J. Makgolane, 1; M.M. Sekonya and others, SC Lydenburg, 9-19/5/1988; M.L.
      Nchabeleng and others, SC,22-27/11/1987; M. Mabotha and others, SC White River
      11-13/11/1987; G. Pelebese and others, SS 33/38 Lydenburg 4/2/1988.
85   *Ibid*; Morokalebole group interview, 1; K.R. Makgolane and others, SC White River,
      9-10/11/1987; M. Thobejane and others; SC 1-2/2/1988; A.T. Kupa and others,
      SS35/88/ Lydenburg, 9/2/1988.
86   R. Sekonya, 1; P. Talane, 1-2; Morokalebole group interview; M. Mabotha and
      others, SC White River, 11-13/11/1987.
87   These statistics are based on material culled from court records and a wide range of
      interview material.
88   R. Sekonya, 1; Morokalebole group interview.
89   P. Talane, 2.
90   *Ibid.*
91   R. Sekonya, 1.
92   P. Talane, 2; see also R. Sekonya, 1.
93   R. Sekonya, 1; see also P. Talane, 2.
94   *Ibid*; B. Molaba, 1; K.R. Makgolane and others, SC White River, 9-10/11/87;
      M.F.Thobejane and others, SC 1-2/2/1988.
95   *Ibid*; A.T. Kupa and others, SC 35/88, Lydenburg, 9/2/1988.
96   P. Talane, 2.
97   R. Sekonya, 1; see also J. Nchabeleng, 3; P. Talane, 2; unrecorded discussions with
      P. Mnisi.

98   P. Talane, 2.
99   J. and J. Comaroff, 'Introduction', in J. and J. Comaroff (eds.), *Modernity and its Malcontents: Ritual and Power in Postcolonial Africa* (Chicago, 1993), p. xxvii. See also Ritchken, 'Leadership and Conflict', pp. 351-72, for a perceptive discussion of these issues in the somewhat different context of Bushbuckridge in the Eastern Transvaal.
100   P. Sebapu, 1-3; J. Makgolane, 1; K. Sekonya, 1; S. Moganedi, 1-2; P. Talane, 1-2; Morokalebole group interview, 1; unrecorded conversations with P. Mbiba, P. Mnisi and C. Rachidi. It was by no means always the case that women were the main targets of witch-hunts in the Northern and Eastern Transvaal. In episodes in the lowveld in the 1990s, men formed the majority of the accused. See Niehaus, 'Witch-Hunting', and Stadler, 'Witches'. What is also clear from the diverse accounts is that it is extremely difficult to generalise about the dynamics of witch-hunts. Within the broad context of belief in witchcraft and the transformation of local-level society, each episode is conditioned by local histories, circumstances and beliefs.
101   Comaroff, 'Introduction', p. xxvii.
102   R.G. Willis, 'The Kamcape Movement', in M. Marwick (ed.), *Witchcraft and Sorcery* (London, 1982), p. 227; see also in this volume A. Richards, 'A Modern Movement of Witchfinders'; and M. Marwick, 'The Bwanali-Mpulmutsi Anti-Witchcraft Movement'; and in J. and J. Comaroff (eds)., *Modernity and its Malcontents* see M. Auslander, 'Open the Wombs! The Symbolic Politics of Modern Ngoni Witchfinding', and A. Apter, 'Attinga Revisited: Yoruba Witchcraft and the Cocoa Economy, 1950-1951'.
103   Morris Nchabeleng, 1; see also R. Sekonya, 1.
104   *The Star*, 5/5/1986.
105   Anderson, 'Keeping the Myth Alive', pp. 38-49.
106   These comments are based on personal observation and discussions with a wide range of students and teachers in the period 1987-1991.
107   K.L. Maredi, 1; M. Phala, 2-3. Tensions between youth and elders were revealed at a number of community meetings that I attended in the period 1988-1990.
108   *K.K. Sekhukhune vs A. Ramodike and others*, SC, Pretoria, Judgment 2078, 20/06/1991. See also the considerable body of evidence in this case.
109   Memorandum to the National Executive of the ANC from the Executive Council of the Ba-Maroteng, nd., 1990. See also Report by Secretary of ANC branch Mohlaletse, 1 March 1992.
110   A. Motsoaledi, 1 and 2; I. Sekhukhune, 4; Nkwana Civic Association launch, 23/9/1990; ANC Meeting with Business Community, 9/12/1990; *The Star*, 12/2/1994.
111   E. Motsoaledi, 1-3; Welcome Rally for J.K. Nkadimeng, Manganeng, 22/7/1990.
112   A. Motsoaledi 1 and 2; I. Sekhukhune, 4; P. Mnisi and P. Mbiba, 1; Nkwana Civic Association launch, 23/9/1990; Abel, 1; M. Sekhukhune, 1.
113   Meeting between NEC delegation and Ramodike Cabinet, 24/10/1990.
114   *Ibid*; See also *Sowetan*, 21/6/1991.
115   Judgment, *K.K.Sekhukhune vs A. Ramodike and others*, SC, Pretoria, 20/6/1991. See also ANC Branch Report Mohlaletse, 1/3/1992; Memorandum to ANC, NEC from Executive Council of Ba-Maroteng, nd., 1992.
116   I. Sekhukhune, 4; A. Motsoaledi, 1-2; P. Mnisi and P. Mbiba, 1; Rally, 14/7/1990; Sayco Council Meeting, Jane Furse, 3/9/1990.
117   A. Motsoaledi, 1-2; I. Sekhukhune, 4; Sadtu pamphlets 1991-1993; M. Nkadimeng, 1; C.M. Rachidi, notes; P. Mogoba, 1-2; A. Mohlala, 1; R. Makgolane, notes; B. Molaba, 2; Apel School Board Meeting, 6/2/1992.
118   *Ibid.*
119   *The Star*, 12/2/1994.
120   *City Press*, 24/4/1994.

Conclusion

In November 1879, Sir Garnet Wolseley observed with grim satisfaction the carnage that accompanied the capture of the Pedi capital. His object was 'the utter destruction of Sikukuni root and branch', in part to ensure that the colonial order born amidst the bloodshed would not contain the 'seed of a weakening ambition for the old rule'. He broke the power of the Pedi Kingdom and achieved a salutary display of imperial might. But neither he nor his successors could erase the memories of their subjects or secure their 'complete submission' to colonial control.[1]

By the 1930s, far-reaching changes had recast the lives of the people of Sekhukhuneland. They were subject to new political hierarchies and were deeply enmeshed in an industrialising economy. The society's lifeblood was the – sometimes irregular – remittances of migrant workers. But Pedi men and women had not simply surrendered to the dictates of this new world. They struggled to limit the intrusion of colonial power and the reach of the market, and crafted continuities between the past and the present and between the countryside and the city. Some elaborated ideologies and associations which conjured an ideal community based on land, cattle and chiefly rule, while others plotted diverse paths to modernity.

The villages and households of Sekhukhuneland were subject to divisions, debates and conflicts, but *Bopedi* was regarded by many of its inhabitants as a place of refuge from abrasive white power, corrosive capitalist relationships and urban moral decay.

From the late 1930s, the residual autonomy cherished by these societies was menaced once more. The threat came from intensified state intervention fuelled by fear of the imminent 'collapse of the reserves' and shaped by both segregationist and conservationist discourses. This evolution in policy and practice (dubbed the 'Trust' in popular parlance) was dressed in the finery of the language of 'development' by officials, but was regarded by most people in the Northern Transvaal as a poorly disguised attempt to force them into abject political and economic subordination. Despite lip service to notions of

216

consultation, the rumblings of popular discontent and even episodes of open revolt, officials pressed ahead in the 1940s, sustained by the belief that 'science' was on their side. By the end of the decade it was only in the oldest reserve areas of Sekhukhuneland that the forces of 'the Trust' had been held at bay. Both officials and villagers believed that the decisive battle was imminent.

The National Party government added powerful new weapons to the official armoury in the early 1950s. The most important of these, from the perspective of Sekhukhuneland, involved Bantu Authorities, designed both to underpin an alternative political order for Africans and to facilitate rural economic restructuring. Migrants and villagers believed this initiative was a stalking horse for 'the Trust' and was intended to co-opt chiefs and disable community defences. Migrant workers who had to run the gauntlet of the pass laws and were threatened by apartheid's urban designs were anxious to prevent further erosion of political and economic possibilities in the reserves. They played a vital role in linking initially the Communist Party and increasingly the ANC to mounting political ferment in both town and countryside. Sebatakgomo, which was forged in this interaction, went on to play a pivotal part in the struggles which culminated in the Sekhukhuneland revolt of 1958.

The history of Sebatakgomo challenges that scholarship which has suggested that national movements remained remote from struggles in the reserves and provides telling insights into the role played by Communist Party activists in building the ANC into a mass-based organisation in the 1950s.[2] But the success of Sebatakgomo in developing a substantial following was both a consequence and cause of political strategies and styles which were not determined by the agendas of national movements. It drew on a lineage of forms of migrant association stretching back to the origins of Pedi migrancy and was grounded in village-based networks in hostels and burial societies. The movement made creative and increasingly heavy use of distinctively Pedi symbolism and history. And part of its appeal lay in its elaboration of an ideology which resonated both with commoner concerns over the fate of chieftainship and with the democratic discourses current within the ANC.

Sebatakgomo also managed to straddle the concern to defend residual elements of autonomy of some of its followers with the aspiration for fuller participation in a common society of others. The range of ideas and members within the movement opens a window on the dynamics of mass mobilisation in this period. They underscore the importance of breaching conceptual boundaries between urban and rural society and moving beyond leaders and formal programmes when analysing the quickening pace of politics in the 1950s.

The state's clumsy attempts first to co-opt and then to coerce the *kgošik-golo* fed mounting popular anger and inflamed divisions within the villages. As processes of social and political polarisation deepened, a minority of individuals – known as Rangers – who were believed to support tribal authorities were increasingly held responsible for the misfortunes that beset the society. This evolution in popular thinking fed on the close connections to the state of some leading 'Rangers' but was also sustained by models of causation which emphasised the temporal and supernatural dangers of internal cleavages. The demand grew, especially amongst young men, that the community should be purged of these dangerous divisions. Plans to kill 'the Rangers' were already in motion when the police opened fire on protesting villagers on 16 May 1958, thereby provoking a partly spontaneous wave of popular violence.

These events not only sent shockwaves through Sekhukhuneland but also had an impact far beyond the boundaries of *Bopedi*. They excited fears of atavistic revolt within white society and contributed to the stirrings of debate about armed struggle within the ANC and the SACP. The willingness of communities to take up arms, and the fact that the mountains and caves of Sekhukhuneland had once again provided rebels with shelter, gave food for thought to men – like Flag Boshielo – who went on to play prominent roles in Umkhonto we Sizwe. And the members of Sebatakgomo proved to be a rich source of recruits for military training and action.

The Sekhukhuneland revolt temporarily halted the advance of 'the Trust' but it did not put a stop to fundamental processes of transformation. Over the next two decades, chiefs were created and co-opted on a large scale and provided one foundation for the evolution of the Lebowa 'homeland'. The combined impact of influx control, removals and in-migration contributed to rapid population growth and a considerable increase in the number of households lacking land and livestock. Households became still more reliant on remittances, but from the late 1970s the flow faltered as some migrants' commitment to the countryside slackened and unemployment grew. Pensions substituted as a frail lifeline for some individuals and families. Female migrancy became increasingly common and the numbers of female-headed and female-linked households expanded.

The experience of growing up in Sekhukhuneland was also transformed by the rapid expansion of primary and secondary education. Forms of socialisation which had been designed to tether youths to their villages were supplanted by schooling which tugged them towards a wider world. But the hopes that education would provide new kinds of security and avenues of opportunity were dashed by mounting unemployment amongst school leavers.

By the 1980s, the social order which Sebatakgomo had fought to defend was in disarray. Multiple processes of change had rubbed old conflicts raw and triggered new disputes in villages and households. The relationship between chiefs and their subjects had soured and cleavages between the genders and generations had widened. Migrant workers increasingly joined trade unions and the importance of a worker identity grew. But the undoubtedly corrosive effects of these processes are not readily captured in crude modernist discourses. Men and women worked with ideas of *setšo* (tradition) and *molao* (the law) to craft new understandings, and the villages and households of Sekhukhuneland remained vivid reference points in conceptions of home and an imagined world of continuity between town and countryside. Fears about the activities of witches flourished and Zionist churches, which offered sanctuary and support in increasingly fragmented and fraught circumstances, expanded rapidly.

Sebatakgomo did not survive the climate of intense political repression in the 1960s, and attempts in the 1970s to draw on its networks to rebuild underground structures were also crushed by the security forces. In the context of national political mobilisation during the 1980s, however, there was a resurgence of resistance in Sekhukhuneland which climaxed in open revolt in 1986. There were some continuities with earlier struggles, most notably in the role of ANC symbols and sympathisers. But, while cadres and migrants played some part, the profound changes which had taken place in the nature of the society and its context moulded a very different pattern of politics.

The uprising was led by youth organisations which were dominated by the beneficiaries of rapid expansion of secondary schooling. The youth movement was grounded in the growing cross-fertilisation of urban and rural youth culture and centrally concerned with the grim circumstances which prevailed in local schools. But the youth also campaigned around other pressing local issues and initially enjoyed widespread sympathy for their demands. Their actions were motivated by the belief that it was their duty to build a new social and moral order purified of the corrupting influence of the agents and institutions of apartheid. But, in the absence of strong migrant, civic or underground organisation, they failed to weld together the broadly based alliance which Sebatakgomo had achieved in the 1950s and their actions increasingly took the form of a generational revolt against all forms of local authority.

The youth saw themselves as ushering in a new world. But their ideology and actions – like those of the soldiers of the Khuduthamaga in the 1950s – were shaped by an eclectic synthesis of the beliefs which prevailed within local-level society and the policies and practices generated within wider political struggles. In some villages, for example, the slogan 'an injury to one is an injury to all' invoked the history of the Congress alliance, resistance to the security forces and the need for a united front against witches. In a minority of settlements, witches were identified as the main impediments to harmony and progress, and were burned. The smouldering tyres which had first been used in the execution of witches in the Northern Transvaal, and had subsequently been employed to provide salutary punishment to suspected informers in the townships, returned to the region, bearing a powerful fusion of meanings.

The patterns of witchcraft accusation were shaped by tensions between neighbours and kin, and by generational and gender-based conflicts. But, while many adults agreed that villagers were infested with witches, they were alarmed by the youths' disregard for established procedures and by the severity of the punishment that they meted out. Increasingly isolated from wider support on this and other issues, 'the comrades' fell victim to harsh repressive measures.

Past and Present

The heart of this book is an account of two rebellions less than thirty years apart. Each episode of resistance poses specific problems of explanation but the continuities and discontinuities between the revolts also illuminate fundamental changes within the society. These processes are not only of academic interest: for, if new generations of policy makers and practitioners fail to understand the nature and trajectory of these transformations, their efforts – like those of their predecessors – are likely to be dogged by misfortune.

One recurring theme is that categorising the population of Sekhukhuneland as peasants or, more loosely, as rural, can obscure the dominant role of income from urban employment and the importance of resources, networks and experiences spanning the city and the countryside. For a hundred years and more, migrant workers pioneered and elaborated these connections; but from the 1960s onwards the movement of youth to schools and between family members facilitated a still wider range of cultural, economic and political exchanges.

Explanations of either of the revolts which do not start with this simple observation make little progress. But, equally, analyses which assume that inter-connection resulted in uniformity of understanding, aspiration and action, also risk being mocked by events.

A related and equally obvious caution is that state intervention accompanied by a rhetoric of 'development' and 'consultation' has a long and chequered history in the Northern Transvaal. The residents of the region have ample experience that declarations of good intentions are no guarantee against destructive or divisive consequences. Some will argue that the existence of a new political order nullifies this legacy. But there is reason for doubt. It might, for example, be supposed that the ghosts of the Native Economic Commission, rehabilitation and other reviled polices have long since been laid to rest. But the partial nature of the transition in South Africa means that the likelihood of old ideas flourishing amidst changed political circumstances is no less than elsewhere in Africa, where colonial models of agrarian transformation have proved remarkably tenacious in the decades since independence. Certainly, no-one who has recently listened to some officials and politicians explaining rural poverty in terms of overstocking, or extolling the virtues of villagisation, self-sufficient small farmers and individual tenure, can be sanguine that past policies will not come back to haunt us.[3]

More significant than these general conclusions is the evidence of fundamental shifts in the dynamics of the society suggested by a comparison of these two episodes. A determination to hold the market and the white state at bay, and a last-ditch defence of land, livestock and chieftainship, lay at the core of the 1950s struggle. The comrades in 1986 barely mentioned land or cattle, and were profoundly critical of chiefly rule. Their primary concern was not with autonomy but with changing the terms of their participation in a common society. Although their ambitions were far from precisely defined, they aspired to secure central power and reshape the national economy.

In particular, the comrades were determined that unskilled and migrant labour, which had so often been the lot of their less-educated parents, should not be their fate. At the very least, their imagined future depicted them in white collar jobs.[4] But these expectations were dashed by the paucity of appropriate opportunities.

This transformation in values and aspirations in a world where the majority of the population is under the age of 15, and can anticipate access to secondary schooling, cannot but have profound implications for the present and the future. But this is not to suggest that the concerns which were so prominent in the 1950s have simply evaporated. Questions of land and livestock, for example, are far from forgotten. Old men still debate the precise boundaries of the Pedi Kingdom at the height of its power and hope for their restoration. Victims of forced removals are determined to regain the land that they have lost.

Bureaucrats, traders and others with agricultural interests also chaff against remaining economic and political restraints. In village forums I attended while researching in Sekhukhuneland, *bakgomana* and older migrants often stressed the importance of initiating or supporting agricultural projects. In private discussion, many women also maintained that cultivating fields formed part of a proper way of life, and made larger claims for the contribution of agriculture to household income than other evidence supports. And youths, asked directly about land matters, emphasised the importance of land reform and redistribution. But it was also striking how rarely women or youths listed additional agricultural land among their priorities in community meetings focused on 'development' initiatives. Water, schooling, employment and clinics were the burning issues.[5]

While the low level of concern with agriculture amongst educated youth is not surprising, it is more difficult to account for the wider silence on these matters. The fact that land reform has only recently been placed on the national political agenda is part of the explanation. But it is also significant that in many villages there was little obvious land shortage, even though a large proportion of households do not have defined land rights. Every year, good or bad, substantial areas of land lay fallow because its custodians were not able to put a plough to the ground. And if a landless household could muster the other resources necessary to initiate cultivation, there were opportunities to hire or borrow unused fields or enter into sharecropping arrangements.

There was also concern expressed by some women about the likely consequences of agricultural schemes. They expressed anxiety that they would be subordinated or shouldered aside by officials or powerful local men should new resources be made available in this form – a far from fanciful fear, given the history of the region.

It might be anticipated that those analysts concerned with the treacherous terrain of policy and practice would place such matters in the foreground. Yet some of the most influential recent models are mute on issues of generation and gender. The Liptons, for example, urge that small 'family farms' should play a central role in rural development partly because of what are blandly termed their 'self-supervisory' characteristics. They do not consider, however, how such a strategy will intersect with domestic and communal struggles. One plausible model of the consequences of such a policy, which is grounded in both local and comparative experience, predicts intensified conflicts as men attempt to assert control over both land and the labour of women and youths. And, while the outcome of such a tussle is not pre-determined, the witch burnings of 1986 provide one particularly grim image of a possible result.[6]

The most important explanation for the limited emphasis on agriculture is the simple point that, without cash, it is not possible to put land under production on any significant scale in places like Sekhukhuneland.[7] There is also, within the society, a widespread recognition of the decisive importance of wages, remittances and pensions to household economies. While money was enormously important in sustaining herds and fields in the 1950s, many households could still derive a significant element of their subsistence needs from the land for limited periods of time. By the 1970s, these economic props had crumbled and households increasingly hoped that the education of their children would offer alternative security and possibilities. In the 1980s, these expectations were undermined by a stagnant job market and declining remittances. Nonetheless, the present prospects of households remain intimately connected to the growth of employment both locally, and in the economy as a whole. The central challenge is thus not to devise means to revive a wounded peasantry but to define strategies appropriate to societies which have been fundamentally restructured around wage labour, and which now face a deepening crisis of unemployment.[8]

In earlier decades, migrant workers contended with low wages and often lived and worked in appalling conditions. Nonetheless, there was ample employment and these times are now remembered as the days when 'it was actually easy for a person to get a job'.[9] In the 1990s, school leavers, who had been led to expect superior employment to their parents, are instead confronted by diminishing possibilities. And their ability to compete for the few jobs that are on offer is limited by their remoteness from the main centres of employment and by local schooling, which rarely provides the skills sought by employers.

These young men and women do not have a ready counterpart to the social networks and willingness to work for relatively low wages which sustained migrant workers in the face of intensifying attempts to exclude them from the urban economy in the 1950s. Thus, at the time when formal barriers like influx control have been removed, new generations growing up in the countryside are in danger of being trapped in bleak circumstances and forced to consider desperate measures.

The difficulties confronting the people of Sekhukhuneland, and places like it, are rooted in historical processes of dispossession and the long-standing refusal of white politicians to countenance large-scale land reform. Both the Native Economic Commission and the Tomlinson Commission tried to find ways out of this *impasse* and failed. But, with the demise of apartheid, it is possible to argue that an ambitious programme of land redistribution can at last provide the key to rural reconstruction.

While few would dispute that land reform can play a part, it is unlikely – at least as it is currently conceived – to provide a panacea for the problems outlined above. The population of the 'reserves' has rocketed, the degree of landlessness is substantially greater than it was forty years ago, and even residual forms of agricultural production have atrophied in many areas. Fiscal constraints, the remaining power of white farmers, concerns for food security and the adoption of a market-led approach to land reform have also placed sharp limits on the amount of productive land which can be made available. These factors make it unlikely that the poorest rural households will be major beneficiaries of land reform programmes. But even if this prediction is misplaced, the problem that remains for many households is that land without the income to put it to productive use is of limited value. And dry land farming in the climatic conditions which prevail in much of the interior of South Africa remains a hazardous enterprise.

In this context, the likely impact of land reform measures on levels of employment is a crucial question from the perspective of the rural poor. Badly designed measures which lead to a reduction in employment may further jeopardise the position of vulnerable households. Processes of land redistribution which boost employment in agriculture and in the broader economy may, on the other hand, provide a lifeline to some struggling families. In some instances, it may also allow currently unused land to be placed under production. But the desperate circumstances of many rural households do not permit policy makers the luxury of wishful thinking.[10]

While a narrow focus on land can obscure the dynamics of rural society, there is also the danger that the currently pervasive rhetoric of 'community' can shroud the countryside in a dense conceptual fog.[11] The diverse and shifting cleavages, conflicts and identities within local-level society highlighted in the history recounted here provide ample warning against the expectation that organic communities lie latent in villages, waiting like Sleeping Beauty for development's kiss. And established networks of patronage and power are often able to monopolise or block new resources, whatever their intended destination.

A striving after community has played a prominent part in the past, and will in all probability have a role the future. But it is worth recalling that 'community' is not only an elusive but also a potentially double-edged ideal. After all, the belief that it was imperative to restore cohesive communities underpinned the decision to kill the 'Rangers' in the 1950s and to eliminate suspected witches in the 1980s.

The two revolts outlined in this book also illuminate broad shifts in popular political consciousness. Chieftainship in the 1950s, although by no means without its critics, remained a central value in the society, partially because of its interconnection with elements of political, cultural and economic autonomy. Faced by the state's attempts to latch on to the legitimacy of the Pedi Kingdom, Sebatakgomo contributed to a remarkable attempt to reconstruct chieftainship from below. It drew both on commoner conceptions of chieftainship and the democratic discourses current within the ANC. The Khuduthamaga in Sekhukhuneland enhanced the influence of commoners and young men, and was able to effect significant changes in chiefly rule. But this attempt to democratise the institution did not challenge either the hereditary basis of chieftainship or the exclusion of uninitiated men and women from the central political forums and processes.

The Sekhukhuneland revolt of 1958 helped to keep Bantu Authorities at bay for a decade, but from the 1960s the majority of chiefs – old and new –

were drawn ever-deeper into the bantustan system. As a result, they were regarded with mounting suspicion and hostility by the majority of their subjects. But, while there was widespread condemnation of the behaviour of individual office holders and popular rejection of the legitimacy of newly recognised chiefs, some villagers and migrants continued to place a high value on the institution and to believe that it could and should be restored. It was against this backdrop that the 'comrades' launched a frontal assault on local chiefs in the 1980s. Even within their ranks, however, there were divisions over the future of *bogoši*. Some argued that it could be reformed, while others suggested that it should be swept aside.

This diversity of views continues to exist. There is widespread support – especially amongst the younger and more educated strata – for an elected system of local government in which chiefs will be stripped of many of their powers. But there are countervailing voices which argue that elected councillors will not be able to manage the complexities of local-level rights, especially to land, or be able to resist the temptations to pursue personal and sectional interests.

A new system of local government will have to contend with a pre-existing structure of chiefly power operating at a local level. This potential contradiction may be resolved by various local accommodations. But rural households may also find themselves at the centre of a protracted power struggle in which legislative and constitutional prescriptions may prove to be very remote allies indeed.

The unresolved position of the chiefs is not the only thorny issue confronting attempts to construct democratic local government. It also remains to be seen whether new institutions will be bolstered by positive transformations in the material circumstances of their constituents, or underpinned by a democratic popular culture. On the latter score, as this study suggests, the historical experience is mixed. There is a proud record of resistance to the designs of authoritarian states and of popularly based attempts to give substance to the maxim that *kgoši ke kgoši ka batho* (a chief is a chief by the people).

While the pursuit of consensus is a virtue often noted within local-level politics, intolerance of divergence and persistent disagreement can be the other side of this political currency. In the 1950s, while the Khuduthamaga enjoyed widespread support and participation, it was also a forum in which dissent was seen as connected to disaster and in which the eradication of internal cleavages became an overriding value. In the 1980s, the 'comrades' commanded a considerable following amongst the youth and committed themselves to democratic ideals. But their actions were marked by a crude enforcement of generational and male power and strongly authoritarian and sometimes violent internal practices. And, while a concern with the 'enemy within the gate' had been an element of the politics in the 1950s, the drive to eradicate witches became a defining aspect in the politics of the 'comrades' in some villages in the 1980s. It continues to be an issue of pervasive popular concern.

It would be foolish to expect to find a flowering of grassroots democracy in a context of repression and revolt. Part of what is remarkable about the story which unfolds in this book is the fact that democratic ideals were elaborated and survived in popular politics in such unpropitious circumstances. There are also a host of developments in community, union and non-governmental organisations which, though not part of the history recounted here, have an important bearing on this theme.

The narrative also touches on elements in popular political culture which may provide a troublesome legacy for those nurturing a new political order. Local-level democracy – like 'the community' – is not a chrysalis ready to fly from its cocoon with the first light of a new dawn. It will have to be built with an awareness of precedents, pitfalls and contemporary possibilities.

But the main moral of the tale told in this book is the importance of understanding the multifaceted processes of conflict and change which have taken place in Sekhukhuneland and comparable districts over the last century. The compendiums of statistics on rural society which have been produced in recent years, and are at every policy maker's elbow, are an invaluable addition to the literature. But they permit only limited glimpses of the interplay over time of the key variables shaping poverty, prosperity and conflict. And programmes of reconstruction, however well-intentioned, which assume that rural societies can be captured by crude, external categories and which fail to recognise the diverse histories, assumptions, identities and aspirations that exist in the countryside, may prove to be no better predictors of the future than was Sir Garnet Wolseley.

Notes

1   Delius, *The Land*, p. 245.
2   This point is more fully developed in Delius, 'Sebatakgomo and the Zoutpansberg Balemi Association', and P. Bonner *et al.*, *Apartheid's Genesis*.
3   For valuable comparative perspectives see Drinkwater, *The State and Agrarian Change*; Moore and Vaughan, *Cutting Down Trees*. The comments about the tenacity of earlier perspectives is based on comments made by participants in a range of policy and development forums held in recent years.
4   Although some youths attended agricultural colleges, this was an alternative mainly pursued by those who could not gain access to other institutions of further education. And many of these students' main goal involved bureaucratic employment rather than farming.
5   Detailed and reliable statistics on these issues are not available for Sekhukhuneland. But more impressionistic evidence suggests that agricultural production meets a very small proportion of the subsistence needs of even the poorest households. And it

seems unlikely that local experience deviates markedly from the national picture which suggests that 'the lowest return from household entitlement generating activities comes from agricultural production'. The fact that it is small does not, of course, prevent some households from seeing it as an important component in strategies to reduce their economic vulnerability. But recent comparative participatory research in a range of rural areas, while stressing diverse regional, gender and generational perspectives, has confirmed the overall relatively low priority attached to agriculture in regions of the Transvaal and the Eastern Cape. Other recent research has shown that, while in some high rainfall areas of the country a number of people are keen to acquire land and farm, in drier areas there is very little interest in farming. For a fuller discussion of these issues, see J. May, M. Carter and D. Posel, 'The Composition and Persistence of Poverty in Rural South Africa: An entitlements approach', Land and Agricultural Policy Centre, 1995, pp. 17, 20; E. Breslin and P. Delius, 'A Comparative Analysis of Poverty and Malnutrition in South Africa', Operation Hunger report (Johannesburg, 1996), *passim*; Operation Hunger, *Northern Transvaal*, p. 2; Centre for Development and Enterprise, 'Response to Government's Draft Rural Strategy Document' (Johannesburg, 1996), p. 6; and personal communication from Rupert Baber, 1995.

6   M. Lipton, 'Restructuring South African Agriculture', in M. Lipton and C. Simkins (eds.), *State and Market in Post-Apartheid South Africa*; M. Lipton and M. Lipton, 'Creating Rural Livelihoods: Some Lessons for South Africa from Experiences Elsewhere', *World Development*, 21, 1993. See also N. Bromberger and F. Antonie, 'Black Small farmers in the Homelands', in Lipton and Simpkins (eds.), *State and Market*. For historical perspectives, see Bradford, *A Taste of Freedom*, and Schirmer, *The Struggle*, Chapters 3-5. For comparative perspectives, see Moore and Vaughan, *Cutting Down Trees*, pp. 206-31; T. Bassett, 'Introduction', in T. Basset and D. Crummey (eds.), *Land in African Agrarian Systems* (Wisconsin, 1993), pp. 17-22; E. Francis, 'Migration and Changing Divisions of Labour: Gender Relations and Economic Change in Koguta, Western Kenya', seminar paper, University of Witwatersrand, 1991.

7   As noted in Chapter 5, most households have to hire the services of tractor owners if they wish to plant their fields, and lack most other forms of agricultural equipment. They also have to purchase seed and fertiliser. However, this does not prevent some crops being grown in gardens situated on residential stands or in the communal vegetable gardens which were established in many villages during the 1980s – often with the assistance of NGOs. Control over these resources was also less likely to be sought or contested by men.

8   For an influential article which merges conceptions of a destroyed peasantry with assumptions about a dormant peasantry, and rounds this off by invoking the spectre of peasant revolt, see H. Binswanger and K. Deiniger, 'South African Land Policy', *World Development*, 21, 1993. It would, of course, be wrong to generalise the experiences of Sekhukhuneland, and there are examples within 'reserve' areas, especially east of the escarpment, where production on the land has retained considerably greater vitality.

9   R. Sekonya, 1.

10   Some commentators have skated over the importance of income from other sources for agricultural production. Christiansen, for example, argues that

> Agriculture will be especially important for some of the lowest income groups who do not have access to remittances, pensions and other non-farm incomes. Such people will be highly motivated to raise production and incomes, although they will be short of resources with which to do so.

See R. Christiansen, 'Implementing Strategies for the Rural Economy', *World Development*, 21, 1993. For valuable comments on the land reform process, see C. Murray and G. Williams, 'Land and Freedom in South Africa', *Review of Political Economy*, 61, 1994, pp. 315-24 and the rest of the articles and briefings on land in South Africa in this issue. See also S. Schirmer, 'The Struggle', pp. 312-17, for a perspective rooted in processes of change in a 'white' farming area neighbouring Sekhukhuneland.

11   These observations are, of course, far from novel. But 'community' continues to be one the most widely used and abused terms in the current vocabulary of a variety of organisations involved in the field of development in South Africa. For an example of the cavalier and uncritical use of the term by people who should know better, see L. Loots and A. Roux, 'An Evaluation of the Relief Development Programme of the Independent Development Trust (Cape Town, 1993), *passim*.

Appendix 1

Research Revisited

The origins of this book lie in a research proposal I presented at the School of Oriental and African Studies in London more than twenty years ago. It aimed to analyse 'conflict and change in Pedi society' from the 1820s to the 1960s.[1] Some of those who attended the seminar suggested that this was rather an ambitious venture. So it proved to be, and a hundred years or so were eventually lopped off the time-span covered. The thesis and the book – *The Land Belongs To Us* – which emerged from it focused on the history of the Pedi Kingdom until its conquest in 1879. But experiences during my research ensured that I did not abandon the larger project entirely. Like many others at the time, I was fired with enthusiasm to recover the historical riches I hoped were contained in oral traditions passed down through the generations.

In 1976, I submitted an application for a permit to do research in Sekhukhuneland and, while I waited for a response, I busied myself in the Pretoria archives. As the weeks and months dragged by, I began to despair of receiving a reply much less a permit. Finally, a letter arrived from the Department of Bantu Affairs which read: 'Enough work have [sic] been done on the Pedi. Pick another tribe and re-apply.' But my plan to pursue oral history was rescued from sudden death by Professor Hammond-Tooke of Wits University, who kindly interceded on my behalf. After an interview with the state's chief ethnologist – C.V. Bothma – I was finally allowed into the area.

Thus, in October of 1976, with the shock waves of the Soweto revolt still reverberating through the society, and local political convulsions under way which are touched on in the body of this book but which I did not at that point begin to comprehend, I arrived in Sekhukhuneland clutching a tape-recorder. In retrospect, it is difficult to judge whether the local population or the ever-present security police were more incredulous at my claims to be in pursuit of pre-colonial history. In the event, conspicuously shadowed by the latter, I made very little progress in persuading the former to talk to me. Finally in growing despair, and having heard that a deputation from the paramountcy was due, I was hanging outside around the magistrates office at Schoonoord when a voice boomed out: 'I hear you want to know about our history.'

I turned around to find a man towering over me. He introduced himself as Godfrey Mogaramedi Sekhukhune and for the next 20 minutes or so he quizzed me about who I was and why I was interested in the Pedi Kingdom. At the end, he said that he would help where he could but he hoped I wasn't planning to add to the 'lies told by the Boers'. True to his word, for the next three months he spent enormous amounts of time travelling around with me, smoothing my way and introducing me to men knowledgeable about the Pedi past. He also enlisted the help of Isaac Segopotše Sekhukhune, who proved equally generous with his assistance.

After a month or so, when he was rather more confident about who I was, Godfrey started to talk, in the long hours we spent driving together, about more recent history and eventually recounted some dramatic episodes of the Sekhukhuneland revolt of 1958, as well as his experiences at the hands of the security police in the 1960s. These stories whetted my appetite to find out more. But, battling to make sense of myriad perspectives on the more distant Pedi past, and running out of time, I did not get very far. While it was clear to me that Godfrey had played an important role in the uprising, it was to be many years before I discovered the full extent of his participation.

In between interviews about nineteenth-century topics, I spent time asking people about their own lives and experiences and was fascinated by the richness of the stories they told, although I was also conscious that contentious issues were being avoided. When I finally left South Africa to return to London University at the end of 1976, I departed wishing that I had been able to pursue twentieth-century history in greater depth and that I could have continued to probe the possibilities of life history interviewing.

When I finally returned to South Africa in the early 1980s and contemplated launching a new research project, these questions and memories tantalised me. I was conscious of the view (forcefully expressed by some of my colleagues at Wits University) that not shifting one's research area, like not changing one's underwear, was a failure of personal hygiene. But I could not avoid the feeling that I had only scratched the surface of the society. In the next few years I made sporadic visits to friends in Sekhukhuneland, set about improving my Sepedi, and did a few interviews. In 1987-8, the luxury of a year's sabbatical leave allowed me to undertake intensive research in the area once again. My central concern was a question I had first posed 12 years

previously: what was the role of migrant workers in the Sekhukhuneland revolt of 1958?

This project ultimately generated hundreds of hours of tape-recordings
and thousands of pages of transcript and translation which form an archive in
their own right and a resource for future researchers. The sad fact that a number of the people interviewed have since died – including Edward
Mothubatse, Kgagudi Lot Maredi, Elias Motsoaledi, Martin Ramokgadi and
Gideon Ngake – underscores the preciousness of the material. This archive,
along with the public records I have drawn on, ensures that those interested
in retracing my steps and re-evaluating my arguments will have rich resources to work with.

I also harbour the hope that I will be able to find a way of publishing a
cross-section of interviews and the unpublished written histories which I was
given access to, in order to make some of the material more easily and widely
accessible. But, beyond that, each interview conducted could bear detailed
discussion of its particular context, form and content. But that would take, at
least, another book. And, of course, virtually every document drawn upon
could be subjected to similar treatment.

However, a sketch of the broad context in which the oral research was
conducted, the approach adopted, the people involved and the rough division
of labour may help interested readers to form a clearer image of the making
of the book and be of some assistance to future scholars.

At the outset, it should be said that 1987 was far from a propitious time to
begin an oral history project in Sekhukhuneland. In the aftermath of the 1986
revolt, the area was under siege by the security services once more, and
events of the previous year had inflamed conflicts within communities.
Tragically, Godfrey Sekhukhune, who had started to prod me to write about
events in the 1950s, had died in 1985 after a car crash. But the fact that I was
known in the area and that I had produced a book which showed that my interest in history was not feigned, eased my entrance. I was initially based at
Mohlaletse village, the seat of the paramountcy, where, with the cautious
support of the *kgošikgolo* and his councillors, I started to interview retired
migrants about their lives. These were, as noted in the introduction, almost
always three-way conversations. Isaac Sekhukhune and Stephen Mothubatse
were sufficiently interested in the project to play a vital role as intermediaries
and interpreters.

Isaac, a businessman and farmer in his late forties, remarkably was both
highly regarded at Mohlaletse and closely connected to leading 'Ranger'
families. He had played a leading part in local business and community organisations since the late 1970s and had a critical role in connecting me to
diverse social and political networks in the region. Stephen Mothubatse had

recently retired from teaching in farm schools. He had been a migrant worker on the Rand in the 1950s and had been involved in both Sebatakgomo and the ANC. He introduced me to a number of key informants and alerted me to important dimensions which I might have overlooked. The standing in the community of these individuals helped persuade men to agree to interviews with a white outsider.

These interviews were mainly conducted in Sepedi. While I was able to follow them in outline, I depended on translation to keep me abreast of more animated discussions and to help me frame some questions effectively. Interviews were subsequently transcribed and then translated – a herculean task in which Cedric Monare Rachidi, a student at Wits who came from the neighbouring village of Ntšabeleng, played a major role. He was present at some of the interviews and also introduced me to valuable informants from diverse backgrounds. He, for example, numbered amongst his relatives both ardent supporters of Sebatakgomo and individuals who had been teachers and agricultural rangers who had seen little point in resisting Bantu Authorities.

Initial interviews took the form of a loosely structured basic life history, with interviewees encouraged to digress or elaborate as they saw fit. These helped me to situate individuals in specific social and political contexts and to establish a chronological framework. The problem of dating was partly overcome by reference to well-known events. But the sequence of named initiation groups in each chiefdom, which can be precisely dated, was also vitally important. As the interviews multiplied, it also became possible to discern broad shifts in the experiences of people born in different decades. Towards the end of the first interview, or in subsequent encounters, specific questions were asked about particular episodes in people's lives.

The additional questions selected changed according to the person being interviewed, and also shifted as the project evolved. For a period of time, for example, a great deal of attention was devoted in interviews to burial societies, but once responses started to become predictable on a topic, other issues were pushed to the fore. These interviews were thus crucially structured by sets of questions posed by myself and the other interviewers, although we did try to be open to issues that our informants wished to discuss and, on a number of occasions, this suggested new avenues of enquiry. And while we were interested in pursuing questions about 'what, when and how', which helped in the painstaking task of trying to reconstruct historical episodes, many of the most important insights were derived from the question 'why'. Informants' own explanations for, and interpretations of, historical processes have been vital to the analysis offered in this book.

I was also fortunate to be allowed to read a manuscript written in Sepedi in 1959 by Mothodi Nchabeleng, a local teacher and supporter of the rebels, which provided a vivid and thought-provoking account and interpretation of the local dynamics of the revolt.

People that we talked to suggested others who might be willing to be interviewed, or who were knowledgeable on specific issues. And while many of our initial informants were of high rank, we soon moved out of this social strata and interviewed commoners. The differing perceptions this revealed – particularly around the issue of chieftainship – are more fully discussed in the body of this book.

Suggestions about further informants ultimately also led us to people in a wide range of villages in Sekhukhuneland and to individuals living on the Rand. However, the main concentration of this part of the research was in Mohlaletse, Ntšabeleng, Schoonoord, Jane Furse and Madibong. As the research evolved, our focus broadened and women who had stayed in the villages or had gone to town were also interviewed. But they remained a minority and also often proved reluctant to discuss events in the public political domain. We were sometimes told that these matters were men's business, and that women had merely been spectators – a comment contradicted by other interviews and evidence.

Part of the explanation for this response may have been that the women were reluctant to discuss episodes which sat uneasily with formal definitions of the role of women in society with male interviewers. Another dimension may well have been the existence of 'a gendered division of genre whereby men tell "true" historical stories while women specialise in fictional narratives'.[2]

In between periods of work in Sekhukhuneland, I spent time reading court records and returned to my old haunts in the Pretoria archives. But while I located valuable sources on earlier decades, the key files on the late 1950s remained closed to public scrutiny. Thus, in contrast to my previous research on the Pedi Kingdom, in which my understanding had been based on archival material and then supplemented by oral traditions, interviews were the principal fuel for my developing historical understanding.

In the early 1990s, when the relevant files were finally made available, I was able to test this perspective against rich documentary sources and open some new windows on the past. When I examined detailed contemporary written reports on structures, meetings and events, it was striking how full the picture derived from oral sources had been. And while the written record provided a considerably clearer view of the workings of the official mind and the inner councils of state, it proved less eloquent on popular organisations, perceptions and explanations.

Initially and unsurprisingly, given a context of intense political repression, people were very uneasy at any discussion of the role of the ANC, PAC and SACP. But over time, some individuals started to talk about the wider connections of Sebatakgomo and Fetakgomo and their own personal political affiliations. They also started to suggest individuals who could tell more about this side of the story. In practice, many of my early informants on these issues were rank-and-file members who had a partial grasp of the composition and connections of the leadership. But they helped put me in touch with individuals who had been in the central structures, and I slowly pieced together a fuller picture.

This larger portrait was also informed by the diversity of views which I encountered. While this was an often bewildering process at the time, in retrospect it increased my sensitivity to the range of perspectives which existed both within the region and within Fetakgomo in the 1950s.

But it must be recalled that the majority of these interviews were undertaken in the late 1980s, before the unbanning of political movements, and it is possible that many interviewees might have been considerable less tentative about the role of the ANC/SACP had they been interviewed in the early 1990s. I was, however, able in 1988 – with considerable help from Hugh Macmillan – to get two lengthy and invaluable interviews in Lusaka with John Kgoana Nkadimeng, who had been a crucial link between the ANC and Sebatakgomo.

After the release of political prisoners, the unbanning of the ANC and SACP and the return of political exiles, I was able to pursue these dimensions much more fully and particularly to probe the role of the Communist Party more deeply. The late Elias Motsoaledi, Hilda and Rusty Bernstein, Walter Sisulu, John Phala and, again John Nkadimeng, were particularly generous with their time, their memories and their insights. John Phala also allowed me to read a fascinating account of Sebatakgomo he had written in Sepedi while incarcerated on Robben Island, and which provided important insights into the nature of the organisation.

My original intention was to deal only with the Sekhukhuneland revolt of 1958. But it was difficult to ignore the context of the aftermath of the 1986 uprising. It also became clear to me that many of my older informants were keen to talk about the 1950s in part because they saw the youth as misguided in their methods, ignorant of previous struggles and contemptuous both of their elders and more broadly of *bogoši*. In a context of high levels of static on intergenerational lines of communication, the interviews which I conducted were seen by some as an opportunity to comment, sometimes obliquely, on the recent behaviour of the youth and to recall a different tradition of resistance. The recent events were, in addition, a topic of conversation and debate wherever I went in the district, and I soon began trying to piece together a fuller understanding of what had happened. I made a point of attending community meetings, made contact with a range of non-governmental organisations working in the area and visited diverse projects.

Late in 1987, I started to work with the Thušanang Study Group, based in Jane Furse, which was composed of local high school students who had come together to provide mutual support and to advance their education despite the chaotic and under-resourced condition of local schools. Some of the group helped with the transcription of some of my tapes, were considerably surprised by the history they heard, and became interested in the project. They looked for informants in their own areas and undertook some interviews. They told me about recent events from their perspective, and students at Wits who were from Sekhukhuneland – especially Cedric Rachidi – also spent time trying to educate me in the recent history of the area.

The upshot of this was the launching of a second phase of research in the middle of 1988 on youth politics in the area. Philip Mnisi and Philip Mbiba, who went on from Thušanang to Kanya College in Johannesburg and then came to study at Wits, played a central role in this programme, along with Cedric Rachidi. The form of interviewing and the process of research broadly duplicated that described above, although many more of the interviews were conducted in English. We also did a number of interviews with groups of young men and women which generated fascinating insights, particularly into gender-based differences of perception and experience.

I participated in a number of the other interviews – particularly with older informants like teachers – and worked on initial and follow-up questions. But the 'two Philips', as they became known, did many interviews alone, often during university vacations, in the years 1988–91. Their connections to, empathy with, and understanding of the youth in the area played a vital part in shaping the research. They, for example, conducted some of the most revealing interviews around the issue of witchcraft, and the fact that Philip Mnisi had close connections to Nkwana contributed greatly to our ability to interview people in that troubled village.

After 1990, they also monitored the quickening political pulse of the area, writing up reports of rallies and meetings, collecting political pamphlets and other documents and interviewing activists. The material they gathered, and the many hours we spent in conversation in Sekhukhuneland, on the road and in Johannesburg, had a powerful influence on my thinking and writing. Once again, this research ranged widely in Sekhukhuneland but the bulk was done in the villages of Apel, Nkwana, Ntšabeleng, Mohlaletse, Madibong and in Jane Furse. Both Philip Mbiba and Cedric Rachidi took teaching posts in Sekhukhuneland when they completed their degrees and continued to do research when they could make time. But tragedy struck in 1992 when Philip Mnisi, who was still studying at Wits, was murdered in Johannesburg. This was a bitter blow for the rest of us, and one from which the research project never recovered.

A number of points emerge from this rather bald account. One is that the research was not based on a random or representative sample of respondents which could be used to generate quantitative data. It rather followed the considerably less 'scientific' method of finding and exploring networks of informants and pursuing qualitative material. But interviews were conducted with a wide range of people from different age groups, economic niches, social strata, villages and religious and educational backgrounds. However, a large majority of the informants as well as all the interviewers were male. None of the people involved in the interviewing were seen within the society as socially or politically neutral. But the diversity of our backgrounds and networks also ensured that a wide range of perceptions of who we were, and what we were up to, affected the responses of informants.

Each of us also brought our own experiences, observations and understandings to the projects which left their mark, but which were also reshaped by the responses of informants and by ongoing discussion and debate amongst the researchers. The perspectives derived from this material were combined with information and insights derived from a wide range of documentary material and secondary sources which, in turn, fed back into interviews. But it should be noted that, because official records remain closed from the early 1960s, the documentary base for the concluding chapters is considerably skimpier than for those on the earlier period. And in the end, much as I would like to transfer the blame (though not, of course, any praise) to others, I have to take responsibility for the blending of all of these ingredients into the particular form served up in this book.

A full list of recorded interviews follows below. In some instances, informants asked to remain anonymous, and in a few cases where particularly sensitive issues are referred to, it has seemed prudent to disguise the identity of informants.

Notes

1   P. Delius, 'Conflict and Change in Pedi Society', unpublished seminar paper, African History Seminar, University of London, 1975.
2   I. Hofmeyr, *We Spend Our Days as a Tale that is Told* (Johannesburg, 1993), p. 6.

List of interviews

1-1   N. Aphane, interviewed (int.) by P. Mbiba, Jane Furse, 4/7/1989.
2-1   M. Bahm, int. by R. Anderson, Johannesburg, 6/6/1990.
3-1   H. and L. Bernstein, int. by P. Delius (PD), Dorstone, England, 18/6/1990.
3-2   Int. by PD, Kidlington, 29/8/1994.
4-1   D.W. Bopape, int. by PD, Johannesburg, 28/10/1987.

5-1   N. Diale, int. by PD, Jane Furse, 18/6/1993.
6-1   D. Goldberg, int. by PD, London, 24/8/1994.
7-1   B. Hirson, int. by PD, London, 14/6/1990.
7-2   Int. by PD, London, 23/8/1994.
8-1   B.K. Hlakudi, int. by PD and I. Sekhukhune (IS), Mohlaletse, 28/8/1987.
8-2   Int. by PD and S. Mothubatse (SM), 18/11/1987.
9-1   C. Hooper, int. by PD, Leeds, 22/6/1990.
10-1   T. Kabu, int. by PD and IS, Mohlaletse, 26/8/1987.
11-1   R. Kaplan, int. by PD, Sheffield, 23/6/1990.
12-1   M. Kgagudi, int. by PD and IS, Mohlaletse, 26/8/1987.
12-2   Int. by PD and CR, 4/4/1988.
13-1   M. Kgaphola, int. by PD and IS, Mphanama, 10/2/1988.
14-1   R. Kgetsepe, int. by PD and CR, Mohlaletse, 9/2/1988.
15-1   S. Kgoloko, int. by PD and SM, Mohlaletse, 2/12/1987.
16-1   D.P. Lebopo, int. by C. Rachidi (CR), Ntšabeleng, 11/7/1988.
16-2   Int. by PD and CR, 8/9/1988.
17-1   N.N. Lebopo, int. by PD and CR, Strydkraal, 7/4/1988.
18-1   K. Lerutla, int. by PD and IS, Mamone, 23/9/1987.
19-1   M. Lerutla, int. by P. Mbiba, Jane Furse, 1/2/1989.
20-1   T. Lerutla, int. by PD and IS, Madibong, 3/5/1988.
21-1   M. Mabiletša, int. by PD, Johannesburg, 20/3/1990.
22-1   S.L. Mabilu, int. by PD and IS, Nebo, 21/1/1989.
23-1   T. Mabogoane, int. by PD and IS, Bothashoek, 7/12/1987.
24-1   N. Mabogwane, int. by PD and SM, Mohlaletse, 1/12/1987.
25-1   M. Mafiri, int. by PD and IS, Mohlaletse, 22/9/1987.
26-1   P. Magodi, int. by P. Mbiba, Madibong, 10/7/1988.
27-1   D. Magomarele, int. by PD and CR, Mohlaletse, 20/1/1988.
28-1   J. Mahlangu, int. by PD, Jane Furse, 3/8/1989.
29-1   N. Maimela, int. by PD and IS, Schoonoord, 9/2/1988.
30-1   J. Makgolane, int. by P. Mnisi, Nkwana, 20/8/1988.
30-2   Int. by P. Mnisi, Nkwana, 23/8/89.
31-1   M. Makotanyane, int. by P. Mnisi, Mohlaletse, 24/9/1990.
32-1   S. Makotanyane, int. by PD and IS, Mohlaletse, 26/8/1987.
33-1   T. Mamokabi, int. by P. Mbiba, Madibong, 4/7/1989.
34-1   L. Mampuru, int. by P. Mbiba, Madibong, 11/7/1989.
35-1   M. Mampuru, int. by PD and SM, Mohlaletse, 9/2/1988.
35-2   Int. by PD and CR, 12/7/1988.
35-3   Int. by PD and CR, 17/11/1988.
36-1   K. Manailane, int. by PD and CR, Johannesburg, 11/4/1988.
36-2   Int. by PD and CR, 30/11/1988.
37-1   T. Mankge, int. by PD, Jane Furse, 15/12/1989.
38-1   L. Manyike, int. by PD, Jane Furse, 17/3/1990.
39-1   H. Maredi, int. by PD, Mamelodi, 25/11/1987.
40-1   K.L. Maredi, int. by PD and IS, Mohlaletse, 10/8/1987.
40-2   Int. by PD and CR, 10/12/1987.
41-1   T.M. Masemola, int. by PD and T. Masikela, Masemola, 6/11/1976.
42-1   J. Mashego, int. by PD and IS, Schoonoord, 2/2/1988.
42-2   Int. by PD, 5/5/1988.
43-1   M. Malata, int. by P. Mbiba, Madibong, 16/7/1989.
44-1   W. Matala, int. by P. Mbiba, Jane Furse, 4/5/1989.
45-1   P. Matjie, int. by PD and IS, Mohlaletse, 10/10/1987.
45-2   Int. by PD and SM, 3/12/1987.
46-1   P. Matlala, int by PD, Jane Furse, 8/12/1989.

47-1　　S. Matlala, int. by P. Mbiba, Jane Furse, 20/7/1988.
48-1　　N. Matlawa, int. by PD, Atok, 9/11/1989.
49-1　　P. Mbiba, int. by PD, Johannesburg, 17/3/1988.
49-2　　P. Mbiba, with P. Mnisi, int. by PD, Jane Furse, 28/1/1991.
50-1　　M. Mbuyane, int. by P. Mbiba, Jane Furse, 11/7/1989.
51-1　　L. Mdingi, int. by H. Bradford, Cape Town, 20/9/1990.
52-1　　W.M. Moadi, int. by P. Mbiba, Madibong, 9/7/1989.
53-1　　M. Moela, int. by P. Mbiba, Jane Furse, 11/6/1989.
54-1　　R. Moetalo, int. by P. Mbiba, Madibong, 3/6/1988.
55-1　　P. Mogoba, int. by PD, Monsterlus, 17/3/1990.
55-2　　Int. by PD, Jane Furse, 11/12/1991.
56-1　　A. Mohlala, int. by P. Mnisi, Jane Furse, 26/12/1991.
57-1　　S. Mokadi, int. by P. Mnisi, Jane Furse, 18/7/1989.
58-1　　R. Mokgolane, int by P. Mnisi, Nkwana, 4/1/1992.
59-1　　S. Moganedi, int. by P. Mnisi, Jane Furse, 10/7/1989.
59-2　　Int. by PD, Johannesburg, 30/11/1989.
60-1　　B. Molaba, int. by PD, Nkwana, 8/11/1989.
60-2　　Int. by P. Mnisi, Nkwana, 4/1/1992.
61-1　　W. Monama, int. by P. Mbiba, Jane Furse, 18/7/1990.
62-1　　M. Monokeng, int. by P. Mnisi, Apel, 26/1/1990.
63-1　　A. Moraba, int. by P. Mbiba, Madibong, 10/6/1989.
64-1　　M. Moreane, int. by PD and IS, 10/8/1987.
65-1　　Morokalebole group, int. by PD and P. Mnisi, Nkwana, 10/11/1989.
66-1　　S. Morwamotshe, int. by PD and SM, Mohlaletse, 29/9/1987.
67-1　　A. Mosehle, int. by PD, Lobethal, 1/11/1976.
68-1　　E. Mothubatse, int. by PD and T. Masikela, Naboomkoppies, 8/11/1976.
68-2　　Int. by PD and T. Masikela, 11/11/1976.
68-3　　Int. by PD and T. Masikela, 16/11/1976.
68-4　　Int. by PD and M. Molepo, October 1983.
68-5　　Int. by PD and IS, Jane Furse, 7/6/1984.
69-1　　S. Motla, int. by PD and IS, Schoonoord, 7/12/1987.
70-1　　L. Mothubatse, int. by PD and SM, Mohlaletse, 29/9/1987.
70-2　　Int. by PD and CR, Mohlaletse, 9/2/1988.
71-1　　S. Mothubatse, int. by PD and IS, Mohlaletse, 12/9/1987.
71-2　　Int. by PD, Mohlaletse, 6/10/1987.
71-3　　Int. by PD and CR, Mohlaletse, 9/9/1988.
72-1　　A. Motsoaledi, int. by P. Mnisi and P. Mbiba, 19/7/1990.
72-2　　Int. by PD, Jane Furse, 5/9/1990.
73-1　　E. Motsoaledi, int. by PD, Soweto, 19/4/1990.
73-2　　Int. by PD, 23/4/1990.
73-3　　Int. by PD, 11/5/1990.
73-4　　Int. by PD, 2/4/1991.
73-5　　Int. by PD, 17/4/1993.
73-6　　Int. by PD, 19/5/1993.
74-1　　J. Moukangwe, int. by PD and CR, Mohlaletse, 29/9/1988.
75-1　　P. Mphela, int. by P. Mbiba, Madibong, 30/1/1989.
76-1　　M. Mpogeng, int. by P. Mbiba, Jane Furse, 4/2/1989.
77-1　　E. Nchabeleng, int. by PD, Johannesburg, 13/4/1989.
77-2　　Int. by PD, 15/5/1989.
77-3　　Int. by PD, Jane Furse, 16/7/1989.
78-1　　J. Nchabeleng, int. by PD and CR, Ntšabeleng, 15/12/1987.
78-2　　Int. by PD and CR, 13/12/1988.
78-3　　Int. by PD and CR, 10/4/1990.

79-1   Morris Nchabeleng, int. by PD, Apel, 22/1/1990.
80-1   Mothodi Nchabeleng, int. by PD and CR, Ntšabeleng, 10/12/1987.
80-2   Int. by PD and CR, 5/4/1988.
81-1   S. Nchabeleng, int. by CR, Ntšabeleng, 22/7/1989.
82-1   G. Ngake, int. by PD, Olifants River, 7/4/1988.
83-1   J. Nkadimeng, int. by H. Macmillan, Lusaka, 6/6/1988.
83-2   Int. by H. Macmillan, Lusaka, 14/8/1988.
83-3   Int by PD, Johannesburg, 3/4/1991.
83-4   J. Nkadimeng with J. Phala, int. by PD, Jane Furse, 17/6/1993.
84-1   Malekane Nkadimeng, int. by PD, Jane Furse, 10/12/1991.
85-1   Mefolo Nkadimeng, int. by PD, Jane Furse, 5/9/1990.
86-1   P. Nkadimeng, int. by PD, Lebowakgomo, 6/6/1988.
87-1   J. Ntsoane, int. by PD and CR, Ntšabeleng, 9/9/1988.
88-1   S. Ntsoane, int. by P. Mnisi, Nkwana, 21/8/1989.
89-1   D. Phala, int. by CR, Mohlaletse, 27/11/1987.
90-1   Johannes Mangope Phala, int. by PD and SM, Mohlaletse, 18/11/1987.
91-1   John Phala, int. by PD, Johannesburg, 14/10/1992.
91-2   Int. by PD, 22/10/1992.
91-3   J. Phala with J. Nkadimeng, int. by PD, Jane Furse, 17/6/1993.
91-4   Int. by PD, Pietersburg, 7/2/1994.
92-1   Marishane Phala, int. by PD and SM, 12/12/1988.
93-1   Martha Phala, int. by PD and CR, Mohlaletse, 2/12/1987.
94-1   Mohube Phala, int. by PD and SM, Mohlaletse, 6/10/1987.
94-2   Int. by PD and CR, 28/1/1988.
95-1   T. Phala, int. by PD and CR, 1/12/1987.
96-1   L. Phokanoka, int. by PD, Pietersburg, 15/10/1993.
97-1   T.M. Phakaogo, int. by CR, Ntšabeleng, 9/7/1989.
98-1   G. Pitje, int. by PD, Johannesburg, 4/3/1987.
98-2   Int. by PD, 12/10/1987.
99-1   M. Puane, int. by CR, Ntšabeleng, 27/12/1989.
100-1   P.M. Rachidi, int. by CR, Ntšabeleng, 9/7/1988.
101-1   C. Radingoana, int. by PD and SM, Mohlaletse, 28/9/1987.
102-1   D. Radingoana, int. by PD and CR, 13/12/1988.
103-1   R. Radingoana, int. by PD and SM, Mohlaletse, 27/9/1987.
104-1   M. Ramokgadi, int. by PD and M. Chaskalson, Johannesburg, 15/5/1988.
104-2   Int. by PD, 24/5/1993.
105-1   M. Raseomane, int. by PD and IS, Madibong, 14/12/1988.
106-1   M. and K. Riba, int. by P. Mbiba, Madibong, 2/2/1989.
107-1   P. Sebapu, int. by P. Mnisi, Nkwana, 8/7/1988.
107-2   Int. by P. Mnisi, 21/8/1989.
107-3   Int by PD, 9/11/1989.
108-1   G. Sekhukhune, int. by PD, Schoonoord, 11/7/1989.
109-1   I. Sekhukhune, int. by PD, Schoonoord, 10/11/1989.
109-2   Int. by PD, 29/11/1989.
109-3   Int. by PD, 11/1/1990.
109-4   Int. by PD, 27/1/1991.
109-5   Int. by PD, Jane Furse, 27/2/1995.
110-1   Mabowe (James) Sekhukhune, int. by PD and IS, Penge, 21/10/1987.
110-2   Int. by PD and IS, 14/10/1988.
111-1   Minaar Sekhukhune, int. by PD, Jane Furse, 5/9/1990.
112-1   Mogase Sekhukhune, int. by PD and IS, Mohlaletse, 12/7/1987.
112-2   Int. by PD and CR, 9/2/1988.
113-1   N. Sekhukhune, int. by PD and IS, Mohlaletse, 9/7/1987.

113-2 Int. by PD and CR, 29/1/1988.
114-1 Phethedi Sekhukhune, int. by PD, Marulaneng, 20/11/1976.
115-1 S. Sekhukhune, int. by PD, Monsterlus, 12/11/1976.
116-1 K. Sekonya, int. by P. Mnisi, Nkwana, 23/9/1989.
117-1 R. Sekonya, int. by PD, Jane Furse, 28/4/1995.
118-1 W. Sekwati, int. by PD and G. Sekhukhune, Mohlaletse, 10/11/1976.
119-1 P. Simons, int. by R. Anderson, Johannesburg, 11/7/1990.
120-1 W. Sisulu, int. by PD, Johannesburg, 15/8/1990.
121-1 P. Talane, int. by P. Mnisi, Nkwana, 27/1/1990.
121-2 Int. by PD, Jane Furse, 28/4/1995.
122-1 M. Tau, int. by PD and P. Mbiba, Jane Furse, 11/4/1990.
122-2 Int. by PD, Jane Furse, 28/4/1995.
123-1 J. Thobejane, int. by PD and IS, Magakala, 13/7/1988.
124-1 Thušanang group interview, July 1988.
125-1 M. Tshesane, int. by P. Mbiba, Madibong, 11/7/1989.

Appendix 2

Population Figures

Population figures for this region are notoriously unreliable. But it is possible to get some sense of broad trends.

- In the 1860s missionaries estimated the population of the heartland of the Pedi state at between 60 000 and 70 000.
- In 1930 local officials calculated the population of roughly the same area, now divided into Sekhukhuneland and Phokwane (later Nebo) districts, at 105 000.
- By 1970 the official population figures for Sekhukhuneland and Nebo totalled 296 000.
- By 1980 the official population figures for Sekhukhuneland and Nebo totalled 504 000.
- By 1985 the official population figures for Sekhukhuneland and Nebo totalled 641 000.
- A more detailed breakdown of the 1970 and 1980 figures shows that the official population of the district of Sekhukhuneland in 1970 was 162 889, comprising 43,8% males and 56,2% females.
- By 1980 this had risen to 298 667 with 44,7% male and 55,3% female. The total population in 1985 was 377 140.
- The equivalent figures for Nebo in 1970 are 133 284, 42,2%, 57,8% and in 1980, 204 714, 43,2%, 56,8%, and by 1985, 264 304.
- By 1980 52,7% of the Sekhukhuneland population was 1-14 years old while the equivalent figure for Nebo was 52,3%.

Sources

P. Delius, *The Land*, p. 48; UWHPL/AD1438/*NEC*, D.R.Hunt, 20/8/1930, p. 654 and J.C. Yates, 22/8/1930, p. 815; DBSA, *Report on Lebowa 1986* and *Regional Poverty Profile; Eastern and Northern Transvaal 1993.*

241

Selected Written Sources

Berlin Missionary Society Archives (BMSA)

Select documents from the diaries and correspondence of the mission stations, Khalatlolu, Phatemetsane and Ga Ratau, 1861-1879.

Transvaal Archives Pretoria (TA)

Selected files were consulted in the following series:

Transvaal Archives Depot

State Secretaries Papers (SS); Superintendent of Natives (SN); Secretary of Native Affairs (SNA).

Central Archives Depot

Chief Native Commissioner (CNC/HKN); Department of Agriculture (LBD/LDE); Department of Justice (JUS); Native Affairs Department (NTS); Department of Bantu Affairs (BAO); Department of Lands (LDE); Evidence Collected by Commissions (K); Director of Native Labour (GNLB).

Court Records: Intermediate Archives

Pretoria Supreme Court:

Supreme Court (SC)/Circuit Court (CC), 1959/185/13/1.

SC/CC, 1959/185/14/2.

SC/CC, 1959/185/15/3.

SC/CC, 1959/185/16/4.

SC/CC, 1959/186/18.

SC/CC, 1959/111.

Institute of Commonwealth Studies, London (ICS)

South African Materials Project (SAMP)

Rhodes House, Oxford

Interviews and documents relating to MK deposited by Howard Barrell.

Wits Historical Papers Library (UWHPL)

Selected documents were consulted from the following collections:

W. Ballinger Papers; D.R. Hunt Papers; Institute of Race Relations Papers; Rheinallt Jones Papers; Xuma Papers; Treason Trial Records; Evidence to the Native Economic Commission; *State vs Mosima Gabriel Sexwale and eleven others*, Pretoria Supreme Court, 1978; *K.K. Sekhukhune vs N. Ramodike and others*, Pretoria Supreme Court, 1991.

Private Papers (copies currently in author's possession)

Sekhukhuneland Murder Matters, 1986-1988; Legal documents; Court records; Interviews. Collected by R. Anderson.

Politics in Sekhukhuneland, 1990-1993: Pamphlets, photographs, correspondence, records of meetings, ANC Branch reports, notes on discussions and interviews. Collected by P. Delius, P. Mnisi and P. Mbiba.

Government Publications

Transvaal Department of Native Affairs *Annual Reports*, 1902-1910.

Blue Books on Native Affairs, 1910-1952.

Government Gazette.

D.L. Smit, *Statement of Land Policy under the Native Trust and Land Act, 1936* (Pretoria, 1937).

D.L. Smit, *New Era of Reclamation* (Pretoria, 1945).

UG22-'32, *Report of the Native Economic Commission, 1930-1932.*

UG61/1955, *Report of the Commission for the Social-Economic Development of the Bantu Areas Within the Union of South Africa.*

Lebowa Department of Education *Annual Reports.*

Newspapers and Periodicals

Select issues from:

Africa South; Bantu; Bantu World; Berliner Missions-berichte; City Press; Contact; Drum; Inkululeko; The Pretoria News; The New Nation; The Rand Daily Mail; Sowetan; The Star; The Sunday Times; The Weekly Mail and Guardian.

Selected Books and Articles

D. Anderson and R. Grove, *Conservation in Africa* (Cambridge, 1989).

A. Ashforth, *The Politics of Official Discourse in Twentieth Century South Africa* (Oxford, 1990).

E. Ayers, 'Narrating the New South', *Journal of Southern History*, LXI, 1995.

M. Basner, *Am I Not an African?* (Johannesburg, 1993).

T. Bassett and D. Crummey (eds.), *Land in African Agrarian Systems* (Wisconsin, 1993).

W. Beinart, *The Political Economy of Pondoland* (Cambridge, 1983).

– –, 'Soil Erosion, Conservationism and Ideas about Development', *Journal of Southern African Studies*, 11, 1984.

– –, 'The Politics of Colonial Conservation', *Journal of Southern African Studies*, 15, 1989.

– –, 'Political and Collective Violence in Southern African Historiography', *Journal of Southern African Studies*, 18, 1992.

– –, *Twentieth Century South Africa* (Oxford, 1994).

W. Beinart and C. Bundy, *Hidden Struggles in Rural South Africa* (London, 1987).

W. Beinart, P. Delius and S. Trapido (eds.), *Putting a Plough to the Ground* (Johannesburg, 1986).

B. Berman and J. Lonsdale, *Unhappy Valley* (London, 1992).

H. Binswanger and K. Deiniger, 'South African Land Policy', *World Development*, 21, 1993.

P. Bonner, P. Delius and D.Posel (eds.), *Apartheid's Genesis 1935-1962* (Johannesburg, 1993).

C.V. Bothma, *Ntshabeleng Social Structure* (Pretoria, 1962).

– –, 'The Political Structure of the Pedi of Sekhukhuneland', *African Studies*, 35, 1976.

B. Bozzoli, *Women of Phokeng* (Johannesburg, 1991).

H. Bradford, *A Taste of Freedom* (London, 1987).

W. Breytenbach, *Tuislande* (Pretoria, 1975).

J. Brown *et al.*, *History From South Africa* (Philadelphia, 1991).

B. Bunting, *Moses Kotane* (London, 1975).

Bureau for Economic Research re Bantu Development, *Lebowa Economic Revue, 1976* (Pretoria, 1977).

M. Chaskalson, 'Rural Resistance in the 1940s and 1950s', *Africa Perspective*, 1, 1987.

R. Christiansen, 'Implementing Strategies for the Rural Economy', *World Development*, 21, 1993.

S. Clingman (ed.), *Regions and Repertoires* (Johannesburg, 1991).

J. Comaroff, 'Dialectical Systems, History and Anthropology', *Journal of Southern African Studies*, 8, 1982.

– –, *Body of Power, Spirit of Resistance* (Chicago, 1985).

J. and J. Comaroff, *Of Revelation and Revolution* (Chicago, 1991).

– – (eds), *Modernity and its Malcontents* (Chicago, 1993).

F. Cooper, 'Conflict and Connection: Rethinking Colonial African History', *American Historical Review*, 99, 1994.

M. de Klerk, *A Harvest of Discontent* (Cape Town, 1991).

P. Delius, *The Land Belongs to Us* (Johannesburg, 1983).

– –, *The Conversion* (Johannesburg, 1984).

– –, 'Sebatakgomo: Migrant Organisation, the ANC and the Sekhukhuneland Revolt', *Journal of Southern African Studies*, 15, 1989.

– –, 'Migrants, Comrades and Rural Revolt: Sekhukhuneland 1950-1987', *Transformation*, 13, 1990.

– –, 'Mapping Histories of Rural Education', *Matlhasedi*, 11, 1992.

– –, 'Sebatakgomo and the Zoutpansberg Balemi Association', *Journal of African History*, 34, 1993.

Development Bank of South Africa, *Lebowa Development Information* (Midrand, 1986).

– –, *Regional Povert Profile: Eastern and Northern Transvaal* (Midrand, 1993).

M. Douglas (ed.), *Witchcraft Confessions and Accusations* (London, 1970).

A. Drew, 'Events Were Breaking Above Their Heads: Socialism in South Africa, 1921-1950', *Social Dynamics*, 17, 1991.

M. Drinkwater, *The State and Agrarian Change in Zimbabwe's Communal Areas* (London, 1991).

F. D'Souza *et al.*, *Operation Hunger: First Report on Estimating Rural Vulnerability in Black Rural Communities in South Africa* (Johannesburg, 1987).

R. Edgar, *Prophets with Honour* (Johannesburg, nd).

S. Feierman, *Peasant Intellectuals* (Wisconsin, 1990).

M. Gluckman (ed), *The Allocation of Responsibility* (Manchester, 1972).

C.L. Harries, *The Laws and Customs of the Bapedi and Cognate Tribes* (Johannesburg, 1929).

P. Harries, *Work, Culture and Identity* (London, 1994).

F. Hendriks, 'Loose Planning and Rapid Resettlement', *Journal of Southern African Studies*, 15, 1989.

B. Hirson, *Yours for the Union* (Johannesburg, 1989).

I. Hofmeyr, *We Spend Our Days as a Tale that is Told* (Johannesburg, 1993).

C. Hooper, *Brief Authority* (London, 1960).

M. Horrel, *African Homelands* (Johannesburg, 1973).

D.R. Hunt, 'An Account of the Bapedi', *Bantu Studies*, 4, 1931.

M. Hunter, *Reactions to Conquest* (London, 1936).

J. Iliffe, *The African Poor* (Cambridge, 1987).

A. Isaacman, 'Peasants and Rural Social Protest in Africa', *African Studies Review*, 33, 1990.

D. James, *The Road from Doornkop* (Johannesburg, 1983).

A. Jeeves, *Migrant Labour in South Africa's Mining Economy* (Johannesburg, 1985).

H. Joseph, *If this be Treason* (London, 1963).

T. Karis and G. Carter (eds.), *From Protest to Challenge*, 1-3 (Stanford, 1972-1977).

T. Karis, G. Carter and G. Gerhart (eds.), *From Protest to Challenge*, 4 (Stanford, 1977).

J. Kiernan, 'Where Zionists Draw the Line', *African Studies*, 36, 1977.

– –, 'Poor and Puritan', *African Studies*, 36, 1977.

N. Kriger, *Zimbabwe's Guerrilla War* (Cambridge, 1992).

M. Lipton and C. Simkins, *State and Market in Post-Apartheid South Africa* (Johannesburg, 1993).

T. Lodge, *Black Politics in South Africa since 1945* (Johannesburg, 1983).

W.M. Macmillan, *Complex South Africa* (London, 1930).

A. Mager, 'The People Get Fenced', *Journal of Southern African Studies*, 18, 1992.

A. Maliba, *The Condition of the Venda People* (Johannesburg, 1939).

N.R. Mandela, *No Easy Walk To Freedom* (London, 1973).

– –, *Long Walk To Freedom* (Johannesburg, 1994).

S. Marks and R. Rathbone (eds.), *Industrialisation and Social Change in South Africa* (London, 1982).

S. Marks and S. Trapido (eds.), *The Politics of Race, Class and Nationalism in Twentieth Century South Africa* (London, 1987).

J. May, M. Carter and D. Posel, 'The Composition and Persistence of Poverty in South Africa', *Land and Agricultural Policy Centre Policy Paper*, 15, 1994.

P. Mayer, *Black Villagers in an Industrial Society* (Cape Town, 1980).

A. Merensky, *Erinnerungen aus dem Missionleben in Transvaal, 1859-1882* (Berlin, 1899).

N. Mokgatle, *Autobiography of an Unknown South African* (London, 1971).

H. Mönnig, *The Pedi* (Pretoria, 1967).

D. Moodie, *Going For Gold* (Berkeley, 1994).

H. Moore, 'Household and Gender in a South African Bantustan', *African Studies*, 53, 1994.

H. Moore and M. Vaughan, *Cutting Down Trees* (London, 1994).

E. Mphahlele, *Down Second Avenue* (London, 1959).

C. Murray, *Black Mountain* (Johannesburg, 1992).

C. Murray and G. Williams, 'Land and Freedom in South Africa', *Review of African Political Economy*, 61, 1994.

T. Nemutanzhela, 'Cultural Forms and Literacy as Resources For Political Mobilisation', *African Studies*, 52, 1993.

I. Niehaus, 'Witch-Hunting and Political Legitimacy', *Africa*, 63, 1994.

A. Odendaal, *Vukani Bantu!* (Cape Town, 1984).

J.D. Omer-Cooper, *History of Southern Africa* (London, 1987).

J. Peires, *The Dead Will Arise* (Johannesburg, 1989).

R. Phillips, *The Bantu in the City* (Lovedale, 1938).

G.H. Pirie and M. Da Silva, 'Hostels for African Migrants in Greater Johannesburg' *GeoJournal*, 12, 1986.

G.M. Pitje, 'Traditional Systems of Male Education Amongst the Pedi and Cognate Tribes', *African Studies*, IX, 1950.

P.J. Quin, *Food and Feeding Habits of the Pedi* (Johannesburg, 1959).

E.M. Ramaila, *Setlogo Sa Batau* (Pretoria, 1938).

E. Schmidt, *Peasants Traders and Wives* (London, 1992).

J. Scott, *The Weapons of the Weak* (New Haven, 1985).

J. Sharp, 'A World Turned Upside Down', *African Studies*, 53, 1984.

J. Small, 'Women's Land Rights', *TRAC Occassional Publication* (Johannesburg, 1994).

South African Institute of Race Relations, *Annual Survey of Race Relations* (Johannesburg, 1952-1994).

J. Stadler, 'Witches and Witchhunters', *African Studies* (forthcoming).

S. Stichter, *Migrant Labourers* (Cambridge, 1985).

The Project on Living Standards and Development, *South Africans Rich and Poor* (Cape Town, 1994).

P. Thompson, *The Voice of the Past* (Oxford, 1988).

S. Trapido, 'Landlord and Tenant in Colonial Economy', *Journal of Southern African Studies*, 5, 1978.

R. Turrel, *Capital and Labour on the Kimberley Diamond Fields* (Cambridge, 1987).

H. van Coller, 'Mampoer in die Stryd om die Bapedi Troon', *Historiese Studies*, 3, 1942.

I. van Kessel, 'From Confusion to Lusaka: the Youth Revolt in Sekhukhuneland', *Journal of Southern African Studies*, 19, 1993.

S. van der Horst, *Native Labour in South Africa* (Oxford, 1942).

C. van Onselen, 'The Reconstruction of a Rural Life from Oral Testimony', *Journal of Peasant Studies*, 20, 1993.

J. Vansina, *Oral Tradition as History* (London, 1985).

H. Verwoerd, *Development and Progress in Bantu Communities* (Pretoria, 1955).

C. Walker (eds.), *Women and Resistance in South Africa* (London, 1982).

– –, 'Women, "Tradition" and Reconstruction', *Review of African Political Economy*, 62, 1994.

P. Walshe, *The Rise of African Nationalism in South Africa* (London, 1970).

M. Warwick (ed), *Witchcraft and Sorcery* (London,1970).

P. Warwick, *Black People in the South African War, 1899-1902* (Cambridge, 1983).

F. Wilson and M. Ramphele, *Uprooting Poverty* (Cape Town, 1989).

J. Winter, 'The tradition of Ra'lolo', *South African Journal of Science*, IX, 1912.

H. Wolpe, 'Capitalism and Cheap Labour Power', *Economy and Society*, 1, 1972.

J. Yawitch, *Betterment* (Johannesburg, 1982).

Unpublished Papers, Manuscripts, Reports and Theses

R. Anderson, ' "Keeping the Myth Alive": Justice, Witches and the Law in the 1986 Sekhukhune Killings', BA Hons dissertation, University of the Witwatersrand, 1990.

H. Barrell, 'Conscripts to their Age: African National Congress Operational Strategy, 1976-1986', D Phil thesis, Oxford University, 1993.

W. Beinart and P. Delius, 'The Family and Early Migrancy in Southern Africa', seminar paper, African History Seminar, University of London, May 1979.

J. Bekker, ' "We Will Plough Where We Like". Resistance to the Application of Betterment schemes in the Pietersburg area, 1937-1946', BA Hons dissertation, University of the Witwatersrand, 1989.

E. Breslin, Operation Hunger, National Nutritional Survey, Johannesburg, 1994.

E. Breslin and P. Delius, 'A Comparative Analysis of Poverty and Malnutrition in South Africa', Operation Hunger Report, Johannesburg, 1996.

D. Everatt, 'The Politics of Non-Racialism: White Opposition to Apartheid, 1945-1960', D Phil thesis, University of Oxford, 1990.

E. Francis, 'Migration and Changing Divisions of Labour: Gender Relations and Economic Change in Koguta, Western Kenya', seminar paper, University of the Witwatersrand, September 1991.

R. Grele, 'History and the Languages of History in the Oral History Interview', History Workshop paper, 1990.

L. Grundling, 'The Participation of South African Blacks in the Second World War', D Litt et Phil thesis, Rand Afrikaans University, 1986.

T. Harding, 'Resistance and Development in Rural Areas', discussion paper, 1990.

D. James, 'Kinship and Land in an Inter-ethnic Rural Community', MA dissertation, University of the Witwatersrand, 1987.

– –, '*Mino wa Setšo*: Songs of Town and Countryside and the Experience of Migrancy by Men and Women of the Northern Transvaal', PhD thesis, University of the Witwatersrand, 1993.

– –, '*Bagagešu*/Those of My Home: Migrancy, Gender and Ethnicity', seminar paper, Institute for Advanced Social Research, University of the Witwatersrand, 11/3/1995.

M.P. Kgobe, 'Resistance to Betterment in the Pietersburg Area: A Case Study of Ga-Matlala, 1940-1980', BA Hons dissertation, University of the Witwatersrand, 1992.

E. Lediga, 'Sekhukhune College of Education: Founding and Development, 1968-1989: Twenty Years of Progress', BA Hons dissertation, University of the North, 1991.

S.P. Lekgoathi, 'Reconstructing the History of Educational Transformation in a Rural Transvaal Chiefdom: The Radicalisation of Teachers in Zebediela from the early 1950s to the early 1990s', MA dissertation, University of the Witwatersrand, 1995.

E. Letsoalo, 'Survival Strategies in Rural Lebowa: A Study in the Geography of Poverty', MA dissertation, University of the Witwatersrand, 1982.

T. Lodge, 'Class Conflict, Communal Struggle and Patriotic Unity: The Communist Party of South Africa during the Second World War', seminar paper, African Studies Institute, University of the Witwatersrand, 1985.

M. Molepo, 'Peasants and/or Proletariat? A Case Study of a Group of Migrant Workers at Haggie Rand Limited from Molepo Village', seminar paper, African Studies Institute,University of the Witwatersrand, 1983.

M. Nchabeleng, *Boipušo*, 1959.

T. Nemutanzhela, 'Cultural Forms and Literacy as Resources for Political Mobilisation: A.M. Malivha and the Zoutpansberg Balemi Association, 1939-1944', BA Hons dissertation, University of the Witwatersrand, 1991.

– –, 'Pulling Out the Sticks and Removing Stones From the Fields. Memory of Resistance to Betterment in the Zoutpansberg, 1939-1940', History Workshop paper, 1994.

Operation Hunger, Annual Report, Johannesburg, 1995.

Operation Hunger, Northern Transvaal Assessment and Planning at Riba, Johannesburg, 1995.

M. Peskin and A. Spiegel, 'Migrant Labour Project: Urban Hostels in the Johannesburg Area', Report of the Institute of Social and Economic Research, Rhodes University, 1976.

J. Phala, untitled manuscript, Robben Island, nd.

G.M. Pitje, 'Traditional and Modern Systems of Male Education among the Pedi and Cognate Tribes', MA dissertation, University of Fort Hare, 1948.

J. Rees, 'Health Patterns in the Northern Transvaal, 1900-1932', MA dissertation, University of the Witwatersrand, 1992.

E. Ritchken, 'Leadership and Conflict in Bushbuckridge: Struggles to Define Moral Economies within the context of Rapidly Transforming Political Economies, 1978-1990', PhD thesis, University of the Witwatersrand, 1994.

B. Sansom, 'Leadership and Authority in Pedi Chiefdom', PhD thesis, University of Manchester, 1970.

S. Schirmer, 'Freedom in Land and Work: Labour Tenancy and the Proclamation of Chapter Four in Lydenburg', BA Hons dissertation, University of the Witwatersrand, 1989.

– –, 'The Struggle for the Land in Lydenburg 1930-1970', PhD thesis, University of the Witwatersrand, 1994.

S.M. Sebekwane, 'The Careers of Black Women Under Apartheid: A Sociological Study of Teachers in Lebowa Secondary Schools', PhD thesis, University of Cambridge, 1993.

D.M.C. Sepuru, 'Succession Disputes, Macongress and Rural Resistance at Ga-Matlala, 1919-1980', BA Hons dissertation, University of the Witwatersrand, 1992.

A. Sitas, 'African Worker Responses on the East Rand to Changes in the Metal Industry, 1960-1980', PhD thesis, University of the Witwatersrand, 1983.

S. Trapido, 'A Preliminary Study of the Development of African Political Opinion, 1884-1955', BA Hons dissertation, University of the Witwatersrand, 1959.

J. Yawitch, 'The Relation between African Female Employment and Influx Control in South Africa, 1950-1983', MA dissertation, University of the Witwatersrand, 1984.

Index

251

Y

youth 29, 30, 159, 161, 176, 180-9, 191, 196, 197, 198, 199, 203, 205, 206, 207, 214;
    see also comrades; education; generational relationships; initiation; witch killings
youth congresses 179
youth culture 159, 199, 219, 220
Youth League see African National Congress
youth movement 194, 198, 204, 206, 207, 219, 220

Z

Zionist Christian Church 165
Zionist churches 159, 166, 219
zombies (*ditlotolwane*) 165, 201
Zoutpansberg 61, 82, 83
Zoutpansberg Balemi Association 61, 84, 97, 226
Zoutpansberg Cultural Association 96